D0479256

"If you are, or aspire to be, a Production Manag⟨...⟩ ⟨bo⟩ok with you in the production office is like havin⟨...⟩ ⟨a⟩way! This book is an excellent Bible, an essential tool⟨...⟩

    — Deb LeFaive, Line Producer/Unit Production Manager

"This book is like a good friend to anyone working in the film and television production sector."

    — Mireille Watson, President,
    Entertainment-Media Consulting, Inc.

"I've always believed that every film that gets made is a minor miracle. Deb Patz's invaluable book is a precious and comprehensive guide to help you navigate through so many of the traps and pitfalls that threaten the creation of your miracle."

    — Martin Harbury, Filmmaker/Sailor/Consultant

"A great guide and reference book, and logically organized. Patz tackles a vast subject professionally while also making it accessible and entertaining. A must-have for beginners and a handy reference for the seasoned; it belongs with you in the production office."

    — Karen Powell, Producer

"Patz delivers an invaluable roadmap in *Film Production Management 101*. Concise and clear, this latest edition makes the leap from traditional production to moviemaking in the digital age. It would take years working in the industry to glean the information presented in this great, readable book. It's a must-have for everyone from aspiring PMs and Coordinators to seasoned Producers. Although directed toward dramatic production, it is an excellent resource for documentary filmmakers as well."

    — Glynis Whiting, Filmmaker, *Weight of the World* and
    Gone Sideways

"A comprehensive, hands-on, practical guide for both emerging and established filmmakers. An essential addition to both the production office and post secondary film programs."

    — C. Leaney, Assistant Program Coordinator, Digital Film
    Production Program, Langara College/Former Producing
    Instructor, Vancouver Film School

"*Film Production Management 101* gives you the "how" and the "why" for production management drawn from Deb Patz's deep and practical experience. It's more than a great guide, it's an indispensable tool."

    — David Hauka, Producer/Director/Production Manager

"I almost hesitate to recommend Deb's fabulous guide — it gives away more inside information than it should."

    — Indira Guha, Entertainment Lawyer/Producer

"An invaluable and comprehensive guide. Deborah Patz has drawn on her own experience and has written a thoroughly researched and helpful book."

— Norman Jewison, Producer/Director, *The Hurricane,*
Moonstruck, Fiddler on the Roof

"If you want to make it as a top-notch show-runner or producer, Patz's book gives you all the info you WON'T get in the writer's room. From setting up a production office and hiring crew to budgeting and contracts, *Film Production Management 101* is a user-friendly, in-depth guide to a world many writers don't know much about, but should: the nuts and bolts of physical production. For those of you who plan on being great writers AND producers, this book should get you there in record time."

— Chad Gervich, Writer/Producer: *Wipeout, Foody Call,*
Speeders, Reality Binge; Author: *Small Screen, Big Picture:*
A Writer's Guide to the TV Business

"Deb Patz's second edition of *Film Production Management 101* has everything a producer needs to get it right. An invaluable guide for the beginning filmmaker or a reference manual for those more experienced, this volume belongs on every filmmaker's desk, not gathering dust on the bookshelf."

— John Churchman, Publisher, *School Video News*

"At last the complex relationship between the creation of a film and the day-to-day production management and coordination of that film is spelled out in clear, readable, and accurate detail. Deborah has written a wonderful book which should be extremely helpful to novice low-budget independent filmmakers and seasoned professionals alike."

— Sharon McGowan, Independent Producer and
Associate Professor & Chair, Film Production Program,
University of British Columbia

"The most definitive production guide I have ever read. A must for anyone who wants to understand the production process."

— Louis Melville, Producer/Director/Writer and former
co-chairman, New Producers Alliance

"An exhaustive overview full of practical knowledge!!!"

— Dan Ochiva, Editor, *Millimeter* Magazine

"Deborah prepares you for any situation the PM and PC will encounter throughout the life of a project. From the initial interview to the wrap party, this book guides you on how to be prepared and how to act professionally in every circumstance."

— Chris Robertson, *www.hollywoodwritersblock.com*

"This is one of the most insightful industry books I've ever seen. Anybody going into this industry should read it."

— Seaton McLean, Producer/Executive Producer

DEBORAH PATZ

FILM PRODUCTION MANAGEMENT 101

SECOND EDITION

management and coordination in a digital age

Published by Michael Wiese Productions
12400 Ventura Blvd. #1111
Studio City CA 91604
tel. (818) 379-8799
fax (818) 986-3408
mw@mwp.com
www.mwp.com

Cover design: MWP
Book layout: Gina Mansfield Design
Editor: Judy Capodanno

Printed by Sheridan Books, Ann Arbor, Michigan
Manufactured in the United States of America

© 2010 by Deborah S. Patz
This is the second edition of *FilmProduction Management 101* by Deborah S. Patz

All rights reserved. No part of this book may be reproduced in any form or by any means without permission in writing from the publisher, except for the inclusion of brief quotations in a review.

Library of Congress Cataloging-in-Publication Data

Patz, Deborah S.,
 Film production management 101 : management and coordination in a digital age
/ Deborah S. Patz. -- 2nd ed.
    p. cm.
 ISBN 978-1-932907-77-3
1. Motion pictures--Production and direction. 2. Television--Production and direction. I. Title.
 PN1995.9.P7P375 2010
 791.4302'3--dc22

                                    2010018594

for Laura
who was there at the beginning

and for Ken, Jordan, and Natalya
who fill my life with love, joy, and inspiration

ACKNOWLEDGMENTS

One cannot make a film all alone... or a book such as this one. My sincere thanks go to the many wonderful people and companies that have assisted in so many ways to make this book possible. Beyond all the crews and the co-workers I have worked with over the years that have given me, and continue to give me, the forum to learn so much about business of filmmaking, I wish acknowledge in name:

Michael Wiese and Ken Lee for making this project come to life around the world.

William Barron, John Calvert, Judy Carroll, Helena Cynamon, Kathryn Emslie, Elizabeth Friesen, Nadine Henry, Eileen Hoeter, Seaton McLean, Rob Mills, Toni Myers, Jamie Paul Rock, Mickey Rogers, Cheryl Wagner, Teri Woods-McArter for the many of the wonderful and varied opportunities of my career.

The Canadian Film Centre for their pioneering support for the book and the Vancouver Film School for being the first to integrate the book in their excellent program.

My many superb Assistants over the years (too numerous to mention each by name – but you know who you are!) for their dedication, hard work, and good humor.

My team of readers and critics for their invaluable input: Charles Braive, Mark Callow, Carrie Chase, Jericca Cleland, Kyle Cunningham, Dixie Cutler, Arthur Cooper, Mike Crain, Kyle Cunningham, Brian de Paoli, Alex Downie, Mary Eilts, Marian Elliott, Lon Hall, Barb Harwood, Debbi-Jo Matias, Bob McGuirk, Robin Mirsky-Daniels, Trish Moore, Tim Moshansky, Leslie Padorr, Deborah Osborne, Richard Patz, Joan Pearce, Eva Schmieg, Barbara Selkirk, Laura Sousa, Kim Steer, Jim Sternberg.

Special thanks must also go to Scott Baker for introducing me to the book that got the ball rolling; to Sue Phillips for seeing my abilities before I did; and to Ann Marie Fleming for never letting me forget them.

Finally, heartfelt thanks go to my mother for teaching me how to reach for my dreams, to my father, in loving memory, for teaching me how to live them, and to my husband, Ken Elliott, for being there to share those dreams, for weathering the challenges to achieve them, and for helping me to balance them with the rest of my wonderful life.

TABLE OF CONTENTS

Sample forms in the Appendix
can be downloaded in full size (8.5" x 11") at:
www.mwp.com
click on "Virtual Film School," click on "Resources"

⋙

Production Manager & Coordinator resource links at:
www.debpatz.com

INTRODUCTION TO THE SECOND EDITION

All of us who work in the film and television industry are storytellers, each with a unique perspective. Filmmaking is a collaborative art that requires the talents of many diverse people in order to come to life: visionaries, inventors, performers, logistics wizards. We all have a role to play.

It's incredible how the technical tools we use to make movies keep changing over time! Long gone is the Moviola, as well as the flatbed. Digital image capture races to fully replace film stock, with 3D technology following closely behind high definition. Digital and social medias continue to change how we communicate on a daily basis, both on and off the set. Pioneers are born all the time, experimenting with new technologies to enhance the movie-going experience and seek new ways to tell stories. Yes, it all comes back to story. Story is the constant.

Look beyond the technology to the reason we are here in the first place: to collaborate in telling stories that entertain, thrill, and educate. We want to make an emotional connection with the audience. Everyone on the cast and crew is part of that magic. The Production Manager and Production Coordinator have the great fortune of being at the very center of the action when it comes to making a film. True logistics wizards, they deal with every department over the course of a production to bring it all together. What an exciting place to be!

Accept changing technologies. The prototype tools of today will be either obsolete or industry standard tomorrow. You may be current on technology as you exit a training facility, but to stay current, you will need to upgrade your skills soon enough. Arm yourself, then, with good practices. These practices are the real tools you need and they take time to fully absorb. Learn what is important behind the technology. By doing so, you are integral to realizing the story on the screen — whatever tools or delivery channels are used. The challenge of learning new technology on the job then becomes the spice that inspires you to re-evaluate how and why you do what you do. Your personal style toward the job evolves.

Immerse yourself in the making of a production from the extraordinary perspective of the Production Manager and Coordinator. I invite you on this journey from prep to post. Start building your enduring personal tool set... become part of the magic using these tools in a digital age.

INTRODUCTION

A film production explodes into life from a mere document – a script – and becomes a thriving expanse of business. Propelling itself forward in a frantic race against time, it captures sound, images, a collaboration of ideas — entertaining, thrilling, and educating. But long before audiences see the final product, production has vanished, and crews are working with different people on other projects. Yet in that brief existence of time and under such frenetic circumstances, a lasting film has been made.

There is glamour in working behind the scenes on a film production. The lifestyle is exotic. It is no regular nine-to-five job. This book is a hands-on "how-to" guide for the management and the coordination of a film or television shoot. A two-for-one book, it is told through the eyes of both the Production Manager and the Production Coordinator, as they are the team in the production office who budgets it all, arranges it all, does it all, reports it all, and double checks that it all gets done... on time and on budget.

The Production Manager ("PM") is the person who is basically handed all the money to make the film, and is responsible to bring it in for the Producer on time and on budget. If you think this sounds like a weighty job, it is. Good Production Managers are hailed as people who know how to keep the money "on the screen" to make the final product look like it cost more than the sum of the budget.

The Production Office Coordinator ("POC" or "PC") deals with everyone during the course of making a film, implementing and coordinating everything from preproduction to postproduction, at head office and on set. If you think it sounds like an enormous job, it is. Good Production Coordinators are hailed as people who "keep the show running."

Together, the PM and the PC form a dynamic producing team. They have secrets on how to do their jobs effectively that tend to remain just that — secrets. This book is written to share those secrets.

This book is designed to be open on your desk at work as you work. Forms, checklists, and samples are abundant throughout the book for your daily use. True production stories are interspersed with the straightforward "how-to" directions. Beyond entertaining, the stories are intended to balance out the simplicity of managing and organizing in the sterile environment of the pages of a book. See how real-life situations happen. You do not have to be perfect. Though their daily accomplishments may make them appear super-human, Managers and Co-ordinators are just like you and me.

The book is written for Executives, Producers, Production Managers, and Production Coordinators. Knowledge and understanding of the management team and its expanse of responsibilities can only help production to proceed with trust, good humor, and a sense of teamwork. Together you are responsible for everything in this book.

Production Accountants, Location Managers, Assistant Directors, Assistant Coordinators, Office P.A.s, and Receptionists will also deem this book invaluable. With it, you will gain a familiarity of the scope of duties that you accomplish together in the production office and bring meaning to and put into perspective the work that you do.

Those entering the film industry will learn about the business side of filmmaking from this book. Not only is there entry-level advice, but also detailed information as you move up the ladder to management. Since the PM and the PC deal with everyone from prep to post, you can acquaint yourself with an overview of the entire film production process in this book.

Finally, this book is for those in and interested in the film industry who are baffled by what the PM and the PC are doing all day long while the set is shooting. It is those people who ask: "How can the Coordinator be that busy?" and "What is it like to be the Manager responsible for all the money on production?"

So, absorb and enjoy! Use this book on your desk as a daily reference. Over time, be inspired to develop your own style of management or coordination. All sorts of unpredictable events on a production are about to come your way. They will test your ability to think on your feet. So you need to know the basics of the job. You are in the right place.

Whether you read the entire book at once or skip over chapters until you are ready for them, enter the world of production management and coordination. Grasp the full production experience, from the perspective of the dynamic team of the Production Manager and the Production Coordinator. No other jobs can compare!

PROJECT DEVELOPMENT

Hire the right people and let them do their jobs.

INTERVIEW NOVICES

Going for my first interview to become a Production Coordinator, I was very nervous. I had jotted down in tiny writing on a cue card all the questions I could muster about the show and my prospective role in production. What I didn't know at the time was that I was being interviewed by a relatively new Production Manager.

He asked me a few general questions. I sputtered out a few answers. Silences and uncomfortable moments crept into the interview. Now and then I referred to my cue card and asked a question myself. The Production Manager was intrigued by the card in my hand. He leaned forward to get a glimpse of its contents, then said: "You seem more prepared for this than I am. Why don't you take over the interview?"

I realized then that he was as nervous as I was about this whole interview. So I blatantly referred to my cue card and continued with my questions, jotting down answers as we discussed the different topics. Soon conversation was lively, direct, and informative. He leaned back in comfort and we lost track of time chatting about film, the project, and the workings of a production office.

By the next day I was working in that office. But it occurred to me that the only question I didn't ask him at the time was: Did I get the job?

GETTING HIRED   1

Before thinking about working as a Production Manager or Coordinator, you first think about getting hired as one. You have exhausted your network of contacts and their contacts and have finally made it to an interview for just that job. Your C.V. is short, to the point, and shows off your experience and education related to this particular job. If it is your first job interview as a PM or a PC, you have worked hard to get here and you are pretty sure you can do the job. You just need the chance to prove yourself. You are trying your best to show how relevant your experience is, how professional you are, and basically emanate all your best working qualities. But what are "they" looking for from you?

YOU AS THE PRODUCTION MANAGER

BEFORE THE INTERVIEW

You have probably already had a telephone interview. You have an idea of what the film is about. You may know some of the key people involved, the overall size of the budget, and when and how long the shoot is planned. You need to know more.

The first stop for your research should be online. Surf the company's website and read up on it prior to the interview. Surf the websites of the company's previous productions. Research the Producer, Director, and any other key members of the team that you know about. How professional are their presentations? Do you want to be associated with these people in your career?

You may also have the opportunity to read the script prior to attending the interview. Take the chance if you can. As PM, or as PC, you will be selling how wonderful the script is to many other people and companies along the production process. You better love it — or something about it — now.

You may also have the chance to read the budget prior to attending the interview. Take this opportunity if you can. You are going to be hired to keep to this budget. You want to know it inside and out as soon as possible. Read the script first, then make notes and questions about the budget while reading the budget. How were these decisions made? You are going to be hired to follow up on these key decisions during production. Can you do it?

Call industry people you know and trust to find out what they know about these Producers or this production company. You are checking their references. You want this job to be a good fit for both you and them. Remember, when checking references, you want information closest to the source. People who have heard rumors, rather than having had direct experience working with those you are checking on, can give you dangerously misleading information. Also remember that personality clashes can give you biased feedback, too. Just store up the reference information you collect, go to the interview, and make a decision for yourself. It is your career, after all, and your prospective employer is calling your references right now, too.

WHAT TO BRING TO THE INTERVIEW

Take notes during your research. You will have questions to ask the Producer(s) about the production. Prepare now so you don't end up leaving the interview saying to yourself, "If only I'd asked...". Use a small note pad, or index cards you can refer to. Bring a pen or a pencil so you can jot down answers or names you collect. You are not being hired to memorize. Reference material is okay. A scripted book of notes would be excessive.

Also bring another copy of your C.V. The Producers should already have a copy, but it may only be an illegible scan or fax, or they may forget to bring it. Be prepared.

AT THE INTERVIEW

The interview could be in a production office, a head office, or even in a restaurant. It depends on the people, their style and situation… and where they can find a private space away from telephones to talk with you. You will be interviewed by the Line Producer, the Producer, the Executive or VP in charge of production, or perhaps a combination of them all. It will depend on the situation.

Ease in with chitchat. Chitchat is an opportunity to find out something personal about the people you may be working with. You can use chitchat as your opportunity to show off your attitude toward life and work and how you balance the two.

WHO ARE THE PRODUCERS?

There are always a number of Producers on a production. They can be: Executive Producers, Co-Producers, Producer, Associate Producers, Line Producers, Creative Producers, etc. Find the complete list of who is on board the production and how involved they are. Some may have worked on the initial assembling of the development package; you may never see them during the course of production. Some may be very "hands-on," showing up daily on set, and attending all meetings. Some Producers work in-house at a production company, while others are freelance and hired, just like you. Include all the Producers' names in your notes. You can research these new names later on at home. Confirm to whom you, as a PM, will be reporting. You should be reporting to the Line Producer or Producer, who will in turn report to the Executives. You will not have time to report to several people. Determine if there is a clear chain of command in place.

WHAT "THEY" ARE LOOKING FOR

The job of the Production Manager is a hugely responsible position. The Producers have been raising money for years to make this production. They have expended a lot of effort developing this project to where it is today. You, as a PM, are being hired to spend the money they have assembled in a superbly short time frame to move this project from script to screen. You better be able to spend the money wisely — on time and on budget. Although you will learn something on every job you do, a Producer is not looking to, and should not, train you as a PM. A Producer wants you for your expertise and professionalism. The company is going to put a lot of trust in you and the team you hire. How wisely do you spend the budget? How well do you track the money as it is being spent? How fast and how accurately do you create cost reports? Can you handle the stress of it all?

KNOW YOUR EXPERTISE

Now, of course, no two productions are identical. Just because you production-managed one show does not mean you can manage any production. Some projects are on a much larger scale than others. Some involve several countries. Some involve shooting with kids, animals, and special effects. Some are shot in HD or other digital format, 3D, or on film. Some specialize in doing everything for "food and favors," while others can pay some of the crew overscale. Do you have experience in production with any of these specialties? Is your background experience compatible with this budget, this script, and this company? Maybe you were working on a production, but not as the Production Manager, and you were the one who negotiated all the rights for the pre-recorded music — and this production is all about music. Though not PM-experience specifically, your knowledge may be superbly relevant to this particular production. You may know more about music clearances than the Producers, so they will need your expertise. You must understand what you can do. Then you can demonstrate how useful your experience is to this production.

WHAT IS THE VISION?

The Producer wants to hire people who are all moving in the same direction, making the same film. Take time to discuss the vision of the final film and the budgetary choices already made in the development budget. If the Producer at the interview has created the current production budget, this is fortunate for you. Bring out your budget questions and start asking. Where does the Producer want the money to be spent? Is the shot with 1,000 extras integral to the story, or can it be cheated with 100 extras, or moved to another location with no extras at all? Now is the time to gather a sense of what has to stay in the story and what is expendable. While asking the questions, ask yourself if you can make this "vision" for this budget. This responsibility will be yours.

KNOW YOUR STYLE

Are you a "paper person" who loves to analyze numbers and report them? Or are you a "people person" who prefers to be on set, physically overseeing production and discussing and observing the status? You will need to balance both abilities; if the Producer you are about to work with prefers one more than the other, be prepared to make the right choice to work most effectively. Also know if you prefer to rule a set in almost military efficiency, or if you prefer a quiet approach to earning the crew's respect. Are you an organizer or do you need an organizer to make it through the day? Know yourself. You will be working in close quarters with the Producer and the Line Producer. Be prepared to determine if your work styles are compatible.

DIFFICULT DECISIONS

Have you ever fired someone? Have you dealt with difficult people or bruised egos? How do you inspire people? Are you confident enough to advise the Producer or Line Producer how to cut costs? Have you ever analyzed a situation and decided that, for the best of the project, someone key needs to be fired? Can you make these difficult decisions? Look into your career history. What have been your most difficult decisions? Share these. The Producer needs someone who can make such decisions. The Producer also needs someone who can deal with widely varied issues both delicately and confidentially.

WHO DO YOU KNOW?

The Producer or production company may have preferred suppliers they already use. They may have names of people they want in key roles or suggest to be in key roles. Others will be looking to you to bring your contacts and crews. Your experience with crews will grow over time, but you should know some reliable crew already. How do these people work? How do they work together? Do they have your respect? A Producer needs a PM who has the crew's respect. As PM, you will often be the "no" person, informing the crew that they cannot have or rent something because of budgetary restrictions. You have to inspire them to think of creative alternatives. Do you have an office team of a Production Coordinator, Assistant Production Coordinator, and Office Production Assistant (Office P.A.) ready to go? If preproduction is fast approaching, it will be good for you to have these people on standby already. You may be starting tomorrow.

WHAT YOU ARE LOOKING FOR

You are part of this interview, too. The fit has to work both ways. Here are some things to consider and to ask yourself during the interview to ensure a good fit. Your questions and participation in the interview will generate further questions and discussions from the Producer, and show the Producer how involved you will be on the production. You will win some trust and assurance with the questions you choose to ask. Notice if the Producer evades some of your questions or is open about the answers. This interview will set the tone for your working relationship.

WHAT'S THE FILM ABOUT?

Have the Producer(s) tell you about the film. Find out both the creative and the financial aspects of the production. Find out the development history of the project. Now is a perfect opportunity for the Producers to show their excitement about the project and sell it to you. If you are to become the PM, you will have to sell the project over and over again to many others. Find out what magic the Producers see in the project.

IS THE BUDGET LOCKED?

Find out how "locked" the budget is. At a certain stage, the Producer has to "lock" the budget for the financiers and begin cost reporting to the locked budget, showing the overages and savings on a line-by-line basis. Hopefully, you will have the opportunity as PM to take a final pass at the budget before locking it, adding your budgeting expertise to it, bringing the estimates per line as close to reality as possible. With all the variables that happen during the course of production, you will never be exact about each line item, but from working on show after show, you will have a better sense each time where money is actually spent instead of just budgeted to be spent. This pass at the budget will also help you become intimately familiar with each budget line and what it is intended to purchase. Ask yourself: Can I hire the crew I need on these wages? Can I rent the equipment I need with this budget?

IS ANYTHING SPENT ALREADY?

Sometimes a Producer will have pre-allocated costs to contingency. Find out immediately if such is the case. Do not wait until you are hired before you find out that contingency money in your budget is already spoken for and will not be there for emergencies.

WHAT COST REPORTING IS NEEDED?

Usually you generate a cost report either bi-weekly or monthly during preproduction, weekly during production, and monthly during postproduction. If you are working on an international co-production, are you reporting on all the costs of production, or just this country's costs, leaving the other costs for the other country's accounting people? How soon in the next week does the Producer expect to see a completed cost report? What will your production office be audited on after the end of production? Ask yourself if you and your accounting team can generate cost reports this soon. Remember that cost reporting is all geared toward the final audit. Plan for the end of the process from the beginning. Is your office going to audit all the costs of production or just the local costs of production?

WHAT IS THE SCHEDULE?

Find out what the production schedule is. How flexible is the delivery date? Does the Producer think the schedule is tight already? Have you shot films this fast before? How fast does the director shoot? Discuss the possibilities and ask yourself if you can bring the project in on time under these circumstances and with these people.

MORE ABOUT THE VISION

You have already discussed the vision of the film with the Producer. Get a sense if you can, prior to your first days on the job, whether or not the Director and the Producer have the same vision. Is the Director known for wide-sweeping, expensive vista shots, yet the Producer is planning an intimate, close, personal story? How do the Director and the Producer communicate? How long have they been working together? Are they making the same film? Any sense you form about their communication abilities will provide you a foreshadowing of how difficult or seamless the production will be.

BIGGEST CHALLENGES OF THE SHOOT

Find out from the Producer what she expects to be the biggest challenge(s) of the shoot. Will there be prototype equipment in use with no back-up plan for when the equipment breaks down? Are there multi-country logistics to be navigated? Does the Star Performer have limited availability to schedule the shoot around? Even though you will read the script and discover other potential challenges or expensive elements for the road ahead, it is good to seek out clues from the Producer's point of view of this particular production's challenges.

WHO IS THE TEAM?

You have already found out about the list of Producers attached to the project. Who else is on board? Find out how involved you are expected to be when it comes to hiring the key crew. Ask yourself if you know of qualified people to fill these roles.

IS THE OFFICE READY?

Find out if the Producer has a production office or a studio already, or if you are expected to find them. More than likely, finding a production office will be your first task.

ANY PREFERRED SUPPLIERS?

Find out if the Producer has preferred suppliers. Is there a computer graphics company already on board? If they have quoted on CGI (computer graphic imagery) costs for the early draft budget created during development, there will be such a company on board already. If the Producer has a track record, he will likely already have a post facility of preference, and an insurance company. Find out and note these names. It will be time to introduce yourself soon, should the job be yours.

WHAT DO YOU GET OUT OF THE FILM? (PC-PM)

Finally, ask yourself what do you get out of this production should it be offered and you take the job? Do you like the project and the people? Are you comfortable with the pay and committed number of weeks and are you confident that you can do the work? Maybe you are being offered this job for less pay than you would rather earn. In that case, evaluate how this show will further your career. Will you be working with someone with whom you want to develop a career contact? Will you be working in a medium with which you have little experience? Does this job fit nicely into your calendar to fill in the space before the high production season begins? Are you particularly passionate about this script or this story? On super-low-budget productions, remember that you have to be getting something out of the production, too. You are about to work extremely long and hard hours, face difficult decisions, and defy all sorts of odds to bring the production in on time and on budget, allowing the creative vision to be realized. Whatever you are paid, you have to be totally dedicated to the project. If you do your job badly, you will hurt your career. You have to find the passion to do it well. Ask yourself: Am I passionate about this project?

THINK ABOUT IT

There is no need to accept a job on the spot if you are offered the position. Thank the Producer or the Line Producer for his or her[*] time, and leave the interview to at least have a cup of coffee and evaluate what you have just learned. It is more likely you will want to sleep on the decision. You are making a career choice. It is a big decision. Take the night before answering.

Once hired, you will be changing seats and first hiring a Production Coordinator to be your right hand during production. This person will put the office together and keep it all running for you. You need an organizer. Have a look over the coordinator interview questions below, and assemble the answers from the Producer before you are faced with these questions yourself. You will be answering them over and over again with all crew interviews.

YOU AS THE PRODUCTION COORDINATOR

BEFORE THE INTERVIEW

As a Production Coordinator, just like the PM, do your research prior to the interview. Searching the Internet is the first step to source information about companies and people.

Bring a pen, paper, and cue cards into the interview. Assemble some questions on them. As a Production Coordinator, you are being hired to organize not to memorize. This is your opportunity to be organized in the interview. On the job you will be walking around with pen and paper anyway, so make this practice your habit now.

---

[*] This is the last time you will read "his or her;" from this point on, I will use one or the other pronoun and assume you understand that at any single time, either sex could apply.

THE INTERVIEW

Relax and enjoy, if you can. The Coordinator and the Manager need to develop an easy communication and working relationship. Here are some questions to start the conversation rolling. Do not be afraid, however, of interview tangents. If these questions spark further conversation and further questions, that is okay. The Coordinator and the Manager will be spending a lot of time together, so you are expected to be able to communicate well. The only warning about interview tangents is to be aware of any time restrictions. Too much chat can warn the Manager that more conversation than work will be done during the shoot.

WHAT ARE THE SHOOTING START AND END DATES?

This will be the first question the crew will ask of you.

DO YOU EXPECT TO HAVE WEEKEND SHOOTS OR 6-DAY WORK WEEKS?

Some films schedule their workweek to include shooting on Saturdays, Sundays, and holidays to take advantage of reduced traffic or greater location availability. If you will be dealing with a 6-day workweek, consider and adjust your fee accordingly.

DO YOU EXPECT TO HAVE LONG SHOOTING DAYS?

The film will be budgeted to shoot a certain minimum number of hours per day. Is it planned to be a 9-hour day or 12-hour day? Note that lunch hour is not included in describing the day's length, so a 9-hour day plus lunch is actually 10 hours long.

HOW DO YOU LIKE THE OFFICE RUN?

Some Production Managers insist that the office be open at least 30 minutes prior to call time until 30 minutes after wrap, with prep and wrap days being a minimum of 9:00 a.m. to 6:00 p.m. Some Production Managers will leave the office-opening schedule up to the Coordinator.

WILL THE FILM HAVE "DAY SHOOTS" AND/OR "NIGHT SHOOTS"?

On night shoots, some Production Managers prefer to have the office open both business hours (9:00 a.m. to 6:00 p.m.) and set hours (all night long). If this is the case, you will need extra office crew to make it happen. Discuss this now. What is budgeted?

HOW ELABORATE IS THE SHOOT?

Will there be a lot of extras, locations, special effects, music clearances? The Production Manager may ask what you mean by this question, which is designed to help you determine how complex your job is going to be.

WILL THERE BE ANY PERFORMERS OR CREW FROM OUT OF TOWN?

This question will determine how much you will need to deal with travel agents and immigration.

WHO IS THE FILM FOR?

Another question the crew will have for you right away — in order to find out who is broadcasting the show or which distributor is handling the feature.

WHO ARE THE PRODUCERS? HOW MANY ARE THERE? HOW INVOLVED ARE THEY?

Executives from many different companies and countries can be listed as the Producers for a film. There can be Executive Producers, Supervising Producers, Associate Producers, Creative Producers, Producers, Co-Producers, Line Producers, or any other "Producer" title newly invented. Since the titles are not standard for describing the duties of each position, you need to find out how each Producer is involved and in what order (often a political decision) to put them on the crew list. As subtext, you will also learn how big a job your documentation distribution to the various companies will be, and you may form an estimate of how long head office decisions take by determining how active each of the various Producers intends to be.

WHAT IS THE COMPANY NAME FOR THIS FILM PRODUCTION?

For legal and accounting purposes, film companies set up separate incorporated companies for each production. You need to know this name to conduct any business, from making letterhead to setting up accounts and contracts.

WHERE ARE THE PRODUCTION OFFICES? HOW SET UP ARE THEY?

Some offices are simply empty rooms that you have to furnish from scratch. Others are fully furnished right down to telephone systems and copier/scanners. This question will determine how busy you will be in your first few days.

DO YOU HAVE A COMPUTER SYSTEM ALREADY? WHAT KIND IS IT?

Often the Production Coordinator comes to a production with a computer. If you do, negotiate a kit-rental fee and find out if your system or training is compatible with the company's. Is there a VPN (Virtual Private Network) or FTP site linking the production and post teams with the post facility and/or head office? If so, what technical requirements and personnel are necessary to connect the required people and locations?

DO YOU HAVE CORPORATE ACCOUNTS ALREADY ESTABLISHED?

Some companies prefer that you use their head-office courier, photocopier, office stationery accounts, etc., whereas others encourage you to bring in your own contacts.

WHAT PRODUCTION DOCUMENTATION IS REQUIRED? ANY PREFERRED FORMS?

These questions are merely confirmation that the Production Manager wants completed production reports, call sheets, production schedules, and so on. Though redundant, the queries should spark further discussion about any existing forms the company prefers to use, digitization expectations of completed documents, and who, between the Assistant Directors and you, will be responsible for certain records. You will also learn how easy it is to talk to the Production Manager and how much the PM will rely on you for the correct documentation on the show.

HOW MUCH OF THE CREW HAS BEEN HIRED?

Here is where your pen and paper prove useful. Write down all names and positions the Production Manager mentions. Also note the status of each person. Often names will be chosen for the various positions, but not yet confirmed. Be aware of who may come on board, but never publish any unconfirmed information on a crew list. This is your opportunity to show how you deal with confidential information.

HOW MANY STAFF WILL BE IN THE OFFICE?

Find out how much the budget allows for Assistant Coordinators, Receptionist, and Office P.A.s. Also find out if you will be hiring the Assistants, or if they will be appointed for you. Some Assistant roles may be already hired or promised by Producers, Managers, or Executives prior to your arrival.

HOW SOON DO YOU WANT THE PRODUCTION COORDINATOR TO START?

This start date will be a budgetary concern for the Production Manager. Be prepared if the date is tomorrow.

WHAT IS THE BUDGET FOR THE PRODUCTION COORDINATOR?

This is the dance of the numbers. You ask the Production Manager how much is in the budget, the Production Manager asks you how much you expect to make. If the coordinator job is union, the dance can be short, as you can look up the scale rate to start; but if the job is non-union, the price range is enormous. If you intend to jump in with the first number, consider the scale and the budget of the film together with your research from other coordinators to determine a starting price. Remember to negotiate your computer and equipment kit rental separately.

You may not be able to have all the answers to your questions right away. That is okay. You can leave some of the questions for the first day of the job. As mentioned in the Production Manager section, you as the Production Coordinator do not have to decide to take the job at the interview. The Production Manager may be interviewing other candidates and will want to make a decision later. You are welcome to think about the possible job overnight, too. Later, review your cue cards and notes. Do you want to be involved with and be a part of this job? It will be a huge commitment. Long, hard hours. Think about it seriously. Sleep on it. Then follow up with the Production Manager the next day.

ABOUT THE PRODUCTION MANAGER & THE PRODUCTION COORDINATOR

The Production Manager oversees everything the Production Coordinator does. This process may seem slow at first, but as the PM and the PC develop a relationship of trust, the Coordinator can be given room to initiate more duties unsupervised. The production office is a very busy place, and everything eventually makes it past the Coordinator's desk. A Production Coordinator should never forget to inform the Production Manager of what is happening. The PM needs to know as much as the PC does about all that is going on in the making of the film. At its best, the PM and the PC will become friends and trust each other with secrets that will help both in excelling at their jobs. At its worst, the PM and the PC will neither inform nor help each other, and the production will stumble along with great problems as everyone finds out crucial information after the fact. Communication is a two-way street, so start off your side as best you can. Work at it. Invest in it.

—⁓—

Congratulations! You made it to the end of the interview as a Production Manager or a Production Coordinator! You have been hired! Celebrate. Take yourself out for dinner and a movie. After today, you are going to give an awful lot of your time and effort to the production. The real adventure is about to begin. You are about to turn an empty set of rooms into a running, thriving film production office. Armed with all the answers you acquired during the interview, you are ready for the adventure.

THE PERSON TO KNOW

Film festival parties are nothing less than schmooze fests. Schmoozing. Not only is it a game, it is an art. But then again, a little luck can help, too.

The goal of schmoozing is to be the Person To Know, or know the Person To Know, or be talking to the Person To Know, or be the person to introduce the Person To Know to others at the party.

Thick in a crowded festival party, I ended up in a circle with an Executive, a Distributor, a Producer, and a Director — all schmoozing at their very best. Not being perceived as being the Person To Know, I was actively ignored, which was rather uncomfortable. And being in a corner, I was unfortunately trapped from leaving the group gracefully.

The Director was the Person To Know. The Executive had his arm around the Director and was schmoozing away. The Producer input some schmooze trying to introduce some of the Director's little known facts to the Executive. The Distributor contributed, too. The Director bathed in the attention. He was the Person To Know. I just watched from my corner, for I did not know the Person To Know. On and on they went. On and on. I was getting thirsty. My drink was long gone.

Then a Big Financier walked by the group. Roles immediately shifted. The Big Financier was perceived by all to be more of a Person To Know than the Director was. The Executive leapt from the Director over to the Big Financier to be the one to introduce him to the group. The Big Financier took in the group's dynamic in a second. Then he waved off the Executive with a "not now" and stepped forward into the middle of the group to greet me... for as luck would have it, I knew him personally. "Hi, Deb. How are you doing?" After exchanging brief pleasantries, he excused himself again with a simple "Sorry, I have to go," and did not stay for any of the schmooze competition.

All eyes swung toward me. In an instant I had become the Person To Know. And they had no idea who I was.

The Executive was first to capitalize on it. He put his arm around me to introduce himself, and more importantly to find out who I was.

I held up my empty glass and answered cryptically, "He's a friend of mine. Now, if you'll excuse me, I need a refill. Cheers!" And I left gracefully... thanks to a little schmoozing luck.

BEFORE OFFICIAL PREP

2

Okay, you have the job, but the production office will not be opening for another week or so. Official preproduction has not really started yet, since it begins when the production office opens. Life before "official prep" is actually the tail end of "development." The Production Coordinator rarely starts prior to the first day of official prep — the day the production office opens — so this chapter is primarily for the Production Manager. If the Producer can afford it, the PM will start in late development. As a PM, here is what you can start accomplishing.

FROM DEVELOPMENT TO PREPRODUCTION

You may be starting work at a desk with a telephone at head office, or, if space is at a premium, you may be starting from your own home. Basically, you need a telephone and your contact lists.

PRIORITY MEETING WITH THE PRODUCER(S)

Meet with the Producer(s) again after the interview. You will have many more questions now that you are working toward production instead of working toward getting a job. What is going to be hard to find for this production? The Producers may have insight from their past experiences. You will have insight from yours. Share. Is it hockey season, and you need to rent an ice rink for three weeks? Is the busy summer season approaching when studio rental space will be at a premium? It is time to prioritize what you first need to find and secure.

BEWARE WHAT YOU PROMISE

The reason so few people are hired during development is because the financing of the production is likely still being assembled by the Producer(s). Not all sources of financing may have committed to paper their financial participation to the project. Because of this uncertainty, there is always the possibility the project could go under before it is made. Keep in daily conversation with the Producer on the status of the financing structure, and obtain approvals on any plans you have for spending preproduction monies at this stage. Remember that every time you make a promise to someone or some company on the telephone, you are spending the Producer's money. If the project happens to fall through at this early date, the Producer is responsible to pay for all your promises. You do not want to over-commit what the Producer is willing to risk. You will spend much of your time "holding" rental spaces and "checking availability," confirming that you are not ordering or booking at this stage.

SINGLE-PURPOSE COMPANY STATUS

Film companies set up a single-purpose company to produce each film they make. It keeps the accounting totally separate from both head office accounting and taxation and all the other films the company happens to be making. You will find that each season of a series will be produced by a different single-purpose company. For example, Production Company Inc., may be a parent company producing a series, but the first season of the series was actually made by Season One Productions Ltd., and the second season made by Season Two Productions Ltd. Both Season One Production and Season Two Productions will be companies owned 100% by Production Company Inc. It makes business sense. If head office or legal counsel has not set up the single-purpose company yet, now is a good time to remind the Producer to do so.

THE PRODUCTION-OFFICE TEAM

Your support team is the staff of the production office: the Production Coordinator (your right hand) with the office staff (the Assistant Production Coordinator and Office P.A.), and the Production Accountant (your left hand) with the accounting staff. The sooner you can hire these people, the more you will be able to accomplish. A Producer or an Executive may have someone in mind for the Office P.A. position already. You may have a team you have worked with before waiting in the wings. Decide on these people early. I will discuss these positions in more depth in later chapters.

PRODUCTION OFFICE

If official prep starts the day the production office opens, one of your first jobs will be to find that office. Consider parking: How many trucks and crew vehicles can you park there? Will you be parking the unit there every night and on weekends? Consider location: Is the office accessible to highways and convenient to potential locations or equipment rental facilities? Consider office space: Will the Art Department and all their computer equipment and/or drafting tables fit alongside Wardrobe and all their storage, and do you have to house the Writer(s) too? Consider security: Is there a system built-in already, or will it be easy to install one? Consider your budget: Can you afford a deluxe office space attached to a high-end studio or are you budgeted for using the basement of a church? Consider the extra costs: Will your production company have to pay for security, a telephone system, Internet access, a copier/scanner and fax, or are these necessities already set up? If the office space has a copier/scanner and fax for you to assume, is the equipment reliable and powerful enough to handle the heavy load you are about to inflict upon it? Film commissions know of office space used for previous productions. Location Managers and other Production Managers are other sources for finding appropriate space. You can also find out which companies are wrapping about the time you want to start official prep, to possibly assume their space.

KEY CREW

While you are waiting for calls back regarding office space, start assembling the key crew. Who is already committed to come on board the project? Start a crew list of your own. A list of key crew positions to start you off is in Chapter 7. In a race for the top of the list, the first jobs you will want to fill are: the Location Manager, the First Assistant Director, the Director of Photography, the Production Designer, and the Construction Manager. The Producer and the Director will be involved in these decisions, too. Key crew are critical to the realization of the project. A lot is at stake with every crew choice for key positions. The Production Designer may be on board already and drafting up designs for sets. A Storyboard Artist may be on board already penciling shots designed by the Director, or a technical previsualization team may be building sequences in 3D on the computer. The First Assistant Director, though it sounds like a Director's Assistant, is actually the Producer's or PM's representative on set. The First A.D. keeps the set running smoothly and efficiently, allowing the Director to concentrate on the creative aspects of her job. This person is the scheduling expert. You will be involved in the choice of First A.D. As your job is to bring the show in on time as well as on budget, choose the First A.D. carefully. I will discuss all the keys in more detail in Chapter 7.

STUDIO

Even if you are shooting many scenes on location, chances are that part of your shoot will be in a studio. You may have budgeted for a warehouse space or for a high-end studio. Either way, you are likely competing with other production companies for the same spaces around town. Book as early as you can for studio space. Meet with the Production Designer and the Producer to discuss the size of space actually needed — both floor space and ceiling height. As with the production office space, consider parking: Will the unit fit in the space allowed, and are the entry points convenient for equipment loading? Consider location: Is the studio close to the office, or have you found a studio with an acceptable office space attached? Consider dressing rooms: Are they decent, or will you be in studio and on location so much that you will be using the mobile units anyway; or can you schedule in such a way so you can stop renting the mobile unit when you move to the studio? Consider hair/makeup rooms: Are they acceptable in the building, or do you have to build a workable space? Consider construction space: Is there enough room for a construction shop on site? Consider multiple studios: Can you rent two studio spaces in the same building, allowing construction or set decoration to be working in one studio while the main unit is filming in the other, and does soundproofing allow it? Consider sound: If you are looking at a non-professional studio space, are you on an airport landing path, or is the space so large that the sound recordings will echo so much that you will have to replace the entire soundtrack expensively in post?

HIDDEN COSTS OF FREE STUDIO SPACE

Remember that when you score something for free or next to free, there are bound to be hidden costs. Find out the hidden costs for this studio space. They could be transparent costs like the place has no power to tap into, so you have to rent a generator. They could be not so transparent costs like the place has skylights that you cannot afford to cover, causing you to shoot at night — so you find you cannot hire the crew you want due to your all-nights shooting schedule. They could also affect other not so immediate costs: The daily rain on the tin roof makes the soundtrack so unacceptable you have to bring in all the performers and dub their voices expensively in post. Always find out how much the "free" space costs you. You may be spending more on hidden extras than if you were to rent a professional studio space. Your job is not about not spending money… it is about spending it wisely.

Film commissions and your local city/town reference sources will have listings of many acceptable studio spaces. Again, you can speak with Location Managers and other Production Managers, or people wrapping productions for their experiences at certain spaces. Find out what worked for them, and what drove them crazy. They will give you a sense of where you may have to spend money to make the space workable.

LOCATION SCOUTING

If you do not have a Location Manager on board, you will obviously need a Location Scout until you can hire the Location Manager. You need to come up with potential locations as well as studio spaces and office spaces. You cannot do this alone. The Location Scout or Manager will visit potential locations and photograph them for review at the office with you, the Producer, and the Director. This person will save you many hours of searching. Film commissions have location libraries filled with pictures of various locations that have been used for filming or would like to be used for filming. This is only a starting point. You need a Scout who can research beyond these files. A smart Scout will consider the locations you need, and come up with potential places where locations can be linked. For example, you can look one way down the street for a certain part of the script and inside one of the houses on that street there is a room that can be used as a boardroom for elsewhere in the script. And in the backyard of another place is a potential location for another part of the script. Driving the unit across town to various locations during the shoot in an expensive waste of time. A smart Scout will also ensure the owner of the location is amenable to a production filming there before you consider the place. Scouting is not just about taking pictures of beautiful places. You do not want the Director to fall in love with a location, and then have the Scout mention that the owner has no idea you were looking at the space, only later to find the owner does not want a film crew there at any cost. Do not waste precious prep time chasing unattainable locations. As PM, do not miss any location meetings. Many decisions are made that radically affect production at these meetings. You have to know about every one of those decisions.

CASTING

The Producer, the Director, and the Casting Director are taking care of casting the stars and the leads. You just need to know it is happening and if any promises are being made that will affect the budget. You will spend more time dealing with locations issues than casting session issues.

PRODUCTION INSURANCE

Arrange for production insurance as soon as you can. There are various insurance brokers who specialize in the film industry. You can compare quotes from different brokers before committing to use one. Since some departments (like

Art and Construction) may already be working, and since some of the insurance covers delays related to key cast illness, you will need insurance coverage as soon as possible. I discuss insurance in more detail in Chapter 17.

EQUIPMENT HOUSE

Camera, Lighting, and Grip equipment houses book packages of equipment like studios book space for a shoot. There is a finite amount of equipment in their stock, and each equipment house will be able to equip a finite number of productions. You will want to book your equipment package, or at least pencil in a booking for your production regarding equipment. If you book too late, you may end up with a smaller package of equipment and be forced to pay for many daily (read "expensive") rentals to make up for what is lacking. Seek out more than one quote for comparison. Decide on a supplier by both its price and its service. When a piece of equipment breaks down on set during filming, you will need service to replace it more than you will need rock bottom prices.

POST FACILITY

If you think it is too early to be thinking about postproduction, you are wrong. It is true that on day one of principal photography you are shooting, but on day two, you have begun editing the footage from day one. You need to assemble quotations from post facilities for backup and transfer (or processing and transfer) of your film.

OTHER SUPPLIERS & SPECIAL NEEDS

Other suppliers to whom you can make initial calls for quotations are: picture (digital or film) stock suppliers, special effects companies, and computer graphic imagery companies ("CGI"). Basically, evaluate what will be the most difficult or most complex to achieve. Start assembling quotations on those items. If initial quotations are showing to be over budget, now is the time to address your concerns to the Producer. The earlier you can warn of potential budget problems, the more time there is for thought that can go into the solution. A script revision or a different way of shooting may solve the problem. With early warnings, you can have time to work out the difficulty the best way for all concerned.

ISAN NUMBER

Do you have an ISAN (International Standard Audiovisual Number) yet? This numerical representation of your production is a growing requirement around the world and incredibly useful to identifying the project (especially for revenue purposes) during distribution even if the production title has been changed or is in another language. You can apply for this number during development of the script, but can only register it once the credits are locked. If you plan on purchasing different version numbers for various cuts, like the Director's cut vs. the Producer's cut, then you need the first work number now.

READ THE SCRIPT AGAIN

You read the script before starting. Read it again. Find out what the revision schedule is. Talk to the Producer about what revisions are planned for the script but are not currently reflected. There is no sense in chasing quotations for a location or an effect that does not exist in the revised script.

BUDGET & CASH FLOW

Although I go into budgeting in more detail in the next chapter, I must mention that you are working on this budget during late development. As you assemble the many quotations from various sources, you will want to reflect these savings and overages in the budget. Find out when the budget has to be "locked" for the Financiers. Make changes until you have to lock it. Read the budget over and over again. You are the budget expert. You are going to report all costs in comparison to this budget. In which lines is there potential extra money? Which lines are tight? Is the budget structured well enough for easy cost reporting? Are the fringes in one easy-to-report account or are they attached to each person throughout the budget? Make any reallocations now so that the budget is easier to read. A first cost report filled with reallocations is not only messy, but makes you look like you did not know how to write a budget in the first place. Also, start a cash flow to find out how much money you may need from a bank to interim finance the bills during production. The Producer will arrange for the interim financing, but will be relying on you to say how much of a loan is needed and for how long.

GET LISTED

Inform the film commission of your production and its contact information and shooting dates. Most film commissions publish a weekly list to the industry reporting on who is shooting what and when. If you do not want to receive unsolicited resumes or calls, ask the film commission to note on their list that you do not want such correspondence. You can wait until you open the production office before calling the commission to get on this listing; if you do that, you can have the Production Coordinator make the call.

—∽—

You may not have a production office yet, but you've chosen one, and you will move in shortly. You have been contacting people and suppliers and assembling a plethora of quotations. Even if you are not listed with the film commission yet, the rumor mill has begun. People will find out about your production any second now. Are you ready for official prep? You bet you are.

THE WRITERS' JOKE

When you work on a series, you have to deal with the issue of the crew's boredom. It is a different story, but it's the same set, the same cast, the same premise, the same crew, the same camera angles week in, week out.

So challenges arise to keep the crew's interest up. How can we push the envelope a little farther becomes the challenge. One time, the Writers got in on the fun. They wrote a shot into the script that involved moving the camera through every single room in the house... without cutting... from the point of view of a housefly. Yeah, right. Cute joke. Now what are they really going to film?

Well, the crew was up for the challenge. Grips and Electrics figured out how to light the shot so that the camera could travel through all the rooms of the house set without seeing a light, a grip stand, or a flag in shot. Camera and Grips figured out how to move the camera through all the sets and keep framing and focus in and the crew out of the shot.

The day came. A rig and harness was set up for the camera operator to start on the balcony, "fly" down to the floor, be unhooked by a grip in hiding on the set, then move through the living room, the kitchen, the dining room, back through the living room, and into the den. And what a shot it was!

So watch out for those "joke shots" the Writers write into scripts. They just might happen!

BUDGETING & BREAKDOWNS

3

There are good books on the market that walk Production Manager's through a budget line-by-line in much detail, some of which provide excellent sample budgets. This chapter will not try to replace those references. Nor will this chapter teach you how to create a budget in record time or even create one for you. The first budget you create will take you plenty of time to do because you will have to look up every calculation and double check all your numbers against quotations and price lists. That is okay. It is normal. In time you will become faster in creating budgets because you will have old budgets and cost reports to refer to, and the memory of creating them to aid you. For now, expect that the learning process will take time. What you do need to know now is what specific issues and questions will help you to understand how to read and write budgets effectively. That is what this chapter is about.

The Production Coordinator will not be nearly as hands-on when it comes to a budget, so the PC can either read this chapter to be informed of the budgeting process, or skip to Chapter 4.

OVERALL BUDGETING ISSUES

WHEN TO WRITE A BUDGET

The Producer may make the first budget, or may hire a Production Manager during development to create one. A budget is required during the process of assembling the financing, months or years before shooting begins. It makes sense to hire a budgeting specialist, like a Production Manager, to create the initial budget. Hiring this individual is the best way to create a realistic cost plan early in the process. Production Managers know the costs of production from being on set and tracking the costs on a day-to-day basis. If you have experience, you may be hired to create a preliminary production budget early in development. You may be hired to create a budget for less than your usual rate in exchange for the promise of being the Production Manager when and if the film makes it to production. If you are new to budgeting, you may offer to write a free budget for a Producer to demonstrate and hone your untried skills.

This preliminary budget, however, will not be the final, locked budget. Some line items will certainly be locked at their cost allocations and the bottom line of the budget will not change (because the financing being raised will be defined), but the script is developing and changing along the way to preproduction. The budget has to change to reflect those script changes. At some point, though, the budget must be locked, and the Production Manager has to know this locked budget inside and out. He must 'own' it and report all costs in comparison to it. As a Production Manager, you will come on board the project most likely just prior to when the budget is locked. In development the Producer and Financiers needed a budget to give them an overview of the feasibility of the project, to comfort them that the budget size would be adequate to complete the production. Now, closer to first day of principal photography, you need to ensure the budget is being prepared for the details of production, and for the reporting of those costs in the audit. If the budget is not locked when you come on board, prepare to revise the budget allocations for ease of reporting during production and audit.

BUDGETING IS ABOUT MAKING DECISIONS

How big is a budget? How long is a piece of string? Both questions have the same answer: It can be anything. Budgeting is about making decisions. Whether you are writing a budget in development or revising one just prior to locking the budget, with every cost allocation you choose, you are making decisions that production will have to follow. The number of extras you choose for a day will affect the lens size the Camera Department will need to capture the shot. The amount of overtime you budget will determine the number of set hours you shoot on a daily basis. The money you allocate to film stock will determine how many takes the Director can have. Needless to say, you cannot make all these decisions alone, and you will be discussing many questions with the Producer and the Director, but during the budgeting process, you will be surprised how many of these "production decisions" you will have to make in isolation. Be prepared to know the ramifications of the money you allocate to each budget line. Be prepared to advise the Producer on areas in the production where money may be saved if certain "production decisions" are effected.

AUDIT-LOGICAL BUDGET LINES

The audit happens long after you as the Production Manager have left the production. Why do you want to think about it at the beginning of preproduction? Producers must account for every penny they spend of the Financiers' money. You have seen the budget. The Financiers have given a lot of money to the Producer to make this film. The production costs must be viable, accountable costs. The Financiers want to know that they financed the cost of making the film and nothing else. If the production ends up under-budget, the Financiers will ask for some of their money back from the Producer. If the production goes over-budget, the Financiers will either give more money to the Producer to finish the film, or — more likely — require the Producer to cover the budget overage. The audit is a report from an outside source that verifies that the costs of production were true and accurate. It will report costs compared to the locked budget. If the locked budget is poorly structured — so that during production many cost allocations were changed to reflect where the money was actually spent, showing huge variances throughout the budget — this problem will come out in the audit and make its interpretation more difficult and therefore more expensive. Allocate costs to lines of the budget logically. Anticipate where you are really going to report on the money being spent. Fringes, for example, are easier to account for in one budget line instead of in each crew member's budget line, as Production Accountants will need only one budgetary code to report on fringes paid instead of fifty budgetary codes — one for each crew member.

DEVELOPMENT BUDGETS vs. PRODUCTION BUDGETS

Development costs are very different from production costs. In development, Producers finance costs with development money. Development money is always a loan until the first day of principal photography. In nearly all cases, if a project never makes it to camera, the loan is never paid back. Yes, that means that financing the development of a script is a very risky investment, and there is no opportunity for profit, only for recoupment of the initial investment. Development loans are to assist Producers moving a project from script to screen; the first day of principal photography is the first day a script is no longer just a script, hence this is why you pay back these loans on the first day of shooting.

As a Production Manager, you will likely never write a development budget. Producers do it. Development costs can include: story rights (so the Producer has the right to develop the project), Writer's fees and fringes, story editor's fees and fringes, researcher's fees and expenses, options or holding fees for stars, legal start-up costs, travel for Writer's meetings, Producer's fees and overhead. In later stages of development, costs can also include: pre-casting costs, pre-location scouting costs, costs for the creation of a production budget and breakdown, storyboard costs, and possibly a pre-shoot. There is a catch-22 when it comes to development costs: The Producer needs money to develop the project, but the more money spent on development, the higher the budget is required for production to pay the development costs back and still have enough money to make the film.

DEVELOPMENT MONEY IS DEVELOPMENT LOANS

Since development loans are paid back on the first day of principal photography, all the development costs are included and itemized in the production budget. Be sure to obtain a proper breakdown of the development costs and receipts from the Producer. In effect, the production is "buying the development receipts" from the Producer on the first day of principal photography. The Production Accountant will need these original receipts to cost report effectively and in preparation for the final audit.

INCORPORATE DEVELOPMENT COSTS INTO THE PRODUCTION BUDGET

There are two ways of incorporating development costs into a production budget. If you do not incorporate the costs carefully, you may be double-booking the development costs and robbing yourself of production money you can spend wisely elsewhere… or worse, you may be paying somebody twice for the same job due to a poorly structured budget!

INCORPORATING THE DEVELOPMENT COSTS - SYSTEM #1

Insert a detailed breakdown of the development budget into the development line of the budget "above the line." Remember when you are noting these costs, you will have to deduct some of these costs elsewhere in the budget; for example, you paid the Writer $25,000 during development to write the script, but her production script fee is $75,000 less any amounts payable in development. In the development line, you budget $25,000 paid to the Writer. In the Writer's line, you budget $75,000 paid to the Writer and you also report "-$25,000" for amounts paid in development. In effect, the Writer's line in the budget will add up to $50,000, and the Writer will also be reported in the development line for the $25,000 balance. The only difficulty of this system is that the Production Accountant will be writing checks on the first day of principal photography to Financiers, not to the line items of the development budget (like to the Writer).

INCORPORATING THE DEVELOPMENT COSTS - SYSTEM #2

This system is very similar to the first system, but it addresses how to keep track of how much is owed to the Financiers on the first day of principal photography and to whom to make the checks payable. Itemize in the development line of the budget the list of Financiers to be paid back and the amount each check needs to be; for example, Financier #1: $10,000; Financier #2: $35,000; Financier #3: $5,000. Also note in the development section of the budget the itemized costs of development, but do not add these numbers to the budget — just note what the costs breakdown is for development. Then, as in the first system, ensure that you deduct double-booked lines of the budget, like Writer's fees paid in development against a future production fee, Performer's options paid in development toward their production fee, and possible Producer fees and corporate overhead fees which may have a cap on allowable levels in the production budget. If you do not take the time to show the breakdown of development costs in this system, you will no doubt double-book items unknowingly.

THE FIRST READ OR PREPARING FOR THE FIRST PASS

THE PHYSICAL STRUCTURE OF A BUDGET

A budget is made up of a top sheet, detail pages, and an assumption page or memo that details assumptions on which the budget was made (the "production decisions" made during the budgeting process).

BUDGET TOP SHEET

The top sheet summarizes the entire budget by category in one or two pages. You never do any budgeting calculations on this page; just summarize the budget attached in a short form. It is the top sheet alone, rather than the complete budget with detail pages and assumption memo, that Financiers require attached to their agreements and signed by the Producer. Few people need ever see the entire budget. The budget is not a public document.

BUDGET DETAIL PAGES

The budget itself is all the detail pages of the budget. Each category from the top sheet is expanded into showing the complete calculations of each cost. The more detail you show on the detail pages, the more you will understand and remember how you achieved these cost estimates when you are in the midst of shooting. You will require this detail when you need to move costs to show savings and to cover overages as you start spending.

HEADER INFORMATION

The top sheet and the first page of the detail portion of the budget have some of these "assumption" notes in the header by the title. These header notes are of global importance to the budget, and include at least the following information:

how many shoot days, how many weeks in post, when in the year is this to be filmed, what format is the shoot and the post, which unions are or are not being used, how much is location versus studio shooting, what is the general location (city) of the shoot, what currency is being used at which exchange rate, what are the names of the production company and the Producer, and who wrote this budget and on what date and what version is it. This header information gives you a quick glance to note if this budget version is the most current or the most accurate. With a notation on a Christmas Special of "Shoot: Summer 2014" in the header, you will know this is the budget that requires a lot of snow special effects instead of the budget that has "Shoot: February 2015" in the header.

BUDGET ASSUMPTION PAGE OR MEMO

The assumption page is a separate page or memo attached to the budget, detailing further why some of the noteworthy calculations in the budget are what they are. Assumptions may mention a global cost for special effects that was not based on a quotation, but based on an allocation as instructed by the Producer to you — or be a notation of any other "production decision" you have made during the course of budgeting. It is wise to draw these noteworthy calculations and "production decisions" to the attention of the reader (especially the Producer), as all these notes make it clear what restrictions you have imposed on the production during the course of budgeting.

BUDGET FORMS

There are many budget forms available. Studios each have their own form of preference for budget structure, each with their own accounting codes. Each format may vary about which categories are above and below the line, or whether the departmental labor costs are budgeted separately from the departmental rentals and purchases, but the differences are minimal. They are all designed to be logical for the purposes of audit. If you budget a non-union production, you will probably want to use a studio-friendly budget format anyway, since the form itself will remind you to budget for categories you may otherwise forget by simply listing all the possible categories you could apply money to. It is also good to get into the habit of using studio budget formats, as this is an accounting language that works well already. In all cases you can remove empty categories you will not be using, and therefore amend the form for your own personal use. In all of Canada, for example, Producers tend to use the Telefilm Canada budget format whether the production is being funded by Telefilm or not, because the separation of labor costs from all other departmental costs simplifies the process of calculating and reporting on labor costs for labor tax credit purposes.

BUDGETING SOFTWARE

Budgeting software is discussed further in the next chapter, but know that if you are planning to budget more than once, you will need budgeting software. There are a host of shortcuts imbedded in the software that will save you the time of re-calculating employee fringes and other amounts every time you modify the budget. Movie Magic Budgeting, the most popular software for production budgeting, is excellent. Take time to become familiar with some of its features, like globals and fringes; if you are just starting, leave the other features for now. There are other key-typing short cuts in the program, but when you are learning to budget, you need the repetition of entries to teach yourself about the act of budgeting. When you have developed a skill in budgeting (you will know when), then you should learn about the other timesaving features of the program. Besides, when you learn the timesaving features later on, you will appreciate them more fully.

SCRIPT BREAKDOWN FOR BUDGETING

If you have the time and the energy, you can do an entire scheduling breakdown and create a production ("strip") board to give yourself a detailed look at the schedule of the production before starting to budget. It is more likely that you will not have the time to do a full breakdown. What you need to do, however, is a "budget breakdown" to assist you in making "production decisions" when creating the budget. There are two systems I have used as "budget breakdown." Neither of these two systems replaces the quality of information you can obtain from doing a full breakdown, but they will assist you in starting the initial budget to determine a production's feasibility at a certain budget level.

BUDGET BREAKDOWN #1 – "THE LISTS"

Have several sheets of paper handy when reading the script, and on each one, create a separate breakdown: a list of locations, noting beside each location how many scenes per location using one tick mark for each scene; a cast list, noting beside each character, the same way, how many scenes each is in; a list of each special item that costs money (like a list of vehicles, animals, children, extras, special effects, CGI, stunts, special locations, songs, etc.). If a scene is hugely long, note it on your breakdowns as more than one scene to account for the extra work that might be involved. Also note with an "N" if a scene is required to be a night shoot. This system gives you a rough idea of the contents of the script, and a rough balance of where the money might be spent. You can look, for example, at the list of locations and determine if you can reasonably achieve a shoot at 35 different locations in a 25-day shoot or not.

BUDGET BREAKDOWN #2 – "THE SPREADSHEET"

If you prefer to be at a computer screen, this system may work for you. Open a new spreadsheet and make columns for Scene Number, Set Description, D/N, # of Pages, Cast, Extras, Special Notes. If you have a large number of stunts or animals, you could create a column just for that item, too. Any special item (like vehicles, animals, children, special effects, CGI, stunts, songs, special locations, etc.) that does not warrant its own column, will be included in the Special Notes column. The information on this spreadsheet is rather similar to that on a one-line schedule, but adds special notes. As you read the script, you need to fill in each line with the appropriate information. Each entry needs to be so brief that it is in code in order to include the information and not to end up with pages and pages of notes afterward. Cast characters, for example, may appear as initials instead of spelling out their entire names. Be rough on page counts. You do not need the detail of counting in eighths of pages at this stage, as you are looking at the global picture and the proportional size of the scene to the script. You may want to round out page counts to half pages to enable this process.

MAKE DECISIONS, MAKE NOTES

While making your breakdowns, and while creating the budget, always have paper and pen or pencil next to you. Jot down questions you need to ask the Producer or the Director before making a "production decision" for them. Note anything unusual for your assumption notes later. If a thought crosses your mind that something has to be shot in a certain way to film the scene on this budget, make a note of it. When someone else reads your budget, they must understand the restrictions you place on them, agreeing to shoot the show using this particular budget. You are making decisions every time you write a budget.

HOW TO READ AND WRITE A BUDGET – THE DETAILS

Perhaps you have not written the preliminary budget. How do you read someone else's budget to understand where the money is allocated beyond a cursory glance? Look at the calculations. If there are no calculations, and only "allowances" for each category, the validity of the final budgeted numbers is questionable. Even on flat weekly rate salaries, it is easy to enter a calculation for how many weeks of prep, shoot, and wrap is assigned to each person. When it comes to postproduction, you can predict to the foot, or to the minute, the footage you need transferred, processed, printed, etc., so you can commit to calculations for nearly all post processes in the budget. Look for entire sections of the budget encompassed by one budget estimate; for example, picture and sound post being allocated a single budget figure. There are many, many steps to picture and sound post that can be itemized in the budget. By encompassing a huge number of steps into one budget number, there is a danger some or many of these steps have been omitted in estimating the cost. Replace these "allowances" with more accurate estimates based on calculations, and detail the breakdown of costs as much as possible. Review the sample budget detail page to see how much detail you can include in one line of the budget. This detail will help you immensely when cost reporting during production.

MORE SPECIFIC BUDGETING ISSUES

WHAT IS THE LINE?

"Line" Producer. Above-The-"Line." Below-The-"Line." What is that darned "Line" anyway and do you want to be above or below it? The Line's placement varies moderately from budget form to budget form, but in general, consider that Above-The-Line (ATL) costs are all the costs associated with the people who made up the creative package that was assembled in development to attract financing to make this production: the Producer, the Director, the Writer and story rights, the Star, the other development costs. Costs associated with these people include not only their pay, but also their travel and living, Assistants, and offices. Everything else in the budget is Below-The-Line (BTL) — starting with the Production Manager. Above-The-Line costs are sometimes called the "fixed costs," because by the time you reach production, these costs have been negotiated. Costs like contingency and the completion bond are often based on a percentage of the budget. They tend to remove the Above-The-Line costs from their percentage calculation because Above-The-Line costs are often above union scale rates, and sometimes are so high they artificially inflate the size of the budget, thereby artificially inflating the costs based on a percentage of the budget.

BUDGET SIZES

How many days can you shoot if you have $1.5 million to make the film? What kind of crew can you hire if you have $1.6 million per episode to shoot the series? Where in the budget will you be spending the most money in a $750,000 feature film? After you have written a number of budgets, you will be able to picture the answers to these questions. Each answer is dependent, too, on the complexity of the script and the production. You may have $1 million to make a film, but you are planning to shoot out of town, so you will have extraordinary costs for travel and living for the crew; you will have to reduce the number of shoot days you had planned to pay for the costs of moving to a distant location. The series may sound simple, but the CGI budget is so high, you may have a tough time finding enough money left in the budget to hire a union crew. The $750,000 feature will undoubtedly be spending most of its money on postproduction costs, unless, of course, something goes wrong during the shoot.

Yet, still oversimplifying, I will give you an idea of what overall budget size means to a production:

> A "$1.6M per episode series" means a union crew, a significant studio build, and great catering.

> A "$1.5M feature" means a below union-scale crew or non-union crew, a superbly tight budget for all departments, and great catering.

> A "$300,000 feature" means a crew working on deferral or for free, everyone cashing in favors in every department to obtain what is needed, insurance costs to enable cheaper equipment rentals, and great catering.

On a big budget it is expected you feed the crew well. They are working long, hard hours on the production, so it is only respectful that you do so. When the overall budget is smaller, the catering must be excellent on the production, too; since you are probably not giving the crew enough time or money to buy their own groceries, you need to feed them well to fuel them through production and keep them healthy for their work.

BUDGET PROPORTIONS

If you like to budget where you take the bottom line budget figure then sub-divide it into rough allocations or targets for Above-The-Line, Below-The-Line production, and Below-The-Line postproduction costs, then you like to budget using proportions. You will therefore need to be aware of the overall proportions of where you will spend the money in a budget. This depends on the overall size of your budget. A "big" budget has incredibly high ATL costs, high production costs, and less high postproduction costs. For a "medium-sized budget," you will have medium ATL costs, medium production costs, and medium to high postproduction costs. For a "low-budget" film, you will find low ATL costs, low production costs, and high postproduction costs. And finally, for a "micro-budget" film, you will find the ATL costs are negligible, the production costs are incredibly low, and the postproduction costs are high. Be prepared for the costs of postproduction. Though you may be able to hire crew on deferrals, and incredibly cheap equipment rentals or borrowed equipment during production, you will find that postproduction has hard costs you cannot ignore. There are stock, equipment and labor costs that have to be paid. Your booking will prevent other paying customers (perhaps paying more than you) at the sound facility in order to mix your production's soundtrack. Also, when shooting digital, editing costs can skyrocket. On the shoot day, shooting digital allows one to be less restrictive in image capture than when shooting film stock (because film stock and processing is more expensive). The extra footage from a digital shoot dominoes costs into postproduction — more footage to review means more editing time is needed — and that means more labor and equipment costs.

QUESTIONS TO ASK BEFORE WRITING A BUDGET

You may have the answers to many of these questions already from your interview, but just in case you are writing the budget early in development and have not yet been hired to production-manage the show, here are questions you need to ask at the start (for a short checklist-format form of these questions, see page 466):

> What is the project title?

> What is the type of production (i.e., a feature film, a TV series and how many episodes, a Movie of the Week)?

> What is the overall budget size? Is the figure locked?

> When is the shoot planned to be? Summer? Winter?

> How many days is the shoot planned to be?

> When is the production's delivery date to the Distributor or Broadcaster (this will tell you how long postproduction may last)? Is the date flexible?

> What format is preferred for the shoot? HD24p? 70mm? 35mm? Super 16? Digi-Beta? BetacamSP?

> What format(s) is/are being delivered? Film finish? Digital finish only? Do you have localization issues to address (such as NTSC, PAL or SECAM formats for video)? Depending on the funding partners involved and distribution channels planned, older delivery formats may be required alongside the "main" delivery format.

> What language versions need to be created?

START BUDGETING BTL

You can start to budget Below-The-Line instead of Above-The-Line. Above-The-Line costs will generate a host of questions for you that only the Producer can answer. Rather than be stalled so early in the budgeting process, start Below-The-Line. You should already know how big a crew you are planning, and how many days you are planning to shoot (as noted above), and since a number of costs

— even Above-The-Line costs — are based on a percentage of the Below-The-Line costs, you might as well start budgeting there anyway.

ATL (ABOVE THE LINE) – "THE PACKAGE"

Though you may be starting the budget Below-The-Line, for simplicity and order, here are questions you need to answer about the budget while finalizing it (The Producer may know most of these answers, or may defer to you to make a "production decision" on them.):

ATL – SCRIPT RIGHTS

How much did they cost? What is the nationality of the original work? (Nationality may affect funding sources.) Do you have to consider currency exchange on the remaining amount payable?

ATL – WRITER & SCRIPT COSTS

Is the Writer union or not? What rights are being purchased up front? Does the Writer need to travel? If so, what for, where, and for how long? What is the nationality of the Writer?

ATL – PRODUCER

Who are all the Producers and how much do they make? Is there a restriction to the overall size of Producer fees (some funding sources impose, for example, a 10% of Production plus Post costs maximum for the total sum of all Producer fees)? Who needs to travel where and for how long? What are the nationalities of the Producers? Do the Producers have Assistants to be included in the budget?

ATL – STARS

Who is/are the Star(s) of the film and what is their negotiated deal? What rights are being purchased up front? Which union has jurisdiction? Are travel, rehearsals, makeup tests, wardrobe fittings, overtime, and ADR/looping included in their deal? Do they need to travel? If so, from where? Are there other extras in their deal, specifying type of on-set dressing room, etc.? What is the nationality of the Star?

ATL – DIRECTOR

Who is the Director and what is the deal? What rights are being purchased up front? Is this person union or not? Does the Director need to travel? If so, from where and when? Will the Director need to travel for postproduction as well as for production? What nationality is the Director?

ATL – OTHER DEVELOPMENT COSTS

What costs have been attached to the project already? Is a breakdown of these costs available, as well as a list of the funding sources from development (i.e.: Writer's costs, Star options or holding fees, travel, budget/breakdown costs, Producer costs, location scout, etc.)?

BTL (BELOW-THE-LINE) PRODUCTION — "PRODUCTION COSTS"

Production ends when you have completed image capture on the set and had the footage backed-up and transferred, and you have viewed the dailies (also known as rushes). Picture editing is ready to begin. Sometimes this section is called Section "B" of the budget. These are questions and notes to ask yourself — or the Producer — while writing the production portion of the budget:

BTL PRODUCTION – OVERALL QUESTIONS

Are you shooting union or non-union? Can you pay the keys above-scale? What rights do you need to buy from the cast? Who of the crew is on board already, like the Director of Photography or the Production Designer? Is the show a period piece or is there a period piece sequence? Are there night shoots or D4N (day for night) sequences? Are there special effects? CGI? Trained animals? How much is planned to be on location versus in a studio? Are there children in the script? Is there money for a B-Camera? For second unit? For cranes? For camera cars? Any other special notes that will cost the production money?

EXPENSIVE PRODUCTION ELEMENTS

When you read a script, you may notice several of these "red flag" or expensive production elements. A few of them, well integrated into the production, can contribute to the special magic of the production; however, too many of them could make the production so costly that there is a threat the production will not be able to be completed on time and on budget:

> **Period dressing** – You definitely pay the price to recreate a period accurately, especially for costumes, uniforms, makeup, cars, and so on; not only are these items hard to find, they often require international customs and courier costs.

> **Vista shots and/or shots with lots of background performers** – For these types of shots you will need lots of crew and communication equipment to lock the set, dress, house, feed, and choreograph the performers.

> **Animals and/or children** – Neither animals or children have the focus and reasoning ability of adult performers, and both tire quickly, so the length of the shoot day is limited, as is the number of useable takes.

> **Prototype equipment** – Since prototype equipment is so unique, its problems are too, and fixing those unforeseeable problems often involves overtime, customs and courier costs, and at worse, down time for the whole set.

> **The special departments: Stunts, Special Effects, SPFX Makeup** – Beyond lots of prep and set up time required, the special departments may require various picture elements to be captured separately (plate shots, Performers against a green screen, etc.) effectively doubling or tripling the set time it takes to capture the screen minutes. Less tangible costs could include stale performances by the cast, since the highly technical environment has very valid needs, but can easily divert the focus off the scene.

> **Night shoots** – At minimum, night shoots require more lighting equipment, power, and crew to light the night.

> **Distant locations** – Obvious distance location costs include travel costs, hotels, and per diems; less tangible costs could mean you cannot hire the crew you want because they would rather be near their families.

> **Weather dependent exteriors** – There is nothing quite like everyone on set standing around waiting for clouds to pass, or clouds to arrive; no one can predict the weather months in advance when you are scheduling, so you need to have backup plans for where to shoot for all exteriors.

> **Lots of scenes** – Lots of scenes translates into lots of company moves and time in those vehicles means precious time not shooting the script.

> **International coproductions** – Beyond the obvious travel, courier, and customs costs of multi-country shoots, legal, bank, and accounting fees skyrocket in the face of complex agreements and reporting requirements for the coproducing partners.

> **Unique scheduling concerns** – Say you want to rent a hockey rink during hockey season, your ice time will probably be both limited and in the middle of the night; or say you want shoot a winter scene in the summer and you need to dress the set with mounds of fake snow and bring in trees that have no leaves. Your script and your circumstances will dictate these unique expensive costs.

> **Inherited costs from ATL deals** – Before you came on board, the Above-The-Line deals struck may have dictated that an entourage for the Star (cast or crew) needs accommodating, or that the Star will work only a limited number of hours. Examine the fine print promises in the ATL deals.

BTL PRODUCTION – CAST

What rights are you purchasing? Refer to your "budget breakdown" to determine how many days per character you are going to budget. Detail out each character name on a separate budget line, no matter how small. Each performer costs money. It is best to see that money clearly detailed, in case a script revision can help ease the cost of production by removing some of the minor talking characters. Create separate lines for rights purchases or advances against royalties, rehearsals, wardrobe fittings, ADR/looping, hair/makeup time, and overtime. They all cost money and add up quickly, whether budgeted or not. If someone has a flat picture fee, still calculate all the scale costs of that person in the budget, so that you can compare the rate with the flat picture rate. Sometimes flat rates sound high until you back-out the numbers; once accounting calculates the actual working cost of that performer after all the overtime is worked, you may still owe him money. Prepare to find out before this situation happens in wrap.

BTL PRODUCTION – CREW

Detail each crew member in the budget with at least 3 lines of budgetary calculations. Mention how many weeks you are hiring this person for preproduction, how many for production, and how many for wrap. By detailing each line separately, you can see clearly in the budget which week before shooting you planned to hire this person. Three lines noting "Prep 5 weeks, Shoot 4 weeks, and Wrap 2 weeks" is much clearer than reading: "Work 11 weeks." You can even detail an extra line for how much overtime you are budgeting for that person. The more detail now, the easier it will be to track labor expenses during cost reporting.

BTL PRODUCTION – NON-UNION LABOR RATE PATTERNS & DEFERRALS

In union shoots, you can negotiate crew labor rates at scale, and there is a pattern as to how much each person makes depending on their hierarchy in their department. On non-union shoots, there are no rules as to how each person must be paid, and each crew member could effectively have a very different rate from another. It is wise to create a "labor rate pattern" for low-budget productions. The key crew in each department earns the same rate, the second in charge receives a lower rate, and the thirds or Assistants an even lower rate, but each different department is structured the same. All keys earn the same. This creates equality on set, and crew will develop a sense of "we're all in this together" rather than looking at each other with suspicion over who negotiated the best pay deal. Another way to create pay equity is to pay everyone the same rate per day and defer the balance of their paychecks. Be sure the deferral language is clear in the crew deal memos, and that it works in synch with the other financing sources of the production.

BTL PRODUCTION – KIT RENTALS

Are you going to hire crew with kit rentals? Crew can augment their paychecks by bringing and using their "kit" on the production and charging a rental fee. Consider this possibility, especially for heads of departments or construction and grips and electrics.

BTL PRODUCTION – EQUIPMENT RENTALS

Equipment houses rent equipment at regular rates, but will likely only charge you 3 days for a weekly rental. This is known as a 3-day week. You can negotiate the number of days in a week for the rental cost, for example, maybe to a 2-day week, and affect a terrific savings. How much you can negotiate will depend on your track record with the equipment rental house, the track record of the technical crew you hire, and the track record of the head office production for paying their bills. It is best to start budgeting at a 3-day week. Extra daily rentals during production may take up the savings you affect by negotiating a short week anyway.

BTL POST – "POSTPRODUCTION COSTS"

Sometimes this section is called Section "C" of the budget. Again, the questions are for you, and for you to ask the Producer while budgeting:

BTL POST – OVERALL QUESTIONS

What are all the versions (digital and film) required for delivery? What are all the language versions required for delivery? What are all the deliverables required (like M&E or Music and Effects track, a transcription, closed-captioned, and described video masters, 100 publicity stills, an EPK Electronic Press Kit, etc.)? Which union, if any, are you using for the postproduction crew? How fancy are the titles/credits planned to be? How much stock footage might be used? What other effects or CGI is planned?

EXPENSIVE POSTPRODUCTION ELEMENTS

As there are expensive production elements that raise a "red flag," so too are there expensive elements in postproduction. Be mindful of these elements so you can carefully budget for them and remember how quickly their costs can skyrocket:

> **Production shot on digital** – Since digital stock is cheaper than film stock, there is an easy temptation during production to shoot more and more footage. In postproduction, that translates to more work hours and equipment rental time to sort, evaluate, and edit the footage.

> **Hidden CGI elements dictated by the shoot** – Though you may have plans for CGI to build obvious and flashy effects shots, you may also need CGI to build other "secret" effects shots, such as painting out animal tethers. Plan to shoot production with these options in mind whenever possible rather than planning to "fix" images in post which will quickly use up your CGI budget on these "hidden" effects shots.

> **Animals and/or children** – Working with animals and children typically means lots of short takes. In post, that means lots of editing time.

> **Prototype equipment** – Prototype equipment (and their associated challenges) can be either on set or in the editing room.

> **The special departments: Stunts, Special effects, SPFX makeup** – If there are several elements captured during the shoot to merge together into one shot, post needs to follow through on the extra time and equipment necessary to complete the merge.

> **Star Performers & ADR access** – The Star went home after the shoot; therefore access to the Star for ADR during postproduction may require a distant location facility and facilitator and/or travel costs.

> **Predictably loud locations** – If you know in advance that you will not capture excellent, usable location sound, be prepared to rebuild — from scratch — the many layers required for the soundtrack, dialogue, and background ambiance during postproduction.

> **Lots of scenes** – The more cuts required to assemble the picture, the more editing time required.

> **Music rights** – Licensing fees can add up. Many rights need to be acquired to license to perform or to play a recording of a copyrighted song.

> **International coproductions** – When dealing with different countries, not only are there many costs associated with the logistics of production and the financing contracts, there are many more delivery elements and formats and versions required – each with its own unique technical specifications.

BTL POST – MUSIC

Is the Composer's fee a flat rate to include the studio and music rights? What songs are in the budget for which you will need to secure music rights?

BTL POST – FACILITIES DEALS

Are there any facilities deals with postproduction houses that include labor costs as an investment to the production? If a post facility is investing in the production, it may provide you with equipment rentals and labor costs instead of a cash contribution to the budget. You must determine the value of the facilities deal, and include and lock those costs in the budget. It is good to make a note in brackets that this is a facilities cost. You will have to account for the cost as it happens to, in effect, "drawdown" the investment. In some cases you can negotiate a flat rate with the facility. Remember to negotiate both time and money. If you can afford to transfer your dailies in the afternoon instead of during the facility's prime and busy morning transfer slots, you will negotiate a better rate.

OTHER COSTS

Sometimes this section is called Section "D." A funny title: "Other." The costs here do not really fit into any other category, but are hugely essential in the making of a production. Such items include insurance costs, legal costs, publicity costs, financing costs, and the all-essential audit. Ask yourself or the Producer these questions:

OTHER – OVERALL QUESTIONS

What are the costs associated with the print and online publicity plan? How many years of E & O insurance needs to be purchased? How much money needs to be set aside for legal costs? Is an allocation necessary for a post Accountant as well as for an audit? Is corporate overhead to be included in the budget? When are the Financiers planning to drawdown money to the production, so you can calculate how much of the budget will need to be interim financed at a bank? Are foreign currencies involved and costs of currency exchange? If there is to be a completion bond on the production, what is the production company's history with previous bonders? Is any treaty office involved in the production that may affect the budget's requirements?

CONTINGENCY

You may hear of contingency as a percentage of B plus C. Since ATL costs can vary incredibly, and "Other" costs (legal, insurance, and publicity) can also vary hugely and are not directly related to production costs, you often calculate costs based on the "production costs" of B and C. The bigger the contingency, the more you are unsure how much the production will cost. If it is too small, it will not be effective enough to cover any unplanned costs. An estimate of 5-10% of B plus C is considered fair.

Check with the Producer if any of the contingency has already been allocated to overages. Contingency should really be spent on unexpected costs in production, not from development. These types of costs might include the deductible on an insurance claim; you never budget for an insurance claim, but you have to pay a deductible if you have one. If some of the contingency is already allocated, try to revise the budget to reflect what is really there, and therefore not give anyone reading the budget a false sense of security that there is a pot of money ready for emergencies. If you leave it allocated, but do not indicate so on the cost report, the contingency can end up being spent several times over, pushing you way over budget. Due to unforeseen circumstances, you can easily end up spending 40-50% of contingency in postproduction, so whatever is pre-allocated now, is robbing you from production costs.

SERIES & CO-PRODUCTION BUDGETS

AMORTIZATION (AMORT) & PATTERN BUDGETS

A series is best budgeted with two budgets that work together: one amortization budget and one pattern budget. The pattern budget multiplied by the number of episodes of the series will add up to the overall budget amount of the show. Here is how they work:

You have a series of 22 episodes. Just prior to shooting Episode #1 you build a set and it costs you $220,000. You do not want to allocate all the costs of building the set to Episode #1, because all 22 episodes will be shot on that set. You want to amortize the costs of that set over 22 episodes, each episode taking $10,000 of the costs. We believe in equality. Now when you are analyzing the costs from episode to episode, there is some common ground on which to do so. Costs you can put into an amort budget include: all prep costs, wrap costs, any hiatus costs during the series, set build, legal costs, audit, and other costs that affect all the episodes equally or seem to affect none of the episodes at all.

In budgeting you create one pattern budget that ends up being template for each episode being shot. When you cost report, you will have a separate cost report for each episode, matching costs to this template. One line at the end of the pattern budget (template) near the contingency will be the amort line. This is the amort budget price divided by the number of episodes in the series. Costs included in the pattern budget include: the crew, Writers, cast, locations, catering, equipment rentals, picture stock, etc. — all production costs, all post costs. Think of the things that cost money during production, or rather during the particular week(s) the show is being shot and edited.

You need to write both these amort and pattern budgets at the same time, remembering to incorporate the amort costs into the pattern budget.

COLUMNAR BUDGETS

International co-productions offer another layer of complexity to budgeting. You will need to prepare for two audits, not one. You want to know how much the whole show costs, as well as each country's costs separately. Therefore, you need a budget with three total columns: my town costs, the Co-Producer's town costs, and total costs. Yes, that means three cost reports each period when in production: my town, the Co-Producer's town, and the consolidated costs. Keep track of any dual costs (like dual citizens); they can help you later when you are going over budget in certain categories and are jeopardizing the cost split balance.

Sub-groups are an advanced feature in the Movie Magic Budgeting software that works well to help create columnar budgets. To do so properly, you need to allocate each line of the budget to one subgroup or another: my town, the Co-Producer's town, dual/either country costs.

Ensure that no line of the budget (and therefore no one accounting code) is shared by two different countries. By separating each line — even separating the Producers by country to separate budget lines — you will make reporting these costs much easier. If all the lines have been separated and marked early, it will be clear which country is to account for which lines of the budget. You will notice that all budget forms have large leaps in account codes for the specific purpose of allowing extra new accounts to be added within a budget without renumbering the entire accounting code system.

A FEW MORE OVERALL BUDGETING ISSUES

MISSING CATEGORIES IN THE BUDGET TEMPLATE

Budget templates' line items are coded consecutively; however, not every number is used; you will notice large gaps in the numbering system, i.e. 12.01 is followed by 12.05, omitting the use of 12.02, 12.03 and 12.04. Reasonably, no one template can predict all the cost categories essential to every production now and in the future. Add missing categories where you need them and next to contextually similar line items. This method works especially well to clearly separate international co-production costs (such as Producer fees) for the two countries.

THE CONFIDENTIALITY OF THE BUDGET

The Producer, the Production Manager, and the Financiers of course need to see the budget. Unions will ask for a copy of the top sheet, too. But do you show the crew their budget lines? Their departmental budgets? Budgets are confidential documents, not public documents. On some productions you will find you have to sign confidentiality agreements if you work with the budget, so that you do not share the information with just anyone. Besides that, what you decided when writing the budget will modify as you head into production. As you spend money, or promise deals, you may be moving money from one line to another to make that deal happen, so the original budget line items become stale very quickly, and the budget no longer truly reflects the cost report. Nevertheless, do not show the budget to anyone who does not absolutely have to see it.

HOW TO CATCH OVERSPENDING

You will be working closely with the Production Accountant, tracking and predicting costs all the way through production. For more on this relationship, see Chapters 19–22. Beyond that, you need to attend all meetings with Location Scouts. Find out what is being promised, especially by the Producer. Have discussions with department heads regarding their departmental budgets and spending status. Make the crew accountable for their spending. If they do not report to you, they do not know what they are spending. If something new is mentioned in meetings, speak up and ask how it is being paid for — what is being removed to make it happen? Be vocal. Be sure the Director and the Producer and the Assistant Director are behind you and the budget. You are the crew's reminder of money being spent.

ABOUT WRITING BUDGETS FOR FREE

When Producers know you are writing budgets, they will ask you to write budgets for free. If you are new to writing budgets, go ahead. The practice is good. Each budget you create will be another you can use for reference in future budgeting work. The practice is invaluable. Be sure to do an excellent job each time. Your work must be as thorough and accurate as if you were being paid. If not, the final budget will not be worth the effort — for you or for the Producer. Budgets take a lot of work and sweat to create. If you cannot afford the time and the energy, or do not need the practice, do not write budgets for free. Like any voluntary work… if you are not getting something out of it, you will end up resenting the time you lose in working for nothing. You have to enjoy even the "free" work.

—⁓—

So, now you have a locked budget, and it is time to spend the money. The production office is about to open. It is time to consider what you need in that office to work effectively.

THE HOLE IN THE WALL

The production office was at the end of the hallway and so its only access was via the front door. The view out the windows was lovely and unobstructed as we were above the first floor and no trees or balconies were in the way. Of course we had security on the front door, but why would we need a motion sensor? There was no other way in..., or was there?

Who would have thought the thieves would break in to the office three companies down the hall (which did not have security on its front door), and then break a door-sized hole through each wall to access all the companies on the floor – ours included? It was almost cartoon-like to peer through the breech in the wall through the series of holes – all carefully lined up – and to see into the offices of each company along our floor. It must have been easy to relieve us of our computer equipment with this access.

They were picky too. They took the latest equipment and left the old stuff. Naturally, our production information was on the hard drives of the new stuff. Naturally, the few computer kit rentals we had around the office were also newer models and designed to be portable. Naturally, we procrastinated doing regular data backups.

Production doesn't really stop for insurance claims, so there is little time to waste. So, after quickly replacing the equipment – thanks to insurance – we had precious little time to rebuild the electronic information on the new equipment while shooting continued, unaffected. All I can say is thank goodness for all that paper on the distribution table.

And, yes, we added a motion sensor to the security system.

YOUR KIT & ONLINE RESOURCES 4

Though a desk and a telephone will suffice for you to start work, it hardly ends there — or rather, it hardly begins there — to work effectively. You probably already have a computer and a printer you will be using on the production. If so, you have already begun to assemble your kit. It is time to think about the rest of that kit: key reference items and material you can bring to the office to start working more quickly and efficiently.

YOUR REFERENCE SOURCES

A key part of the kit you bring to a production is your reference sources: both online and in print. Besides this book, let us have a look at other reference sources for the Production Coordinator and the Production Manager.

THE COORDINATOR'S REFERENCE SOURCES CHECKLIST
- ☐ Your personal crew & contact lists from past jobs
- ☐ Telephone books (White Pages & Yellow Pages)
- ☐ Your library of production resources
- ☐ Other city production resources
- ☐ Non-Production reference sources
- ☐ Crew & union reference information
- ☐ Cast & union reference information

THE MANAGER'S REFERENCE SOURCES CHECKLIST
The Production Manager may have a copy of all the reference books the Production Coordinator has, plus a few extras:

- ☐ Budget reference material
- ☐ Crewing reference material

YOUR PERSONAL CREW & CONTACT LISTS FROM PAST JOBS

Over time, you will collect a wealth of reference documentation (such as contact lists, crew lists, and crew resumes) from every film you complete. Storing paper copies of these documents in a binder for future reference means you will never have to worry about changing technologies, the readability of old file formats, or networks being down, but the binder does become more bulky over time than keeping the files electronically on a portable drive. Find a system that works for you because the information in these documents will be most relevant to you in the future and will end up being your first and foremost research tool.

TELEPHONE BOOKS (WHITE PAGES & YELLOW PAGES)

Next to your own collection of crew lists and contact lists, these are your first and foremost research tools. Never underestimate their value in helping you find something or someone.

YOUR LIBRARY OF PRODUCTION RESOURCES

Many online guides to local resources are available, including *www.la411.com*, *www.newyork411.com*, *www.reelwest.com* (for Vancouver), the "Ontario Production Guide" at *www.omdc.on.ca* (for Toronto), and *www.mandy.com* (for multi- and international locations), to name just a few. Categories span accommodations, animals, crew, equipment, studio listings, and more. See the PM and PC links pages that I have set up for you at *www.debpatz.com* for other online production resources. You may customize your own unique set of Internet site bookmarks or favorites on your kit computer or online at sites such as *www.delicious.com* for easy access from production to production. Print versions of some of these online guides are available, which can be handy in your kit so that you are not tied to Web access to seek a certain contact number. Government liaison offices often have publications that you can add to your reference library.

OTHER CITY PRODUCTION RESOURCES

If you deal with another city repeatedly, you would do well to bookmark resources specific to that city or buy the guide to that area, too. From these sources you can find, for example, that limousine company or costume shop you need.

NON-PRODUCTION REFERENCE SOURCES

Other online (or print) resources that will prove useful to you during production include: zip code/postal code look-up, reverse telephone number look-up, mapping sources to map out your shooting zone and create location maps, especially when the Locations Department cannot, traffic conditions, and the list goes on. A good place to start for such a list is the PM and PC resource links I have provided at *www.debpatz.com.*

CREW & UNION REFERENCE INFORMATION

Unions and guilds (for technicians to directors to writers) have a variety of online reference material that you will find useful including, standard production agreements, template agreement forms, and membership lists. However, not all the information may be available online. The PM will refer to these resources when looking to hire and negotiate with crew; the PC will refer to them when looking for daily crew and when completing the crew deal memos.

CAST & UNION REFERENCE INFORMATION

Performers' unions have agreements and forms you will need in completing cast contracts. The union's pictorial membership list may be available online or in print form and it depicts Performers by photograph. Since this list is so useful to Producers and Directors during casting, it is nice to have a copy of the print version in the office for reference.

BUDGET REFERENCE MATERIAL

As a Production Manager, you will not only be needing your old contact lists in the future, you will also find it helpful to save rate sheet and flyers from former suppliers. Some of this information may be irrelevant to your current production, but may prove useful in the future. Be prepared to store some of this reference information electronically (on your kit computer and/or portable drive) as well as physically (in a set of physical files in a binder or box). You will bring this information from production to production. The collection of budget-related information will help you estimate quotations and assess the feasibility of acquiring a specialty item before committing the time to detailed research. Government Liaison Offices or payroll companies may also publish a "budgeting reference" as a quick guide to pricing just about anything to do with producing films, sometimes including floor plans and dimensions of the all studio spaces in your city. After using these guides for rough initial estimates, remember to seek proper quotations in order to obtain more accurate pricing and the best deal.

CREWING REFERENCE MATERIAL

Old crew lists are useful reference when crewing future productions because you are already hugely familiar with the members of the crews you have hired. You will, however, also have met or considered numerous candidates that you have not hired but could prove to be excellent potential hires in the future. Collect these candidates' resumes and contact information as well, either online and/or in print. For the in-print collection I suggest the file-box storage method. Due to the volume of documentation that you will accumulate, date each resume so you when you refer to it in the future, you will be aware of how stale the information might be. Then, just drop the document in the box, keeping the latest on top, and the files will stay organized longer than you can imagine.

YOUR START-UP SUPPLIES

Every time you start up a new production office, you find that production has to buy all sorts of the same supplies over and over again, from the rental computer all the way down to the paper and the pen to write down the first telephone message. The Production Manager may do well to add photos and a calendar to the PM kit to feel more at home, but the Production Coordinator would do well to add a number of office supplies to the PC kit to start the office up and running swiftly.

THE COORDINATOR'S DETAILED START-UP SUPPLIES CHECKLIST

Upon first arriving at the production office, here is what the Production Coordinator will need: (For items that are "expendable," bring them with you in your kit, then top them up to the same starting level at the end of production, preparing for the next office you will need to start-up.)

- ☐ Date stamp and pad (for date-stamping the mail)
- ☐ Three-hole punch
- ☐ Stapler and staples
- ☐ Heavy-duty stapler (for thick scripts; depends on your funds)
- ☐ Box of pens and pencils
- ☐ Fat permanent marker (for labeling courier packages)
- ☐ Eraser
- ☐ Electric pencil sharpener
- ☐ Manual pencil sharpener (for backup when electric one fails)
- ☐ In-trays
- ☐ Scissors
- ☐ Glue stick
- ☐ Matte clear tape (shiny clear tape becomes tacky in time)
- ☐ Packing tape
- ☐ Telephone message pad ("duplicates" so you retain a record)
- ☐ Paper clips and dispenser
- ☐ Ruler

☐ Pad of lined paper
☐ Desk or wall calendar
☐ Manila envelopes
☐ Letter-sized envelopes (for before letterhead is printed)
☐ File folders (to furnish the files on your desk)
☐ File folder labels
☐ Plastic or tin box for storing copies of keys
☐ Extra printer cartridge/ink
☐ Some of your usual courier waybills and packaging
☐ Pictures and knick-knacks to make you feel at home

YOUR COMPUTER & OFFICE EQUIPMENT

Not all of the following equipment is necessary to complete your kit. You decide how extensive a kit you would like to maintain.

THE COORDINATOR'S COMPUTER & OFFICE EQUIPMENT CHECKLIST

☐ Computer & Printer
☐ Essential and nice-to-have software
☐ Paper-cutting board

THE MANAGER'S COMPUTER & OFFICE EQUIPMENT CHECKLIST

The Production Manager will not likely have the cutting board, but will have the rest of the items the Production Coordinator has, plus a few extras:

☐ Budgeting software for the computer
☐ elephone headset
☐ Smart phone

COMPUTER & PRINTER

In most cases you are expected to provide your own computer (and sometimes printer) to use during the course of production. If you need to build a network of computers, renting might still be the way to go to ensure full computer compatibility around the office and various nodes of the network. The photocopier is likely also to be the scanner and network printer of the production office; however, you may still choose to bring your own printer to use when the copier/scanner is wall-to-wall busy copying other production documentation, or to print confidential material more discreetly.

Three important considerations to keep in mind when purchasing your kit computer: (1) the film industry uses both PC and Mac systems. If you work with one or a few companies repeatedly and you have not already committed to personally owning either Mac or PC, find out which system they use for maximum compatibility; (2) since technology changes so rapidly and what was considered top-of-the line a few months ago becomes ordinary today and outdated a few months from now, it is best to buy the latest equipment you can afford. It will maximize the useful term of your equipment and minimize the time you will need to learn and re-learn the nuances of working on your most useful tool; and (3) freelance life demands portability; though desktop computers provide more options for less money, if it annoys you to take four trips to the car to move your computer parts (CPU, monitor, printer, keyboard, and accessories), the frequency of your jobs should make you consider notebook computers and portable printers.

If you are really keen, you could even include a typewriter in your kit. This machine is still useful for typing envelopes, forms, and even the odd check.

ESSENTIAL AND NICE-TO-HAVE SOFTWARE

What programs do you really need on your kit computer? You want flexibility to excel at the tasks of your job. You also want compatibility with the other computers on your network during production and with the computers your production files will be going to after production.

The essential list includes: word processing software (such as Word) to cover roughly 80% of your production documentation needs; spreadsheet software (such as Excel) to make simple forms and handle numbers; database software to track your contacts (which you can also do online or in your word processor or spreadsheet program). For the Internet, you will need at least: a web browser (such as Internet Explorer or Safari); security software (such as Norton or McAfee); Adobe Reader to read PDF files; and email-managing software unless you only access webmail.

On the nice-to-have list, for working with scripts, you may need specialty script formatting software (such as Final Draft or Movie Magic Screenwriter). This type of software is rather useful as it will force a professional script format on the material and can automatically number both the scenes and pages (even A & B scenes and pages during revisions). Changes to the locked script will also automatically be marked for easy identification. Nevertheless, some Coordinators prefer to work in a word processor to publish the locked shooting script and manually track the script revisions because their familiarity with the word processor's features allows them to manipulate and fine-tune the presentation of revisions in a way that the specialty software cannot. For example, when the specialty software forces an "A" page during the revision to display one line of text, a manual change could expand the margin slightly on one line of the preceding page to remove the need for the extraneous "A" page. Note, however, that once you move the script into a word processor for manipulation, the trip is one-way; you lose the ability to go back to the script formatting software.

Another nice-to-have specialty software is production-scheduling software (the most noted being Movie Magic Scheduling). This type of software is simply a database program written specifically to schedule film productions. Basically a customized database software, this program takes the input of AD breakdowns of each scene and creates a production schedule for manipulation and printing. Assistant Directors will most likely have this software on their computers and they will output the schedule themselves, thus requiring only photocopying and distribution. The software is expensive, and as PM or a PC, you will rarely use it. Still, it is wise for the Production Coordinator to be familiar with this program should you have to revise the schedule in the AD's absence; and it is wise for the Production Manager to be familiar with this program should you have to generate a detailed schedule for budgeting purposes, or because you are on a super-low-budget film and you need to be the one creating the shooting schedule.

Network connectivity software is useful if you are going to host or connect to a VPN (Virtual Private Network) to link your computer to perhaps head office or just elsewhere around the production office. When you do, ensure to work in a secure, password-protected, encrypted network. FTP (File Transfer Protocol) software is also useful if you are going to have access to upload or download material from the production's FTP site for elements such as dailies and/or production documentation. It could also be useful if you will be one of the contacts charged with uploading content to the production's website.

There are many other software choices available to you, and how much you choose to load onto your kit computer and maintain will depend on your technical ability, interest, and style.

PAPER-CUTTING BOARD

After reduce-photocopying script sides, you will need to cut them. A cutting board makes this job much easier and faster than using scissors. It is not necessary for the PC kit, but advisable.

BUDGETING SOFTWARE FOR THE COMPUTER

The Production Manager will no doubt need budgeting software on the kit computer. Though it is possible to write a budget in spreadsheet software such as Excel, custom budgeting software (like the best known, Movie Magic Budgeting) has many features that address the nuances of the film and television industry. This software knows that writing the budget is only the beginning. There will be hours of tweaking, reducing, re-allocating, and comparing scenarios. As a tool for the Production Manager, custom budgeting software is so worthwhile that it could be considered essential to all but the super-micro budget productions. Once you own such software, it behooves you to learn all the shortcuts the program has to offer so you can write budgets efficiently, with integrity, and with the ability to make easy modifications.

TELEPHONE HEADSET

Since the Production Manager spends so much time on the telephone, it is wise to have a headset to hook up to the telephone to save neck and back trouble. Though the telephone rental company may provide headsets, the best fit, most comfortable and easiest to use will be the headset of your own choosing.

SMART PHONE

Not really mandatory requirement, smart phones provide excellent telephone and email access to the PM when not in the office. Besides that, once one starts using a smart phone on a regular basis, it is apparently exceedingly difficult to continue working without one.

IDENTIFY & INSURE YOUR KIT

A folder label with your name can be attached to almost anything in your kit for identity. This system will help you to collect all your equipment at the end of production. As for insurance, your kit belongs to you. Properly insure expensive equipment. If the software you have purchased is hugely expensive and comes with a serial number, you can insure the software, too.

—m—

You now have virtual or physical boxes of reference material standing by. You are prepared to start work in the production office. Get set to enter the empty office and turn it into a functional, living, breathing production office. You are ready.

PREPRODUCTION II

Fail to prepare... prepare to fail.

SWEATY, THE BURGLAR

Most break-ins are memorable for the grief they cause. Critical office equipment is stolen, yet you must continue on with production at the same frantic pace. You feel your privacy has been invaded, knowing that someone was in the office routing through your things in your absence. You are not alone.

Well, my most memorable break-in was by a fellow we never caught. We didn't even know this guy broke into the office four times, until a month after he'd done so! He left no trace of his presence and took no office equipment of any kind. Yet a month after his first deed we had an exact record of his movements and written proof. At this point, I dubbed him "Sweaty," because this is what he was up to:

Sweaty broke into the production office every Thursday morning precisely at 2:00 a.m. Each time he came in, he used our office for a solid three hours. He spent his time dialing and re-dialing "1-900" phone-sex numbers.

We never discovered the way Sweaty got into the office, and by the second month, he was gone and never returned. His signature? He left us his $750 telephone bill.

SETTING UP THE
PRODUCTION OFFICE

5

The Production Manager has found the production office. An empty office. The Production Coordinator is about to bring it alive, setting up the physical office. The Production Manager is about to bring it alive, setting up the financial backbone to it. After production wraps, the production office is to become empty again. But where do you start now? Turn to your bedside table. Put a pen and paper beside the bed. This is for when you wake up in the middle of the night panicked that you have to remember to do something in the office the next day. Next, set up two alarm clocks (one battery-operated) so that no matter how tired you are, and no matter what power outage may happen, you can wake up on time. Finally, go into the office, open the book to this chapter, and begin.

THE COORDINATOR SETS UP THE PHYSICAL PRODUCTION OFFICE

Though it is the Production Coordinator who actually ensures this setup happens and does most of the hands-on work, the Production Manager needs to know the answers to the Coordinator's questions before they are asked. Both should read about setting up the physical production office (including the virtual components that link various teams).

You have an empty office and a group of people that will be using it. Your first order of business is to place everyone logically in that office. Draw a rough sketch of the office floor plan. Your artistic skills are not being tested here, so have fun with it.

THE OFFICE FLOOR PLAN

The office likely will have a large open area and several offices with doors and locks. Do not worry about creating a drawing of exceptional quality or even a floor plan to scale, but do note which offices are larger than others and which ones have windows. You will use this floor plan extensively in this chapter, and again for marking the placement of telephone extensions, so legible is the key word.

LIST CREW WHO WILL NEED OFFICES AND/OR DESKS

Make a list of who will be using the office, who needs a desk, who needs a lockable room, and who has already been assigned a desk or a room. The Production Manager's input will increase accuracy.

PLACE NAMES ON THE FLOOR PLAN

With pencil and eraser, or with names marked on sticky (post-it) notes, place the crew on the floor plan. Talk to each department for their wish list regarding office placement. Move the names around and around until you achieve an appropriate compromise for all wishes. Using a modest production as an example, here are some likely initial minimum concerns about crew placement:

> **Producer** – Private office

> **Director** – Private office

> **Production Manager** – Private office, near Production Coordinator for frequent access

> **Production Accountant** – Private office that locks

> **Assistant Production Coordinator** – Near entrance door to act as reception

> **Production Coordinator** – Near the entrance if there is no Assistant Coordinator; in a place of high traffic, so that crew and Coordinator have frequent access to each other

> **Office Production Assistant** – Desk

> **Assistant Director Department** – Desk and telephone, near Director

> **Locations Department** – Room for maps on walls; room for storage of tables, chairs, and other Location Department purchases

> **Art Department** – Room for computers and printer (or drafting tables), plus at least one spacious work table and large filing cabinets

> **Set Dressing Department** – Room for storage of purchases

> **Wardrobe Department** – Room for wardrobe racks and wardrobe purchases; dressing rooms and fitting room for studio shoot; laundry room

> **Hair/Makeup Department** – Room with makeup mirror for studio shoot

> **Transportation Department** – Desk and telephone

OFFICE FURNITURE & EQUIPMENT

Once the crew is placed on the floor plan, make a list of required furniture to be rented or purchased. Have the Production Manager approve the list, then order the furniture immediately. While you wait for the furniture to show up, use pencil and eraser or more sticky notes to add further decorating concerns to your office map. Some items are too small to be drawn on the map, but can hardly be called insignificant, so arrange for them too, imagining them on the map.

THE FURNITURE & EQUIPMENT CHECKLIST

- ☐ Copier/Printer/Scanner
- ☐ Printer(s) for Digital Photos
- ☐ Facsimile Machine
- ☐ Telephones
- ☐ Computer & Other Printer Equipment
- ☐ Copier/Printer/Scanner & Facsimile Machine Supplies
- ☐ Office Supplies – Photocopier Paper Storage Shelf
- ☐ Office Supplies – Stationery Shelf/Cabinet
- ☐ Filing Cabinets
- ☐ Playback Machine & Television/Monitor (Office)
- ☐ Playback Machine (Producer or Director)
- ☐ Office Craft Service Area
- ☐ Water Cooler
- ☐ Washer/Dryer
- ☐ Distribution Table
- ☐ Wall Envelopes (Crew)
- ☐ Wall Envelopes (Forms)
- ☐ "To Set" Box
- ☐ "To Head Office" Box
- ☐ "PA" Box
- ☐ "Mail" Box
- ☐ Dailies/Rushes Sign

COPIER/PRINTER/SCANNER

You will be making up to 10,000 copies per week. Honestly. Rent the best high-volume and fastest machine you can. This means the machine will be loud, so do not place the copier next to the Reception telephone. Put it in its own room, or at least in the most remote place in the office with dividers around it for sound containment. You will be double-sided copying the call sheet, collating masses of scripts, copying on letter-size, legal-size, 11" x 17" size (for the Art Department), enlarging and shrinking, and clearing out paper jams with great frequency. You may also link the main printer to your computer network to serve as the default printer for the production office. With this set up you can scan physical documents to your computer as PDF files to aid with electronic filing and distribution of documentation. Some companies will loan you a second such photocopier machine at no charge to have on hand in case the main copier breaks down (which it usually does on Fridays after 5:00 p.m.). Secure a service contract.

PRINTER(S) FOR DIGITAL PHOTOS

Continuity, Wardrobe, Hair and Makeup take many documentary photographs during production to supplement their production notes with much-needed visual reference. A couple of printers dedicated to printing out these digital references are essential. Polaroid film used to be the norm for these digital references; however, the film was very expensive. Now with the use of digital cameras, a printer or two is required for hard copy prints. During prep, Locations may use this printer to strike panorama prints of the short list of potential locations.

FACSIMILE MACHINE

With the ability to scan and email documents, the fax machine has become a less popular machine than it used to be for information distribution; however, it still proves useful, and can even serve as an emergency photocopier for small jobs when the main copier/printer/scanner is too backlogged with a string of jobs in the queue. This machine is not loud. Keep it accessible so that the office staff can monitor it from their desks.

TELEPHONES

Make a list of who needs a telephone before you approach the telephone company. Note that you will need a fax line. Also keep in mind what line requirements you may need for your Internet connection. Note, too, who really needs to have access to long distance on their telephone sets and who would just like to have it. You can restrict long distance and directory assistance on individual sets. It is amazing how many long distance calls happen on a telephone that is on an unmanned desk in an open concept office. It is also amazing how many times you will pay for directory assistance no matter how many telephone books are stacked by each telephone set. (More on choosing a telephone system is in Chapter 9.)

COMPUTER & OTHER PRINTER EQUIPMENT

Are you using Mac or PC? Are you bringing in your own equipment or renting? How many people need a computer? With so much use expected of the default copier/printer/scanner, might you need a secondary printer or two around the office? Is the Accounting computer and printer updated and fast enough to run the payroll software and print all the checks? Keep the name of a repair company and your I.T. contact handy. When you look at the price difference between renting and purchasing, does purchasing make more sense? Check if head office will want to buy back the purchased computer equipment at the end of production before committing to renting versus purchasing.

COPIER/PRINTER/SCANNER & FACSIMILE MACHINE SUPPLIES

Both machines need toner and paper. Store these supplies near each machine for efficiency of replacement and for frequency of monitoring them. Supplies can come from your office supplies source, from an independent source, or be included in your service contract. Check around for best rates and accessibility. Most places deliver.

OFFICE SUPPLIES - COPIER PAPER STORAGE SHELVES

Have plenty of shelving available for the various colors of paper you will need for script revisions. Store the paper near the copier for ease of access. Label each shelf for each color and stack the reams of paper so that at a glance you can see which colored paper is running low.

OFFICE SUPPLIES - STATIONERY SHELF/CABINET

Place a cabinet or a shelf in a visible area of the office for storage of all the supplies. Have a pen and paper (preferably attached to each other) on hand for crew requests. Make sure there is a space on that paper for crew to note their requests and their names so that the right supplies make it to the right people. To prevent crew overindulgence (especially nearing wrap), the Production Manager needs to approve the requests before ordering. Many companies deliver office supplies. Delivery is a great way to cut down on the Office Production Assistant's runs. Check how long the turnaround for an order is, what conditions are inflicted on the order, and if the price makes it worthwhile.

FILING CABINETS

Note everyone who will require cabinets from the Producer to the Production Accountant to the Production Manager to the Coordinator. The top of a two-drawer lateral filing cabinet can serve a great second purpose as a shelf for the facsimile machine or a set of binders. An empty filing cabinet drawer can serve as a locking drawer for supplies you or the Accountant will need hidden and secure.

PLAYBACK MACHINE & TELEVISION/MONITOR (OFFICE)

How will dailies be viewed? To make them accessible in the production office, a playback machine with television or monitor is essential. Discuss with the Production Manager the type of machine and features required, for example, does the playback machine need access to the FTP site to download the dailies directly from postproduction, or does it only need the ability to play a portable copy of the dailies (such as DVD)? Would it be useful to have a set up where you can burn copies of the dailies and final shows right there in the production office? When you know what you need, shop around. Depending on the term, renting or buying will be the better option. Remember to add a stand with or without wheels for the equipment to your shopping list, and decide if the unit is going to be kept in the Producer's or the Director's office, or in the main office (for everyone's access). Remember to assemble plenty of extension cords and patch cords. Does head office want to buy back the equipment after production?

PLAYBACK MACHINE (PRODUCER OR DIRECTOR)

Visiting Producers or Director may need a playback machine in their hotel rooms. The Production Manager should know if this is necessary, or find out. A second playback machine in the office (when not at the hotel) can double as part of the set up to burn dailies and final shows.

OFFICE CRAFT SERVICE AREA

Often this area is where the office playback machine and television/monitor are kept. Impromptu meetings happen here as people talk over a cup of coffee. Place a couch or a few chairs in this area to make the area more like a lounge or waiting area. Use a coffee table, end tables, lamps, and posters as other decorating ideas. Be creative. Set up the food and drink section with some or all of the following:

> **Coffee Machine** – so mandatory, the coffee machine could be a union requirement; keep in mind you'll be ordering a second one for use on set

> **Tea Kettle** – good for instant soup, hot chocolate, and, of course, tea

> **Refrigerator** – to store milk, cream, brown bag lunches, and, of course, after-work beer

> **Other Equipment** – cappuccino maker, toaster, toaster oven, microwave oven, hot plate, and any other equipment your heart desires and the budget allows

> **First Aid Kit** – when shooting, the set will need one, so buy one early for use around the office; when shooting begins, you can scale down the size of the office First Aid Kit and give the big one to set

WATER COOLER

The water cooler is just about as necessary as the coffee machine. You can choose from cold water only to hot -and cold-water machines. Either way, water and coffee machines have a love-hate relationship. It is not a good idea to have them next to each other. The high mineral content of bottled water creates a build up and plugs the coffee machine in such as way that water will pour out its side cracks. You can check with your coffee company and find out if your machine is designed, like most, for tap water. If the crew does not like the taste of the coffee, try a new coffee bean. Also note that you will likely be ordering a second water machine for use on set.

WASHER/DRYER

The Wardrobe Department will need these. Louder and hotter than the copier, this duo needs its own room. Check whether renting or buying makes more sense. You will need a plumber for installation.

DISTRIBUTION TABLE

Place a folding table in the highest traffic area of the office. Position it so that everyone will trip over it. You want them to do just that, because on the distribution table you will be laying out all the latest paperwork that the crew wants and needs (copies of scripts, crew lists, call sheets, and so on). Make sure that you (the Coordinator), Assistant Coordinator, and/or the Office Production Assistant can see the distribution table so that you all can keep the document copies topped as the hoards of crew descend on this table daily.

WALL ENVELOPES OR CUBBIES (CREW)

For wall envelopes, assign wall space near the Assistant Coordinator's or the Coordinator's desk. Use heavy-duty envelopes, mark them for each department, and use them to gather paperwork for those departments that are currently not in the office. A paperclip on front can also serve to gather each department's telephone messages. For a wooden rack of cubbies, simply label each slot with the name of each department. (A list of possible departments for wall envelopes or cubbies is in Chapter 30.)

WALL ENVELOPES OR CUBBIES (COMPANIES)

For wall envelopes, assign wall space for these, too. Similar to the crew envelopes, these are used to gather physical documentation for the various producing and outside companies involved (if you are not sending information electronically). Collect appropriate documents over the course of the week, and send these packages at week's end. (A list of possible companies for wall envelopes or cubbies is in Chapter 30.)

WALL ENVELOPES OR CUBBIES (FORMS)

Assign more wall space for these envelopes, or label more available cubby slots. These are blank forms that crew will ask you for constantly, from letterhead (if pre-printed) to time sheets. (A list of forms for wall envelopes or cubbies is in Chapter 30.)

"TO SET" BOX

This box can be made out of a wonderfully big paper box top and can be placed on the distribution table, or near the entrance door. Use it to collect paper, notes, and all those various items that must go to set on the next run. Everyone (such as the Drivers and the Office Production Assistant) en route to set should check this box before leaving the office. Make it convenient for them to stumble across and check.

"TO HEAD OFFICE" BOX

Like the "To Set" box, place this box so that it becomes the last place to check before going to the head office. This box can be made redundant if all items to go to head office are put into the "P.A." Box.

"P.A." BOX

This is the in-tray for the Office Production Assistant. Place it on the P.A.'s desk, and make sure it is big enough to hold parcels as well as paperwork.

"MAIL" BOX

Place this in the office to gather mail to be posted (near the "P.A." Box or the "To Set" Box). Ensure that each night someone takes the contents to a real mailbox. Set a policy about buying stamps so that crew do not fall into the habit of leaving you their unstamped mail for production to mail.

DAILIES/RUSHES SIGN

Some people call them "dailies," others call them "rushes." On some productions, dailies take several days to ship, transfer and synch, and so the term becomes a misnomer. Dailies also means those crew that are only working today, and so the term sometimes is just plain confusing. Whatever you call the captured image that has just been transferred and synched and is ready for first viewing, be familiar with both terms and make and place a sign by your desk that reads: "Dailies Tonight Will Be At _____" — and leave a space for the time and location. The time will change daily and even hourly. Having it posted saves you remembering the latest change and informs people around you without their having to interrupt to ask you. Typically dailies are screened on a television or monitor, but for feature films you may also wish to arrange regular viewing of the dailies on a bigger screen (like at the post facility) to preview the big screen experience.

INVISIBLE OFFICE REQUIREMENTS

Your handy office map can take a break. "Invisible" office requirements are services that you must have on hand to complete the office setup. Over time you will have a contact list of these companies that you use from show to show. On your first show, take the time to start this list early... before something happens and you need a plumber at midnight.

THE INVISIBLE OFFICE REQUIREMENTS CHECKLIST

☐ Internet Requirements: Access, VPN, FTP site, Domain Name Registration
☐ Security (Office Alarm System)
☐ Security (Locations & Studio)
☐ Cleaners
☐ Plumber
☐ Production Assistant Car
☐ Keys
☐ Circuits & Electrician

INTERNET REQUIREMENTS: ACCESS, VPN, FTP SITE, DOMAIN NAME REGISTRATION

Internet access and email are essential to a functioning production office. Consider the needs you have for a Virtual Private Network and, primarily for postproduction, an FTP site. Does the post facility provide the FTP access? For production, who will be arranging the technical requirements of setting up a VPN (and providing support) and which crew needs how much access to the network? Include the copier/printer/scanner as a network printer. Decide who will control the administration of the VPN and its password. Set up a generic email address for the Assistant Coordinator to answer, and discuss with the Production Manager who else really needs email on the crew to do their jobs. Regarding domain name registration for the production, check with the Producer to see if it has been registered yet. If not, now is the time register it. The domain name that perfectly describes your project may be snapped up quickly. The publicity department will likely be involved for these discussions, as they have their finger on the online and print visibility plan.

SECURITY (OFFICE ALARM SYSTEM)

An alarm system in the production office is very wise indeed. Though film shoots are transient, unprotected computer equipment is asking for trouble no matter how short a time you intend to be there. The cost of an alarm system makes sense. You may think that replacement through insurance is adequate, but imagine working for weeks without any computer equipment until the insurance company completes administration of the claim.

SECURITY (LOCATIONS & STUDIO)

If there is no Locations Department, you will be arranging for a security company to watch the set after hours. You can find names and references in your film reference books or from your Location Manager friend.

CLEANERS

It is usually best to arrange for them to clean the office at least twice a week.

PLUMBER

Have a plumber's name on hand. It could be the same plumber you use to install the washer/dryer. Know what hours she is accessible — especially for those after-hours bathroom jobs in old buildings.

PRODUCTION ASSISTANT CAR

The sooner you arrange for this car, the sooner the Office Production Assistant can run wildly around the city taking care of business. Well, not too wildly, you hope. Check if the Production Manager already arranged for an account for the production vehicles with a car rental company, so that you can rent the office car from the same agency. You may arrange for the office car to be the Assistant Coordinator's, the Office Production Assistant's, or your car after hours.

KEYS

The Production Manager may want to change the locks when you first move in. Arrange this procedure as soon as possible. As for how many copies you will need, start a list for one key per department head as a rough estimate. Keep a log of who receives which keys. Keys are lost, so keep a master set for yourself. Track security pass cards along with office keys. There is no sense in providing someone a key to the production office without security access at the same time.

CIRCUITS & ELECTRICIANS

Pull out the office map again. Mark on it where each wall plug is. Take the time to do a circuit check and label each wall plug, the breaker panel, and the map. This is a great job to delegate to the Office Production Assistant when few people are using the office (and therefore few using the electricity). Have an electrician's name on hand for after hours. Heavy drains on a circuit are:

> **Copier/Printer/Scanner** – Most high volume, fast copiers require a dedicated circuit, i.e., a single wall plug that is connected to a single breaker. Have an electrician install one.

> **Craft Service** – Any electric appliance that prepares food is a big drain on the circuit (this includes coffee machines, tea kettles, microwave ovens, refrigerators, toasters, etc.). Have an electrician install a few dedicated circuit plugs in the craft service area.

Though this project sounds like a lot of work, it will be time well spent. When you turn on the coffee machine and blow a circuit someday, you do not want to find out that the Accountant's computer is sharing that same circuit.

SUPPLIER ACCOUNTS & CONTACTS

The office map aside again, it is time to set up supplier accounts. Armed with the corporate name of the film company and help from the Production Accountant in filling out account applications, you are ready. However, before committing to a new company right away, do a price check on three competing companies. From this process you will be able to judge how suppliers are to deal with, and how affordable they are.

THE SUPPLIER ACCOUNTS & CONTACTS CHECKLIST

- ☐ Courier Account
- ☐ Stationery Account
- ☐ Taxi Account

☐ Walkie-Talkie Account
☐ Cellular Phone Account/Negotiations
☐ Travel Agent
☐ Limousine Account
☐ Hotel Account
☐ Research Company
☐ Customs Broker
☐ Credit Card Number

COURIER ACCOUNT

You will need three couriers: a local courier, a national courier, and an international courier. Some couriers can cover more than one of these needs, but beware that the price differences can be excessive in the overlapping territories.

STATIONERY ACCOUNT

Set up an account with an office-supplies company that delivers, or a discount store of your choice. An account will save the Office Production Assistant from keeping copious amounts of cash on hand.

TAXI ACCOUNT

Taxi account chits are simple, convenient, and often misused. But there is an administrative cost involved in using an account, so the taxi charges are usually higher than if you pay cash. Decide with the Production Manager whether or not to go with a taxi account.

WALKIE-TALKIE ACCOUNT

The Assistant Directors will have their preferences about who should have walkies and accessories such as headsets, speaker mics, and holsters. Make a list of who needs what on set and approve that list with the Production Manager before contacting walkie-talkie suppliers. When negotiating the account, you will often be able to score an extra walkie-talkie or two rent-free to cover yourself for inevitable equipment breakdowns. Maintain excellent records of who has which walkie-talkie equipment (including serial numbers), so that none are lost by the end of production. Walkie-talkie equipment is very expensive and very portable. Know the replacement value.

CELLULAR PHONE ACCOUNT / NEGOTIATIONS

Crew members typically come with their own cell phone and negotiate reimbursement of all or a portion of airtime costs as part of their kit rental. Since there is a cost to both sending and receiving calls and text messages, the PM will be busy with these negotiations. As for who will use the cell phone the most, consider your crew and start with the Location Manager, Transport Coordinator, and Transport Captain. In some cases you can arrange a temporary change to an existing phone plan (such as the Office P.A.'s phone, for example), to secure the best rate for the heavy usage that will be needed for the job.. Take advantage of after-hours and weekend rates where appropriate, but be cautious about locking into long term contracts.

Pagers are rarely, if ever, used anymore; however, setting up an account and providing pagers can offer an inexpensive alternative to reimbursing everyone's cell phone usage.

TRAVEL AGENT

This is one of the Coordinator's best friends. Yes, you can book flights and travel online; however, the time invested to do so will have you delegating this job to a travel agent in no time. Producers, Guest Stars, and Directors are very busy people who usually change their travel plans at least 100 times before boarding an aircraft. Booking the cheapest flight is rarely the way to go with all the restrictions attached to cheap flights. Allow your travel agent work for you — and obtain a home number if you can.

LIMOUSINE ACCOUNT

Either you or the travel agent can arrange for limousines. Since spellings of names and specific directions can become muddled when several people are involved in the chain of communication, arranging for limousines yourself is the best way to ensure accuracy. It is also wise to have the name of a limousine company in any other city you that you deal with repeatedly.

HOTEL ACCOUNT

Go to see the hotel rooms in early preproduction. See their facilities. As production nears, you will not have the time. Take your camera and take pictures like a location scout. You will find it easier to talk about the hotel to a visiting guest when you have actually been there and have photographs to remind you and to show them.

RESEARCH COMPANY

Check with the Production Manager to determine if you will be clearing the script for legal purposes, then find a company best able to serve you. Clearance companies read the script and note potential trademark infringements, for example.

You will find names of companies in your reference books. (More about script clearances is in Chapter 33.)

CUSTOMS BROKER

This is one more of the Coordinator's best friends, helping you to bring all sorts of items across the border. Find a broker and prepare a letter giving them power of authority to clear packages through customs for you, and collect a home number if you can. (More about customs is in Chapter 32.)

CREDIT CARD NUMBER

The Production Manager may furnish you with the company's credit card number for use with discretion in emergencies when only a credit card will get the job done. Keep this number well protected.

THE MANAGER SETS UP THE FINANCIAL BACKBONE TO THE OFFICE

With the physical office in good shape thanks to the Production Coordinator, the Production Manager is busy setting up the financial backbone to production. Here is some of the information you will need, as the Manager, to ensure this set up:

☐ Incorporation Documentation
☐ Financing Structure, Status & Agreements
☐ Recoupment Schedule (optional)
☐ Locked Budget
☐ Cash Flow
☐ Audit Discussions

INCORPORATION DOCUMENTATION

Find out from the Producer if the production company has been incorporated yet or not. If not, arrange with legal counsel to do this immediately. Have a copy of the incorporation documents on hand. Though the whole crew needs to know the legal name of the company, you and Accounting need to have proof of that legal name in your hands and files.

FINANCING STRUCTURE, STATUS & AGREEMENTS

If you have not received the one-page financing structure summary from the Producer, listing all the financing sources participating in production, obtain it immediately. You need to know to whom you are reporting, and which documents each Financier needs during the course of production. The financial structure should also detail the type of money being supplied: equity participation, a grant, a distribution advance, a broadcaster pre-sale, a Producer investment or deferral, etc. Assemble a copy of all the financial agreements, too. Accounting will need them. You will need them. The Agreements detail when the money is paid out to production and on what conditions or triggers. Since the Financiers are basically investing in a product that does not exist yet, they will have a payment schedule for their participation. Some payments may be triggered, for example, by production reaching the first day of principal photography plus delivering the latest cost report to the Financier, or by reaching wrap of production plus delivering the latest cost report to the Financier. You need this information to generate an accurate cash flow. Find out (from the Producer) the status of each of these financial contracts. It often takes plenty of time to bring all sources to signed contract to start the money flowing to production in a speedy manner. You may have drafts of these contracts to start your work, but whatever you obtain, you need this documentation to know how soon the money will be flowing.

RECOUPMENT SCHEDULE (OPTIONAL)

This document details, in the form of a chart, a list of the equity partners and Distributor(s) with advances, along with who needs to be paid back their investment from monies earned during distribution (in proportion and in position compared to other investors). Since recoupment happens long after production, this schedule is not necessarily relevant to you on a daily basis. It is still good to have a copy of the final, approved recoupment schedule in the Production Manager's and/or the Production Accountant's files for completeness. The Producer will negotiate the Financier's placement on the recoupment schedule.

LOCKED BUDGET

As mentioned in Chapter 3, you should be trying to lock the budget as soon as possible, so you can move onto cost reporting in comparison to the budget. Going to production without a locked budget is like going to camera without a script. Meet with the Producer to finalize the budget allocations.

CASH FLOW

With information from the financing documents, the Producer, and the locked budget, it is time to create a cash flow to see when you might need to arrange for interim financing from a bank to help you through the monetary demands of production. Sometimes Accountants create this document on their own, but usually it is the Production Manager who is heavily involved in its creation. (More on creating cash flows is in Chapter 20.)

AUDIT DISCUSSIONS

Discuss with the Producer the plan for audit. Prepare now to set up the accounting system for an easy, clear audit. These discussions are especially important if you are on a co-production involving two or more Accountants and audits in two or more cities or countries. (More on audits is in Chapter 36.)

WHEN INFORMATION IS CONFIDENTIAL

Realizing that you talk to all the departments of the production, you will often be trusted with confidential information from everyone. Some information will need to be forwarded on to others under the cloak of continued confidentiality, other information you will wish you never heard because you cannot tell anyone even though it drastically affects everyone. Some information the Production Manager should not tell the Production Coordinator, even though the Coordinator is the Manager's right hand. Everyone should be very, very careful handling confidential information. When confidential information must be shared among the office staff, consider the following advice:

USE A CODE WORD OR PHRASE

With your closest staff, use a code word or a phrase (like "you didn't really hear that") to inform them that the information they just heard, whether on purpose or by mistake, is strictly confidential, and they should not pursue the subject. Have the staff respond with another phrase to let you know they understand.

USE ENVELOPES OR FILE FOLDERS

Never have confidential information left face up on your desk. Use sealable envelopes, or put such paperwork into file folders to hide from view, thereby quelling people's curiosity as they pass by your desk or enter your office. If there is no time to use an envelope or a file folder, place the document face down on the desk. Make sure all the office staff understands and uses this system.

BE CAREFUL WHEN FAXING & PHOTOCOPYING

Avoid faxing confidential information, if at all possible. If necessary, do not fax anything else at the same time, and do not use speed dial. A confidential fax going to the wrong recipient by attaching it to the back of another fax, or by pressing the wrong button, is inexcusable. When photocopying a confidential document, take the same care. Take the time to copy it on its own. Without distraction, chances are you will not leave the original in the photocopy machine. Make sure the office staff understands and abides by this system, too.

MAXIMIZING EMAIL CONFIDENTIALITY

Avoid emailing confidential information too, if at all possible. However, in an environment with so many virtual workers on computers and smart phones, some in different time zones, there will, no doubt, be a need to email confidential information.

WRITE THE EMAIL BODY FIRST

First, write the entire email message with no address in the recipient (or "to") box. Keep the email to one topic. This practice helps retain the confidentiality of the topic both now and in the future when the email may grow into a chain. Keeping to one topic also helps with filing the email later. Save the unsent draft email to retain your work.

LABEL THE EMAIL DESCRIPTIVELY

Descriptive subject lines for emails are both useful for filing the information and keeping the email to a single topic that will fit in the short text box.

IDENTIFY THE EMAIL AS CONFIDENTIAL

Include the word "confidential" both in the subject line and at the top of the email body. If you wish, you may also add a confidential disclaimer to the bottom of the email body reminding readers that this email is intended only for the person to whom the email is addressed; however if the wrong person receives the email, by the time they read the disclaimer at the bottom, they have most likely already scanned the email itself. Still, the disclaimer can remind the reader not to forward this email on to other people.

INSERT REQUIRED ATTACHMENTS

Insert any required attachments, and once attached, open them inside the draft email to double-check you have included the right one(s).

ADD THE DESTINATION EMAIL ADDRESS LAST

Once the draft email is complete, only then add the recipient's email address. This practice prevents you mistakenly hitting the send button too early and firing off an incomplete and possibly embarrassing email. If you have an auto-complete feature turned on for addressing emails, do not trust the shortcut – the correct recipient's email address could easily share some (if not many) of the letters as another email address in your address book. Triple check the destination email address is correct before hitting the send button.

ANOTHER NOTE ABOUT EMAIL CHAINS

Since subject lines can be amended over time, a confidential email can no longer be labeled as such later in an email chain. Indeed, topics of discussion naturally branch out over time or change focus, so it is good practice (for confidentiality and for ease of filing and finding information in the future) to respond to email chains keeping the focus on the original topic. Open new email chains with newly descriptive subject lines when you see new topics are developing.

—⁓—

As a house becomes a home, so these empty rooms are becoming a production office. Be proud. In essence, you have a production office ready to function already! Over time, you will find that each office has slightly different needs — not all offices will require a full setup from bare floors and walls. Revise this chapter to suit each production's needs and your own personal style as it develops. But now is the time to add people to the office and stir.

LOST & FOUND

When the Office P.A. calls in sick, you have to hire a Daily P.A. very quickly. There is no time to review qualifications or check references. In such an instance I hired a fellow who had been begging me for his chance to "break into the film industry." And as with many such P.A.'s, I'm sure he embellished his merits in order to get the job. Embellishing is okay. Lying is a bad career move. He said he was a very experienced driver and knew the city well.

Run #1: First up in the day, I sent him to our payroll company to drop off the payroll. The company was right downtown. The trip normally takes fifteen minutes to get there from the office in the east end and fifteen minutes back. We didn't hear from the Daily P.A. for over four hours. He never called. He never wrote. I was confused, then concerned, then worried. The PM needed him for another important run and, in the P.A.'s absence, I had to send the Assistant Coordinator.

When he finally called, he was at a telephone booth in an industrial area of the west end. He was lost. Didn't have a map. Didn't know the city at all. Didn't know that downtown was a small collection of very tall office buildings, and when he wasn't driving in that vicinity, he wasn't downtown. I directed him back downtown and asked him to buy a map en route. He returned to the office — run completed — another three hours later. That was seven hours for a 30-minute run. I hoped he was just having a bad day and decided I would schedule the next run for him closer to the office.

Run #2: I asked him to pick up some stamps at the drugstore one block away from the office. He borrowed the Production Manager's car and took forty-five minutes to get there and back. He could have walked faster. Another important run came up in his absence. It had to be delayed. Upon the P.A.'s return, he broke the key in the ignition thereby making the PM's car undrivable. He finally admitted that his driver's license was considerably newer than he had originally let on and that he didn't know the city at all. At this point, the PM asked me to send him home.

We've never seen him since. We just hope he got home all right.

HIRING CREW 6

The roles are now reversed. You are sitting in the chair across from the seat you occupied a short time ago. You are about to hire crew and support staff. You may not be sure how to hire and manage staff. You may not be sure how to be a good boss. It may seem daunting to have the responsibility of hiring, managing, and sometimes even firing people, but it is not as difficult as it first appears. Whether you are hiring experienced department heads or someone green to the industry applying for his first Production Assistant position, the essence is the same: Hire a good team and let them do the job.

WHO HIRES WHOM

The Production Manager will tend to hire the Production Accountant, other departmental heads, and key creative crew alongside the Producer, and may also have a voice in the staffing within the departments. Though Chapter 7 details all the departments, here is a list of the first priorities in hiring for the Production Manager, presuming these people are not on board already: the Production Designer or the Art Director, the Construction Coordinator, the Director of Photography, the First Assistant Director, the Casting Director, the Location Manager, the Editor, the Set Decorator, the Property Master, the Wardrobe Designer, the Hair and Makeup Artists, the Continuity Supervisor, the Gaffer, the Key Grip, the Transportation Coordinator, and the Post Sound team or facility.

The Production Coordinator will tend to hire the Assistant Coordinator, the Receptionist, the Office Production Assistant, and perhaps the Craft Service Person — usually in consultation with the Production Manager, since both of you are, after all, a team working together. The Production Manager has the budget that the Production Coordinator is trying to spend and honor.

REGARDING RESUMES, COVER LETTERS & THE INTERNET

Resumes and cover letters are the first step in finding crew. You want to read them to narrow down your search so that you bring in only selected qualified people to interview for the job. This is a paring down process. Naturally, a discussion about resumes and cover letters may lead you to review and revise your own, but this chapter deals with what you need to know about how to read resumes and cover letters. What are you looking for in the pages that come in? Do Production Assistant and other entry-level resumes differ hugely from First Assistant Director and other department head resumes? How do you read a resume?

RESUMES

When you read resumes, especially lots of them at one time, your attention cannot help but wane. Resumes in general should not exceed one page; however, if there are huge numbers of relevant film credits to list, they can be two pages long. You want to read resumes that are short, to the point, and perhaps demonstrate a little of the person's personality. Every crew resume is basically structured the same way.

CONTACT INFORMATION & PROFESSIONAL ASSOCIATIONS

Near the name and contact information (address, cell phone and telephone numbers, email address, web page or blog, etc.), you want to see professional associations, or the crew position this person most associates herself with. This is especially important if the person has a diverse resume. With a resume that notes a huge variety of film positions in past experience, you need to know for which position or department this person is applying.

MOST RELEVANT EXPERIENCE AT THE TOP

You want to read resumes that are structured so that the most relevant (and therefore hopefully the most recent) film-related information is at the top, just after name and contact information. This way, as your attention wanes, you will have read the most relevant experience to this job without having to search for it. If education is noted at the top, this person is likely to be a recent graduate. If education is noted at the bottom just above references, this person's recent experience is more likely earned working in the industry than in a school environment.

DIFFERENT RESUMES & SKILLS FOR DIFFERENT JOBS

Because of this structure, crew members will have different resumes for different jobs. That is okay. For certain jobs you need to see certain skills stressed. You do not want to read a notation and description of every single position this person has ever held — especially if much of it is irrelevant to this job. For Office Production Assistants, you would like to know if they can drive standard should the production car have a standard transmission. For First Assistant Directors you would like to know with which Directors they have worked, and which shows were completed on time. For Production Accountants you would like to know if they are fluent in the payroll software you are intending to use. Different skills are for different jobs. You want to see these skills on the resume. Other skills of use might be: safety training, fluency in a language, fluency using a specific software, knowledge of certain production paperwork, typing speed, certification to use a certain piece of equipment, a license to drive a certain type of vehicle, and so on. Know what you need from each department skill-wise, and read the resume looking for that type of experience.

THE FILMOGRAPHY

The majority of the page will be taken up with a filmography: a list of film credits, the production titles, the year produced, the production company names, the key supervisors, and any other key, short relevant information regarding each production (like awards). You, as a Production Manager, are looking for names you recognize in this list of supervisors. You will tend to call these people for references over the list of references at the bottom (if there is a list at the bottom).

HOBBIES OR INTERESTS

After the list of experience and a notation of skills, you may see a line noting hobbies or interests. This is a good line to use for conversation starters at the interview.

REFERENCES

Finally, if there is room, about three references may be listed at the bottom. More likely, however, references will be noted as "available on request." With a well-structured resume, you will not need to ask for extra references. There will be enough names and companies on the resume for you to do your due diligence.

PORTFOLIOS OR REELS

Art Department staff and Set Photographers may note there is a portfolio on request. Directors of Photography and Second Unit Directors will have a reel available on request, whether noted on the resume or not. As you narrow down your search, you must review these support materials, too. This type of creative experience cannot be demonstrated in the resume format.

COVER LETTERS

Cover letters give the opportunity for applicants to demonstrate their style, their awareness of the demands of the job ahead, their preparation to put in the hours it takes to make a film, and to basically tell you what is not on the resume due to format restrictions. Read the cover letter and ask yourself if this person is professional enough and prepared enough for the complexities of this particular film production.

If resumes do not have cover letters, toss them — well, certainly for people applying to P.A. positions. You will learn more about a P.A. by the cover letter than by the fact that the resume says he delivered a newspaper at age 16. The P.A. position is an entry-level position, so chances are the resume will not have any "Office P.A." credits on it yet. You must look to the cover letter to determine the person's working style and attitude. As crew members work up the ranks, cover letters become somewhat less frequent. This situation is okay, as the resume is now more clearly demonstrating skill level with a growing number of credits in the filmography.

ONLINE PRESENCE

Next step is to review the prospective crew member's online presence. Start with a simple Internet search and then move on to the social networking sites. The site *www.imdb.com* may not have the complete information, but it is still a worthy stop to look up credit lists for people who have moved past entry-level positions. Basically you want to know if this person's online presence supports the image portrayed in their resume and cover letter. Is there a match? What is your impression of this person's public, Internet footprint in the world? One look at what you can find out about someone will remind you how careful to be about your own online presence... your public Internet persona.

QUESTIONABLE RESUMES

It is always easy to remember the questionable — or bad — resumes first... but you will not remember them as people you wanted to hire, but as people you want to avoid. Still, you may be mildly entertained by some of the resumes that come to you, like the resume that was sent in a shoe in order for the prospective Production Assistant to "get a foot in the door." Maybe you like this kind of humor and would consider hiring this person to keep you laughing in this manner, or then again, maybe you prefer to find crew who work first and play second. It all depends on your management style. But do be sure they can do the job. Is there substance in the resume alongside the humor? Having someone keep you laughing is fine unless you have to make up for her slack at doing a bad job. Remember you are building a team to work together. You are producing a film together. This work is not play. It is an industry and you first have to do a job. Consider how each member of the team will fit and do his part. What is his working style versus yours? Though we work in a creative industry, a resume typed all in italics stating why that person was fired from every single job in her life might seem funny at first, but do you really want someone to be that much of a rebel against conventions? If hired, maybe that person will be equally rebellious of authority or of the hierarchy on the set, thinking she is being funny. If so, this is not a team player, and most certainly someone you do not want on the crew. Think about the barely-out-of-adolescence Production Assistant that sends you a student's directing reel as a P.A. resume. Do you think this person will be happy enough and therefore do a good job of photocopying and driving when it is obvious he would rather be directing your production? Very unlikely.

REGARDING CREW INTERVIEWS

After reading all the resumes and the cover letters, researching their online presence, and calling some references, you have narrowed down the search to a few people for each position. It is time to bring them in for interviews.

DUE DILIGENCE BEFORE THE INTERVIEW

Even if the credentials are incredible, call to check with former employers. The resume may seem impressive, but this person may have been fired from all those fabulous previous jobs. If you recognize names of people you know and trust on the resume, call them. But call other people, too. Try to build a rounded view of this person. Be aware that you may learn about bad experiences that came from personality conflicts due to working style, so some bad references may be misleading. Find out what contacts these people have for their field of work. Will this person, her skills and contacts, complement the team you are assembling?

THE TELEPHONE PRE-INTERVIEW

Before committing to an interview time and date, find out if the potential crew member is pleasant on the telephone, and ask him if he is available for the term. No sense in wasting your time and his in coming in for an interview if your schedules do not mesh. If there is a specific skill that is required for the job (like use of certain computer software or of certain equipment), ask now for proficiency to see if this person is qualified.

CONDUCTING THE INTERVIEW

You need to structure this interview the same way yours was structured: (1) ice-breaking conversation, (2) questions relevant to production asked and answered, (3) conclusion and thanks.

The ice-breaker starts the flow of conversation. You are both likely to be nervous at this interview. You are looking for the right person to fill the role, and this person is hoping for the right job to suit her experience and career. Look for any notation of hobbies or interests on the resume or from your online research to help you break the ice. If not, invent a starter. Weather is a boring subject, unless, of course, you have just experienced an earthquake or a heat wave. As conversation flows, you can begin to discuss the production's needs in more detail, the team you are assembling, and how this person may or may not fit into that team.

Here are questions to ask yourself during the course of the interview. You will learn some of these answers from asking outright questions, and others will come from your own observations:

> **Team Player**: What is not on his resume? Who is this person? What is this person like? Will this person fit into the team you are assembling? How has this person worked in a team environment previously?

> **Part of a Team Already**: Is this person part of a team that moves from production to production, or does this person need help in finding a team of Assistants?

> **Resume Value**: Are the credits on the resume overstated, or are there more credits omitted? Are the past work experiences relevant to working on this production?

> **Job Requirements**: Can this person fill the requirements of the job? For example, can this First Assistant Director schedule a show? Does this Assistant Coordinator enjoy answering the telephone and is she familiar with production paperwork? (See more about job requirements below and in Chapter 7.) What does this person think is key to be able to do this job?

> **Skills**: If there is no list of skills on the resume, ask what relevant skills this person has for this job, like language fluency, software or equipment proficiency, and so on.

> **Stress & Long Hours**: How does this person deal with the stress of a film production? Does this person think a long day is eight or eighteen hours? How does this person deal with difficult people?

> **Ambition**: In what direction is this person's career headed? If this person were to find a better offer elsewhere one week into filming, might he leave your production?

> **Price**: How much does this person expect to make? Can the budget support this person? Is there a kit rental to augment the fee?

Take your own mental notes during the interview. Learn about this person's manner, attitude, honesty, and maturity. Can you work with this person? Will she put forth the type of professionalism you expect? Do not be afraid to take notes. A word scribbled here and there on the resume during the interview will aid you later in evaluating the people you have met.

AFTER THE INTERVIEW

Make written notes about each person after the interview and review them later. Before making a decision, the Production Coordinator can discuss these notes with the Production Manager, and the Production Manager can discuss these notes with the Producer.

Also, do not be afraid to do more due diligence by calling references for more information after the interview. The more responsible the job you are trying to fill, the more due diligence is necessary.

REGARDING THE OFFICE STAFF & CRAFT SERVICE

The Production Coordinator is the Production Manager's right hand. Therefore, the Production Accountant must be the Production Manager's left hand. The Coordinator's key Assistants are the Assistant Production Coordinator and the Production Assistant. As these people are so critical a team together, it is worthy to look at them in more detail. Because Craft Service is a unique entry-level job, it is worth a further look at this position, too.

If any or all of these positions are unionized in your city, go to the union as a source for a potential crew for your production. If they are not unionized, there will likely be a list of such non-union personnel at the local film commission. It is also wise to speak with other Production Managers, Producers, and contacts at film organizations and clubs for recommendations.

THE PRODUCTION ACCOUNTANT

For a Production Accountant, you are looking for someone to track the money being spent during production even more closely than you! This person has to understand the budget, payroll, petty cash, cash flow, financing inflows, and cost reporting in great detail. The less you know about any of these issues, the more the Accountant needs to be the expert. You want someone who is: organized, a good communicator, detail-oriented, fast, accurate, and understanding of the nuances of film production budgeting and accounting.

When interviewing and doing your due diligence on the Production Accountant find out if this person:

> **Payroll Issues**: understands the complexity of payroll, and knows the computerized payroll system inside and out;

> **Budget Issues**: knows when and why it is required to lock a budget, and understand columnar budgets if your production is a co-production, or pattern and amortization budgets if your production is a series;

> **Communication Issues**: knows how to communicate often and effectively with you regarding all accounting issues, including budget savings and overages, both actual and predicted;

> **Petty Cash Issues**: understands that petty cash is not petty at all (the first time you approve $5,000 cash to be handed to a crew member to go shopping for the production, you will understand how petty it is not), and knows how much to hand out to which departments to keep them functioning efficiently, but not keep them in excessive cash — thereby putting an unnecessary drain on your cash flow;

> **Cost Reporting Issues**: knows how to report on actual costs as they are incurred during production, both efficiently and accurately;

> **Cash Flow Issues**: understands how Financiers pay out money on triggers; knows how to read and write a cash flow; knows which bills can be pushed and for how long if cash flow is tight; and both knows and uses the purchase order system right through to the cost report;

> **Reporting & Filing Issues**: knows how to keep impeccable books to affect a seamless transfer of the accounting files to the Post Accountant and/or the Auditor (allowing the Producer to trigger all financial drawdowns as fast as possible);

> **Prioritizing Issues**: knows how to say "no" to the crew or to the Producers or to you for the good of the production, and can prioritize effectively;

> **Stress Issues**: knows how to handle a lot of stress (the Accountant is often harassed by crew and Producers for various money and reporting demands);

> **Working-Team Issues**: has an accounting team or can pull together a team if the project is large enough to warrant and has worked together with any of the keys already on the production.

THE ASSISANT PRODUCTION COORDINATOR

For an Assistant Production Coordinator, you are looking for someone to work with the Production Coordinator effectively and effortlessly, easing the huge workload of running the production office. How that workload is divided is rather hazy and very personal between the Coordinator and the Assistant. Typically the Assistant Coordinator is responsible for: telephone reception; paperwork distribution to all crew, cast and related companies; shipping and receiving; organizing the P.A. runs (to be sure the P.A. is not overloaded by too many input sources from Coordinator, Production Manager, Producers, and various crew departments). This person also may be the one to type up the last minute changes to the call sheet every day. But no matter what the Assistant Coordinator does, he should constantly report to the Coordinator what jobs are in progress, so the Coordinator can be informed, aware, and able to prioritize those jobs. You want someone who is: organized, a good communicator, a team player, good at answering the telephone while doing much other work, and understanding of the running of a film production office.

When interviewing, and doing your due diligence on the Assistant Coordinator, find out how the candidate fits the bill pertaining to these issues:

> **Telephone**: Does she enjoy answering the reception telephone (you will be surprised how many hate answering the telephone and will tell you so) and can she figure out how to use the many telephone system features? Remember this person will give the first impression about your company to anyone who calls in.

> **Communication**: Will she communicate with the Coordinator often and clearly, be able to take direction, and fit into the team?

> **Production Paperwork**: Is she familiar with production paperwork such as production reports and call sheets (because you will not have time to teach this person from scratch on the job)?

> **Organization & Filing**: Does she know how to file, track paperwork distribution as it happens, and deal with the reams of paperwork that flow through the production office?

> **Computer System**: Is she fluent on the computer system and the various software programs you are using on production? (If you can test this person,

all the better, as a number of people will inflate their computer skills in order to win the job.)

> **Handwriting**: Does she have legible handwriting for telephone messages?

> **Boredom**: Does she understand this is a "hurry-up-and-wait" industry?

> **Stress**: Does she know how to deal with stress and work with difficult people?

> **Work Day:** Does she understand that a long day is closer to sixteen hours rather than eight and is she prepared to work it if needed?

> **Career**: Is she prepared to stay with this job, not taking this job only until a better offer comes along, and is she expecting a paycheck that is in line with what is budgeted?

2ND ASSISTANT COORDINATOR, PRODUCTION SECRETARY & RECEPTIONIST

When there are two Assistants to the Coordinator, the main Assistant is called the First Assistant Production Coordinator and the second one can be called: the Second Assistant Coordinator; the Production Secretary (though "Secretary" is a fading term); or the Receptionist. If budget allows, you could have an office team with a First and Second Assistant Coordinator, plus a Receptionist. It is also possible (unless a union contract specifies otherwise) that when the main Assistant to the Coordinator is also relatively inexperienced, he may be called the Production Secretary and earn the "Assistant" title after growing into the job.

THE OFFICE PRODUCTION ASSISTANT

You will probably hire a wider variety of Office P.A.s than Assistant Coordinators in your time, because the Office P.A. is the entry-level job that everyone who wants to break into the film business covets. Unfortunately, many are disillusioned when they discover the job — once achieved — is not a creative position after all. They take orders all day long, drive around the city like a courier, make coffee, and learn how to remove paper jams from the photocopier. At this point they may become bored, feel unimportant in the making of the film, lose interest, and so do the job badly. They were looking for that mythical creative job that comes with great pay and lots of responsibility, because they think film work is easy and film pay enormous. You are looking for a team player, not a self-imagined leader. You are looking for Assistants. And Assistants do just that... they assist. On a crew of ten people, it is true that each person has great responsibility and a varied set of tasks to do. That is the beauty (and the nightmare) of low budget. On a crew of 50 or 75 or 120, the same set of tasks has to be divided between many people; on individual analysis, each person's job may seem small and pointless. You need people who can see themselves as an integral part of the whole picture, because that is exactly what they are.

Here is information you need to know prior to and during the interview to narrow down the search for genuine workers. The requirements may not sound like much, but you will be surprised who is out there looking to break into the film industry. You will interview P.A.s who think they deserve your wage and more per week, P.A.s who think they have to be hired because they know someone on the show, P.A.s who are ready to start their own production company but want to make a quick buck before doing so, and even P.A.s who think that answering phones, making coffee, and fixing the photocopier is beneath them. Remember: attitude, attitude, attitude — then choose accordingly.

> **Read the Cover Letter**: Read the cover letter to learn the most about this person. There are bound to be next to no relevant film credits on the resume to tell you about this person and what she is like. If there is no cover letter, this person has not spent much time, if any, applying to work with you. Do you want this kind of person as a P.A.?

> **Internet & Social Networking Search**: Does this person's presence on the Internet support the impression you have from the resume and cover letter or is it diametrically opposed?

> **Attitude & Work Day Issues**: Does this person have a good attitude towards working long, demanding hours?

> **Workload Issues**: Does this person have some idea about what an Office P.A. does?

> **Memory Issues**: Does this person have some intelligence and remembering ability?

> **Boredom Issues**: Will this person enjoy the job and atmosphere, not growing bored within two weeks? Is this person prepared to work in this "hurry-up-and-wait" industry?

> **Driving Issues**: Does this person have a license to drive the production car you have, or does he own a car you can rent from him? What is this person's driving record?

> **Stress Issues**: Can this person deal with stress and be able to work with difficult people?

> **Teamwork Issues**: Can this person deal with the many sources of requests for runs (from Producers, Manager, Coordinator, and other crew departments) and work with the Coordinator, and Assistant Coordinator as a team to ensure the jobs are prioritized together?

> **Career Issues**: Is this person prepared to perform this job, not taking this job only until a better offer comes along, and expecting a paycheck in line with what is budgeted for the P.A. position?

Since the P.A. position is entry-level, there will be teaching required for this person during the course of the job; therefore, here are tips for working with the P.A. on the job to ensure her efficiency and responsibility. Though the Assistant Coordinator may be the one monitoring the P.A. runs in detail, the Production Coordinator is responsible for the whole office team, so I have used only Coordinator references below:

> **The P.A. should write everything down** – First things first: Make sure the Office P.A. has a notebook and pen at all times. The Coordinator will give this person lists and lists of things to do, and each task may sound simple, but the sheer number of them dictates that something will be forgotten if not written down.

> **The P.A. should keep in constant contact with the Coordinator** – Ensure that the Office P.A. has a cell phone at all times and that the phone is turned on and accessible at all times in case there is a change in plans for the office runs. An Office P.A. out of touch for hours at a time is a gamble that nothing will change in this ever-changing business.

> **Double-check the P.A. did the tasks** – Take nothing for granted. Tell the Office P.A. a task and explain why it has to be done in a certain way, have her re-tell it back to you so that you know she understands. By contextualizing the tasks you show respect to the Office P.A. and give her information from which to learn both the how and the why, and even to make emergency decisions about priorities when you may be unavailable. In time, such detail and double-checking may not be necessary, but at the beginning of a production, the detail is hugely helpful. If you tell half a tale, expect half a job.

> **Check the detail of the P.A.'s paperwork** – Teach the Office P.A. about purchase orders and petty cash reports. Teach them detail.

> **The P.A. should know who to report to/take orders from** – The Office P.A. takes orders primarily from the Coordinator. Do not let the P.A. do runs for any other crew member, including the Producers and the Production Manager, without talking to the Coordinator first. The Coordinator is responsible for the prioritizing the P.A.'s runs, even if it is the Assistant Coordinator that is listing and tracking these jobs. Sometimes the P.A. must sit waiting in the office until the next task is ready. But that is the true nature of film... hurry up, then wait.

> **The P.A. should have things to do when waiting** – Give the P.A. some responsibilities. This way you can learn if he is indeed responsible or not. Put the P.A. in charge of the weekly photocopier paper count (so you never run out of any color), fax supplies, coffee and water supplies, the status of the distribution table, and so on. He can make more coffee during a "wait" period, help with answering busy telephones, or ask the Assistant Coordinator and Accountant if they need help. Have him to report back to you on these responsibilities. If all else fails, there are still plenty of learning opportunities for the P.A. who wants to succeed, like learning how to read a production board instead of reading the comic section of the daily newspaper.

> **The PA should know which runs happen on a regular basis** – The responsible P.A. can anticipate runs that happen on a regular basis, and help you manage her time, like: delivery and pick up of the payroll for Accounting, weekly runs to the companies that have wall envelopes, petty-cash runs, cast-contract runs, script-package runs, grocery runs for office craft service, and lunch runs for office people too busy to leave their posts.

Since many P.A.'s dream about that mythical creative job, you can dream about that mythical perfect Office P.A. Let me paint one for you now:

Always has a map book of the city. Knows the nearest liquor store, beer store, and post office — and their hours of operation. Knows how to fix a jammed photocopier and fax machine and understands many of the features of these machines. Knows how to use the telephone, fax machine, copier/printer/scanner, coffee, and water machines. Makes coffee first thing in the morning and when the coffee is low. Buys a few snacks for the office as allowed by petty cash and the Production Manager and the Coordinator. Never lets the car run out of gas or windshield-washer fluid, especially if borrowing the car from another crew member. Never lets petty cash run too low. Never leaves the building or the room without letting the Coordinator know where he is going and for how long.

Anticipates what runs happen on a regular basis. Knows how to open the office or close it by himself, in case he has to do so on a weekend. Treats original scripts with great respect so that the paper will not be chewed up in the photocopier. Always looks for something to do to help pass the time — because there always is something to do.

THE CRAFT SERVICE PERSON

Though the Craft Service Person works on set making refreshments available to the crew and the cast between meals, the Coordinator can be the one to hire this person. Often a non-union position, the Craft Service assignment is another entry-level job, and the only true entry-level position that works every day on set. If attitude is key in hiring the Office P.A., it is double-key in hiring the Craft Service Person.

Many craft service companies save you the trouble of hiring crew for this position and possibly teaching someone from scratch. Their staff is usually prepared and knowledgeable about the job and their role on set. Make sure you meet and introduce yourself to this person on your set.

When interviewing the Craft Service Person, discuss the following:

> **Work Day Issues**: Coffee must be hot and ready on set fifteen minutes prior to the first pre-call. That means that the Craft Service Person is on set about a half hour before call time, and it also means she is the person on set with some of the longest hours of all the crew.

> **Entry-Level & Paycheck Issues**: If the job is paid a flat rate, tell this person not to calculate the hourly wage. You can tell him right now, as an entry-level position on set, Craft Service is paid the least and works the most hours of any crew member. It is a fact. But know that the position is excellent for observing many jobs on a working film crew, so when the Craft Service job is done well, the crew will help that person move into any department he wishes.

> **Food Issues**: Imagine feeding fifty different people with fifty different food preferences and numerous dietary restrictions. No one can ever satisfy them all, so do not exhaust yourself trying. Present fresh food to the crew to renew their energy throughout the day. Address food allergies. Serve the food in a pleasant manner. Picture how much food the number of crew will eat, double it, and double it again. Crews eat a lot.

> **Craft Service Budget Issues**: It is very easy to go over budget in this department, so you need someone who can monitor a budget responsibly.

> **Driving Issues**: The Craft Service Person needs to be able to drive a cube van (or not be afraid of driving one), unless the production budget only allows a panel van. Does this person have a license to drive the production vehicle you have, and what is this person's driving record?

> **First Aid Issues**: Does this person have a first aid certificate and is it still valid? What experience does this person have in first aid? Typically craft service is the keeper of the set first aid kit and point person for first aid.

> **Responsibility Issues**: If the Craft Service job is done well and professionally, you will find yourself treating this person as a department head instead of as an entry-level position. The job is as responsible as the Craft Service person wants to make it.

> **Stress Issues**: Can this person deal with stress and be able to work with difficult people?

> **Attitude & Career Issues**: If someone is always looking to do the next job up the ladder, that person will never fully enjoy the work she is doing at the moment, since when she moves up to the next job, there is always another rung to look toward. Enjoy the steps along the way. This is advice for any job, including for Craft Service's. The bonus of the Craft Service role is the opportunity to watch what happens on set and learn like a fly on the wall. The weight of the position is that the Craft Service person can set the mood of the set with her attitude, just like a morale officer.

UNION & NON-UNION CREWS

It is the Production Manager more than the Production Coordinator who will deal with the various crew and cast unions, if applicable, but it is essential that you both know and understand them. Is production going to hire a union or a non-union crew? If the choice is to go with a union crew, the production company has to become signatory to the appropriate union(s) and guild(s) when the hiring is about to begin.

If you choose a union crew, you will find that unions are terrific for helping you when hiring crew. They are especially able to find people with specialized skills, as they have banks of resumes and lists of qualified workers. Unions are also wonderfully helpful in the budgeting process, since they have scale rates from which you can start budgeting. There are unions and guilds that represent technical crew, camera crew, accounting and coordination crew, directors and production staff, and so on. Some unions compete with other unions in the same city, so you may find an arena of competitiveness for union negotiations.

UNION AGREEMENTS & NEGOTIATIONS

Though union agreements may be boring to read, the Production Manager has to know them. You must understand the many terms and conditions these agreements encompass, and how those terms and conditions affect the production. For example, how many hours is a minimum requirement for crew turnaround (the hours a crew is required to have between going home at night one day and starting work the next day) without monetary penalty? It is therefore most wise to read and to understand these agreements prior to initial budgeting, to ensure you address all the money triggers of the decisions you are about to make during the budgeting process. Also know that not all the terms in these agreements are carved in stone; some are negotiable to address the specific needs of each production.

BECOME SIGNATORY

Find out if head office has already become signatory to one or more of the unions or the guilds. Some unions and guilds will ask you to sign up the head office of the production company as signatory to their agreement for all future productions. Head office may not want to commit to this type of agreement when it reviews all the various types of productions the company produces. Beware. You may want to ensure only the single-purpose production company is signatory to the unions or the guilds.

UNION NEGOTIATIONS

Most union or guild agreements have an enabling clause in them to allow you to modify some of the terms of the master agreement to suit the specific needs of your production after you become signatory. If there is no enabling clause, be sure to ask for any concessions you need prior to becoming signatory. Imagine your production has two days of its shoot five miles outside of the allowed free-travel zone; if you used the master agreement as written, production would be required to house the entire crew and pay travel time and per diems for those two days, but with the enabling clause, you ask for a concession to allow this travel outside the zone for only the cost of travel time. When you read the agreements, you will find other clauses that hinder your production unreasonably. List them all and discuss them with the union to negotiate which modifications can be made. There will be some give and take, so be prepared. Have some things on your list you can give up. Amend the union agreement early in preproduction to make it work for your production.

AFTER UNION NEGOTIATIONS

After negotiations, the Production Coordinator should be the one to keep in touch with the union, sending them informational paperwork about production as it proceeds. More on this paperwork is in Chapter 30.

NON-UNION

There are no rules when you shoot non-union, but remember you need to respect the crew whether it is a union or non-union crew. You do not want to burn out the crew. Once tired, they will perform badly. This performance will show onscreen, and/or worse, will cause crew to have accidents due to tiredness: accidents where people are hurt; accidents that production has to pay for. If you are shooting non-union, become familiar with the union structure. It works. Emulate it. Being non-union you do not have to be heavy-handed about union-type rules, but you can schedule regular meal breaks. You can schedule the availability of substantial snacks three hours into the day to keep the crew's energy up until lunchtime. You can wrap at a reasonable hour so the crew will have enough turnaround to go home, rest, and return to work the next day. Respect is the key.

NON-UNION DOUBLING UP ON JOBS

The size of a crew can vary enormously from production to production, depending on the budget size. On some films the budget is so restrictive and the production simple enough so that the Production Coordinator is also the Assistant Coordinator and the Receptionist, while the Production Manager doubles as Line Producer, Location Manager, and Production Accountant. On other films, you will have the luxury (or the necessity) of having people report to you in these other positions. The Production Manager can sometimes double for the First Assistant Director, but only on very short shoots, since someone has to be doing the Manager's job in the office while the Assistant Director is running the set. On union shoots there is less flexibility about crew doubling up on jobs. If you are going to double-up jobs, be sure the jobs are compatible and you are not asking someone to be in two places at the same time. This suggestion may sound obvious, but remember: Sometimes you have to spend money, like hiring an extra crew member, in order to save money, like saving time.

HIRING UNION CREW ON A NON-UNION SHOOT

Any crew or cast working on a non-union shoot requires special dispensation from the union to do so. It is the crew's or cast's responsibility to arrange for this. If they do not receive dispensation, there will be a penalty; if the penalty is money, it may even become your production's expense. Other penalties can include that crew member being thrown out of the union, so be cautious — this is dangerous territory. Crew members, however, are generally eager to upgrade their skills, and can often do so on non-union shoots, with the union's permission. The union primarily wants to know that you are not going to abuse this member. Since you are not a signatory, they cannot legally step in to protect their member from your production, should you treat the crew member unfairly, like refusing to pay him after work is done. Respect, again, is key. Structuring your production to work similar to a union shoot structure is helpful. Doing so, you may have an incredible crew available to you. Look for crew members that are experienced enough to move up to the next union level, and let them try their wings on your shoot at that higher level. Your production gets fabulous crew for less money, and the crew member gets the experience he needs to boost his career.

MENTORSHIPS AND INTERNSHIPS

There are a number of funding programs where the production company can be subsidized to mentor new crew members in certain jobs. These programs are not designed to provide cheap labor to the production (though that is partially what they do), but to build the capacity of the industry through contextual learning experiences. Basically, the mentor has to make the time to work with and teach the new crew member in line with a specified career plan, and not treat him as a hired assistant who should already know the job. There is usually an application procedure for both the mentor and the "mentee," and typically the "mentee" seeks out the right mentor for the experience. With the right people-matching, the learning experience of mentorships is unparalleled, and the contribution of the new crew member is exceedingly valuable and affordable to the production, paving the way for a longer lasting business relationship.

Internships tend to be less structured (and less funded) than mentorships. For a typical internship, a production company takes on an unpaid new school graduate for a fixed number of weeks in exchange for on-the-job training. The usefulness of the internship experiences varies widely depending on the individual participants, so it is best to set clear goals in advance with all participants to maximize the experience and rewards.

FIRING STAFF

Sometimes you will have to fire someone for poor job performance or poor attitude. There is nothing easy about doing so. Imagine that someone falling down on her knees and begging for you not to fire her. Imagine firing someone and not realizing it is her birthday tomorrow. If you think firing has to be done, consider the following:

WEIGH THE PROS AND THE CONS AND DO DUE DILIGENCE

Film production contracts are basically short, so you have very little time to teach someone the job he has been hired to do. In some positions you cannot expect to need to teach the person the job he has been hired to do. Have you given this person the chance to improve? Have you talked to him about the seriousness of the situation? Is this person's poor performance or attitude creating other problems on the set or in the office? Do your due diligence in giving him space to improve, and preferably document your steps and discussions. If this person is with a union, you will need this documentation to prove the firing was justified. If you weighed the pros and the cons, have done your due diligence, and there is no change, you cannot keep covering for this person.

DECIDE WITHOUT EMOTIONAL INVOLVEMENT

Never fire someone out of an emotional reaction, like anger or frustration. Cool off and decide logically if firing is the right solution. Talk this situation over with your superior.

IS THERE ENOUGH TIME OR MONEY TO HIRE SOMEONE NEW?

If there is only a week or two to the end of the production, firing the person may not be worthwhile. Flying in someone to fill-in for the final two weeks may be more work for you than putting up with a poor worker. There may be a costly contract pay-out to consider. Evaluate how much damage this person has caused or is causing. If you replace this person now, can the damage be repaired or at least stopped? If you do not replace this person, will the damage become greater or remain stable? You may feel that replacing a person at such a late date does not make sense. It is for this reason that you should always check references with previous employers before hiring someone.

HOW TO FIRE SOMEONE

After all your consideration, if the decision is to fire the person, pull her aside, explain why, and fire her. It is not easy, but know that you have done all you can. If your reason is valid, the next person you hire will excel at the job, and the person fired will go on to excel in the next job she achieves.

—⁓—

The crew is now coming together. You are no longer alone in the office preparing for the shoot. Give positive feedback to the crew when you see them excelling at their work. Do not make a habit of private talks only being critical. Managing staff will always have its ups and downs, since both managers and staff are all humans, after all. You will all make mistakes, but realize that your Assistant today may be your boss tomorrow. Together you must create a team that works together to prepare for production.

DOLLIES, REDHEADS, AND BEST BOYS

The film industry... it's the only place where...

You can play with dollies as an adult.

You can put pancakes on the floor.

You won't find any fruit in an apple box.

You know the similarity between a giraffe and a tulip.

You can use cookies, but not eat them.

You can have babies, juniors, seniors, redheads, or blondes on set — but none of them are people.

You can work alongside Gaffers, Best Boys, Gennie Ops, and TAD's — and know what that means.

You can open two barn doors with one hand.

You know Red as a noun, not as a color descriptor.

You can hire a Greensperson to bring in and set up trees in a forest.

And... you can hire a wrangler for bugs.

What an industry!

CREW DEPARTMENTS 7

You run into someone in the hallway and exchange information. You have just had a meeting. Meetings in production can be a casual or even accidental get-together. As the Production Manager or the Coordinator, you will talk to everyone on the crew in order to do your job. Talk as much as possible to keep your finger on the pulse of the production: Find out what is going on and what is being spent.

Let's look at these departments in more detail, and how you interact with each of them:

OFFICE PEOPLE

"Office People" are the people with offices in the production office or in head office, who retain those offices actively throughout production, and are associated with overall production issues rather than specific departmental ones.

PRODUCER

The Producer, who answers to the Executives, is responsible for the whole production, and is involved in balancing both creative and financial decisions to ensure the project is completed, maximizing the creative vision within the financial restrictions of the budget. The Producer, therefore, is your source of information about big production issues, plus the casting status of Performers and the revision status of the script. Producers come in many forms: Line Producer, Executive Producer, Supervising Producer, Co-Producer, Associate Producer, Producer, Creative Producer, and Consulting Producer. In general, the Line Producer is usually heavily involved in the budget and can be seen as an experienced Production Manager ready to move into producing, and the Executive Producer is usually key to the financing of the production, but most producer titles vary from production to production. Some Producers are attached to the project because they were key in setting up the initial deal to make the project happen; you will never hear from them. Other Producers are heavily hands-on during production, overseeing every day on set personally. Still other Producers supervise the series postproduction process closely, because the Producer on set will not have time to devote to the needs and the decisions of postproduction while supervising on set. Find out the list of Producers that are on your production, and identify what roles each will play; identify whom you need to meet regarding, and whom you must keep informed of, various production issues.

PRODUCTION MANAGER & PRODUCTION COORDINATOR

As this entire book is about the Production Manager and the Production Coordinator, there is not much to say here. You work hand-in-hand together. Meet every day for approvals, direction, and to keep each other informed. The Production Manager is responsible to ensure the film is made on time and on budget, and oversees everything the Production Coordinator does.

DIRECTOR

The Director has the overall creative vision of the project, and meets with each department to realize that vision (within the restrictions of the budget). The Director will be involved in location choice, set design, casting, and script revisions early in preproduction, and will be involved at least until the first cut (known as the "Director's Cut") of the production in the picture-editing phase. He knows what script revisions and casting choices he wants, though the Producer must confirm these choices before the Production Coordinator can proceed with publishing script changes or issuing cast lists. If the project is director-driven, like a feature film, the Director may also be a Producer. If the project is a series, the Director will be hired by the Producer. If the Director has no Personal Assistant, the Production Coordinator will be covering such needs for him.

WRITING DEPARTMENT

In the Writing Department, there may be a Creative Producer, Executive Story Editor, Story Editor, and Story Consultants, along with a team of Writers — depending upon how complex a production or series you have. Since the Writing team has a handle on the official script revisions that may affect the budget, the Production Manager needs to be in communication with this team often. The Production Coordinator may be typing up the script revisions into script format for this team; if so, they will likely want to know the page count of the typed script as soon as possible. It is wise to ensure that both the Writing team and the PC use the same software. As PC, you may have to correct their grammar, too. Make sure the Producer approves each draft you receive directly from them.

PRODUCTION ACCOUNTANT

As discussed previously, the Production Accountant is key to the Production Manager, and they meet more than daily with each other. This person can output cost reports, cash flows, and basically track real costs and promises (purchase orders) as they happen. As with the Coordinator, the Production Manager needs to work hand-in-hand with the Accountant too, for accuracy of cost reporting and estimates. The Production Coordinator discusses with the Accountant which individual will track purchase orders. The Coordinator may have the Accountant arrange to complete an exemption from sales tax form, and help determine how much petty cash the office will need, and who, of your team, is going to keep and monitor it.

ASSISTANT PRODUCTION COORDINATOR

The Production Coordinator, more than the Manager, tends to hire the Assistant Coordinator, as this person is the Coordinator's right hand. As mentioned previously, the Coordinator and Assistant need to keep up a constant conversation, meeting at least daily to give direction and approvals, and to keep each other informed.

OFFICE PRODUCTION ASSISTANT

The Production Coordinator also tends to hire the Office P.A. — or at least highly recommend this person to the PM for hiring — as this individual is the other critical person in helping the Coordinator manage the production office. Be clear who in the office gives direction to the Office P.A., so the latter will not be confused with having multiple bosses. As discussed previously, there needs to be a constant flow of communication between the Coordinator and the Office P.A. to keep the office and the office team running smoothly.

HEAD OFFICE/CO-PRODUCTION OFFICE PEOPLE

There may be Executive Producers, Co-Producers, Legal Counsels, and Controllers at head office who need to be kept abreast of the goings on of production. The Producer should be the point person to keep head office informed, but there may be times when the Production Manager is brought into these conversations. Discuss with the Producer. Head office Legal Counsel may be a source of advice for production decision-making, and that office may be the place where long-form Performer contracts are generated. Most meetings with head office are done by telephone, often conference calls. Find out what paperwork and reports these people need and when. The Production Coordinator can ensure the paperwork is sent to them regularly.

CAST & CASTING PEOPLE

The only reason that "casting" has anything to do with "fishing" is because casting people are always fishing for the right talent to fill all the acting roles in a film.

CASTING DIRECTOR

The Production Manager needs to keep atop who is being hired for how much, and what bonuses the Performers want that will no doubt affect the budget (dressing room requirements like a Winnebago and transportation needs like number and class of flights, type of car rental, etc.). The Producer tends to hire the Casting Director(s); you may have one for the guest star-type leads and a different one for the main cast, but at least one per city where you are shooting or casting. The Production Coordinator needs to keep the Casting Director apprised of the latest script revision and she will keep you apprised of the latest status of Performers chosen. Casting Directors make the deal with the Performers' agents, and then send the deal memos to the Coordinator. The Production Manager needs to be kept in the loop prior to the commitment of the deal letter, since once the deal is on paper the money is as good as spent. The Coordinator turns these deal memos into cast contracts, and may also be involved in helping the Casting Director set up audition sessions, and in making and distributing audition sides to be read at the auditions.

CAST

Though the Production Manager may not actually meet the cast until they are on set, or when they visit the office looking for their per diem, the PM signs the cast contracts. Go figure. The Production Coordinator, however, may be the first person to deal with the Performers, and therefore give them their first impression about the company. The Coordinator is responsible for sending them all the paperwork necessary for them to act in the show. Keep them updated on all script revisions immediately. They are the ones who have to memorize the lines. You may also have to arrange for immigration, travel, and accommodations for them.

EXTRAS & EXTRAS CASTING DIRECTOR

The Production Manager never really interacts with the Extras (also known as Background Performers). The Extras Casting Director tends to be hired by the PM on strong recommendation by the First Assistant Director. The A.D. Department keeps up the communication with this person, and the First A.D. directs the background action on the set. Extras are cast with that have no speaking parts and that fill the background of scenes. On screen, they pass by, walk dogs, or comprise crowds. Special Skills Extras (or Special Business Extras) are paid slightly higher rates because they have a unique skill to perform on screen; for example, they play hockey, ride horses, and do other things on film that require some special skill. The Production Coordinator will, however, deal with the Extras Casting Director in order to coordinate the Extras' arrival on set.

SET PEOPLE – ASSISTANT DIRECTORS

Both Production Manager and Coordinator deal with Assistant Directors several times each day, funneling any information you have for set through them; therefore, they warrant having their own section. A.D.s are in charge of running the set, so that the Director can be creative without worrying about the time or gathering the people and props together. That is why Assistant Directors seem to do an awful lot of running around.

ASSISTANT DIRECTORS

While the Production Manager is overseeing the budget, the Assistant Directors are overseeing the schedule. Between the two of you, you cover it all: time and money. Work together. Together you report on the daily activities of the set on the Daily Production Report, both signing the official, completed form. Discuss the schedule. How flexible is it? The First A.D. is running the set, trying to keep it to schedule, so he is the source of information on how fast (or not) set is moving through the day's work. The Production Manager may hire the First A.D., but the Director may have approval or choice of this person, depending on the Director's agreement. The Director and the First A.D. work hand-in-hand. Some A.D.s prefer a military style of running the set, but others have a softer approach. Some use screaming to keep people on their toes, and some find other ways of earning the crew's respect and focus. Some can be considered "production-hostile." There are many different styles of Assistant Directing. This person will be key in determining the mood of the working set, so find out what style you are in for before hiring the First A.D. Discuss working styles with the Director and the Producer to be sure all are looking for the same style. Assistant Directors tend to own their own scheduling software and have their own computer equipment. Often the First A.D. comes with a full team of Seconds and Thirds. Is this a long-running team, or is this A.D. constantly replacing his A.D. team? Does the Director have a history with the First A.D.? Sometimes the First A.D. will pick up the Director in the morning on the way to set to discuss the day prior to shooting. No matter how they do it, the First A.D. and the Director need to be a team, so the First A.D. can worry about moving the schedule along, leaving the Director to worry about the creative issues of each shot.

For the Production Coordinator, the A.D.s have the lowdown on the schedule. They make it. You have the lowdown on casting status. You can swap information. Inform them of special agreements in the cast contracts that affect the set (like private dressing rooms that have been promised for the length of production, and driver pick-ups promised daily). Decide together which call-sheet form, schedule form, day-out-of-days form, and production-report form to use. Find out if you have compatible computer equipment. Discuss the shoot day responsibilities in detail: Who is to call crew with the next day's call times; who is to inform Performers of change of dates; who is to inform the crew when the call time is pushed or pulled in the middle of the night. Before the shoot, the A.D.s will come to you to stock up on all the paperwork from the distribution table and forms from the wall envelopes or cubbies for their portable office on set. Give them a hand and work as a team.

OTHER SET PEOPLE

Many of these people float from office to set, but their primary responsibility is to set.

LOCATIONS DEPARTMENT

Briefly, these people scout and survey potential locations, then once chosen, make the location deal with the owners and secure permits for permissions. They also ensure that the location remains protected and clean during the shoot day, that lunch arrangements are made, that the unit trucks have accessible space to park, and that there is parking available for the crew, too. If owners have had a bad experience with a film crew, the location may become "burned" from any film crew ever going back there to film. "Burning" locations must be avoided at all costs, as it has a negative effect on the entire industry. Instead consider ways of being "green" and of giving back to the community. When it comes to hiring the Location Manager, ask yourself, or the interviewee, how does this person deal with the public? How has she protected locations from being burned? Has she ever had access to film in a burned location and turned the public's attitude around regarding filming? How well does this person know the city? Can she creatively find and use locations, like finding one location that links two different sets from the script in one place, cutting down on unit moves? During preproduction, the Production Manager needs to look over the location contract and approve it. If it is complex, you may even want Legal Counsel to review the document. As Production Manager, you should attend at least all major location scouts and surveys to learn about costs being planned. For the Production Coordinator, the Location Manager will often ask you to type up the agreement letter or the contract, and arrange for insurance certificates for each location. She will usually need these documents hurriedly. She will also give you location maps to attach to the call sheets. Ask for the maps early, unless you enjoy making maps at the last moment. (More on Locations is in Chapter 16.)

CONTINUITY SUPERVISOR

This person is basically the Editor's representative on set to make sure that each shot will be able to cut to the next without faults, like arm movements that do not match and burning cigarettes that change length. Continuity, therefore, makes many, many notes about and photographs each and every shot during the course of the shoot day. The Production Manager needs to hire someone who is incredibly organized, diligent, and detail-oriented. The Production Coordinator will deal with this person in prep, making sure that the Continuity Supervisor and the Editor meet. Find out what forms need to be printed, have them made, and ensure the equipment exists to print out the continuity stills efficiently. Also discuss a procedure for the most seamless continuity document flow from set to the editing department and back to set.

TRANSPORTATION DEPARTMENT

The Transportation Department basically arranges for truck, car, and picture vehicle rentals, then drives and parks the units. But wow, what a unit it is, made up of numerous huge trucks and trailers that locations has asked to be parked into the most incredibly tight spaces! It is an amazing feat. They also courier items and make purchases throughout the day, ensure the vehicles are working properly throughout the day, and take the film to the lab nightly. They may also provide security for the set between shooting hours. Since the Transportation team is on set first in the morning and last at night, they work some of the longest hours. The Production Manager needs to keep a conversation going with the Transportation Coordinator to minimize overtime and keep the Drivers fresh and functional for the daily work. The Production Coordinator will see Drivers every day in the office during the course of their many runs. Talk to them often, because you can usually help them out with use of the Office Production Assistant, just as they can help you out with use of a Driver.

CRAFT SERVICE

As already discussed, Craft Service supplies snack foods to the crew all day to keep them energized between meals. Since it is the Production Manager who receives all the complaints about food from the crew and the cast, ensure you hire a fabulous Craft Service person or company. If the person is new to the industry, he will have a lot of questions that the Production Coordinator can field. Help by discussing the accounts you have with coffee and water companies. Since the Craft Service person is typically also the certified first aid representative on set, make sure a sufficient-sized first-aid kit for the set is purchased.

CATERER

The Caterer brings a hot lunch to set for the crew. If not Craft Service, the Caterer may also be the one to supply substantial snacks three hours into the day to keep everyone energized until lunchtime. The Locations Department will help set up the lunch, including chairs and garbage cans. You may hire a Caterer who can supply craft service, too. As mentioned, the Production Manager will have to deal with any and all complaints about food. Be sure the Caterer can address food allergies. The caterer must be reliable and serve good, healthy food with lots of variety. On long shoots, it can be a good idea to alternate between two Caterers on a weekly basis to keep variety in the diet. The Production Coordinator will be calling the Caterer every day with the time for lunch the next day, along with the particulars for where, when, and how many. Find out from the crew if there are any special needs (not requests) for catering, like those food allergies.

DESIGN, BUILDING & DECORATING PEOPLE

Depending on the needs of the production, these people may have been hired before you begin and are already working when you start.

ART DEPARTMENT

This department can be made up of the Production Designer, the Art Director, the Assistant Art Directors, and the Art Department Coordinator, or any combination thereof. They design the whole physical look of the film, especially the sets. The Production Manager needs to discuss the art budget with the head of the Art Department. Since a Production Designer can be involved not only in the creative design and building of the sets, but also in overseeing the set dressing, props, and greens — and may even be involved in overseeing wardrobe and makeup — the art budget is a sizable chunk of the entire budget. Keep in conversation with the head of the Art Department on the status of this budget being spent. Find out, too, how big a studio space is required for the set plan. As you find locations, modifications may need to be made to that location so that the place works for filming. Be sure the Art Department is preparing for these modifications, by allocating time or planning to hire more people to cover these needs. For the Production Coordinator, the Art Department can make beautiful, artistic letterhead for you. They will need items couriered by you and cleared through customs. They also need you to arrange for a speedy script clearance so that once the names in the script are legally approved, the correct signs can be made.

SETS DEPARTMENT

These people buy and rent the set furnishings, from lamps to furnish a house set to fake garbage to furnish a location alley set. The Set Decorator is hired in consultation with the Production Designer. The Production Manager may deal more with the Production Designer than directly with the Set Decorator, but should be no stranger to either in order to keep atop production spending promises. The Sets Department may arrange for a set sale (along with wardrobe and props) at the end of production, or for set storage, as needed. You need to discuss these details. The Production Coordinator primarily interacts with the Sets Department to arrange for couriers and customs clearances for them. This department also needs cell phones (or affordable air time packages) to keep in touch with each other.

PROPS DEPARTMENT

Props are anything the Performers handle as written in the script, from cigarettes to food to suitcases to clothing they carry, and so on. There are a lot of overlaps between various departments and Props that are ironed out during preproduction. A chair, for example, is set dressing, except when the Performer has to pick it up and throw it – then the "breakaway" chair (made to break easily) becomes a prop. The Production Manager will likely deal with the Production Designer, rather than with the Property Master directly, to oversee the spending in this department — but again, the PM should be no stranger to this department. The Production Coordinator will arrange for couriers, customs clearances, and cell phones or air time packages for these people, too.

CONSTRUCTION DEPARTMENT

As the name suggests, these people build the sets. The department can be made up of a Construction Manager, a Construction Coordinator, various Carpenters, Scenic Painters, and Laborers. Hiring of the Construction Manager is done in consultation with the Production Designer, then the Construction Manager tends to bring together his entire team. As time draws short to complete sets prior to shooting, taking all set and location modifications into account, this department often goes over budget in overtime. No matter what the set design, actual building of sets takes longer than originally planned. Be prepared for this situation. Ensure you have hired a Construction Manager who can deliver what the Production Designer plans in a timely manner, so that you are not lighting while the last coat of paint is still being applied. The Production Coordinator does not have to deal with this department very much, as they are usually working before the Coordinator is on board and have their own system of organization in place. It is still worthy to talk to them now and then to keep in touch with the progress of production.

GREENS DEPARTMENT

If you shoot in a forest, no doubt the trees will be in the wrong place for the camera, and you will have to hire Greenspeople to place trees and shrubs to augment the forest location. The same rings true for gardens, and Greenspeople are especially needed for studio sets that must show a bit of the "outside" through set windows. If production is small and simple enough, the Props or Sets Departments may cover greens work. Since this is another team under the Production Designer, the Production Manager and Coordinator may not deal directly with these people often.

TECHNICAL PEOPLE

Technical crew is hired toward the end of preproduction and report directly to set. If they are not in the production meeting, you will have to visit set to meet them.

CAMERA DEPARTMENT

The Director of Photography ("DOP" or "DP") designs the technical look of the production. As the Production Designer oversees all the Art Departments, the Director of Photography will oversee all the technical departments — Camera, Sound, Electric, Grip — and will be heavily involved in issues relating to Special Effects and CGI. The camera team can be made up of the DP; the Camera Operator; the Focus Puller (since focus is measured with a tape measure, not by eye), who is also known as the First Assistant Cameraperson ("1st AC"); the Second Assistant Cameraperson ("2nd AC"); the Camera Trainee; and the Data

Management Technician ("DMT") or Digital Image Technician ("DIT") who backs up the footage on set and ensures the image is indeed captured. On smaller shoots, the DP may also operate the camera. The Production Manager will interact with this department regarding choice of image capture format or film stock, size, and nature of equipment package rental, and will listen to the DP's design of shots. Are they expensive? Do you need second camera, second unit, cranes, steadicams, jimmy jibs, camera cars, scaffolding, and are these wishes in the budget already? In prep, the Production Coordinator needs to find out what film stock is being used, as it is the Coordinator who will do the ordering. If it is digital, typically the camera department takes care of ordering the hard drives, cards or disks, but will require a purchase order from the PC to do so. Keep informed, too, when the camera equipment and tests are scheduled, because you will likely be asked to help in those arrangements. From the Camera Department, you can also receive a battery order and an expendable order (like camera tape and lens tissues).

SOUND DEPARTMENT

Another obvious department, the Sound Department is made up of the Sound Mixer (or Sound Recordist), the Boom Operator (who holds the microphone at great heights and for inhumanly long hours), and sometimes includes a third, the Cableperson. Because sound recording is essentially much cheaper than filming (camera), the sound team is often placed second or forgotten on set when it comes to production issues. The Locations Department may have found a fabulous location, but not considered the flight path that will ruin your location sound recording at regular intervals. As a Production Manager, be sure you hire a production team that considers sound issues, and also a sound team that is excellent at capturing location sound — a very difficult job. If you manage to achieve good location sound, you will save production loads of money in postproduction as they try to rebuild the soundtrack. Research their past projects. Discuss the merits of radio mics versus booming. Sound Mixers often have their own equipment but may need specific elements rented to augment their kit. When you visit a set, the Sound Mixer is a great person to visit... he hears everything the microphone is pointed at! For the Production Coordinator, find out and order which sound stock the Sound Department intends to use, unless the Sound Mixer is planning to arrange for purchase of the stock himself. Sound always has an extensive battery order for production.

ELECTRIC DEPARTMENT

The Gaffer is the head electrician, and the Best Boy is next in charge. The rest of the team is called Electrics. These people, obviously, are in charge of the lights on the set. The Production Manager may be the one hiring the Gaffer in consultation with the DP. Discuss the wish list for rental package with the Gaffer. You may need to negotiate the list down, depending on your budget. Be sure you have enough crew for the equipment. Renting a huge equipment package and being short on crew will cost you time on set. The Production Coordinator will address the order of expendables, i.e., for gels (colored-gelatin sheets or rolls to color the lights), black wrap (to shade the light), and clothes pegs (to hold the gels onto the lights).

GRIP DEPARTMENT

Grips move all sorts of things around on the set, and create the most beautiful rigs to enable the camera to dolly around, in, and through just about anything. They also set up flags to block or pattern some of the lights. The Key Grip heads the department, the Dolly Grip pushes the camera dolly, and there can be a Best Boy Grip who is second in charge. Again, the Production Manager may hire the Key Grip in consultation with the DP or the Gaffer, and you need to discuss the wish list and the crew list to make the beauty happen. The Production Coordinator needs to arrange for the expendable order for tape and sash, etc. Grips may also have specialty rentals they will ask you to arrange, like scaffolding and cranes. Obtain necessary approvals from the Production Manager.

HAIR, MAKEUP & WARDROBE PEOPLE

Affectionately known as the Pretty Department, its members dress and makeup the Performers into character for on screen.

WARDROBE DEPARTMENT

Obviously, this department designs the wardrobe (or costumes), shops for wardrobe, makes wardrobe, does laundry of wardrobe, dresses the Performers, and keeps notes and photographs of who wore what for which scene. Knowing the retail price of clothing, you must be aware that it is hugely easy to go over budget in this department. As Production Manager, discuss the wardrobe budget with the Wardrobe Designer and how they plan to keep to the budget. Can any of the wardrobe be sold after filming, or must it all be stored? Be sure you hire a wardrobe team that has designed similar costumes: Period wardrobe differs radically from contemporary glamour or grunge. As Production Coordinator, find out if they need production support for their camera's photographs. Also, keep them abreast of the casting status as soon as possible, because these people never seem to have enough time to fit the cast.

HAIR & MAKEUP DEPARTMENT

Again, the job of this department is obvious. The Hair Designer and Makeup Artist should be budgeted to come to some preproduction meetings to meet the Director, the cast, and possibly to do screen tests. As Production Manager, find out if these people have worked with any of the Performers you are planning to cast. From their previous projects, find out how fast (or slow) they are in doing their work on the day. An entire crew waiting for a Performer to come out of hair/makeup is an expensive wait. Do you need any special needs makeup for this shoot, like glamour makeup or wounds? How adept are these people at production's special needs? For the Production Coordinator, these people also need to be kept informed of the casting status, but not quite so hurriedly as the Wardrobe Department.

SPECIAL DEPARTMENTS PEOPLE

Depending on the scale of the production, you could have any, all, or none of the following departments to create the magic of movies.

STUNTS DEPARTMENT

When the script calls for someone to walk through fire, the script calls for a stunt double. The Production Manager must consider safety as a first priority when hiring the Stunt Coordinator. Naturally, you want to see a track record of stunts performed that look good for the camera too, but safety is always your primary goal. Also, when looking for a Stunt Coordinator (or company), does he (or they) have access to people who will double for the necessary Performers? Stunt adjustments in the budget are bonuses beyond the stunt price for particularly difficult stunts. As Production Coordinator, you need to know from the Stunt Coordinator who is going to play which role, so that you can inform Wardrobe and also can whip up the appropriate stunt contracts. Discuss the nature of the stunt with the Stunt Coordinator and the Assistant Director to determine if a Nurse or an Ambulance Attendant is required on the day. If so, order one. As for insurance, you may need to acquire sufficient coverage, as specified by their union.

SPECIAL EFFECTS DEPARTMENT

Special Effects can include fires, snow, rain, and more created on set. These effects are sometimes known as Physical Effects, to differentiate them from computerized special effects. This is another department where the Production Manager has to be concerned with safety first. Special Effects people need to work hand-in-hand with at least the Art and the Locations Departments initially;

larger effects require lots of planning to do them cost effectively. In order to ensure accuracy, be specific about your needs when you ask for quotations from Special Effects companies. Keep updated on the quotations to keep the spending in line. For the Production Coordinator, these people often come from a supplier that does not work in the production office with you, so it is your job to keep them informed of meetings and script changes that affect them. Find out the nature of the effect, and how you can help. You can arrange, for example, for a representative from the fire department to be on set, or for someone to have a fire extinguisher handy. Discuss all arrangements with the Assistant Directors.

COMPUTER GRAPHICS IMAGERY (CGI) OR VISUAL EFFECTS & ANIMATION

Different from set special effects, visual effects or CGI are usually computer effects or motion-controlled camera equipment (to enable computerized matching of camera movements). You may have one department creating 3D computer effects and another creating 2D computer effects. This team has to work hand-in-hand with at least the Art Department. Again, the more planning time, the more cost effective the effects will be. Beware on set, as it is easy for crew to say "fix it in post" and do a sloppy job on set to rush forward. Imagine if a tether is left on a bird for the shot to save the crew five minutes in removing it (because the bird was trained for this action already). You save the five minutes of shooting, but find that to remove the tether in CGI, the cost equals that of one of your fancy effects; so you have to remove a fancy effect from the script to cover the cost of the tether removal — leaving you with a CGI effect that is in effect, invisible. "Fixing it in post" is expensive. Avoid it. As Production Manager, keep an eye on CGI quotations and the changes that affect the original quotations at all production meetings and in all script revisions. Keep an eye on crew that likes to shift responsibility from set to CGI, too. For the Production Coordinator, the CGI people are rarely in your office fulltime, though they may have a representative on set for all effects shots. Keep them informed of meetings and script changes that affect them.

PREVIS TEAM

You may only cross paths with the previs team and/or Storyboard Artist during preproduction. They are busy testing and refining the director's vision of the script. From their work you can preview the scope of the production plan. They are there to help plan shots and sequences in advance of shooting, so they happily contribute to maximizing the production's budget making it to the screen. On more complex productions, the previs team may also have a presence on set to help test changes to that vision on the fly. (More on Previs is in Chapter 26.)

SECOND UNIT

Second Unit may be dedicated to being the Special Effects Unit, the Stunt Unit, the Action Unit, or the Animal Unit. Whichever unit they are, whatever shots they are achieving, they do not require the lead cast nor any meaty dialogue scenes, so they can be a reduced-size unit capturing shots that would be expensive for the entire Main Unit to be standing around waiting to capture (like an establishing shot of the sunrise, or a dog fetching a stick). They take direction from the Main Unit Director and the DP to ensure their shots will match seamlessly in style into the whole picture. They can also work closely with the Editor for the same reason. Have Second Unit start after Main Unit begins, to be sure that Second Unit is capturing shots that Main Unit missed — instead of getting ahead of the Main Unit shooting schedule, and locking Main Unit in to Second Unit's choice of camera angles for matching. If both units schedule to finish on the same day as wrap, this situation will be a bit tricky. Try to schedule so that Second Unit finishes a few days into wrap to ensure they are available to capture last minute pick-up shots that Main Unit could not. When Editors ask for shots to help with transitions that did not work as originally planned, Editors often create a video reference for Second Unit's playback reference on set. As the Production Coordinator, keep Second Unit informed of meetings and script changes that affect them.

POSTPRODUCTION PEOPLE

The term "postproduction" sounds like "after production," but the process actually starts long before the end. The Editor is usually aboard cutting the film together while the film is still being shot — from the second day of principal photography!

EDITING DEPARTMENT

There may be a Postproduction Supervisor, a Postproduction Coordinator, Editors, and Assistant Editors in postproduction. The Supervisor is hired by the Production Manager or the Producer, and it is to this person you hand over the running of production after wrap. The Supervisor will manage the post budget; if not, the Producer will. Supervisors know how postproduction works. They have contacts with post facilities. They are responsible for monitoring the budget. They are highly organized. The Editor, being a key creative on the production, may have already been chosen prior to your arrival in preproduction. On a series you may alternate Editors on each episode to more efficiently move postproduction along. Though production has managed to film shots on set, it is in the editing room where the story is actually created. This is the reason many Editors make the transition to Director. As the Production Coordinator, you have already made sure that the Continuity Supervisor and the Editor connected during preproduction to discuss the continuity paperwork flow. Other things to discuss with the editing team are: a system for the information flow regarding the arranging for and screening of dailies, and who is to call the post facility for the daily check on the transfer or negative.

MUSIC DEPARTMENT

Another key creative, the Music Composer is often part of the team assembled by the Producer in development. This person often negotiates a flat fee to include her work and music rights, studio rental, musicians hired, and their rights. If the Production Manager is still on board in postproduction, he should ensure that a music spotting session happens where the Director and/or the Producer sits with the Music Composer and a cut of the film to decide when music is required and what it might sound like. If production's plan is to fill the soundtrack with pre-recorded music instead of original music created by a Composer, beware of music rights. They are expensive. (More on Music Rights is in Chapter 33.) As the Production Coordinator, you likely will not need to deal with the Music Composer very often. She will tend to deal with the Producer directly. If a piece of music is to be played back on set for filming, you need to arrange for a transfer of music – in the appropriate format – to send to the Sound Mixer on set. Make sure you have an extra copy of this music in the office in case of emergency on the shoot day.

POSTPRODUCTION FACILITY

If you are shooting digital, the post facility receives the digital original from the set every night. By morning, they transfer it to a working copy (the "dailies") for you to view. At the time of this transfer, if funds permit, you may have the entire negative backed up as well. If you are shooting on film, the post facility (the lab) receives your negative at night and processes the film, transferring it to video in the early morning. As Production Manager, you need to set up the post facility deal and book processing and/or transfer time slots for production. You will also want to store your digital original or negative at the post house for safekeeping. The Producer may have set up a facilities deal with the lab, trading some facilities costs for investment participation in the production. Discuss with the post house which costs are associated with the facilities deal, and which costs are to be paid for with cash; then discuss with the Accountant how to track those non-cash expenses. Decide how dailies are to be viewed: projected onto a screen at the post facility, or available on a portable format like DVD, or downloadable from the FTP site to the production office or head office, or a combination of any of these methods? When the camera test happens prior to shooting, be sure that the work flow of postproduction is tested using the test's output. Also, if you are using film stock, ensure you are informed of the negative check or "neg report" daily (stating if the film negative was processed okay with no scratches). If there are negative problems, address them urgently. How big is the problem? How expensive the fix? Investigate the severity of the problem before committing to re-shooting all of yesterday's footage and filing an insurance claim. There may be ways to cut around much of the troubled images. (More on insurance claims in Chapter 17.) The post facility or lab is also required to sign a letter for the Completion Bond, granting access to the digital original or negative should production be taken over by the Completion Bond.

Because of the Postproduction Supervisor, the Production Coordinator may not have to deal directly with the post facility very often. The Coordinator, though, may be the one to call the post house first thing every morning for a digital check or neg report, and pass on that information to the Production Manager and the Producer. Another reason to be in touch with the post house is to arrange to screen dailies at their facility, as you need to make plans for the screenings to happen following the shoot day's wrap to allow the key crew to attend.

POST SOUND FACILITY

You may have a Sound Designer, Sound Editors, Dialogue Editors, Sound Effects Editors, Music Editors, a Mixer, and a Foley Artist. The work of the Sound Editors is obvious, as it involves cutting the sound into separate tracks so the quality of each sound can be treated separately in the mix. The Mixer is different from the Location Sound Mixer, in that he sits at the sound facility's control panel literally mixing all the numerous soundtracks (you can easily have over 100 different tracks of dialogue, sound effects, foley, music, and atmosphere) down to a mere few tracks for marrying with the finished master or print for playback (in mono or stereo). This person will also ensure you mix a separate music and effects (M&E) track to allow for dubbing the film into foreign languages. The Foley Artist is that cool person who watches the film from a sound studio and recreates sounds live to tape to add richness to the soundtrack — sounds like footsteps (on various surfaces), clothing rustles, door slams, kisses, and so on. As this happens far in postproduction, only on a series might you as a Production Manager or Coordinator still be on board when sound post is happening. The Coordinator may still be around to assist in setting up ADR sessions (Additional Dialogue Recording, also known as Looping) with the Performers. Make sure that the Performer's work reports are filled out so that the Performer will be paid for this work. There will not be an A.D. around in post to do this task.

PUBLICITY PEOPLE

Though it may seem that publicity arrangements get in the way of filming, a film would have a hard time finding an audience if publicity people failed to do, or were not allowed to do, their job.

PUBLICITY DEPARTMENT

The Unit Publicist and the Publicity Department conduct interviews, arrange for publicity shots (action shots on set), arrange for gallery shoots (the Performers in character in a studio setting), create one-sheet and other promotional material, arrange for or make an EPK (Electronic Press Kit or behind-the-scenes video), arrange for press to visit the set, and issue press releases, too. The Producer or studio typically hires the Unit Publicist, though the PM and/or Coordinator may influence the decision based on past experience. The Producer will be key in designing how much publicity needs to be assembled for the production. Be sure that the A.D.s schedule time for publicity shots and interviews. The Production Coordinator can be involved in arranging for the Publicity Department to visit and work on set. Keep them informed of the shooting schedule, and keep them in contact with the Producer to discuss the best days to be there. Keep the Assistant Directors in the loop with these communications also.

STILLS PHOTOGRAPHER

As this person is likely to be on set a lot more often than the Unit Publicist, it is worth dealing with her separately. If the Producer or studio has not already chosen a Stills Photographer, seek recommendations from the Unit Publicist and review potential applicants' portfolios. Note that both the Stills Photographer and the EPK Cameraperson will be covered under the Camera union if you are using a union crew, and also note you may require Executive approval in the hiring process of either or both of these positions. As Production Manager or Coordinator, be sure that stills are both scheduled and captured. Make sure, too, the Producer and the Director are involved in the choice of what is most interesting to shoot. Be sure the Assistant Director is in the loop to give input to the lighter workload days (to schedule a gallery shoot). Keep the Stills Photographer aware of the shooting schedule and stills time windows.

DIGITAL MEDIA TEAM

There may be a production website and blog under design or already live for the production that requires a constant flow of fresh content from the set. This means more interviews, B-roll, photographs, and stories. Beyond the production's website, there are multiple channels of Internet communications (such as behind-the-scenes marketing websites, various social networking platforms, and other blogosphere destinations) further fragmenting the ways that the film's marketing messages can be disseminated. Communications with the digital media team associated with your production is typically funneled through the Unit Publicist. She will have a handle on managing the messages and overall publicity plan... well, as much as you can manage publicity on the Internet and in the blogosphere.

—⁓—

This chapter has been a micro look at the whole crew. Okay, so I am leaving lawyers and bankers and auditors to be dealt with in the money section of the book. I know you know what they do! The more you deal with each department the more you will understand the nuances of what they do, and respect them for their work. There is always trust. You earn their trust and they give you trust in return. Keep talking to everyone on the crew. The constant input will be helpful and educational. There is always something to learn from the professionals you hire.

MIDNIGHT CREATIONS

- -

An excerpt from notes from the Production Coordinator to the Assistant Coordinator, penned during one of those late night shoots:

1. 1:28 a.m. The call sheet is done and faxed. Office P.A. is on his way to set with it.
2. 1:34 a.m. A ginger ale is opened.
3. Please call the female lead with call time change: It's now 5:30 p.m., not 3:30 p.m.
4. Office P.A. will be in at noon; I'll work at 2:00 or 2:30 p.m.
5. Office P.A. needs to return the standard picture vehicle at 2:00 p.m.
6. Only after having cleaned both vehicles. With a toothbrush.
7. Just kidding! About the toothbrush, that is.
8. I'm returning your script pages used for "siding."
9. Oh, and one more thing for Office P.A. First thing: Camera is sending back the 2nd unit equipment tonight and having it put in the P.M.'s room. Please have him take it back to the equipment house first thing.

A little later...

17. A production report to distribute... really.
18. And some lovely state of the art deal memos for that "distrib thing."
19. 1:54 a.m. Heart failure. I've been all alone since the Office P.A. left. Then I heard a voice. Of course I knew that someone was trying to make their presence known, but who? It's pretty dark and scary here sometimes... the Office P.A. came back for the craft service water.
20. 1:57 a.m. Heart resumes, and I'm alone again.
21. Please find out from the Location Manager, or whomever, when the A.L.M. is coming back to visit the office. I need something from him.
22. No, only a signature.
23. 2:36 a.m. And now what? Another ginger ale.
24. A note to the Daily 3rd Electric from the Gaffer: Please bring the other Daily Electric in with you.
25. An equipment house order and purchase order: 200 amp 3-phase disconnect for today.
26. 2:57 a.m. I realized the Art Department copier was still on.
27. 3:03 a.m. Found the off switch.
28. 3:12 a.m. I get my second wind. Or is it the third?
29. 3:14 a.m. False alarm.
30. You might as well send the Office P.A. out to post the mail. It keeps getting forgotten.
31. 5:14 a.m. A slew of call time changes. Please call all the actors with changes in their times.
32. As for them editors: I didn't call the Post Coordinator at night and just as well. At 1 a.m. they didn't want rushes on Thursday. At 5 a.m. they want RUSHES AT 7:00 P.M. Let the Post Coordinator know.
33. Please note the call sheet is pink. The Location Manager and Set Decorator know. Everyone else is to find out in the morning.
34. Gotta run to take pink call sheets to set. I've only faxed pink to head office and technical union...

WORK SPACE ORGANIZATION

8

You are sitting at your desk. If you are the Production Manager, you will likely be in an office, as nearly all the issues you deal with are highly confidential. If you are the Production Coordinator, you could be in your own office or working in open concept, as you need to be near the traffic of the active production office. In either case, this is your personal space and you need to set it up to work best for you.

How you organize your personal work space is most certainly up to you and your own personal style. Yet, are you ready for the reams of paper that will flow onto and off your desk? Will you be able to find every single document or piece of information with lightning speed or will much of it become lost amid the abundance? Will passing crew members be able to read Performer contracts left face up on top of one of the great many piles? What you want are tips on handling your work space before it handles you. Since even the Production Manager relies on the Production Coordinator's organization, the Coordinator's work space is more structured than that of the Production Manager's.

ELECTRONIC vs. PAPER WORK SPACES

As the office increases the use of electronic processes, even more of your work will be on the computer or Internet. Paper, however, may still be required for a number of reasons: for wet signatures on hard copy contracts; distribution of documentation to a group of people without constant computer access (yes, "the set"), and so on. Paper may also still be desired for a number of work style reasons: for penciling in notes on a hard copy of the document;

for carrying a paper document for review where you do not want to bring an electronic device; for reviewing a document prior to scanning into the system, and so on. Typically part of your work space will be electronic and part of it will remain paper-driven.

THE PM'S WORK SPACE

Basically the Production Manager needs to keep on top of tons of issues and deal memos and long-form contracts without dragging documents in and out from files in a cabinet, because all issues are current and immediate in preproduction. You also want to be organized enough to find anything quickly and for the Coordinator to be able to come into your office to find something if you need her to do so while you are on set. Your work space organization cannot be too complex.

First, we will look at managing the paper side of your work space. Here are two systems that work well:

LATERAL FILING ON THE DESK

If you like to spread paper out over a wide, lateral surface, this system is for you. Since you have an office where you can close the door, you do not need to enclose every bit of paper in file folders for confidentiality. Flag sticky notes dry side up atop each stack of paper and offset the piles in a column down one side of your desk. You can now view many differing stacks of papers at once by their sticky note labels. Though this system uses up maximum desk space, it is good for hiding confidential information lower down on the stacks of paper — a bit like hiding documents in plain sight. If you want to organize further, you can use colored highlighters to code the sticky notes by subject or departmental matter, or by level of urgency. The only downside is that if you have so much paper in this system, the piles can slide off the desk.

IN-TRAY FILING

If you prefer a vertical look to your organization, tuck stacks of paper away in in-trays as your organizational system. This system works for keeping similar issues together, as you will no doubt have a limited number of in-trays stacked on your desk, each labeled with a different subject or department: Locations, Casting, Cost Reports, and so on. Since you cannot see everything at once, you may find that you lose track of an item or two, or at least spend a little time looking for it. This system, however, does keep your desk surface relatively clear of stray paper.

THE PM'S FILING PILE

In both cases, you can allocate a space or a box as a filing pile. As you finish dealing with issues, put the related paper in the filing pile for archiving at a later time or date. (To keep on top of filing, it is advisable to do this once a day.) Determine between you and the Coordinator who will be maintaining the Production Manager's files. Do you want the PM files to be folded into the production files? Also, when placing documents into your filing pile, if you want to keep a particular one only until a certain date, use a sticky note to mark a "trash date" on the document; that way, when the files are being purged at a later date, no review is necessary to remove this temporary document from the files.

THE PM'S ELECTRONIC FILING SYSTEM (ON EMAIL)

Documents you generate yourself tend to be stored on your computer's hard drive, whereas all other documentation tends to arrive via email, especially if you use both computer and smart phone to keep up to date. To maintain consistency, first organize your email into folders and then mimic that folder structure on the hard drive.

Descriptively label emails you wish to keep for future reference. You may need to find an email client that allows you to change subject lines of existing emails. You can file nearly everything in your email client, sending yourself important items to provide access to all necessary information while mobile. Yes, doing so means you will have a huge inbox or many folders of emails. Of course you can sort email by sender's name, receiver's name, and date sent, but email has a unique feature that makes it a superior filing system for information: priority and colored category flags. Use them. Red is typically for high priority items and blue is for low. Beyond these two, green could represent budget issues, purple for cast, and yellow for items where you are awaiting a response from someone. Define your own color shorthand. Remember, too, to backup your email filing system to another format on a regular basis. (see a list of email folders in Chapter 10).

THE PC'S WORK SPACE

On to the much more structured environment of the Production Coordinator's workspace. It is wise for the Production Manager to read this section too, to gleam hints of organization that may prove useful to his own organizational style.

The surface of the Production Coordinator's desk may look like a sea of paper. A big sea. Documents will be constantly moving to and from your desk. Not only that, but at any given time, you will need to be able to find any one document from that mess. Separate your desk surface into sections.

THE "TO DO" LIST

The "To Do" list is not actually a section of your desk because it should be portable, but when you are at your desk, it should sit center stage. There are many styles of "to do" lists, from calendar books, to steno pads, even to scraps of paper. Choose a method that best suits you.

CALENDAR BOOK

Choose a calendar book that shows one week for every two pages. Though it gives you the illusion you can plan one week in advance, you will probably be thinking one day at a time anyway. Still, this is my favorite method. It keeps a history of what you have done, as well as allowing you to plan for future events. If you write small, each day has enough space or lines to jot down the sometimes fifty-odd things to do for that day. Use the margins to note important names and numbers you may want to add to your contact list. Prep the calendar, labeling the days of the shooting schedule with day number, set name, and approximate call time. During production you can correct the call times and add the wrap times. This will be a handy reference when you are completing the production reports. Always write in a pencil dark enough to read and hard enough to not smudge. You will make lots of changes.

LEGAL-SIZED LINED PAD OF PAPER

Letter-sized pads of paper will not have enough lines for the number of jobs you will do in a day. Legal-sized pads are big, and hard to lose on the desk. Use one page per day, and one line per job. You will not have to write as small as you would in the calendar book, but you also cannot glance at the full week to see what is approaching. If you find the stress of one-day-at-a-time is the best for you, this is your system. Tear off the pages that are done and file them in case you need to refer to them again.

LINED NOTEBOOK

A combination of the legal-sized pad of paper and the calendar book, a notebook works best if you want to refer back to recent days without having to dip into the filing cabinet, and you do not worry too much about the future. Since this system is not in a calendar format, you will not have the same feeling of schedule that comes with a calendar — and it is hard to plan too far in advance, since you do not know how many pages in advance you need to write about a triggering event.

STENO PAD

The portability of a steno pad cannot be matched. The drawback is that you will be constantly flipping pages back and forth, as the pages are much too small to hold all your jobs for one day. You can use this drawback to your advantage, however: it is a fine way to look organized but a little frantic at the same time, thereby letting the frantic crew members relate to you.

ONE STICKY NOTE PER JOB

If you love to post sticky notes all over your desk, the telephone, and the walls around you, this method is for you. This is a good system to make people think you are totally disorganized and totally busy. When things get done, you come across as a miracle worker. When you delegate something, just hand your Assistant the note. Drawbacks are: losing sticky notes that have lost their stickiness and have fallen behind furniture, and having no record of what is completed — since you throw out the notes as the jobs are finished.

DESK CALENDAR

A blotting paper desk calendar is not recommended. The squares are too small to list even a portion of what you have to do, and it will spend most of the time on your desk covered by the reams of other paperwork that your desk supports.

ELECTRONIC CALENDAR TASK LIST

This system is not recommended because of its lack of portability and flexibility. A computer is cannot be carried around as easily as a pad or sheet of paper and the on-screen display of a computer or smart phone is not large or flexible enough to display the information you need on such a constantly changing "to do" list.

TYPED NOTES

This is another method that is not recommended, but mentioned only because on my first coordinating job, I actually typed myself a list of things to do every night for the next day. Call me crazy. I have never had the time or the inclination to do it again. The Production Manager from that show still shakes his head in remembrance.

GENERAL NOTES FOR ANY "TO DO" SYSTEM

Remember that you will need to refer to your "to do" list daily, and may reference it later in production. Take the advice you gave the Office Production

Assistant and note down absolutely every task you need to do, no matter how simple each may seem. Imagine trying to remember fifty different things to do without the aid of written notes. It cannot be done. With a list you can check off each item as it is completed, so that you will be able to see both what is left to be done and what you have already accomplished.

THE "IMMEDIATE" NOTES

Always carry around sticky notes and pen for when you do not have your "To Do" list handy. These are your "Immediate" notes. As people ask you to do something, write it down on a note for transposing onto your "To Do" list as soon as you have time. If it is a job that requires a question of someone on set, you can put it into the "Set Square."

THE SET SQUARE OR BIG STICKY MEETING NOTES

Mark off an area on your desk near the telephone (about six inches by six inches) with any colored tape. Write all questions for the set on separate sticky notes for when you next talk to them. The set always calls when you are in the middle of doing something else, so with this system, all the questions are immediately handy; you will never have to waste time hemming and hawing trying to remember why you left them a message to call you in the first place.

The Production Manager can adapt this system to have big sticky notes with different names on each for meetings or discussions to have with people like the Producer, the Executive Producer, the Production Coordinator, the First A.D., the Production Designer, and so on. When an issue comes up and you have to talk to someone — but now is not the time — note it on the big sticky notes (big, because you will need the size for all you need to write). Then, when you meet with that person, you have a collection of questions to ask at once, rather than returning to that person over and over again.

THE "DESK" FILE FOLDERS

These files hold ongoing issues that generate a lot of documentation and can take over the Coordinator's desk if you let them. Most of the documentation is confidential, so by using file folders, you will never have contracts exposed on your desk for passing crew members to glimpse. By name, the desk file folders are:

> Cast Contracts
> Crew Deal Memos
> Credits
> Script Revisions
> Legal Clearances

One file folder per issue, they sit stacked to one side of the desk with all the most current information for each issue inside. Since the documentation comes from both electronic and paper sources, you may file the information in a fragmented way making it difficult to find the latest, most relevant information at any given time. Since these desk file folders are a hard copy system, it is worth printing the electronically-received information to store all relevant documentation together (and easier than scanning all paper sources). Try to print only the last email in a decision chain, though knowing when someone has had the last word may be next to impossible. And, if an email branches into more than one topic, cut the email or print it twice in order to file the relevant information in the appropriate two folders. If you highlight the most important information in an email chain, you will be saved from multiple re-readings of the entire chain as you look for the necessary kernel.

More on the topics of these movement folders will be covered in later chapters: Crew Deal Memos in Chapter 23, 25 & 26, Cast Contracts in Chapter 24, Script Revisions in Chapter 27, Credits in Chapter 29, and Legal Clearances in Chapter 33.

THE "MOVEMENT" FILE FOLDERS

Use a file-folder color that contrasts with the "Desk" file folders. These files are used to move stacks of paper to and from the people you most deal with as the Coordinator. They should be placed so that passing crew can access them easily.

THE COORDINATOR-TO-COORDINATOR FILE

Okay, this may be stretching the topic of movement, but this folder holds all the backup to the items listed on your "To Do" list. It will become a really fat file, so paperclip groupings together, and give each a label with a sticky note at the top. Then lay them in the file one grouping slightly lower than the next so you can see most of the grouping names as soon as you open the file folder.

THE COORDINATOR-TO-PM FILE

This file will be most used and become ragged, since you have daily meetings with the Production Manager. Inside put all documentation to be signed by, approved by, and discussed with the PM. Encourage the crew to put items in for signature so he can have a single signature session, instead of one for every member of the crew. Once this system is in place, the Production Manager may not want any other in-tray. Paper clip telephone messages to the front.

THE COORDINATOR-TO-PRODUCER FILE

Like the Coordinator-to-PM file, this file collects paperwork and telephone messages for the Producer. This one may not find as much usage as the Production Manager's, but it will probably be close.

THE COORDINATOR-TO-DIRECTOR FILE

As it sounds, this file works the same as the above crew files, but for the Director.

THE COORDINATOR-TO-PERFORMER FILE

If you have a visiting star or guest star, this file is a great way to have a temporary in-tray for her. Do not wait for the Performer to come to you in search of the file's contents. Regularly deliver the contents yourself. The personal treatment will be appreciated.

IN-TRAYS OR BOXES

With the movement file folders, you will find that you do not need a traditional in-tray. By not using an in-tray, people will have to hand you every item, thereby giving you the opportunity to quickly glance at it and determine its level of priority. But there are some in-trays or boxes that you should use. Place them on or near your desk for use by you and your Assistants only.

TO-BE-FILED TRAY

Dump all the paper to be filed into this tray for you or your Assistants to do the actual filing when convenient. Pencil in the file name where you would like the page to go at the top right hand corner (especially near the beginning of production), so that both you and your Assistants are on the same track filing–wise.

ORIGINAL SCRIPTS TRAY

The second tray houses the original white pages of each script revision that is current. These pages go through the photocopier many, many times, so make sure they are treated with respect so they can continue to do their job. Label each revision with a sticky note indicating what color the revision is (even though the title page will clearly say so). The more double-checks in the system, the less likely mistakes will be made.

ORIGINAL FORMS TRAY

Like the original scripts tray, this one houses the original white copies of all the types of paper on the distribution table (from crew lists to contact lists to schedules, and so on). Label the color of the respective item with sticky notes, and move outdated versions immediately to the to-be-filed tray to avoid confusion. Electronically, you can duplicate this collection by setting up an original forms folder to store the copies of documents and forms to print as needed. Since your electronic filing system will typically house all versions of crew lists together, but in a separate folder from, such as "schedules," for example, use short cuts to get to the folders where the documents are actually stored.. This method reduces the risk of your accessing the wrong version of the original document.

THE PC's HIDING PLACES

If the Coordinator's desk has a section underneath that is enclosed, celebrate. You likely are working in open concept and need space for hiding items. Under the desk is a perfect hiding spot. If you are not blessed with such a desk, the bottom drawer of a locking, lateral filing cabinet is good, too. The Production Manager's office may also prove useful for hiding spots. As for items worth hiding:

VIEWING COPIES OF DAILIES OR FINAL SHOWS

Viewing copies of final shows (like DVDs) are borrowed for personal consumption, and therefore the inevitable loss. Copies of dailies will not disappear as fast as master copies of final shows. Even with a sign-out sheet, people forget to note which ones they have borrowed. By "hiding" the disks, crew members must ask you personally to borrow them. You can keep the sign-out sheet accurate.

EXTRA CREW GIFTS

Hats, t-shirts, sweatshirts, jackets. Crew members love crew gifts, and many love having more than one per person. Keep any spares hidden.

THE PRODUCTION OFFICE WALLS / SPACE

The Production Coordinator already has wall envelopes posted or cubbies stationed for crew and for companies. Add a regular wall calendar, displaying several months at a time. Mark down the production schedule, noting prep weeks, shoot weeks, hiatus weeks (if applicable), and wrap weeks. Crew will often come to look at this calendar. So will you.

THE DOORS

Decide with the Production Manager what is the wording needed for the sign on the front door. Production may want a sign as simple as a photocopied sheet of paper naming the production company or as fancy as a professionally engraved door plaque. Should the sign list the show title along with the production company name?

Next, choose the most artistically inclined person in your department and have them make paper door signs for all the doors in the company (every department and every door, including dressing rooms). Note the company or the show name (ask the Production Manager) and the description of the room. Door signs are great for looks, to help when you describe to someone how to find a certain room, and to teach you why wardrobe tells you they need seven different rooms for storage.

CREATING A DOCUMENT TRAIL

To the Production Manager and Coordinator, there is nothing like having information recorded for future reference. When you do something and there is no one to memo about the task done — but it seems an important bit of information — send a memo "To File." You may be teased for the thoroughness, but those around you will soon learn that if you have dealt with a matter, you have completed it and recorded it. This system is very comforting in such a transient way of conducting business.

Imagine that you have been looking for the owner of a certain piece of music to negotiate a legal clearance, and you have spoken with thirty different people in five different countries over three weeks — all to no avail. When the Producer and the Legal Counsel ask for a report on your research, you can remember only three contacts. You are advised to continue searching. The search takes up a lot of your time and production's time. Record what you need to do, what you are doing, and what you have done. Do this on paper or electronically, filing it in a manner so you can find the information again — using the desk files, for example, or using descriptive electronic file names that mimic the organization of the desk files. You will never know what piece of information you will need to access in the future, but you will not be sorry if you are thorough, and consider (when filing) the question: "if I were to look for this information in the future, how would I look for it?"

—∿—

Some people think organization is hereditary; okay, my mother is hugely organized too. But systems can be learned, and now you have a system of dealing with the everyday information and paper flow that will cross your desk during the course of production. You are already well on your way to developing your own working style, keeping on top of the ever-flowing paper of production.

MANNERS, MANNERS

When several telephone lines light up at the same time, I help the Assistant Coordinator by answering a few myself. We work as a team.

One day an Office P.A. Hopeful called in and I happened to answer the phone. He asked some detailed questions about production before introducing himself. When I asked who was calling, he insisted that he needed to talk to the Production Manager or the Producer to apply for work. I explained that as Production Coordinator, I handle all the incoming resumes and hire the Office P.A. position, since the position reports to me. I would be happy to talk to him more about it. He became very insistent about speaking to the PM or the Producer, and, shall I say, got very irate about the matter, insulting me and my position very pointedly along the way. I pleasantly put him on hold, then explained the situation to the Assistant Coordinator. She took the call.

The Office P.A. Hopeful was as sweet as pie to her. He was happy to be passed along to whom he thought was the Production Manager. Never questioning her identity, he just assumed that his ranting would get him results. She asked him to send in a resume, and he agreed to do that right away. Then she asked for his name so that she would recognize the resume when it came in.

We did.

TELEPHONE ETIQUETTE 9

It is in your office, it is in your home, and it haunts you long after production has finished. It is the telephone ring. There are many particular rings of differing telephone systems. You will be haunted for years by the ring of whatever system you intend to use, because the production office telephone will ring incessantly. Hope it is not the same ring as your house phone. Now, talking about telephone etiquette may seem overly basic, but it is through the telephone where the public gains first contact with — and a first impression of — your company. Email communication is passive, whereas telephone communication can (and should) be instantly interactive. Executives call the production office. So do crew, cast, suppliers, and the general public. Are you portraying a professional image?

CHOOSING A TELEPHONE SYSTEM

If there is a telephone system already in place when you start, you are fortunate. If not, make it one of the Production Coordinator's many first priorities. Know the features you need before you start looking.

HOW MANY EXTENSIONS (TELEPHONE SETS) WILL YOU NEED?

You will never have enough for all the crew that will request one — especially for the week before filming, when everyone is in the office — so review the list with the Production Manager.

HOW MANY TELEPHONE LINES WILL YOU NEED?

Twenty-four extensions and three lines will not work. Also keep in mind you will need a line for the fax machine.

WHAT TELEPHONE FEATURES DO YOU NEED AND HOW INTUITIVE ARE THEY?

You will want the ability to do conference calling without using the conference operator, the ability to restrict long distance and directory assistance on some extensions, and some sets to be speakerphones. Do you want direct dialing to extensions and/or voice mail? Can you plug a telephone headset into any of the sets?

WHAT NETWORK FEATURES DO YOU NEED?

If you go with a Voice Over I.P. (VOIP) system, how much speed and bandwidth is required for the telephone system along with the computer network you have in mind? Are you planning on using video calling or conferencing to connect people (like Director and Editor) during the production? Will your access to a post FTP site affect your VOIP requirements? How much I.T. support and set up is provided?

List your requirements and arrange for delivery as soon as humanly possible.

RECEPTION: THE JOB

Reception has to be the most underrated job on the film production. Good Receptionists know who wants the calls screened and who wants certain calls to interrupt any meeting. They recognize people's voices, are pleasant and professional, and do not lose their cool when eight lines light up at the same time. They never volunteer information to any unnamed person who calls, and on and on. They basically have a mature attitude.

These are further specifics about what the person who answers your telephone should know:

WHO WILL ANSWER THE TELEPHONE

On small productions, the Coordinator is the Coordinator, Assistant Coordinator, and Receptionist all rolled into one. On large productions you could have enough support staff to cover each job separately. Though hard to judge accurately, know that answering the telephone will likely take up about 30-40% of your workday.

"HELLO, PRODUCTION"

This generic phrase is the best way to answer the telephone if you are working on multiple productions out of the same office, or you do not want to advertise what production you are at this phone number. Other options are: "HELLO, SHOW NAME" or "HELLO, PRODUCTION-COMPANY NAME." Find out which the Production Manager or the Producer prefers.

"HELLO, PRODUCTION. HOLD PLEASE"

When the telephones become extraordinarily busy, you will have to put people on hold as soon as you answer. That is okay. Just get back to each one as soon as humanly possible. Imagine all the calls coming in might be long distance, or from cell phones with low batteries.

ANSWER BY HOW MANY RINGS?

Some people become angry if you cannot answer by the first or the second ring. If eight lines light up at the same time, we all know that is impossible. Just answer as soon as you can.

TELEPHONE EXTENSION MAP OR LIST

You have two choices here: (1) the map. Retrieve that floor plan map you made of the office. List the people and the telephone extensions on the map, and copy (or reduce copy) the map for reference at each telephone set. Or, if you prefer lists, (2) the list. Type up a list of crew (alphabetical by first or last name) and their telephone extensions. The map often works best because with the speed that the crew is hired on a production, people tend to identify where someone is located in the office first and their name second. Another feature of the map is speedy access to alternative extensions in the same department, if you have trouble finding someone.

KNOW HOW TO USE THE FEATURES OF THE TELEPHONE

The Coordinator and the Assistant Coordinator should know how to do conference calling, last number redial, and any other useful feature. Read the telephone manual because the crew members will not; they will come to you for lessons in how to use the telephone.

DO NOT HAND OUT INFORMATION FREELY

Some productions are more confidential than others. Often callers will not identify themselves and ask a fair amount about the production. These people could be anyone, including reporters attempting to gain information that the publicity department wants to keep secret for some reason. Do not let the staff (Assistant Coordinator or Office P.A.) hand out any information. Depending on how confidential the information might seem, have the Production Coordinator or the Production Manager take the call. Find out who is calling. If you are still uncomfortable with the call, hand it over to the Producer.

SCREENING CALLS

The Receptionist should find out who on the crew wants to have their calls screened. Chances are it will be Producers, Director, Production Manager, Production Accountant, and the Performers.

TAKING MESSAGES – WHEN SOMEONE CAN'T TAKE THE CALL

Generally, if someone cannot come to the telephone, do not volunteer information as to where that person is and when she is expected back. Occasionally you will find that certain crew members are avoiding certain phone calls until a certain time.

TAKING MESSAGES – SPELLING

This may sound basic, but get the correct spelling of the caller's name, where he is calling from, the phone number, the reason for the call, and note the time and the date. Thoroughness is essential. Imagine having to decipher a phonetic message with no phone number or time, like "Gerie called" — and you know a Jerry, Gerry, Geraldine, and Jahri. Who do you call back?

TELEPHONE MANNER

It is absolutely essential to be pleasant and professional every time you and your staff answer the telephone. If you do not ensure this approach each and every time, it will come back to haunt you. The old saying still rings true: You only have one chance to leave a first impression. When you answer the telephone, you are representing the company.

TO VOICE MAIL OR NOT TO VOICE MAIL

Voice mail is a terrific invention that allows Receptionists to go to the bathroom, to handle extremely busy telephones, and to give them more time to complete the other tasks now swamping them. The negative side effect is that voice mail is not personal. Machines cannot tell how important the call is, and so cannot interrupt someone on another call because this call is more important, cannot tell if you are calling long distance, cannot tell that it is the one person you have been trying to reach for days, cannot tell that it is the set calling and the low battery warning is displayed on their cell phone. Consider the importance of a person as a Receptionist. Use voice mail as a tool, not a crutch.

HOW TO LEAVE A MESSAGE

Imagine the A.D.s have charged you with informing the crew of a revised call time for the next day because wrap happened in the middle of the night and you are the one in the office first thing in the morning. Be responsible. When you leave a message on voice mail and/or with a text message, leave the following critical information:

1) The time you called (for voice mail only)
2) Why you are calling
3) A request to return the call for confirmation

You need to know each person received and understood the message. Do not presume that because the message is left in voice mail or sent by text message that the person actually received the message. People do not always check their messages; people do not always have their cell phones on. Make a list of the people you called, when you called them, and if you talked to them personally or left a voice and/or text message. Try to reach them hourly until you make contact personally. If you do not speak to someone personally, you will have proof in your notes of how hard you tried to reach this person. If they do not show up to set on time, and happen to cause an expensive set delay because of their absence, you want to prove how hard you tried to reach them.

—⁂—

Even with the prevalence of cell phones, direct-extension calling, voice mail, and text messaging, do not forget the importance of the central person that answers the production office telephone. If you have never answered a system telephone that rings wildly every day while trying to do your daily work, try it. You will learn a new appreciation for the brave soul who does.

ANY FILES AT ALL

I love two-drawer lateral filing cabinets. Filing boxes are great for those low-budget we-have-to-be-portable shows, but you can't beat a solid two-drawer lateral filing cabinet to double as a TV stand, a fax machine table, or even a distribution table. And the big drawers? Well!

The Production Manager came up to one of the filing cabinets one day deciding to look for a specific file himself. Knowing that I am an organized person, he was confident that he could find the file he needed without a problem and wouldn't have to interrupt me on the telephone.

The first filing cabinet drawer he opened was stacked with Polaroid film and a sign-out sheet on a clipboard. The second drawer he tried housed VHS copies of all the episodes to date and a few patch cables. He paused. There were only two drawers to this filing cabinet.

When I was off the phone, he asked me: "Do you keep any files at all?" He told me which file he needed, and I produced it right away from a filing box behind my desk. He looked from the filing box to the filing cabinet one more time. Then he shook his head and took the file into his office.

SETTING UP A FILING SYSTEM

10

When all the dust is settled, the sets all broken down, and the crew gone home to live their lives again, the production files are some of the only source material depicting what happened during the making of the film. When you set up the filing system, you are making it up for more than just yourself. Rather than waste busy production time creating new files one by one and chance making too many duplicate or similar files, you can prepare the filing cabinet early in prep.

FILING ELECTRONICALLY & PHYSICALLY

There is a slew of information that you about amass over the course of a shoot and at any given time you will need to find specific information quickly. Legal counsel could ask you about research conducted regarding music rights. Set could ask you to find that excellent daily crew member they hired two weeks ago. Not only that, the auditor is bound to have questions long after you are gone, and your files and filing system need to speak for you in your absence.

Information, however, arrives via many, fragmented sources (paper and email being the major two) and documents you create are typically on a hard drive. You will, then, have at least three filing locations to set up and maintain: physical; email; and hard drive. If you have a shared drive, your filing systems are further fragmented. Make the file structure in each location correspond so you can file documents in the same, logical folder no matter the physical/electronic location.

The physical files still make up the main filing system, and are the first stop when auditors look for information. Physical files do not require computer access or even electricity. Open the filing cabinet and all the information is there... well, if you have filed it there.

DESCRIPTIVELY NAME EMAILS

Email is convenient, as it is right there in front of you at all times. Your email folders should mimic the physical files folder structure. A good start. You should also use an email naming protocol: use descriptive file names, and keep to a pattern so that you can use the email "sort" function on the subject heading to find information later on, for example:

[topic] – [description] – [date and/or version description]
Call sheet – Day 1 – draft
Budget – Columnar – version 4.2

EMAIL CHAINS

The last email on an email chain is a great reference of the entire path to making a decision on an issue. You can delete all previous emails in the chain, and keep only the last one. There is a challenge, however, in determining which email is indeed the last one since people tend to pipe in with a few more words when the issue appears to be resolved. And then a few more. OK, many times. Really. Other folks respond to a parallel copy of the chain (not the main chain itself), forcing you to keep two copies of the chain if you wish to keep a copy of everyone's voice on the topic.

Another challenge is when the topic of an email chain branches into more than one issue (to be filed now in two places). The easiest solution is to copy the email twice and properly file the two issues of discussion separately.

PRINTING & ARCHIVING EMAILS

Typically you do not need to print emails. The odd one, however, with a particularly critical decision path recorded should either be printed, or moved from your email client into your official electronic file folders. To remind yourself which ones need to be, or have been, archived in this manner, you can mark the affected emails with flags. During wrap, it is a good time for a second look through your email folders to see if there are any other emails that would be good to archive. If on a series, a hiatus is a good interim time for electronic filing catch up to avoid an overwhelming job during wrap.

SHARED DRIVE

If you have a shared drive between a network of production computers, you can house a folder on this drive for all the latest documents on the distribution table, as well, the list of who receives which documentation. Remember during wrap to move any unique files on this shared drive back to your official set of electronic files.

PHYSICAL FILES

Between electronic and physical, the physical files are still your main set of production files. It is much faster to place a document in a paper folder than to scan the document and file it electronically. Contracts that need wet signatures mean you still have physical files to archive no matter what. Keep all drafts of a document, where appropriate, and have the latest version on the top so you will see it as soon as you open the folder. You can cull the extra versions later, when you have a moment, or during wrap.

BACKING UP

A paper copy of an electronic file is an automatic back–up, but that only covers selective files. Regularly back up your electronic files! Your email folders! Your address book! If you store all your folders in one centralized electronic location, and include a short cut to quickly find all your email folders and address book with one click, backing up becomes a simple task that takes only a few minutes.

THE PRODUCTION COORDINATOR'S FILES

The Production Coordinator and the Assistant Coordinator will keep the bulk of the files, but the Production Manager needs files, too.

THE PC'S PRODUCTION SERIES FILES

For a television series or a mini-series, divide the filing cabinet and computer folder structure into four sections as follows:

A-Z FILES

These alphabetically-labeled files do not refer to any specific episode of the series. A more specific list of file names for this section is noted below. Electronically, these files are folders and as a group (or section) are called the "Production Office Files" for the particular production. You may not wish to create all the empty computer folders at the outset, but instead post the list (below) of file/folder names near your computer to make the new electronic folders as the need arises. Using this method, you will know at a glance if there is documentation in the folders or not.

EPISODE BY EPISODE FILES

Make a section/folder for each episode, labeled by episode number and title.

In this section, collect cast lists, schedules, credits, locations, memos, and any other information specific to that episode. These file names are marked by (★) in the file list below.

PRODUCTION REPORT FILES

Mark this section/folder for production reports. Each shooting day needs a separate file (for the physical files) to house all the production report backup information, the draft, and final copies of the production report. Note the shooting day as well as the date on the file folder label for future reference. Electronically, you can scan and house the final and signed version of each day's production report into one folder. Production Reports are important enough documents to ensure you collect digital copies as well as physical ones.

ORIGINAL FORMS

Since you will be making numerous forms, store them in their own section.

THE PC'S PRODUCTION FEATURE FILM FILES

Feature films or single-episode productions require files simpler than the series files, in that you can include the episodic files section in the A-Z files section.

THE PC'S PRODUCTION A-Z FILES

Use this list to start your filing cabinet. You can substitute actual names for general descriptions — like "John Doe" can replace "Lead Performer" — and re-alphabetize accordingly.

Accounts & Credit Applications
Accommodation
Animals
Art Department
Breakdowns – A.D.'s
Breakdowns – Continuity
Broadcaster
Call Sheets (one complete set)
★ Cast
★ Cast Contracts
Catalogues
Catering Menus
Clearances – Script Research Reports
Clearances – Music Rights

Contact List

Correspondence

Correspondence – Fan Mail

★ Credits

Courier Waybills/Acct

Crew List

Crew Deal Memos

Crew Union or Guild

Customs

Distributor

Director

Director Union or Guild

Document Distribution

Equipment – Set (e.g., cell phones, walkie-talkies)

Equipment – Office (e.g., copier/printer/scanner, fax machine)

Fax Top Sheets

Funding Agency

Immigration

Internet (email accounts, Web page, ISP/network)

Insurance

Insurance – Accidents

ISAN Registration

Lead Performer

★ Locations & Agreements

★ Memos

Music & Cue Sheets

Parent Production Company

Performer Union or Guild

Postproduction

Postproduction – ADR

Postproduction – Schedule

★ Previs / Storyboard

Production Reports (one complete set without Production Report backup)

Publicity

Publicity – News Clippings

Resumes – Crew

Resumes – P.A.'s

Resumes – Other

Second Unit

★ Script – White Draft
★ Script – Pink Draft (etc.)
★ Script – As-Produced
★ Schedule – Preproduction
★ Schedule – One line
★ Schedule – Shooting
Special Effects Company
Stock Footage
Studio
Synopsis
Technical Specifications
Travel
Vehicles
Visual Effects Company (CGI)
Wardrobe Department
Wrap Party
Wrap – Inventory

THE PRODUCTION MANAGER'S FILES

The Production Manager or Coordinator may set up these physical files, but the Production Manager will use them, plus the PM will have to set up his own electronic file structure to effectively find information during production. Most of the documentation in these files is more confidential than the Coordinator's production files, as they include more financial and accounting-type paperwork. You can combine both sets of files in wrap, throwing out duplicates to reduce clutter and to increase efficiency of information retrieval after production is completed. Below is a starter list. As with the PC, you may not wish to create all these empty electronic folders immediately during prep, but may instead post the list below near your computer to create the logical folder structure on an as-needed basis — checking off each topic as each new folder is created. The posted list can duplicate as a visual reminder of subject matter you may need to address when you find that you have not created certain relevant folders as production advances.

Art Department
Audit Preparation
Auditor
Breakdowns
Broadcaster
Budget – Early Drafts

Budget – Locked and Signed by Producer
Call Sheets
Cash Flow
Cast
Cast – Leads or Stars
Casting
Chain of Title & Writer's Agreements
Clearances – Script Research Report
Clearances – Title Search
Completion Guarantor (or Completion Bond)
Conference Calls
Correspondence
Cost Reports
Cost Split (between companies or countries)
Credits
Crew
Crew – Key Creatives
Crew Union or Guild
Currency Exchange
Director
Director Union or Guild
Distributor
Financing Plan
Financing Agreements
Incorporation Documentation – Production Company
Incorporation Documentation – Parent Company
Insurance – Entertainment Package
Insurance – Production Liability
Insurance – E & O (Errors & Omissions)
Interim financing
Interparty Agreement
Legal
Legal – Corporate Opinion
Marketing
Memos
Parent Production Company or Head Office
Performer Union or Guild
Personal (obviously, remove this folder from the production files during wrap)
Production Reports

Postproduction
Postproduction – Schedule
Recoupment
Schedule (per episode)
Script (per episode)
Studio
Synopsis
Treaty Coproduction Documentation
Writer's Guild

—∽—

Now you have cabinets of empty file folders and a nearly empty computer drive both waiting for documentation. It will not take long for you to do just that. Use and revise these starter lists as you develop your logic of filing. As you do, remember to keep in mind the question: "Where would I look for this information if I were looking for it?" Also ask yourself: "In a year from now, where would someone look for this information if I were not around?" When you can answer that question, you will file the information in the right place.

BALCONY PAPERWORK

For one low-budget show, the entire crew and cast were housed in three cottages by a lake. Breakfasts, meetings, dinners, and social time were usually held in the big cottage's living room. I had the room with a balcony that overlooked this room. On that balcony, I set up my "office." While I was completing the production paperwork, I could also participate in the meetings and the social activities.

I was known for keeping up with all the paperwork in spite of the surrounding diversions, and the crew got used to looking up at the balcony if they wanted to find me. Time slipped away on that picturesque balcony. I never knew how much until the day that the crew bombarded me with paper airplanes made from old call sheets.

I got the hint and came down for dinner.

FORMS, MEMOS, LOGS, CHECKLISTS

11

Reports, sign-outs, requisitions, logs, and checklists flow back and forth across the production office desks creating the document trail of production. There is a form for every purpose and new forms are being made constantly to keep up with the speed and the complexity of production. Where do you begin finding or designing all these forms? And where do you begin to decide which forms and documentation earn a spot on the distribution table?

The answers are right here. Checklists are provided so you can mark your progress. Samples and blank forms of many of the following forms are in the Appendix, which begins on page 457. They can also be downloaded from the Web at *www.mwp.com,* click on "Virtual Film School," click on "Resources."

FORMS & MEMOS-TO-ALL TO CREATE

There are a host of different forms to create. I have divided them into the following categories to make it easier to tackle: Letterhead & Office Forms, Accounting-Related Forms, Schedule & On Set-Related Forms, Memos to All Concerned, Sign-Out Forms, Log Forms, Weekly Office Checklists, and the Inventory List. Store the original template files on your computer in the "Original Forms" folder as backup, but also house a hard copy original of each form in the "Original Forms" physical files. This situation allows anyone to make extra copies of forms regardless of computer access.

LETTERHEAD & OFFICE FORMS

The Production Coordinator arranges for or creates each of the following forms, and then should save the original on the computer as well as store a hard copy original of each in an "Original Forms" file. With this system, each form remains as pristine as possible, photocopy after photocopy, and the PC does not have to be the only person to print additional copies of the form from disk. Using a shared drive is another way of sharing these templates among crew members.

☐ Letterhead
☐ Letterhead Envelopes
☐ Address Rubber Stamp
☐ Business Cards
☐ Big Letterhead Labels
☐ Memorandum Form
☐ Fax Top Sheet

LETTERHEAD

First up, make letterhead for the company. If the Art Department is too busy to aid you, design it yourself. Include: film title, company name, address, telephone, fax, email, website, and any other appropriate contact information. Even if the Art Department does the design, review the design and information with the Production Manager and the Producer before printing. The design may be inspired by or inspiring to the production company's website for the production. Find out if the budget allows printed, colorful letterhead, a small graphic file, or if you need to design letterhead that uses existing computer fonts and prints directly from file each time. Even if your letterhead is an electronic file that you distribute to all crew, print a few copies for the distribution table to allow the crew ready access to letterhead, especially for hand written purposes where they do not need a printer.

LETTERHEAD ENVELOPES

If production has the money, make letterhead envelopes at the same time as letterhead. Check if Accounting needs window envelopes.

ADDRESS RUBBER STAMP

Make a rubber stamp with the company name and address. It is a functional, affordable, multi-purpose labeling device that can be used to label purchase orders, or even to create very cheap letterhead envelopes. Consider the amount of mail you will be sending out and select a self-inking stamp.

BUSINESS CARDS

Some productions arrange for business cards, and some prefer not to. Locations, Sets, and Art Departments use them constantly. Considering how quickly productions set up, shoot, and wrap up, business cards validate the professionalism of the company. Order blank cards (i.e., those not identifying any employee by name) to give you the option of typing any crew name on them. This tactic will avoid your being left with hundreds of useless named cards midway through the show, while you run out of other named cards.

BIG LETTERHEAD LABELS

These labels are about 3" x 5". They have the letterhead information printed on them, and are great for addressing script packages, other courier packages, and for labeling viewing copy cases (unless you plan to make custom labels for viewing copy cases, too).

MEMORANDUM FORM

Once you have letterhead, use part of it by removing the address and the contact numbers to make a memorandum form. Include in the heading:

Memorandum
Date
To
Cc (carbon copy to)
From
Subject

FAX OR FACSIMILE TOP SHEET

Take another piece of letterhead to make a fax top sheet. Leave the address and the contact numbers on the form. Be sure you leave spaces large enough for people who write big. Include in the heading:

Fax Cover Sheet
Date
To
Company
Fax Number
From
Number of Pages (including cover sheet)
Subject
Notes
Confidentiality Note (optional)

If you are working on a series and know the air date, include this information on the fax cover sheet too (and as part of your email signature), as a way of informing every single person you contact when to catch your show on television.

ACCOUNTING-RELATED FORMS

Often Production Accountants come with their own forms. If not, they and head office will have definite preferences about the design of forms that relate to them. The Production Coordinator needs to talk to them before designing the following forms:

☐ Crew Deal Memo – Union
☐ Crew Deal Memo – Non-Union (sample on p. 503)
☐ Time Sheet (sample on p. 468)
☐ Check Requisition (sample on p. 495)
☐ Petty Cash Report (sample on p. 491)
☐ Sales Tax Form
☐ Accounting Procedures Memo

CREW DEAL MEMO – UNION

These forms are available from each union directly and become part of the "start pack." (More on "start packs" is in Chapter 23.)

CREW DEAL MEMO – NON-UNION

Accounting, the Payroll Company, or Legal Counsel has a form or specific requirements for this form. Be sure you leave enough space for the crew member and the production company to sign and date it. There will be different forms designed for "employee" crew and "corporate" crew. (More about employee versus corporations is in Chapter 23.)

TIME SHEET

Flat weekly rates make for easier time sheet forms than hourly rates and their many calculations. Design a form that works for both. Always have plenty of these forms on hand. Payroll companies often have their own forms and will supply them to you.

CHECK REQUISITION

This is another form that Accountants use all the time. They will have very specific preferences about design — because they will be coding the costs to the cost report based on the information presented. Make sure there is space for the appropriate approvals necessary for the check and contact information of the company, in case this form becomes the only backup paperwork Accounting will ever receive for this purchase.

PETTY CASH REPORT

It is best to design this form and have it printed onto 8.5" x 11"- envelopes for use. When crew submits their expenses, the envelope serves to collect all the receipts applicable to the report on the front of the envelope. Be sure there is a column for splitting out any refundable tax that is paid, and columns for Accounting to code the receipts to cost report/budget accounts. If you cannot afford envelopes, just photocopies of the form will do fine. (More on Petty Cash is in Chapter 19.)

SALES TAX FORM

If production's purchases can be exempt from sales tax, obtain the appropriate form from the tax office, and have the Accountant or the Production Manager assist you in completing it. Sometimes you will be able to apply for a tax number to use for the exemption, and other times you need to have a "blanket" tax form that crew must attach to each purchase to effect the exemption. In either case, you will need plenty of copies of the number or the form for the crew's usage when purchasing.

ACCOUNTING PROCEDURES MEMO

Some Accountants will spell out in a memo to all crew exactly how to fill in a purchase order, how to complete a check requisition, and so on. If your Accountant does not do this, find out the procedures anyway and write it down for yourself, the Coordinator. Each Accountant has a different style, and you will be explaining that style to crew, including the office staff and dailies (daily crew), over and over again throughout production. (More about money issues is in Chapter 19.)

SCHEDULE & ON SET-RELATED FORMS

Though the use of these forms overlaps many departments, the following forms are to be designed or acquired with the help of the Production Manager, the Assistant Directors, and the Accountants. The Production Coordinator usually designs them with the Production Manager's input. Think about what information you might want to refer to later when looking back at and analyzing production.

☐ Call Sheet Form (samples on p. 483–485)
☐ Daily Production Report Form (the "DPR") (samples on p. 486–488)
☐ One-Line Schedule Form (sample on p. 515)
☐ Shooting Schedule Form (sample on p. 516)
☐ Performer's Union Forms
☐ Accident Report Forms (sample on p. 469)

CALL SHEET FORM

Simply put, the call sheet tells the crew what is being filmed on the day, where set is, when everyone is to report there, and the weather forecast. There is no one single format for making a call sheet. Collect versions from past productions and solicit input from the Assistant Directors; then the PC can design a form. The First or Second Assistant Director will probably have the most input in the design of this form. Second Unit call sheets are separate from Main Unit call sheets. It is best to print Second Unit call sheets on a different-colored paper to differentiate them from Main Unit's at a glance. All call sheets tend to be printed (double-sided) on legal-sized paper to stand out from all the other production paperwork on the day. All call sheets are required to have a map-to-location attached (describing, in both pictures and words, how to find the location from the production office). Also included on the map should be directions and contact information for the nearest hospital. (More on call sheets and location maps is in Chapter 13.)

DAILY PRODUCTION REPORT FORM

At the end of every shooting day, the Production Manager and the Assistant Director must report to the Executives and to Accounting what transpired that day (so the Accountant can give an estimate of how much the day cost to the Executives and the Production Manager). Executives are rarely on set and must keep abreast of the running of production: Is it on schedule? Which scenes were shot? What is the updated timing of the entire script? What events happened that caused delays? Accounting needs to know what was spent daily to keep on top of costs as they happen: How much film and sound stock was used? What hours did the cast and crew work? How many daily crew were working? The A.D.s and Production Coordinator are in charge of completing the form daily with input from all departments, then the First A.D. and the Production Manager give their approval to the document (by signing it) before it is distributed. It is expected the completed report is approved and distributed by the end of the next day's shoot. The Production Coordinator should design this form with the Production Manager and the Assistant Director. Just as Second Unit requires a separate call sheet, they also require a separate production report. It is wise to print Second Unit production reports on different-colored paper to differentiate them from Main Unit's reports. Treat completed production reports as confidential information. They are. (More on Production Reports is in Chapter 14.)

ONE-LINE SCHEDULE FORM

Assistant Directors typically have their own computers equipped with scheduling programs, and they make one-line schedule forms themselves. If this is not the case, design a one-line schedule to show the schedule of scenes to be shot during the entire production, with, naturally, one line of text per scene. Include: scene number and description (including interior/exterior and day/night), cast (by number code), script day, and script page count. This form expresses the entire schedule to the crew with the fewest number of pages. In a manual process, the A.D.s will give you their scene breakdown pages, shuffled into shooting order, to create this schedule. (More about schedules is in Chapter 28.)

SHOOTING SCHEDULE FORM

This is also a form that Assistant Directors tend to generate themselves. If not, design a shooting schedule as an expanded version of the one-line schedule. Also include the character names and the various set requirements of each department, as indicated on each scene breakdown page. Due to the detail of this schedule, when completed it may be as thick as the script.

PERFORMER'S UNION FORMS

Contact the performer's union, find out who your representative is, and collect the following forms for the Assistant Directors to use on set — and for you, the PC, to use in postproduction:

> **Performer Work Reports**: These are for the A.D.s to report which hours the Performers worked each day, and you (production) to report which hours the Performers worked for postproduction looping.

> **Performer Contracts**: There are likely several versions of Performer contracts to address various genres, so choose the correct one for your production.

> **Extra Vouchers**: These are like contracts for Extras and often too for Stand-Ins; make sure you have enough copies for production.

> **Permit Forms**: These forms may be needed for non-union Performers.

> **Union Agreement**: This is the agreement that the Production Manager signs to make the production company signatory to the union. It is filled with details and requirements you must know when hiring Performers. Print sufficient copies of this agreement and have the link handy for your reference. This document is invaluable to the PM when budgeting and cost-tracking, to the PC when completing Performer contracts, to the A.D.s when working with the Performers on set, and to the Accountant when calculating meal penalties.

MEMOS TO ALL CONCERNED

Most documentation the Production Coordinator generates is approved by the Production Manager and is, in essence, from the Production Manager. You two are a team. But, here are two things the Coordinator may generate alone:

☐ Color Revision Order Memo
☐ Episode List & Synopses

COLOR REVISION ORDER MEMO

As the script is revised, you will copy the new pages on another color paper for clarity and speed of recognition. Make a memo to "all concerned" what the colored-paper order is of the script revisions. Know that some head offices have preferences. Here is a suggested order:

> White
> Blue
> Pink
> Green
> Yellow
> Any other pastel-colored paper of your choice, until...
> White Again
> (etc.)

Remember that non-pastel-colored paper does not photocopy well, and you need the ability to re-photocopy pages over and over again (i.e., do not use cherry-colored paper).

EPISODE LIST & SYNOPSES

When you work on a series, after several episodes, it is difficult for anyone, Writers included, to remember all the episode numbers, episode titles, and stories. Make a list of the episodes noting episode number, title, former titles, and a one- or two-line synopsis for each. You will be surprised how useful this list is to the entire crew and to head office, including Publicity. If the list, however, is distributed to Publicity – even on a "for-your-information" basis, be sure the Producer approves all wording for publication. Publicity is bound to use the information (publicly) somewhere.

SIGN-OUT FORMS

Track all equipment rented or even exchanged when broken. Many people during the course of production will handle a lot of equipment, and it is very easy to misplace an expensive piece or two if you do not know who had the equipment last. Production is responsible to return all that is rented. The Production Coordinator needs tools to help track the use of these items by whom. Sign-out sheets work wonderfully. Completed, the Production Manager and the Accountant will also find them useful reference tools.

☐ Walkie-Talkie Sign-Out Form (sample on p. 470)
☐ Cell phone Sign-Out Form (sample on p. 471)
☐ Keys & Security Cards Sign-Out Form (sample on p. 472)
☐ Scripts (By Label)

WALKIE-TALKIE SIGN-OUT FORM

Walkie-talkies are essential on set, very expensive, and very portable. Track serial numbers and each accessory alongside each crew name. The Assistant Directors are primarily responsible for these forms on set, but a double-check tracking system in the office is also wise. When you rent a large number of walkie-talkies, you should expect a large number of parts constantly being exchanged for repair. Know where all the pieces are at all times.

CELL PHONE SIGN-OUT FORM

Another very portable item: the cell phone. They may be purchased or rented. Track telephone numbers and serial numbers alongside the appropriate crew names. Identify any accessories and chargers that are included in the package. It is also worth noting the service, data plan, and effective date.

KEYS & SECURITY CARDS SIGN-OUT FORM

Track on a crew list the keys and security cards each person receives beside their names, or make a simple log form for people to sign out copies of keys and security cards. Using a crew list, you have to transpose all the information each time the crew list is updated, but it is an easy reference by department of who has access to the office. The act of using a sign-out form hopefully makes crew realize that there are a select number of keys and security cards, and therefore they will try not to lose them. Either way, label each key copy with indelible ink for future identification, then cover the inked label with clear tape to prevent its being rubbed off. Security cards typically have serial numbers for you to track. There should also be one master set of every key kept safely away in a locked space. The Production Coordinator should have the key to that locked space. If a password is required as part of security, be sure to pass along the information personally (not in writing).

SCRIPTS (BY LABEL)

Though scripts do not fall under the heading of "equipment" when it comes to signing equipment out, signing out scripts is a terrific way of cutting down on over-photocopying the long document, and thereby saving a few trees. Put each crew member's name on file folder labels for marking each script: one sticker, one script. When crew sees that the scripts are specifically named, they will realize that the copies are limited in number, and will likely take better care of the one given to them. It is heartbreaking to see piles of discarded scripts tossed in the garbage. Discuss the names for this scripts-by-label list with the Assistant Directors.

LOG FORMS

Using log forms is another tool for the Production Coordinator. Keeping logs inspires people to put a higher value on the item(s) being tracked. Since all items indeed do cost money and do add up rapidly if left unchecked, the use of log forms will keep costs down. Also, logs report on where money is currently being spent, and this process enables Accounting to keep updated with the "spending status" of production.

☐ P.O. Log (sample on p. 492-493)
☐ Equipment Rental Log (sample on p. 473)
☐ Courier Log (sample on p. 474)
☐ Long Distance Log (sample on p. 475)
☐ Photocopy Log

P.O. LOG

If you keep no other log, keep a log of every purchase order you handle! A purchase order is a promise to pay for the item ordered. Blank purchase orders are like blank checks. With enough detail, your P.O. log can assist your listing everything that has been rented when it comes time to do the returns during wrap. (More on Purchase Orders is in Chapter 19.) Include the following columns:

Purchase Order Number
To Whom
For What
Episode Number
Department
Date
Price

EQUIPMENT RENTAL LOG

If you keep a detailed P.O. log, you will not need this log. If not, note the following each time production rents an item, whether on a daily basis or for the length of production:

Date
Rental Company
Equipment

Department Ordered By
Episode Number
Rental Start/End Dates
Price

COURIER LOG

If you have an efficient Office Production Assistant, you will not need a courier around town very often, but when you do, track couriered packages. Fill out detailed waybills, or keep a separate log including the information below. The person in charge of shipping and receiving should be in charge of this log. You may need proof that an item was sent to someone. You may have to report who received a certain piece of paper, on which date, and when. There is no sense in trying to tax your memory for this information when you have incomplete waybills or the absence of a courier log. You may not refer to this log often, but when you do, the work you put into it will be invaluable.

Date
To Whom
What Sent
Courier Company
Waybill Number

LONG DISTANCE LOG

Though it is near impossible to track all long distance charges, you can make a miniature log form to attach to each telephone set. Encourage the crew to complete it, especially when making personal calls. Long distance on all sets in the office can slip out of hand. You may find you will need to restrict long distance on certain sets to keep the situation under control. This log is particularly handy when you are working on two different productions simultaneously; it also helps the Accountant code the long distance charges incurred to the appropriate productions.

Date/Time
Phone Number
Your Name
Personal/Business

PHOTOCOPY LOG

If you have several companies using the same photocopy machine, have a log by the photocopy machine with pen attached to fill out each time the machine is used. If you have a code system built-in to the photocopier's hardware, you may not need this log.

Date
Company or Film Title
Department
Number of Copies

WEEKLY OFFICE CHECKLISTS

As the variety of supplies diminishes with use, few people will remind you when it is time to order more until the shelf is absolutely empty. Check supplies on a weekly basis. Give the Office Production Assistant the opportunity to show you if she can be responsible by taking charge of the weekly checks, keeping track of that information, and reporting the results to you, the Coordinator, regularly. These checklists will also help you both learn how much of these items are being used — information you will use on future orders, or on your next production.

☐ Craft Service Supplies
☐ Coffee Supplies
☐ Water Supplies
☐ Photocopy Supplies
☐ Copier Paper Count (sample on p. 476)
☐ Fax Supplies
☐ Office Stationery Supplies
☐ Cleaning/Paper Supplies

CRAFT SERVICE SUPPLIES

If Craft Service is ordering coffee and water through the office supplier, talk to set weekly about Craft Service's supply needs.

COFFEE SUPPLIES

Check supplies a day before the coffee company is scheduled to call you for an order.

WATER SUPPLIES

Like the coffee supplies, check before the company calls you for an order or before the company's automatic delivery. Water companies tend to put all companies on an automatic delivery. Beware if you make a one-time order of 27 bottles; the water company may automatically send you 27 bottles every two weeks until you tell them otherwise.

PHOTOCOPY SUPPLIES

Keeping in mind which colored revision is due next, check the amount of colored paper and toner you have. There is little worse than running out of toner on a Friday night of a weekend shoot.

COPIER PAPER COUNT

When checking the paper supplies, jot down the number of copies used to-date on the machine. You will need this number for your photocopy service agreement, for Accounting, and if you have several companies using the same machine. It is also enlightening to discover how many thousands of copies you actually do on a weekly basis. Have an office lottery, if you like.

FAX SUPPLIES

Check fax paper supplies and toner.

OFFICE STATIONERY SUPPLIES

Have an order form hanging by the office supply cabinet with a pen attached to it. Check the general supplies, such as pens, on a regular basis also.

CLEANING/PAPER SUPPLIES

Does the office have enough paper towels, cleaners, bathroom tissue, and first aid supplies?

THE INVENTORY LIST

The Production Coordinator should start making an inventory list as production acquires items during preproduction. You will find out this information quickly from the P.O. log. The chance of your remembering everything that was rented or purchased throughout the entire film after the fact is slim... or, rather, impossible. The Coordinator already has a file in the cabinet labeled "wrap," so both Manager and Coordinator can use this file to collect notes to trigger you both later to address certain things. The work you do now leaving notes for future reference will save you hours of searching after the film is done and any crew that could help you has gone home. If your P.O. log is very detailed, it can double as your inventory list. Make and use the P.O. log! Did I say that already?

THE DISTRIBUTION TABLE & OTHER PLACES FOR DOCUMENTATION

Basically, where do you put all this paper so it is used efficiently? You have a distribution table, wall envelopes, and your desk drawer. Here is a recap of the forms mentioned in this and other chapters, and where to put them for appropriate access.

WHAT'S ON THE DISTRIBUTION TABLE
> Script & Script Revisions
> Crew List (including cell phone numbers)
> Cast List
> Contact List
> Telephone Extension List
> Episode List & Synopses
> Schedules (all kinds)
> A.D. Breakdowns
> Accounting Procedures Memo
> Crew Deal Memo "Start Packs"
> Color Revision Order Memo

WHAT'S IN THE "FORMS" WALL ENVELOPES OR CUBBIES (OR ON A SHARED DRIVE)
> Letterhead
> Fax Top Sheets
> Memorandum Forms
> Check Requisitions
> Exemption From Sales Tax Forms/Proof
> Time Sheets
> Petty Cash Reports

WHAT'S ON THE PC'S COMPUTER (OR IN THE PC'S DESK DRAWER)
> Everything else (logs, checklists, accident reports…)

—m—

If not before, you probably now have the sense that the Production Coordinator's desk is quite a hub of document activity. It is. The Coordinator has lists to jog the memory about what is going to happen, forms to take care of all that is, and logs to keep track of all that was. Store templates of these forms for future use. Assemble more from every production you know. Create your own collection and preferences. You are ready to anticipate, analyze, and organize. You are ready to record it all for a reliable document trail. And you can sleep at night too, because you are not trying to keep it all in your head. Being part of a team with the Production Manager, the information can be shared. You are ready to move forward.

HOT COPIES

- -

Yes, a photocopier does have a mind of its own. It is only trying to be an artist when it jams and folds fifty sheets of paper into tiny little accordions in the duplexer. It wants to be fed when it runs out of paper or toner. And its favorite pastime will always be complaining about the weather by feeding multiple sheets of paper through at the same time. But understanding the mind of the photocopier, you are on your way to a mutually beneficial relationship.

The Production Manager decided that no production office needs air conditioning in the summer. Summer is too short. Even heat waves last only a few days. He simply had to put up with the office staff's complaining and all would be well sooner than later.

Heat wave day #1: The office temperature started in the morning at 115 degrees Fahrenheit. The air was thick with humidity. Even a sauna would have been more refreshing. People moved slowly and the photocopier decided enough was enough and stopped working. It refused to feed any less than five humid stuck-together sheets of paper at any one time. No production information could be copied to anyone on the crew. No scripts. No schedules. No deal memos. We went home early.

Heat wave day #2: 113 degrees. We bought and rented fans to cool off the copier. It appreciated our attention and copied about three sheets of paper before shutting down. Tempers quickened. Work pace slowed. No information got to the crew this day either.

Heat wave day #3: 115 degrees. A balmy 110 outside. We tried to trade in the photocopier for a more hardy machine, but no copier would submit itself to this working environment. Added more fans. Kept holding on to tempers. How long can humans or machines put up with this heat? Five copies today. Not even a dent in a full script.

Heat wave day #4: PM arranges for air conditioning. Copier is happy and starts to work again. Coordinator decides that a photocopier has the power to save human lives.

COUNTDOWN TO PRODUCTION

12

You have an office. You have a crew. You are in preproduction. Go. This chapter will help you to do just that. Far in preproduction, the pace of work seems easy throughout the crew, but as the date of first day of principal photography nears, stress heightens and nerves tighten. There is nothing like a deadline to change the feel of the workplace. Rather like preparing for a wedding, these checklists will count you down to the first day of shooting as a team, flagging what you need to work on each week.

THREE WEEKS OR MORE BEFORE PRODUCTION

The Production Manager is busy closing out development and assembling the framework for production, while the Production Coordinator is busy dressing the distribution table and filling the shared drive with documents of information (approved by the PM for distribution). Go through this list every day to check if you can revise, update, or do something on it.

THREE WEEKS OR MORE BEFORE PRODUCTION – PM CHECKLIST

- ☐ Locked Budget Matches Cost Report Accounts
- ☐ Development Cost Report (sample on p. 477)
- ☐ Start The PM-Only Cost Report (sample on p. 499–502)
- ☐ Accounting Procedures
- ☐ Payroll Service
- ☐ Cash flow & Interim Financing
- ☐ Union Negotiations
- ☐ Crewing Keys & Rest of Crew
- ☐ Casting – Stars & Support Cast

☐ Studio
☐ Locations Scouting & Surveying
☐ Previs (Previsualization)
☐ Completion Bond

THREE WEEKS OR MORE BEFORE PRODUCTION – PM & PC CHECKLIST

☐ Crew List (sample on p. 478-479)
☐ Cast List (sample on p. 480)
☐ Catering Choice
☐ Script Research Report
☐ Shooting Schedule (sample on p. 516)
☐ Production Schedule (sample on p. 334)
☐ Preproduction (Prep) Schedule
☐ Insurance
☐ Customs
☐ Equipment Orders
☐ Picture Stock (Digital or Film)
☐ Audio Stock
☐ Other Suppliers (Animals, Stunts, CGI, SPFX…)
☐ Post Facility
☐ ISAN Number
☐ Unit Publicity Plan

THREE OR MORE WEEKS BEFORE PRODUCTION – PC CHECKLIST

☐ Set Up Office, Files & Network
☐ Contact List (sample on p. 481-482)
☐ Crew Deal Memos (Start Packs) (sample on p. 503)
☐ Script Revisions (samples on p. 507-511)
☐ Director Medical
☐ A.D. Breakdowns (samples on p. 513-514)
☐ Continuity Breakdowns
☐ Cast Contracts
☐ Nurse/Ambulance Attendants
☐ Cast Packages
☐ Travel for Crew/Cast
☐ Immigration
☐ Cast Medicals
☐ Digital Camera(s) & Supplies

THREE OR MORE WEEKS BEFORE PRODUCTION – PM DETAIL
LOCKED BUDGET MATCHES COST REPORT ACCOUNTS

Ensure the budget is locked and check with the Producer to be certain all the Financiers have the same budget. Prior to locking it, ensure all the fringes are coded in one "line item" in the budget for easy reporting in accounting. Discuss with the Accountant any other reallocations that will make cost reporting easier prior to locking the budget. Now is the time to do so. The two of you are going to be working with the locked budget a lot from now on. Double check, too, that the Production Accountant is using the account codes from the locked budget. A cost report with totally different code numbers from the budget defeats the purpose of writing a budget in the first place. The budget is not revised anymore. From now on, you take savings from and show overages against the various budget lines on the cost report. The budget is locked. Time will show how well the budget was made… by you or whoever wrote it.

DEVELOPMENT COST REPORT

It is time also to find out where you are, cost–wise. What has been spent so far? The next cost report you do after the development cost report will probably be the end of preproduction cost report, so you need to know what has been spent up until now — especially since it is on the first day of principal photography that you have to pay back all the development loans acquired. Better know now in which "line items" the money was spent. Closing out the development costs may also trigger the last development money inflows from Financiers. You can use this money now, so report it soon. Even though development money is only a loan until the first day of principal photography, at least it is money in your bank providing cash flow to you through preproduction. You will need it. (See a sample on page 477)

START THE PM-ONLY COST REPORT

Yes, the Production Accountant is monitoring and accounting all the costs. Accountants are accurate and detail-oriented, reporting on purchase orders, check requisitions, and actual money inflows and outflows. You, however, may need to monitor costs before they happen — when the costs are still words and ideas exchanged between people and are only estimates of the future. You need a "work-in-progress" or "PM-Only" cost report to track down all the promises as you spend them and before the Accountant reports them. The DP has agreed to come on for a flat rate that is lower than the budget amount; note it in your PM-Only cost report and note the savings you can take for this. The Production Designer is worried that a certain set may cost an extra $5,000 because of the initial supplier quotes for materials. You note the suspected overage in your PM-Only cost report. You may mention the DP savings on the official cost report the Accountant creates, but you may not report the suspected overage on the official cost report yet — because the overage is not yet confirmed, and the Production Designer is working on other suppliers or finding other ways to build the set and avoid or minimize the overage. Two weeks later the Production Designer finds a different supplier, and the overage will only be $150. You approve the purchase order, and change the overage in the PM-Only cost report to a $150 overage. The Accountant notes it in the official cost report because now the cost is official — the amount is on a signed purchase order, and you have not worried anyone about a suspected overage that never happened anyway. (More on PM-Only Cost Reports is in Chapter 22.)

ACCOUNTING PROCEDURES

Identify with the Production Accountant what the accounting procedures are. Which Producers and Executives are you reporting to? How often will you be publishing official cost reports? Ensure the purchase order system is explained to the crew in a memo, and ensure that you use the system. What else might you add in a memo to the crew regarding accounting procedures — rules about per diems, about receipts, about petty cash reporting? What day and by what time each week must payroll be paid? Review the inflow schedule from the Financiers' agreements, and review the requirements that trigger each inflow. Is interim financing involved? Are you working on a co-production that requires two audits? Set up the accounting system now to prepare for it.

PAYROLL SERVICE

If the Accountant is more closely related to payroll service than you, she may set up the deal for you. If not, contact a few payroll companies to discuss your production. Basically, production pays them a percentage of the payroll, and the payroll company writes the payroll checks (doing all the fringe and union calculations) and generates proper tax forms in wrap, loaning you the accounting software to create cost reports. When you consider fringes, union dues, retirement payments, cast buyouts, overtime, meal penalty calculations, and so on, a payroll company is worth every penny — especially with frequency of weekly payroll.

CASH FLOW & INTERIM FINANCING

Start the cash flow soon. If the Accountant is too busy to start it, you do it. You need to know when and how much interim financing is needed. You will probably need the bank loan sooner than later. When is the money flowing in from financiers, and when is it flowing out as production expenses? Arrange interim financing as needed with the Producer. (More on cash flows and interim financing is in Chapters 20 and 21.)

UNION NEGOTIATIONS

Are you shooting union or non-union? It has already been decided in the budget, and issues regarding the union have been covered previously (Chapter 6). Call up the unions now and negotiate any concessions you need with them right away. You are already assembling the key creative crew. By next week you will want the union's help in finding support crew.

CREWING KEYS & REST OF CREW

Look over the empty crew list and discuss crewing with the Producer and the Director. Do you have a DP and a Production Designer on board already? Do these people have teams? Start finding the rest of the heads of departments and lock up a great crew. How solidly you can offer a job to someone may be contingent on the financing closing, so keep in close conversation with the Producer so you can turn availability checks into job offers. Note all deals made on the PM-Only cost report.

CASTING - STARS & SUPPORT CAST

Again, how solid is the financing to allow the cast to be confirmed, instead of your checking their availability and interest only? Find out what bonuses the cast may be asking for, like a private dressing room, a motor home, a driver to and from set and home, and so on. Can the budget cover it? Do you have the crew to cover these extras? Note all deals on the PM-Only cost report.

STUDIO

Secure a studio. Be sure it is large enough for the sets that the Production Designer is designing. Is there construction space on site or do you need to rent another space nearby and have the crew travel the partially built sets from the shop to the studio? What is included in the studio cost and what is extra? How much insurance do you need?

LOCATIONS SCOUTING & SURVEYING

Attend location scouts and surveys. Learn what is being promised during the discussions that occur while walking around the potential sites. Script changes happen. New items to build happen. All sorts of ideas are formed during scouting and surveying that cost money. Discuss the potential changes with the Producer, along with their cost ramifications.

PREVIS (PREVISUALIZATION)

The creation of previs elements and story sequences may be well under way by the time you start work on the production. For the PM, these tools provide an especially accurate scope of the Director's vision. It is useful to stay updated on the previs to ensure the production budget and crew can achieve that vision. Previs may range from 3D computer animation by a small Previs team to 2D storyboards by a Storyboard Artist to miniature toy people placed in a model of the set by the Art Department. If the budget allows, you can previsualize the entire script, or only the action and effects sequences. (More on previs is in Chapter 26.)

COMPLETION BOND

Are you purchasing a completion bond? Start assembling the required documentation now: post facility/lab access letters, locked budget, schedule, director letters, and so on. The Producer will likely do most of this work, but the Bond will want updates on the running of production from you. They will need daily production reports and cost reports at the very least. (More on completion bonds is in Chapter 18.)

THREE OR MORE WEEKS BEFORE PRODUCTION – PM & PC DETAIL
CREW LIST

Blast a crew list onto the distribution table as soon as possible. On page one list the addresses of all the production companies involved, then start the crew list itself with the all Producers in order of importance. The Production Manager needs to approve the crew list being published. You only want to publish names of confirmed crew on the list. Do not publish names of people with whom you are still negotiating.

CAST LIST

This list includes the character names, Performer's names, home addresses and telephone numbers, respective agent names, addresses, telephone & fax numbers and email addresses. Do not identify any Performer on the cast list who has not been approved, or until you have a signed deal memo in your hand to prove he is on the film. Some Performers prefer not to list their home addresses and telephone numbers. Often they will let you and the A.D.s have the information for emergency use only. Honor their wish for confidentiality.

CATERING CHOICE

The Production Manager can choose the caterer from a list of choices the Coordinator generates from experience or film reference sites and books, and from referrals.

SCRIPT RESEARCH REPORT

If it is in the budget, send off the script to a script research company as soon as the Producer says the draft is ready for clearing. Keep the research company informed of all script changes after that draft. In order to get speedy results, it is wise to telephone first to warn them about impending changes. Art Departments wait with bated breath for these reports, so they can make signs with "clear" names for set. (More on clearances is in Chapter 33.)

SHOOTING SCHEDULE

With the A.D.s on computer, the Coordinator rarely has to type up a shooting schedule, just copy it. The only downside to this situation: You must keep making sure that the present schedule you have is the current one. If the A.D.s happen to not have a computer, type up this form from their breakdown notes. Distribute the information onto the distribution table as soon as possible. (More on schedules is in Chapter 28.)

PRODUCTION SCHEDULE

Simpler than a shooting schedule, this schedule lists the production's plan on a weekly basis. Identify which weeks are prep weeks, which are shoot weeks, which are wrap weeks, and which weeks production is on hiatus. Also include reference to statutory holidays. Amass all this information onto one page. This form is very useful to all sorts of departments in production and in the head office.

PREPRODUCTION (PREP) SCHEDULE

The A.D.s will have a list daily of what is going to happen tomorrow and for the rest of the week. The Prep Schedule is another item for typing, copying, distributing around the office, and putting on the distribution table very quickly. Confirm with the A.D.s if anyone affected by the schedule needs to be called with the information. (More on Prep Schedules in Chapter 28.)

INSURANCE

Are all the insurance certificates in to cover production and the Financiers? Most Financiers have particular wording for each of their certificates. Are the insurance certificates worded correctly and does the coverage indeed cover the cost of production or the needs of the locations you will be using? Also, keep blank accident reports in the Coordinator's filing cabinet. Have even the most reluctant crew fill them out for any type of accident or injury. You never know when a small accident is going to develop into a larger problem. Memory fades with time. Fill out the forms immediately. The Production Manager can decide which reports need to be forwarded to the insurance company.

CUSTOMS

Appoint a customs broker. Brokers help you with moving equipment, clothing, or basically anything across the borders of the world. They alone know what reams of paper need to be filled out each time. Be aware that clothing has to win the award for most complex to cross a border, so when Wardrobe starts shipping clothing in, preserve as much lead time as you can for customs clearance. (More on Customs Clearances & Brokers is in Chapter 32.)

EQUIPMENT ORDERS

The Production Manager will deal with the basic equipment packages; if the Coordinator is tracking the purchase orders, the Coordinator can be hit for the specialty equipment orders, like cranes, man lifts, and jib arms. The Production Manager should approve all special requests (so they can be noted on the PM-Only cost report too).

PICTURE STOCK (DIGITAL OR FILM)

When you know what the Camera Department needs, the Coordinator can order the film with a purchase order. Know that the Camera Department will be doing camera tests and post workflow or film stock tests before first day of shooting.

AUDIO STOCK

Discuss the needs of the Sound Department and arrange for audio stock purchases and battery purchases when you know what is needed and how much. Some Sound Mixers supply these needs themselves.

OTHER SUPPLIERS (ANIMALS, STUNTS, CGI, SPFX...)

If you need any of these specialty suppliers, it is time to look for them now. Identify what exactly you will be requiring from these suppliers with the Producer, the Director, and whomever else you need to ask. Suppliers cannot quote effectively if you give them generalities. Be sure you seek quotations from at least three sources, and conduct due diligence researching them with previous Producers before committing to one. Track all your research on a memo for ease of reference and comparison later.

POST FACILITY

Find a post house and negotiate the deal for postproduction facilities and services. On which formats do you need to deliver the final production (i.e. film, HD, BluRay, DVD, etc.)? Are there localization issues to address — like PAL and NTSC — for international delivery elements? What is the specialty and the expertise of this post facility? Do they have an FTP site for sharing dailies and other post elements? How is their service? You will no doubt be asking them for favors later on.

ISAN NUMBER

ISAN stands for "International Standard Audiovisual Number" and in really basic terms, it is a (relatively new) global, numeric identifier for your production. Represented as both a number and a visual bar code, the ISAN number is superbly useful during exploitation of a film because the title of the film may change over time and across borders, whereas the ISAN number remains constant. For festivals and distributors, a scan of the bar code on a film can will tell them all they need to know about the production and the delivered elements. For producers, it increases the ability to track down revenue sources, especially in foreign countries. Numerous versions of the ISAN number can be registered under the same ISAN work number to track, for example, the director's cut separately from the producer's cut, the international version, and so on. Though the ISAN number cannot be registered into the system until the credits are locked, it is possible to reserve a number during development of a script, so your production may have one already. If you do not have one, it is a good idea to arrange for one during preproduction so you can start tracking all the versions you are about to create. This number is not only a global standard, but is also fast becoming a globally standard delivery requirement for all audiovisual productions.

UNIT PUBLICITY PLAN

The Producer will have a handle on the unit publicity plan, including a digital media publicity or communication roll-out. Since this plan has to synch with the production schedule, especially for collection of behind-the-scenes material, now is the time to start discussions on the contents of the plan and the roll-out schedule for publicity announcements. Find out if a communications policy needs to be set for the cast and crew to harmonize with the production's publicity plan and schedule.

THREE OR MORE WEEKS BEFORE PRODUCTION – PC DETAIL
SET UP OFFICE, FILES & NETWORK

Setting up the office, files, distribution table, and so on, have been covered by all the previous chapters, so I will not recap any of the detail here. Is there a shared network to tap into, or do you need to set up a virtual private network for this production? Arrange for I.T. support as needed.

CONTACT LIST

Once you start generating accounts, you can put this list onto the distribution table, too.

CREW DEAL MEMOS (START PACKS)

Have blank union and non-union deal memo forms ready. Approve the forms with the Production Manager. The head office Legal Counsel may have blank forms that office prefers. Make sure crew members fill out the correct forms. Rather than tackle crew members several times for several different forms, make a "start pack" all stapled together to include all you need: crew deal memo, payroll company information page, tax forms, corporate forms, citizenship forms, permit forms, and confidentiality forms. (See more on Start Packs in Chapter 23.) Once signed by the crew member, each deal memo can be gathered in the Production Manager's file on your desk for countersignature by the Production Manager at one of your daily meetings. Keep an extra crew list as a checklist as deal memos are completed. Chase down missing deal memos and keep in touch with Accounting in case the missing forms end up there before they come to you for countersignature.

SCRIPT REVISIONS

Trying to keep up with script revisions is like trying to hold on to a waterfall. In time, you will learn who is affected most by which change, and you will be able to inform the appropriate department before the revision is distributed. Until then, keep in touch with the Producer about the estimated arrival of the next wave of revisions, and publish the changes as fast as possible. Hand them out to each department and place them on the distribution table.

DIRECTOR MEDICAL

Check with the Production Manager if the Director is to be covered in the insurance policy. If so, arrange for a medical with a doctor approved by the insurance company. Note that some Directors have a kind of illness called "Gosh-I-forgot-the-appointment-again."

A.D. BREAKDOWNS

A.D.s basically generate a lot of information to distribute to the crew. If it is in the script, they break it down. You distribute it to the crew.

CONTINUITY BREAKDOWNS

The Continuity Supervisor cannot come close to the A.D.s in the amount of paper generated in prep, but the day/night breakdown and script timings are memos you will need to distribute right away.

CAST CONTRACTS

The deal memos come from the Casting Director. Know the performer's union agreement before typing them up. The agreement may not be the best for late-night reading, but you will find it incredibly useful before working with cast contracts. Arrange for permits as needed. If the Performer is young enough, check with the Production Manager about arrangements for a Tutor.

NURSE/AMBULANCE ATTENDANTS

Check with the A.D.s if a Nurse or an Ambulance Attendant is required on set for any specific days. If so, arrange for one. Nurses are on set for minor stunts, Ambulance Attendants for major ones.

CAST PACKAGES

As the cast is contracted, send the Office P.A. to each one with a "Welcome Aboard" package including: script, schedule, cast list, crew list, call sheet (if available), and a personalized welcome letter. Keep track of which version of each item you sent to each Performer.

TRAVEL FOR CREW/CAST

For visiting Performers or crew, the Coordinator is a travel agent. Once a visitor is confirmed, you will need: flights, limousines (both ends), hotel, flowers in hotel room, per diem from Accounting, script package (sent by courier), and possibly an immigration permit.

IMMIGRATION

Inform the Immigration Department early! Warn them that you are going to use a Foreign Performer or crew even if you do not yet have a name. Then keep them abreast of the information as it unfolds.

CAST MEDICALS

Like the Director, most Lead Performers are insured and need medicals. If Performers live out of the city, your insurance agent can furnish you with approved doctors closer to where they live. The sooner these medicals are done, the sooner the Performers are fully insured.

DIGITAL CAMERA(S) & SUPPLIES

Wardrobe takes documentary photos on set and in fittings, Continuity takes them for each shot, Hair and Makeup Department takes them, too. If the cameras and picture cards are not provided through a kit rental, ensure the teams are equipped to do their job.

TWO WEEKS BEFORE PRODUCTION

Review your list for three weeks before, plus address these issues:

TWO WEEKS BEFORE PRODUCTION – PM CHECKLIST
☐ Pre-calculate Costs of Extra Days & Extra O/T
☐ Hot Costs prep
☐ Daily Production Report Evaluation prep

TWO WEEKS BEFORE PRODUCTION – PM & PC CHECKLIST
☐ Script Research Report Is In
☐ Cast Medicals In
☐ Forms for Call Sheet & Production Report Chosen
☐ Rehearsal Room
☐ Arrange Preproduction Party

TWO WEEKS BEFORE PRODUCTION – PC CHECKLIST
☐ Picture Stock (Digital or Film) Is In
☐ Audio Stock In
☐ Craft Service Order
☐ Continuity Forms
☐ Battery Stock
☐ Expendables Order
☐ Catering Deal Memo
☐ Stunt Contracts

TWO WEEKS BEFORE PRODUCTION – PM DETAIL
PRE-CALCULATE COSTS OF EXTRA DAYS & EXTRA O/T (OVERTIME)

You must prepare now to answer questions on set during shooting like: "Can we afford to shoot an extra hour or two today?" or "How much will it cost if we stop shooting now, and rent this location again tomorrow to finish up at straight time?" You should have hired most of the crew by now, so you can estimate these scenarios. Prepare an estimate sheet on a spreadsheet program, like Excel, so you can revise it as more confirmed crew costs come in. Pre-calculate the cost of an extra hour shooting after wrap time. How much is two hours? How much is an extra day? What if that extra day were a Saturday (or sixth day)? Run through some scenarios and estimate costs now, so that you can confidently — at a moment's notice — say that overtime tonight makes more financial sense than returning to this location tomorrow or not. You need to be able to advise the Producer on the day. You need to know the budget and costs inside and out.

HOT COSTS PREP

Do you need to generate "Hot Costs" for Producers and Executives on a daily basis to keep them in touch with the daily cost of production? Find out what costs need to be tracked. Usually the costs that fluctuate the most on a daily basis warrant a close eye, for example: How many hours of overtime did you work?; How much film stock was used and processed? These cost report estimates are fast, dirty, and therefore not always terribly helpful, plus they keep the Accounting staff busier than ever. If you manage to output official and accurate cost reports in a timely manner, hot costs may not be necessary.

DAILY PRODUCTION REPORT EVALUATION PREP

It is worthwhile for you to pre-calculate the daily average for things like overtime predicted or film stock to be used, to find out if production is on budget or not when you evaluate the very first daily production report ("DPR"). Review the DPR and decide which items you need to track for this production. What is budgeted? How much is used on day one? Prepare your budgeted daily averages as a template now.

TWO WEEKS BEFORE PRODUCTION – PM & PC DETAIL
SCRIPT RESEARCH REPORT IS IN

The research report for the script should be back and distributed. Keep the research company informed of any script changes, especially any changes to character or company names.

CAST MEDICALS IN

Depending on casting status, this process should be done, too.

FORMS FOR CALL SHEET & PRODUCTION REPORT CHOSEN

Choose or design a set of forms that suit both the A.D.s and the Production Manager. Once chosen, give plenty of blank copies to the A.D.s. (More on Call Sheets and DPRs is in Chapters 13 and 14.)

REHEARSAL ROOM

If extensive rehearsals are going to happen, book an appropriate room. If the room is near the production office, you can tap into the office craft service supplies for their breaks and develop a close link between the preproduction office and staff and the rehearsal participants.

ARRANGE PREPRODUCTION PARTY

Is there a budget for a preproduction party for the crew? If so, commit to a date, decide on a budget for it, and let the Coordinator start planning it now.

TWO WEEKS BEFORE PRODUCTION – PC DETAIL

PICTURE STOCK (DIGITAL OR FILM) IS IN

Depending on the Camera Department, this should be in by now.

AUDIO STOCK IN

Some Sound Mixers arrange to pick this up themselves. Check that it has been done.

CRAFT SERVICE ORDER

If Craft Service is using any of your accounts (like coffee and water), the orders should be in with enough time for delivery before the first day of shooting.

CONTINUITY FORMS

Review the forms that the Continuity Supervisor is going to use. You may need to arrange for printing of NCR ("no carbon required") forms by the hundreds before shooting.

BATTERY STOCK

If not already arranged, collect orders now from the Camera and Sound Departments, then use your battery supplier.

EXPENDABLES ORDER

Grips, Electrics, Camera, and Sound will have orders. Expendables are everything from sticky tape to gels to black wrap to clothes pegs. Try to assemble all the orders together. One call to your supplier is better than four. Approve the extensive request list with the Production Manager.

CATERING DEAL MEMO

When the Production Manager has struck a deal with a caterer, make sure a deal memo is made.

STUNT CONTRACTS

Check with the A.D.s when Stunt Performers are being used and generate the contracts. These daredevils tend not to be booked through Casting Directors, so their deal memos can be forgotten. Also check: is there sufficient insurance coverage for their specialized work?

ONE WEEK BEFORE PRODUCTION

Review your previous lists for completion, plus address these items:

ONE WEEK BEFORE PRODUCTION – PM CHECKLIST
- ☐ Preproduction Cost Report

ONE WEEK BEFORE PRODUCTION – PM & PC CHECKLIST
- ☐ Final Production & Safety Meeting
- ☐ Final Location Survey
- ☐ Prep Production Report
- ☐ First Call Sheet
- ☐ Camera Test

ONE WEEK BEFORE PRODUCTION – PC CHECKLIST
- ☐ Who Is The Crew Representative?
- ☐ Who Is The Safety Representative?
- ☐ Crew Deal Memos Done

ONE WEEK BEFORE PRODUCTION – PM DETAIL
PREPRODUCTION COST REPORT

The end of preproduction (start of principal photography) is a trigger for financing inflows. Your final prep cost report ends at the end of this week. Are you and the Accountant prepared to generate it quickly? Meet with the Accountant, reviewing the PM-Only cost report against the actual costs incurred to date. You are a team.

ONE WEEK BEFORE PRODUCTION – PM & PC DETAIL
FINAL PRODUCTION & SAFETY MEETING

Usually held a few days before shooting, the final production meeting often takes place on the same day as the final location survey, typically including or followed by the safety meeting. The Coordinator arranges for an appropriate table or room for this meeting, with plenty of chairs and refreshments. Both of you should attend the meeting. The Coordinator needs to arrange for clean-up afterward.

FINAL LOCATION SURVEY

Usually the Locations Department, Transport Department, and the A.D.s take care arranging for this procedure. The Production Manager needs to attend. The Coordinator needs to keep in touch.

PREP PRODUCTION REPORTS

Production reports in prep are for the day of the final production meeting and location survey, and for all rehearsal days. Are there any other days for which you would like production reports completed? The A.D.s can help the Coordinator complete them, but the Production Manager needs to approve and sign them before distribution.

FIRST CALL SHEET

In the ideal world, the first call sheet — complete with location map — will be generated in time to distribute at the final production meeting. Not so ideally, a scribbled, handwritten version will be given to the Coordinator a few hours after the meeting for deciphering, typing, and distributing. Work with the A.D.s to disseminate the necessary information to all the cast and the crew.

CAMERA TEST

The Camera Department tends to arrange the camera test a few days to a week before shooting. For digital, this test is the first step in testing the postproduction workflow as well as the standard testing of all the technical nuances of equipment and playback. If film stock is being used, the Coordinator should ensure that after the test, the final film stock order is collected from the Camera Department, and make sure that order arrives before shooting.

ONE WEEK BEFORE PRODUCTION – PC DETAIL
WHO IS THE CREW REPRESENTATIVE?

The Crew Representative needs to be named at the bottom of each call sheet. Find out who it is.

WHO IS THE SET SAFETY REPRESENTATIVE?

Find out who from the set crew will volunteer or be appointed the Safety Representative, though typically it is the Craft Service Person. Name the designate at the bottom of each call sheet.

CREW DEAL MEMOS DONE

Except for the crew that starts on the first day of shooting, you should have all the deal memos completed. Let people know that a time sheet is useless without a deal memo, and chase down the stragglers.

— ∽ —

That is it. On different production teams, you will find differing expectations of a Production Manager and a Production Coordinator. No matter how much work you take on, someone will always be surprised that you take care of certain matters, and that you do not take care of others. Leave that to style. You cannot do everything for everybody. But right now, it is the night before shooting. You have a crew, cast, script, equipment, picture and sound stock, vehicles, post facility, location and/or studio, and a call sheet. You can go to camera tomorrow morning. Relax.

PRODUCTION III

Spending money during principal photography is like standing on a street corner throwing $100 bills into the wind.

THE DAILY CHUCKLE

I'm proud of the fact that I have never published a call sheet without a joke on the back. It's an incentive. Crew make sure they get a call sheet at the end of the day when they know they are going to get their daily chuckle. Then one day the hydro building across the street from the production office blew up.

The office power went out and we were left with one emergency telephone in a darkened, silent place of work. Without a telephone system and computers, there was little to do but watch the black smoke billow out of the remains of the building across the street. Our front step afforded us a picture-perfect view. The wind was blowing the smoke away from us.

The emergency crew arrived quickly and got to work breaking windows and, I suppose, drawing straws for who was to go inside. The police soon noticed us, came over to give us ten minutes to leave the building and area. If not, they would seal us in. Several blocks already had been closed off for the crisis. Oh boy.

We could only grab what was portable and absolutely necessary. The Production Manager took the budget, the Accountant took the crew deal memos and cost report, and the Assistant Coordinator grabbed a selection of office supplies. I looked at my computer. It was a desk-top model. Too big. I still had the call sheet to do today, so I grabbed a copy of the shooting schedule, a typewriter, and... the joke file.

Later, in a makeshift space at head office, the call sheet was completed, the evacuation was lifted, and my reputation for supplying the daily chuckle remained intact.

THE SHOOT DAY & CALL SHEETS

13

Shooting has begun. Most of the daily action happens on set now. There is a different routine. You have to adapt to a new daily schedule. The set runs on time that does not really exist on a clock. Times like morning and afternoon are all relative to the start of your set day and set lunchtime. For instance, 11:00 a.m. falls in your morning if the set started at 8:00 a.m., but it falls in the afternoon, if set started at 2:00 a.m. Keep this in mind as you walk through the following explanation of a set day.

SHOOT DAY FORMAT

The set's shoot day is basically structured into four phases that repeat over and over again: blocking, lighting, rehearsal, and shooting — all orchestrated by the Assistant Directors. Because of this structure, not everyone is active at all times and it appears there is a large number of people standing around doing nothing; in fact, some people are preparing for their jobs, and others are on standby to do their jobs. Because of the structure, too, there will be time to speak with nearly anyone on set should you need to.

BLOCKING

Everyone on set — especially the keys — watch the Director walk the Performers through the scene. This may be the first time the Performers have walked through this location, so it is an orientation for them, too. The Camera Department finalizes where the camera positions are going to be. Everyone makes note of the action and where and when it is planned to happen; for example, a Camera Assistant will put markers on the floor during blocking to mark the Performers' positions for various lines to prepare for focus points. At the end of blocking, the Director and the Performers leave the set (where they can discuss the scene, or the Performers can finish in Hair, Makeup, and Wardrobe) and the technical team can move on to the next phase.

LIGHTING

With Stand-Ins on the set instead of the cast, the technical team (Camera, Lighting, Grip) prepares for the shot. Depending on the complexity of the shot and the planned movement of the camera, this phase can take a very long time.

REHEARSAL

Once the shot has been lit, the Director and the Performers come back to set for rehearsal. The Sound team has their first opportunity to practice, too. They have to find a spot or two to record the sound where they create no shadows — always a challenge — and they can preview the recording level from the Performers' run through of the lines. Everyone, Camera and Focus included, has a chance to practice before committing the shot to film. The Lighting and Grip team are on standby in case lighting needs to be tweaked for perfection.

SHOOTING

Finally the camera rolls… or rather, sound rolls then camera rolls. This time before "action" is called the "pre-roll," and it is necessary because it takes a while during the synching process for the time code to lock. The A.Ds will "lock up the set" to keep it quiet like they did for rehearsal and even more so than they did for blocking. All work on set, save the action related directly to the shot, ceases and the magic is captured. After the take, if the shot is wanting in any way, they will shoot again; if it is okay, they move back to blocking for the next shot.

EARLY MORNING

Early morning for the office usually starts about thirty minutes before crew unit call time, or 9:00 a.m., whichever is earlier.

WHAT THE PM IS UP TO...

The Production Manager usually starts the day on set, but will not be the first person there, guaranteed. Unit call time is the "default" time for crew and cast to show up for set. There are usually so many pre-calls you will wonder if having a unit call time makes any sense. Makeup, Hair, and Wardrobe are busy prior to unit call dressing and making up the Cast. Drivers are already on set, having parked the unit, some having driven Performers to set. A.D.s and Locations people are already opening up the location for use. Electrics and Grips are already pre-lighting for the day's work. Craft service beat them all to set to ensure that a welcoming cup of coffee awaits the early risers. You will find you can meet anyone and everyone at craft service this early in the morning.

DAILY SAFETY MEETING

Often the A.D.s host a daily set meeting at the start of each shooting day to run through the safety concerns and procedures for the day's requirements. As PM, attend this meeting. All cast and crew are required to attend.

OVERSEE PRODUCTION

Oversee how the team works together. Oversee how fast they prepare for the first shot. The faster a first shot is achieved, the higher energy the crew has for the pace and the tone of the day. The A.D.s are doing much more hands-on overseeing than you are. You are here in case there is any trouble to be fixed… with money. If you have just moved in to a new location, set may discover that a certain piece of equipment does not fit as originally planned, and a specialized piece of equipment has to be rented. You are there to approve it, or to encourage a different line of problem solving. Who knows what the trouble will be? Time to test how you think on your feet. How fast can you calculate the extra money being spent? Is weather holding you up? Are you reliant on sunrise and sunset to capture the shots needed this day? You may need to do nothing at all. Relax, if you can.

PROBLEM-SOLVE

Hopefully nothing goes wrong, and you can just have an enjoyable visit to set. Chat with crew as you can, without preventing them from doing their jobs. If you have hired the right people, then you have hired the right people. Let them do their jobs. In a good scenario, you can primarily watch the magic unfold. If it is falling to pieces and horrible things are happening, do not panic. It is merely time to evaluate the size of the problem. Will the problem grow bigger in time? How much will it cost to change (for example, to fire someone)? During principal photography, you are at the stage of filmmaking that costs the very most per minute. You do not have the time to be leisurely about fixing problems on set. Evaluate quickly and thoroughly. Act fast to stop a problem, but do not act before thinking through the consequences. Talk over your concerns with the Producer. If the Producer wants to refrain from action at this stage, write a confidential memo documenting your observations and recommendations. It may seem drastic to be thinking about radical changes even on the first day of shooting, but you will recognize problems sooner when you have lived through a few nightmares; if you do not fix it early enough this time, you may at least be able to fix it next time. Do not cry wolf, either. It may be thin ice you step on, but that is the responsibility of the job. You are responsible for lots of money. You are responsible to complete the project on time and on budget. Remember the phrase "good, fast, cheap… pick any two," and you will realize that any money you spend during principal photography will be expensive money.

DIGITAL CHECK OR NEG REPORT

From day two onward, find out the report on the digital original or negative from the Production Coordinator (as noted below).

DAILY PRODUCTION REPORT EVALUATION

Evaluate the DPR's information daily against the averages you expected per day for film stock, number of scenes completed, and so on. How much overtime are you shooting daily? Especially for a series, have a look at the continuity top sheet — if the DPR is regularly late — to find out the estimated running timing for the entire show. If the show is estimated to come in too long, why shoot the extra footage that will have to be cut out of the final show? Cut scenes now and spend more time on what will end up in the show. If the show is coming in too short, maybe the Writers will have to add lines or a scene to fix the problem. Discuss with the Producer. (More on DPRs is in Chapter 14.)

GO BACK TO THE OFFICE

After a while, you can head back to the office to tackle all the urgent business sitting on your desk waiting to be completed.

WHAT THE PC IS UP TO…

Back at the ranch, uh, office, the Production Coordinator and the office staff are busy opening the production office.

PUT COFFEE ON

The first person in the office makes the first pot of coffee; like any other crew member, you will probably want a cup to start your day. Most people come to set or office before having had breakfast at home, and need some. Put a sign on or near the machine asking people to clean up after themselves, but expect to do the job anyway. Ceramic mugs are preferred to save trees and garbage dumps, but do have a few disposable cups on hand for times when all the ceramic mugs are dirty and guests come to visit.

HIRE DAILY STAFF

Have a list of Production Assistants and Assistant Coordinators handy so that you can call one in when a member of your office staff calls in sick first thing in the morning. The A.D.s may also call from set to ask you to hire daily crew for other departments. For union positions, start with the union office. For non–union positions, ask for preferred names from the departmental heads. It is for this purpose that you should meet and interview Production Assistants and Assistant Coordinators even when you have no job to offer. You will have no time to interview crew you call in on a daily basis. Note all of these daily crew names down on your copy of the call sheet or "To Do" list so that you can send each one the correct deal memo start pack, and you can be accurate in completing today's production report later.

CALL FOR A DIGITAL CHECK OR NEG REPORT

As mentioned before, call the post facility (or have Postproduction staff call them) to collect the morning's report to find out if any problems surfaced regarding the precious, recently captured images. For digital, these problems could include dead pixels or video hits, for example. For film negative, they could be irreparable negative scratches or light fogging of the negative that obliterates the entire image. Forward the information, good or bad, onto the Production Manager.

FORWARD EXTRAS LIST TO SET

Extras Casting Directors typically send a list of Background Performers who will be reporting to set in the morning and at what times. Forward this list to set with the first run, but keep a copy for yourself in case the original is lost or delayed.

FIRST RUN (FROM SET)

The A.D.s should send you the draft copy of the production report with all its backup paperwork, usually by a Driver. If you do not have it by now, call set to ask for it. Review the entire package while the Driver is waiting in case there are items that must be copied and returned to set immediately.

FIRST RUN (TO SET)

You likely already have items to return to set in the "To Set" box. Some of those items are the draft call sheet (explained later in this chapter) and the Extras list. Have the Driver wait for you to address the immediate requests that just came in the envelope from set. Ask Accounting if there is anything from their department that needs sending to set. Send all office/set packages to the A.D.s for distribution on set.

DAILY PRODUCTION REPORT (DPR)

You receive a draft from the A.D.s first thing in the morning. Check it over for accuracy and completion. Add to it any notes you made on your copy of the call sheet or "To Do" list. Accounting will be grateful if you make sure daily crew names are listed. Photocopy the "corrected" draft copy for the A.D.s and Accounting. They need the form immediately. If you are new to production reports, review the report with the Production Manager at this point. Then create a final version for approval signatures by the First A.D. and the Production Manager. Once approved, you can finally distribute it to all who need it.

MORNING

Morning is an hour to a few hours after call time.

WHAT THE PM & THE PC ARE UP TO...

You may both be back at the office, or the Production Manager may still be on set.

SET CALLS THE OFFICE WHEN FIRST SHOT HAPPENS

One of the A.D.s will call the Production Coordinator when set has rolled film on the first shot of the day. The Coordinator needs to note this information down on your copy of today's call sheet. You will need this information to keep Producers and Executives informed, and to complete the production report tomorrow. Before hanging up: always ask the Production Manager, the Producer, and the Accountant if they need to talk to set.

MORNING AND/OR AFTERNOON

These events can happen in the "set" morning and/or the "set" afternoon. The timing of some items is up to your discretion, or some will be dictated for you.

WHAT THE PM IS UP TO...

Review ongoing issues mentioned in the Countdowns, because issues like interim financing are never solved quickly. Make notes in the Set Square of any questions you may have for the A.D.s or others on set for when they call.

COST REPORT & DAILY PRODUCTION REPORT STATUS

Review how much yesterday cost. Read and evaluate the production report. Calculate figures on the PM-Only cost report. How does the PM-Only cost report match (or not) the official cost report? Meet with your buddy, the Accountant, if need be. Keep the Producer informed of the spending status. Depending on the time of the week, you may have a full-out cost report meeting with the Production Accountant today.

WHAT THE PM & THE PC ARE UP TO...

The Production Coordinator may initiate most of these issues, but the Production Manager is heavily involved in them, too.

MAIL DELIVERY

When the mail comes in, the Production Coordinator can open it, stamp it with the date received, and distribute it to the rightful recipients. Leave confidential mail sealed. Some people prefer their mail to be opened for them, others not. Check with Producers, Production Manager, Accountants, Director, and Stars before doing so. Some productions will open fan mail for some Performers (like children) to edit out any pieces that might be upsetting. Find out.

EMAIL DELIVERY

For email sent to the generic production address, the Production Coordinator can review it, and should forward it on to the rightful recipients by email, print it out and forward it on by hard copy, or act on the contents personally. If you use an automatic junk email filter, check the junk email folder frequently for email that is mistakenly identified as spam. It is recommended you keep deleted emails for several months because topics you may think are closed tend to resurface after time passes and memories fade about the decision that was made. To be even more vigilant, mark key email chains (even in the deleted folder) with a flag or category marker if you think there may be a chance the topic may resurface for discussion in the future.

DAILIES TIME & PLACE

The Coordinator needs to discuss with the postproduction team when and where yesterday's dailies will be screened. Keep the A.D.s informed of the changes as they happen throughout the day. Are there any people in head office you have to keep informed? Depending on the timing of arrival of the dailies, the Manager and/ or the Coordinator may be the first to see the dailies and give feedback to Producer and to set. Hopefully, the Editor will see them this quickly also.

A.D.s CALL THE OFFICE

Whenever an Assistant Director calls the office to speak to anyone, the Production Coordinator is usually first to field the call. Ask where set is on the call sheet and note it down. Find out who (of the producing team) is presently on set.

Refer to the notes you have been gathering in the "Set Square" by your telephone to make the conversation useful and brief. Chances are the A.D.s are calling from a cell phone, and they may be limited on battery time. Always check if the Producer, the Production Manager, or the Accountant needs to talk to set before hanging up.

When the A.D. calls from set, the Production Manager should always get the latest update on the status of set. What is happening? Find out the schedule of shots. Did they stop for lunch on time or generate a meal penalty? How far ahead or behind are they on the day's schedule? How much time might they need tonight to complete the day? Can shots be carried over until tomorrow because this scene needs lots of attention, or do you have to leave this location tonight and therefore have to finish the slate of scenes no matter what — because a few hours of overtime is cheaper (or is the only possibility) compared to returning for another day to this location and adding a day to the end of the shooting schedule? Will set be able to catch up if they fall behind schedule? How decisive is the Director? Does the DP seemingly take forever to light? Does the Director ever stop the DP from tweaking lights to over-perfection? Note down on your copy of the call sheet when the latest set update was, with details about it. You may need to relay updates to head office frequently, or you may just need to be prepared to update head office when they call you to ask what is happening on set.

HEAD OFFICE CALLS

Someone from head office, parent production company, or co-production company may call — even on a daily basis — to keep in touch with the production. The Production Manager will likely be the person of contact, but if he is not there, the Production Coordinator should have some information to give. The Coordinator talks to the A.D.s as constantly as the Manager does, knows when first shot happened, and knows if set has broken for lunch yet or not.

PUBLICITY EVENTS & VISITORS TO SET

As the Production Coordinator sets up events with Publicity or visitors to set, remember to discuss with and keep the A.D.s informed. Regarding publicity events, the A.D.s need to know about these early so that they can arrange for time during the shoot day for the Performers, Director, and/or specific crew members to be available for interviews. A.D.s will also help identify which locations and days are most appropriate to fit publicity into the schedule. Gallery shoots may end up being on a weekend, incurring sixth-day overtime fees for the crew needed, like Makeup and Hair. Web publicity or behind-the-scenes teams may shadow such a significant portion of the production that you may come to think of them as additional main unit crew.

The Production Manager and the Producer need to decide who can approve visitors to set, and how closed a set it will be. Some sets like to shoot on a set closed entirely from the public, while others do not mind the odd family or friend visiting set and staying out of the way. All sets welcome visitors from the financing companies. Make your "set visitor" policy clear to the crew before they bring visitors to set to enjoy free lunches on the production budget. You may find you will have to be host to a visitor or two for the first day that the Publicist is on set, as she may need an introductory tour. Be ready to play host.

OFFICE PETTY CASH

The Office P.A. may need to do a petty cash report daily to avoid a float getting too low. The Coordinator should review the report for enough detail before the Production Manager does, so you can answer any questions the PM may have about it later. The Coordinator needs to know what is happening in the office department.

UNUSUAL TELEPHONE REQUESTS

The Producer may call the office with unusual requests, like finding a monkey that can retrieve things on command, or finding fluorescent-colored contact lenses. These are requests that do not seem to fit into any department on the crew, so they tend to fall into the lap of the Production Coordinator and team. Here is where you can be creative in researching the oddest of things. Refer to your kit of references books and you can find pretty much anything. If not, ask fellow Production Coordinators. Have fun!

VISIT THE SET

The Production Manager will visit the set on a daily basis. If the Production Coordinator can do the same, do so. There is no better way of keeping in touch with what is happening on set than being there yourself. Use your visits to keep in touch with the crew, to gather information first hand to aide you in completing the production report, or to have the latest production report signed very quickly.

REVIEW OTHER CHAPTERS

A number of chapters are worth reviewing daily. Chapter 11 has a list of supplies the office team can check on a weekly basis. Use these checklists when the day allows. Chapter 7 has lots of information about how to deal with each department. Review this chapter from time to time. Chapter 15 is the countdown through production to identify events before they are about to happen. Chapter 22 deals with ongoing accounting issues for the Production Manager.

LUNCHTIME

Lunchtime means the crew is being catered a buffet lunch. The office staff often has to purchase their own lunch, unless unionized. If set is nearby, ask nicely for take-out.

WHAT THE PM & THE PC ARE UP TO...
SET CALLS IN LUNCH BREAK

The A.D.s will call when the set has stopped for lunch. Even if neither of you has any more news than that, talk to each other — set and office. You may remember something during the course of a conversation. How many lunches were served (since lunch is usually charged to production by the number of plates used)?

The Production Manager often has lunch on set. Lunchtime is an ideal occasion to meet with crew and to discuss with the A.D., the Director, and the Producer the morning's achievements (or not) and the afternoon's plan (often to catch up). What is the target for wrap time tonight? The A.D.s are committing to tomorrow's call sheet over lunch. Is the plan to carry any shots over to tomorrow or to another time? Depending on the day's schedule, the A.D.s may even create two different call sheets so they can commit to the call sheet later in the afternoon.

AFTERNOON (INCLUDING CALL SHEETS & LOCATION MAPS)

How soon the draft call sheet comes to the office will determine how busy the Production Coordinator's afternoon will be. The Production Manager looks more and more toward are they "getting their day"?

WHAT THE PM & PC ARE UP TO...
THE FIVE O'CLOCK REPORT

This report rarely happens exactly at 5:00 p.m., but does occur after lunch and before wrap. An A.D. calls the Production Manager to report on the present filming status, and what is expected to be completed by the end of the day. This is the Coordinator's opportunity to learn an estimated wrap time, or an approval to copy and distribute the call sheet. The Production Manager and the Coordinator should share information regarding potential wrap time.

CALL SHEET

After lunch, the A.D.s send the Production Coordinator the call sheet for photocopying (typically sent electronically). The Production Coordinator needs the Production Manager's approval, and the A.D.s' "go-ahead" before copying and distributing it to the many people who need it every day. There may be revisions the Coordinator will have to make to the call sheet before committing it to the photocopier. As the Production Manager has already had discussion on set regarding this call sheet (likely at lunchtime), the call sheet's information should not be news.

WHAT IS A CALL SHEET?

The call sheet tells the cast and the crew what time and where to show up on set the next morning, and includes the weather forecast. It also informs everyone of what scenes are to be shot, and what special requirements (like specific props, wardrobe, lighting effects, etc.) or daily crew each department must have arranged for to accomplish the day. Finally, an advanced schedule of what is planned for the following day ends the call sheet. All call sheets need to have a location map attached to be complete.

A WORD ABOUT PRE-CALLS ON THE CALL SHEET

There is a unit call time for everyone to arrive on set in the morning, plus there are specific call times prior to unit call (pre-calls) for certain departments to arrive earlier to ensure the most efficient start to the shooting day. Having a crew wait around for one department to finish their on-set preparation is an expensive wait, so pre-calls work. Experienced A.D.s are superb at giving the minimum number of crew pre-calls and still ensuring a fast start to the day. Though the PM reviews and approves the call sheet anyway, if the A.D. team is inexperienced, the PM has to review the call sheet very closely, and ensure a good look at the pre-calls. Are 90% of the crew being called prior to unit call time? Question the need for each pre-call. Are they truly necessary and efficient, or are you just pre-scheduling overtime on the bulk of your crew for the sake of comforting a nervous A.D.?

WHAT THE PC IS UP TO...

Now that the call sheet is happening, the Coordinator and the office team are rushing through a sea of related paperwork.

LOCATION MAP

The Locations Department will create a map to location to attach to the call sheet. If they cannot do this, make a map from the production office to location, depicting instructions in both pictures and words. The easiest way, of course, is to print out a map and directions from an online mapping source. Long distances from office to set force you to display a large-scale map that omits useful detail, so you will need to create multiple maps at various scales on multiple pages, which is easy, but a waste of paper. Drawing a custom map (with the help of online sources) that fills one page or less is the best way to go. Start with the local map as reference, and trace out a route from the production office to the shooting location. Include all major streets and ensure that north is to the top of the page for customary orientation. If the location is far from the production office, create two maps: one of large scale to show where the location is in reference to the production office, and one in small scale — which can be displayed separately or as an inset – to show the detail as you approach location. At location, note where crew parking is and any loading instructions the crew or the cast needs. The map should also include the location of the closest hospital, along with its address and emergency telephone number. Do not forget to have the actual address and contact number for the location itself. Finally, supply written instructions to location on the map for those people who understand directions by words more than by pictures. Though scale can be approximate instead of exact, be very clear about your instructions. Imagine trying to drive to location at 3:00 a.m. to a place that you have not been to before. Do not write small.

SIDES & SIDE COVER

Sides are selected pages from the script. For shooting on set, you need to reduce photocopy sides to pocket-sized for portability. Make them at the same time as you make the call sheet. Pull the pages from the script that correspond to the scenes on the call sheet, and reduce-photocopy them to pocket size. Use the first page of the call sheet as a cover sheet. It informs the cast and the crew what the shooting planned order is. Because sides are small, they are often treated as dispensable and become lost with great frequency. Label each set to the people that you and the A.D.s deem require them on set.

CAST & CREW CALL FOR TOMORROW'S CALL TIME

Clear up with the A.D.s who is going to contact whom with call times on a daily basis. You may fax the Caterer and the Extras Casting Director, while they may telephone the Cast, the Stunt Performers, and the Specialty Daily Crew. Some crew will phone the office for call times without identifying themselves. Find out to whom you are talking before handing out the "unit call time." These people may have a special call different from the majority of the crew, and you may have to telephone these people back should the call time change later in the afternoon. Write down their names and numbers. Keep the A.D.s informed of whom you have given call time information. Never give out the wrong call time.

LATE AFTERNOON

Call sheet and plan for tomorrow done, you are now waiting for wrap. If set slips into overtime, the wait could be very long.

WHAT THE PM & THE PC ARE UP TO...

As time grows closer to wrap, the Production Manager finds the time to go back to set.

PREPARE FOR TODAY'S WRAP ISSUES

Catch up on the status of set in readiness for wrap issues. How is the day's shooting going? Will you "get the day" (capture all necessary shots)? Do you need to approve overtime? Does call time tomorrow have to be pushed to avoid expensive turnaround costs and to give the crew enough time to go home and rest before tomorrow? You already know how much an hour or two will cost. Can you find the money in the budget to cover it? How does this day fit in to the whole schedule? What are the extenuating circumstances of today's shoot? Did weather hold you up? Is the crew becoming too tired to work the overtime effectively? Might accidents happen because they are tired? Weigh the odds. If all is going well, it will be another pleasant visit to set. If all is going superbly well and Producer is on set, you may stay in the office and complete more of that office work that is piling up on your desk.

WHAT THE PC IS UP TO...

The Production Coordinator is back at the office, holding the fort.

DRAFT CALL SHEET (FOR THE FOLLOWING DAY)

If the A.D.s do not prepare the draft call sheet themselves, after the call sheet is completed, type a draft copy (with no times on it) for the following day to send to the A.D.s on set for completion tomorrow. Create this draft from the information on the advanced schedule and on the shooting schedule. The draft call sheet is a great timesaver for A.D.s who do not have the luxury of a stationary desk and predictable weather on location.

AT WRAP

When the A.D.s call the office with, "We've wrapped," at the end of the day it is not always time to go home.

WHAT THE PM IS UP TO...

By the time the shoot day wraps, the Production Manager's part in wrap decisions are made. There may be a quick meeting after wrap to plan for the future day's work, or to discuss a future location or a schedule need or issue, but if not, go home. Rest up for tomorrow. You will need to be able to think clearly then. A whole new set of decisions and challenges await you.

WHAT THE PC IS UP TO...

The Production Coordinator and the office staff are still in the production office. There may be more work to be done after wrap.

SET CALLS IN WRAP TIME

Note wrap time on your copy of the call sheet, for reference when completing the production report tomorrow. At this point, the A.D.s will also tell you if call time tomorrow is pushed or pulled or remains the same. If it stays the same, ask them how long they need someone to wait around the office (in case someone who does not have a key needs access to the building).

WHEN CALL TIME CHANGES

If tomorrow's call time has changed from the call sheet (e.g., to one hour later), use a big fat red marker to write boldly at the top of all call sheets in your possession: "ALL CALLS +1HR" (of course, you could even have a self-inking stamp or two in your kit to serve this purpose); then re-distribute the call sheet to everyone necessary. Next, telephone all department heads not on set with the new information. If it is too late to make telephone calls, leave a list for the person opening the office to make the calls in the morning. Double-confirm with the A.D.s who is contacting whom with the call time change. Find out from the A.D.s which crew were not on set at wrap or left set early and therefore need a telephone call about the call time change.

WHEN THE CALL SHEET REVISES TO PINK

Sometimes the changes to the call sheet at wrap are so extensive that you need to make a "pink revised" call sheet. This is the reason having two people in the office until wrap is useful. Collect the changes from the A.D.s and whip up the new call sheet as quickly as possible. Select and reduce-copy the new sides. Indicate in bold at the top of both sides and call sheet that this is "pink revised," so there is no confusion about which call sheet to use (even when faxed, or photocopied onto the wrong colored paper). If there is no Driver standing by, and if time permits, you or your Assistant may be charged with driving the new call sheet out to set.

—⁂—

You made it to the end of the day. That is cause for celebration in itself. Pat yourself on the back. Go home. Prepare two alarm clocks beside your bed (one on battery power, in case of power outages), and rest before you come back to tackle tomorrow. Shoot day routine is different than prep day routine, and perhaps a little more predictable in its form, so you will become used to it very quickly. Just remember: Now that the cameras are rolling, you must be prepared for the unexpected.

PRODUCTION REPORT ENTERTAINMENT

The notes section of a daily production report can be its most informative section. In the shortest words, set has to report what happened yesterday, how long specific delays were on set, and what those delays were.

There is no room for humor on these reports. You are reporting to Producers, Executives, Accountants, and possibly Lawyers. If there ever is an insurance claim, these production reports are the legal representation of what happened on the set. Yet sometimes these reports cannot help but be entertaining, because naturally a day comes when it is difficult to sum up the day's events and delays on the production report and remain tactful.

My favorite day was... filming a family story, the star horse was in his stall and all was going fine. Heck, we had filmed scenes with him before with no problem. This day, however, no one noticed – well, until it was too late – that there was a mare in the next stall. A very attractive mare, apparently. So here we were making a family show, and the star horse was on screen in all his glorious maleness. I don't think so. So, set incurred a delay, and the crew stood around doing nothing while the star horse – a feisty, enamored stallion – was given a cold shower.

Just write about that on the production report...

DAILY
PRODUCTION REPORTS 14

They are published daily. The information on them may make them seem dry, but they are essential. They become the record of what officially happened on a daily basis on set during the most expensive time of filmmaking: principal photography. They are the daily production reports, also known as the DPRs.

WHAT IS A DAILY PRODUCTION REPORT?

Nearly every department creates a daily report on set detailing what happened in their department that day. Continuity creates the continuity top sheet; the Camera Department creates a camera report summary; the Sound Department generates sound reports for each roll of sound used; and the A.D.s generate or collect the Performer's work report (time sheet), Extra vouchers, and various other reports. The king of all of these daily reports is the daily production report or DPR. It summarizes all the departmental reports in one place, reporting, quite naturally, an official daily report to Accounting and to the Executives of what transpired during that set day. It is important to be clear in reporting everything on the DPR — from how much picture and sound stock was used, to how long the film's running time is estimated to be, to the hours of all crew and cast members, to general and specific notes about what happened on set. Note that the daily production reports are the first documents examined in great detail if production ever has a legal battle or an insurance claim, so fill them out accordingly. (See samples of DPRs on pages 486-488)

WHO GENERATES THE DPR?

The A.D.s on set collect the departmental information and generate the draft report. They send the report and all its backup paperwork to the Production Coordinator.

The Coordinator distributes the backup information to the appropriate departments (Continuity information to Editing, and so on — see Chapter 30), keeps a copy of all production report backup paperwork in the production files, and checks the integrity of the information on the draft production report. Accounting may need a copy of the draft ("unsigned") production report to review even incomplete information immediately in order to estimate the cost of yesterday's shoot. This protocol is not unusual. While finalizing the report, the Coordinator can also add notes to the notes section from her observations; once the report is complete, she gives it to the Production Manager.

The PM reviews the report, includes more notes, or revises notes as needed. The PM can evaluate the report in detail to garner information about the daily cost of production for the PM-Only cost report. How many hours of overtime was worked by the crew? How many daily crew were hired? For more on how to read and evaluate a DPR, see below.

Both the PM and the First A.D. need to sign the official report to approve it for distribution. The Production Coordinator takes care of arranging for the signatures, and for the distribution of the final, official report.

WHO ELSE READS THE DPR?

The Producers, the Executives, the Financiers, and the bonding company read the DPR to see how production is moving along. What is set achieving during the day? Is the shoot on schedule and on budget?

The Production Accountant uses the DPR to estimate how much the shoot day cost so that he can set aside money to pay for these costs when the bills come in or payroll is due.

If there is an insurance claim, the claim adjusters refer to these reports as the official word for what happened on set that day. Because of this procedure, there is no place for humor on the reports.

HOW TO READ A DPR

As mentioned, the DPR is made up of a variety of departmental reports. Here is a look at how to read those mini-reports (and who generates the information for them) as they are presented on the DPR. Update the PM-Only cost report as needed with what you learn from this report.

THE GENERAL DAILY INFORMATION (FROM THE A.D.s)

The header information of the DPR notes the day and the date of the shoot and the production title and key crew. Just beneath this is a notation reporting actual call time, time of first shot, lunch time, first shot after lunch time, wrap time, and last-man-out time. There should also be a notation of what the weather was like, which sets were used today, and on which locations they were filmed.

How fast is the crew getting the first shot off? Are the days regularly starting slowly? Is there a way to speed this up, like using a pre-call for Electrics and Grips to do some pre-lighting prior to the main unit's arrival? How much main unit overtime is being done per day? How long does the last person take to leave set after wrap? Is this overtime budgeted? What are the extenuating circumstances of today? Might weather have held you up?

THE CONTINUITY REPORT

Just under the header information is usually a chart that reports the information from the Continuity top sheet. This mini-report details what scenes were planned versus shot, how many pages of the script were planned versus shot, how much screen time was planned versus shot, what is the running time of the whole show estimated to be now, which specific scenes were shot today, and which wild lines were recorded.

Review this section to determine: How many setups are you achieving? Is the Director planning an unreasonable shot list of 45 setups per day, but the main unit is working at top speed and achieving only 18-25 of them? Is estimated timing of the each scene similar to final timing of master scenes? Are you capturing lots of scenes but little page count? As long as you are achieving something, that will be okay, because lots of camera placements (setups) take time. Heavy dialogue scenes will be low on scene count and high on page count to balance these days. What are the average scenes and screen minutes you are achieving per day? How many scenes were not shot and need to be carried forward to a future day's work? Can you move them later into the schedule without adding a day to your shoot? Did you achieve any target shots (unplanned bonus shots) from the call sheet? You are formulating good questions to discuss with the First A.D., the Producer, and the Director when next you meet or talk.

Especially for television series, look at and track estimated final show timing. If the show is coming in too long, why shoot the extra footage that will end up on the cutting room floor anyway? Cut scenes now. If the timing is too short, maybe the Writers have to write more scenes or more lines. Find out the plan. If the timing is just right, it will be broadcast length plus some extra to edit out in post to punch up the pacing.

THE CAMERA REPORT

Each day, the Camera Department summarizes the amount of picture stock used and remaining in inventory on the Camera Report Summary. For digital, information also includes: number of takes, circled (selected) takes, and which tape/card/drives were used. For film, information includes: the type of film stock(s) used; the number of feet of film that has run through camera detailing how much was exposed, printed, or wasted (unexposed and too short to be used again); how much film became short ends (unexposed partial rolls that may be used again); how much film remains in the inventory; and how much of the inventory has been used since you began.

Film stock is expensive. Since digital is less expensive than film stock, you can shoot more; however, editing time will need to be extended in order to sift through the extra footage. Consider if you are pushing the shot choices into the editing room instead of being decisive on the shoot day. Also consider the following: What is your budget for how much picture stock will be used daily? Is a lot of film being wasted? Are short ends being used or just stockpiled? As you approach the end of production, is the inventory growing smaller?

THE SOUND REPORT

The only information that makes it to the DPR from the sound reports is how many sound rolls were used.

Since film is more expensive than sound, the number of sound rolls tends not to be reviewed very closely. Still, it is wise to remember to check with postproduction if the sound quality is good. It is very expensive to replace sound and re-create a complex soundtrack in postproduction. Ensure you are recording good sound now.

THE CAST REPORT (FROM THE A.D.s)

The A.D.s are in charge of making sure the work report (time sheet) for the Performers is completed. The information that is transferred to the DPR from this report includes: a list of all cast members and each Performer's call time, travel time, lunch time, and wrap time. Wardrobe fittings may happen for Performers at the production office (not on set), so the Production Coordinator can track this information and ensure it is included on the DPR, too.

When reviewing this section, ask yourself: How much overtime is the cast doing? Are you budgeted for this overtime? Are there any meal penalties payable? Any extra hours payable to the cast is hugely expensive.

THE EXTRAS REPORT (FROM THE A.D.s)

The A.D.s also ensure the General and Special Skills Extras are all accounted for on vouchers or on a cash report form. On the DPR you will read how many Background Performers of which type were on set, their call time, lunch time, wrap time, and travel time. You will also learn the set times for the Stand-Ins.

Review this information. How many Background Performers were there? Did they work overtime? Is this information in line with what was budgeted?

THE CREW REPORT (FROM THE A.D.s)

The A.D.s report on the DPR the arrival to set time and wrap time of every crew member. They also include a listing of daily crew hired beyond the regular unit and their work times.

Check this information to see who is working how much overtime. Are some of the times unreasonably excessive? Is there a pattern as to who is working excessive overtime? How many daily crew were hired? Are they covered in the departmental budgets?

THE LUNCH REPORT (FROM THE A.D.s)

The A.D.s talk with the Caterer to discuss how many lunches were purchased that day (the plate count), and report this on the DPR. They will also note on the DPR how many substantial snacks were purchased (three hours into the morning), and — if set went to a second meal that day — how many second meals were purchased. This information will be near the crew work times.

Again, review this section to determine if the meals being purchased are in line with the number of meals budgeted. The call sheet will have a notation of how many meals were ordered. Is the Caterer serving many more meals than were ordered?

THE NOTES (FROM THE A.D.s, THE PC & THE PM)

And finally, the A.D.s have a large note section in which to detail a miscellany of information. What is the list of specialty daily equipment rented? What delays occurred, how long were they, and why did they occur? What is the list of scenes to be rescheduled, and the plan for folding them into the schedule? Did set achieve the day? The section also needs to report all accidents that happen, minor or not.

The notes section has to be the most-read section by Executives and Financiers. This is the section you as a Production Manager must review in detail, add your notes, and edit the notes that are there as needed. There will be set delays. Mention them. Report the plan to address them, too. Mention if someone was late on set due to traffic and that caused a set delay 10 minutes. Whatever. What accidents happened? Even if it is only a finger that was caught in a piece of equipment and needed a bandage, mention it. As you read DPR after DPR, are you noticing that the minor accidents are becoming more frequent? If so, the crew is becoming exhausted. Address the source of the problem. Is a particular cast or crew member difficult to work with? Mention how so, but be tactful. If someone is to be rightfully fired later in production, the justification must be evident here in the production report notes. The Production Coordinator may add notes to this section before the Production Manager sees the report to review and approve it. This is terrific, as the Coordinator has a finger on the buzz of production, too. Just think of what might have cost money, and report it. Discuss with Producer if you are not sure if a note should be included, or how it should be worded because of its sensitivity. When you are ready to commit to the wording, sign the report… but be speedy, because you have to publish a new report each day.

PUBLISHING THE DPR

For some productions the DPR is handwritten, completed in legible ink. Computer printed documents, however, are the easiest and the clearest to read, and therefore most advisable. Whatever you choose to do, never complete and sign the official production report in pencil. The DPR is a legal document. Be permanent.

The Coordinator will take care of distributing the official, signed DPR. (More on the distribution of the DPR is in Chapter 30.)

THE SECOND UNIT DPR

Should you have a second unit shooting as well as main unit, you need to create a separate DPR for second unit. Track the information from second unit separately. Print the DPR on colored paper to differentiate it from the main unit DPR. Second unit has less information to report, anyway. They usually have no sound and small crew, but are furnished with their own First A.D. and their own shooting schedule. Beware that main unit may push shots to second unit and overload them. Second unit is not a miracle unit. Keep both units talking to each other.

—⁂—

When reading daily production reports, remember the big picture, too. Day one takes longer to achieve than other days because new patterns are being forged. People are working together for the first time. Unforeseen problems are being ironed out. Some props or sets might be rushing to set completed just seconds before shooting has begun. In this hurry-up-and-wait industry, this is normal. You will find that overtime worked is probably greatest in week one. If the overtime becomes a pattern, though, you may not be able to afford to support it. Changes must happen. Discuss with the Producer a plan of action and put it into place.

THE CUSTOMS POLICE

This is the story of how I nearly got arrested for carrying the wrong customs documents.

Enlisted to hand carry a number of post elements to Los Angeles, I sat down in my plane seat — still on the tarmac in Toronto — and heard my named paged. The flight attendant told me that the company I worked for had just called the gate to tell me that I had the wrong elements, did I know what that meant? I said yes, thanked her for the message, and asked to de-plane. She said that it was too late and closed the door right in front of me. Since wrestling with her at this point would have been useless, I sat back down and resigned myself to a lovely, fruitless day of traveling to and from Los Angeles.

Upon my arrival at the Los Angeles airport, my contact examined the elements I brought and declared that all was well. I had the correct elements, I just had too many. He gave me four items to return to Canada. Fine, I agreed, and looked at the customs documents in my hand. Written in clear, bold, underlined, block capital letters was the phrase: "Not to be returned to Canada." My contact gone, I called head office for advice.

They consulted their experts and reported back to me this simple procedure: "When you arrive in Canada at customs, the officer will examine the documents and arrest you." Arrest me? "Then he will take you to a holding room where we will have someone there to bail you out and clear the whole thing up." Arrest me? Great.

Fifty minutes later, I boarded the exact same plane to go back. For the next four and a half hours, I sat down and rehearsed over and over again what I might say to the customs officer.

At customs in the Toronto airport, I handed over the offending document and spewed out as fast as possible — and in way too many words — my case, along with an explanation of the events of my entire day. The Customs Officer interrupted me, returned the paperwork, and said he didn't want to hear my story. I should just go away. Speechless, I did just that.

Then I remembered that there was someone waiting for me in a holding room. I had to go back and ask in my sweetest, most innocent manner: "Uh, if you were to have arrested me, where might you have taken me?"

He paused before answering. I smiled. He told me. So I thanked him and trotted off to the holding room, entering it from the visitor's side (not the prisoner's side).

Upon my entrance, the promised contact was there. She belted out fast and loud, "It's not her fault!", accompanying her declaration with grand gestures. The officers on duty regarded her with curiosity. I jumped in to shut her up and dragged her out of the room to explain. I did not want the officers to change their minds about arresting me.

COUNTDOWN THROUGH PRODUCTION | 15

You think about work day by day now. You initiated a lot of happenings during preproduction and you are wondering what you can initiate during production. As a continuation of Chapter 12, this chapter will count you down through the shooting period, stepping back from a day-to-day focus and seeing the elements that develop or trigger over time.

FIRST DAY OF PRINCIPAL PHOTOGRAPHY

This is the first day that the project is a film instead of a script. The cameras are rolling — an event that triggers a number of requirements that the Production Manager must address.

FIRST DAY OF PRINCIPAL PHOTOGRAPHY – PM CHECKLIST
- ☐ Visit the Set
- ☐ Memo Financiers that Principal Photography Has Begun
- ☐ Repay Development Loans
- ☐ Pay Production Fees to Writers & Others
- ☐ Update Producers/Executives & Bond

FIRST DAY OF SHOOTING – PM DETAIL
VISIT THE SET

First of all, visit the set! You have helped prepare for this wonderful day, so show up and see how it is going. There may be a few problems to iron out, as this is the first day these people have worked together on set for this production, and first days always reveal something to be addressed that was not dealt with before. Be on standby to assist in solving these last-minute problems.

MEMO FINANCIERS THAT PRINCIPAL PHOTOGRAPHY HAS BEGUN

Send a memo (by email or letter) to the Financiers informing them that principal photography has officially begun. This memo is likely part of the triggers for the next money inflow you need to receive. In many cases, a copy of the first day's production report will suffice, but that document will not be ready until the end of shoot day two. Have the Coordinator copy the memo to all Financiers and to head office immediately.

REPAY DEVELOPMENT LOANS

As mentioned before, development money is only loaned to you until the first day of principal photography. You must pay back the Financiers today for the money they loaned to you, so that you do not start generating interest on the unpaid balance. Some Financiers will allow you to do a "check swap" between the repayment of the development loan and their next payment to you that is triggered on first day of principal photography. Find out if you can do this and preserve your bank balance.

PAY PRODUCTION FEES TO WRITERS & OTHERS

A number of people will have payments triggered on the first day of principal photography. Discuss these payments and to whom they are to be made with the Production Accountant. Writers, for example, are paid for their writing work in development, but they have a production fee payable on the first day of principal photography — because the script they wrote is technically now a film, no matter how short it is at this point! Directors often have a payment triggered on this day. As you will have created a cash flow in preproduction, none of these payments will be a surprise to your bank account. Just ensure they happen on time, and note what has been paid on the PM-Only cost report.

UPDATE PRODUCERS/EXECUTIVES & BOND

The Producer and some Executives will likely be on set with you on this, the first day of principal photography. It is quite a celebration to move a film from development into production. For those who are not or cannot be on set, it is good to give them a telephone call to update them that you have begun shooting. Call Executives and the Completion Bond to keep them informed. They will appreciate the call.

FIRST WEEK OF PRINCIPAL PHOTOGRAPHY

This week the Production Manager will tend to be working very much in the present, while the Production Coordinator focuses on items for the future. You are both still meeting every day to touch base; soon you will be in the new routine of the more structured production days, instead of the less-so prep days. Even though you will still be tidying up issues from preproduction, there are other issues you need to address, starting now.

FIRST WEEK OF PRINCIPAL PHOTOGRAPHY – PM CHECKLIST
- ☐ Review Cash Flow
- ☐ Approve Payroll
- ☐ Approve Petty Cash
- ☐ End of Prep Cost Report

FIRST WEEK OF PRINCIPAL PHOTOGRAPHY – PM & PC CHECKLIST
- ☐ Credits
- ☐ Crew Gifts
- ☐ Wrap Reel

FIRST WEEK OF PRINCIPAL PHOTOGRAPHY – PM DETAIL
REVIEW CASH FLOW

Thinking of cash flow, this week is a good time to review it. How close are actual bills to the projected bills as noted in the cash flow? Review this alongside the PM-Only cost report and with the Production Accountant to keep you updated on the financial health of the production.

APPROVE PAYROLL

Payroll will not be terribly big this week, as you will only be paying for the crew that was on the last week of prep, but it is increasing rapidly. Find a routine in the week to approve the payroll to keep the Production Accountant working efficiently. Note payroll amounts in the PM-Only cost report.

APPROVE PETTY CASH

Crew have been spending, and spending. Keep on approving petty cash. You may find you have to teach people how to be detailed while filling out the form, or teach them what a valid receipt is. Be prepared for this situation. You can track petty cash in the PM-Only cost report by monitoring their floats as they go out, or spends as they come in. Whichever way you do it, keep track of it. Petty cash is far from being petty.

END OF PREP COST REPORT

You prepared for this cost report during the last week of prep. Meet with the

Production Accountant, bring your PM-Only cost report notes when you review the draft, and arrange to publish the official end-of-prep cost report as soon as possible to trigger your next inflow from the Financiers, updating your PM-Only cost report as you do. Be ready, because by the end of this week, you will have to generate another cost report!

FIRST WEEK OF PRINCIPAL PHOTOGRAPHY – PM & PC DETAIL
CREDITS

Though you may initially believe this is too early to think about credits, know that credits will have to go through many drafts and approvals from many companies before they are final. The Coordinator can start the first "pre-draft" to show the Producer and the Production Manager only. Consult the crew deal memos, cast contracts, and any other information you have gathered in the credits file folder on your desk. Double-check all spellings. Call those people if you are at all unsure about the spelling of their names. Do not promise them a credit (you do not have the authority), just check the spellings. Everyone is happy to confirm the spelling of their names when credits are being discussed! Credits are very sensitive information. Treat them with the utmost confidence.

CREW GIFTS

Crew gifts can be t-shirts, jackets, hats, bags, or doormats imprinted with the production name. Delivery of ordered items can take four to six weeks, so consider what you might want now. The Coordinator, the Production Manager, and the Producer can discuss this procedure. Some productions will pay for the gifts, and others will sell them to the crew. Some productions want them to be a surprise, others not. Find out how crew gifts are to be treated on this production, and order the items immediately. If the crew is to pay for all or part of the order, collect payment in advance.

WRAP OR OUTTAKE REEL

The Production Manager, the Producer and the Coordinator can discuss if production is going to create a wrap reel or outtake reel. If you are going to create one, bring the Editor and Continuity into the discussion to ensure you include interesting or funny takes flagged for use as you proceed through production. Finding outtakes at the end is a time-consuming process. With enough notice, Continuity can flag appropriate takes for the editing team as they happen during the shoot.

DURING PRODUCTION

Much of what you do on a daily basis is covered in Chapter 13 about the shoot day, but there are issues that come up during production that do not come up regularly day after day.

DURING PRODUCTION – PM CHECKLIST
☐ Weekly Cost Report
☐ Weekly Payroll Approval
☐ Petty Cash Approvals
☐ Daily Production Report (DPR) Approval
☐ Extra Equipment or Crew Approvals
☐ Overtime Approvals
☐ Unexpected Problem-Solving

DURING PRODUCTION – PC CHECKLIST
☐ Call Sheet & Draft Call Sheet
☐ Daily Production Report & Backup
☐ Daily Equipment
☐ Daily Crew
☐ Stunt Contracts, Nurses, Ambulance Attendants

DURING PRODUCTION – PM DETAIL
WEEKLY COST REPORT

Every week you need to meet with the Accountant, and publish the official cost report detailing how much has been spent. Update your PM-Only cost report each time.

WEEKLY PAYROLL APPROVAL

Along with the weekly cost report — or rather prior to — you need to approve the payroll for the Accountant. Take this opportunity to update the PM-Only cost report with the information.

PETTY CASH APPROVALS

Petty cash comes in when petty cash comes in. How well are the departments managing their money? Keep up discussions with them as you approve their petty cash reports. Update the PM-Only cost report as needed.

DAILY PRODUCTION REPORT (DPR) APPROVALS

Though this does happen daily, I mention it here again, as it is another approval you have to schedule for your workday. Compare the DPR information to the estimated averages you pre-calculated during preproduction. How is production doing?

EXTRA EQUIPMENT OR CREW APPROVALS

Now and then, crew will ask for extra help or extra equipment for which you had not originally budgeted. These requests are natural. Because you are keeping current on the PM-Only cost report of what may be the final cost picture for the entire production, you can decide if it is wise or not to approve such extra cost. The more you dip into contingency approving these extras, the more you must keep the Producer informed of the declining balance. Save at the very least 40-50% of the contingency for postproduction use.

OVERTIME APPROVALS

You may have budgeted for some overtime, but not for all of it. This is what contingency is used for. You have already pre-budgeted how much overtime will cost per hour. Use this information when advising if you can afford production to work overtime or not. Keep a close eye on how much overtime the set is working. The first week is bound to have the most overtime during the production as the team irons out how to work together. But if you keep the hours up, the crew will become tired and burnt out and not perform well, plus the budget will not be able to handle consistent over-spending. You will be robbing contingency from postproduction to pay for it. Not wise. Problem-solve too much overtime early with the Producer and the First A.D.

UNEXPECTED PROBLEM-SOLVING

Speaking of problem-solving, you will encounter other events too numerous and of too much variety to mention here. Most of these problems, if not all of them, will cost money. Be ready for the unexpected, and be ready to find a way out of it, minimizing the impact on the budget so that the maximum amount of money in the budget ends up "on screen" for all to see.

DURING PRODUCTION – PC DETAIL
CALL SHEET & DRAFT CALL SHEET

In review, send the draft copy of the call sheet you created to the A.D.s on set in the morning. Receive the "penciled-in" copy after lunchtime. Type up the call sheet as soon as possible, seek approvals, add the location map to it, make script sides, and distribute it.

DAILY PRODUCTION REPORT & BACKUP

The draft production report comes from the A.D.s in the first run of the morning. Check and complete it using the backup paperwork provided and the information you gathered yourself yesterday. Seek approvals as necessary, type a final version, collect signatures, and distribute it. Treat it with confidentiality.

DAILY EQUIPMENT

Purchase order any special equipment requests, remembering to get approval from the Production Manager as you go.

DAILY CREW

Be prepared to call unions or suggested people first thing in the morning to replace absent crew members.

STUNT CONTRACTS, NURSES, AMBULANCE ATTENDANTS

If a Stunt Performer is scheduled for the next day, check that you have already completed his contract. Also check with the A.D.s if a Nurse or an Ambulance Attendant is needed. If so, order one.

TOWARD THE END OF PRINCIPAL PHOTOGRAPHY

As production draws to a close, you think more and more about completing the show, about getting it "in the can." Crew should not be buying much in the way of office supplies now, except perhaps for boxes to wrap up their files. Before wrap begins, plan for it now.

TOWARD THE END OF PRINCIPAL PHOTOGRAPHY – PM CHECKLIST
☐ Finishing on Time & on Budget
☐ Cost Report Savings & Overages
☐ "Pink Slip" End of Production Notification
☐ Wrap Plans Per Department
☐ Plan Wrap Sale or Set Storage
☐ Prepare Memo to Financiers That Principal Photography Has Ended

TOWARD THE END OF PRINCIPAL PHOTOGRAPHY – PC CHECKLIST
☐ ADR Sessions (Looping)
☐ Credits Continue
☐ Crew Gifts In
☐ Wrap List
☐ Wrap Party Prep

TOWARD THE END OF PRINCIPAL PHOTOGRAPHY – PM DETAIL
FINISHING ON TIME AND ON BUDGET

There will be lists of shots on the DPR that are being carried forward from one day to the next. You want to know these are addressed, and the list of shots being carried forward is rapidly diminishing. Have meetings with at least the Producer and the First A.D. to ensure you will be finishing on time and on budget. If there are any flags you are not going to finish on time or on budget, address those concerns now. Do you need a reduced unit for pick-up shots for a day in wrap? Do you need an extra shoot day for the entire unit? What will it take to finish principal photography? What ramifications do these decisions have on the budget — some cast or crew contracts will be very specific noting their stop date, inflicting a high monetary penalty should you shoot beyond that date. Weigh the odds and prepare now.

COST REPORT SAVINGS & OVERAGES

As production nears the end of shooting, you will be closer to closing out a good portion of the budget lines in the cost report, and will have a more accurate idea of where you are saving money versus going over budget. Coming in heavily under-budget is just about as bad as going over-budget, since the Producer will have to give back any budget "underages" or savings to the Financiers. If being under-budget is your problem, target now how production is going to spend any savings on valid production or postproduction costs.

"PINK SLIP" END OF PRODUCTION NOTIFICATION

This is a payroll issue. Using a memo or a letter, officially notify the crew of the end of principal photography and the end of their particular wrap on the show. Typically one week in advance of production wrap, unions often require such notification, even if production is very short in duration. Whether you are required to do so or not, this is your opportunity to thank the crew for their hard work and dedication to the project. You can include this notification in the crew's paycheck envelope.

WRAP PLANS PER DEPARTMENT

While the Production Coordinator plans for the wrap party, the Production Manager should meet with each department to discuss their plans for wrap. As crew is no longer needed, are the departments letting them go off the payroll? What are the actual last days of work needed for each department? You can use this information to update cost projections on the PM-Only cost report.

PLAN WRAP SALE OR SET STORAGE

Are you going to sell the sets, dressing, props, and wardrobe, or are you going to put them in storage? If you are going to put them in storage, how long can you do so, according to the budget? Research the cost ramifications now. If you are planning a sale, make sure the various departments synch their dates to sell at the same time to ensure the most profit. Monies that come in from the set sale go into the production bank account and can offset overages in the respective categories. Find out other productions that are starting up as you are wrapping. They may need to buy a number of your items, and selling to one source is very convenient for you.

PREPARE MEMO TO FINANCIERS THAT PRINCIPAL PHOTOGRAPHY HAS ENDED

Just as the first day of principal photography is a trigger for financing inflows, the last day is often also a trigger. Though you will still need a cost report for the period ending on the last day of shooting, you can at least prepare the memo (by email or letter) to the Financiers that will inform them that principal photography is completed. For maximum speed the Coordinator can send this memo to all concerned on the morning of the first day of wrap.

TOWARD THE END OF PRINCIPAL PHOTOGRAPHY – PC DETAIL
ADR SESSIONS (LOOPING)

After a Performer has completed filming, expect the postproduction team to ask you to arrange an ADR session ("Additional Dialogue Recording" or Looping) for that Performer. Postproduction may coordinate the studio arrangements while you coordinate the Performer's presence. Be sure that the proper time sheet or contract is completed at the session so the Performer can be paid. Distribute a memo announcing the session and attendees.

CREDITS CONTINUE

Drafts and drafts of credits will continue to fill your files. If you do not receive approvals from the people you need, call them to speed up the process.

CREW GIFTS IN

With luck, the crew gifts will be ready early. The easiest way to distribute them, whatever they are, is to label each gift with each crew member's name, and order them into alphabetical (but decorative) boxes. Imagine handing out one hundred black sweatshirts to a crew that is working all over set. Unlabeled, the sweatshirts are identical and unidentifiable when crew members put them down temporarily as they work. Some will get lost. Few crew, if any, will mark their gifts with their names as soon as they receive it. Also note that the Producer usually says a few words to the crew as the gifts are being handed out.

WRAP LIST

Make a list of everything you have rented, leased, and bought during the course of production. You will have to return or sell all of it come wrap. The earlier you do the list, the more accurate it will be. Start by reviewing the P.O. log. The Production Accountant can help add to your list with a look over the petty cash reports for purchased items. Review the list with the Production Manager.

WRAP PARTY PREP

Finalize a budget from the Production Manager for the event, and budget a party accordingly. Start to think about appropriate venues. (More about wrap parties is in Chapter 34.)

—⁂—

Now you can see the big picture of production and plan ahead. You find that it not as daunting as you once thought it was. But before you think too far into wrap and postproduction, there are ongoing issues that you need to explore further during production.

MORE MANAGEMENT & MONEY ISSUES

IV

Know how to spend money in order to save money (like saving time).

GRANDMOTHER ON THE SET

There was a day I brought my grandmother to visit the set. I don't normally bring visitors to set, but my mother, who had been once before, was insistent that my grandmother see filmmaking first hand. My mother, you see, sees roses in everything in life, and will always see the magic created on a film set. She wanted to share this magic with her mother.

My grandmother was predictably very silent and observant on her visit. The crew and the cast were very friendly to her and she saw a fair amount before going home.

Afterward she made only three comments about the day. About the crew: "Nobody bothers to dress up for work; they're all in jeans." About the time when the cameras are rolling: "Everyone seems to be standing around doing nothing." And about filmmaking in general: "I don't know how the show comes out in order; everyone looks so disorganized."

To anyone in film that I have mentioned these three observations, I get the same response: "How very astute of her."

LOCATION MANAGEMENT

16

Traditionally, shooting on location is a cheaper alternative to building a set and shooting in a studio, but it is not always the case. You may choose to shoot on locations for other reasons. On existing locations, you may find a richness of production values (all the detailed dressing of the location) that would cost too much time and money to reproduce in a studio environment. On existing locations, you can film and have the cast interact with a real vista, not a painted backdrop. In any case, you will be renting locations at some time during a film shoot, and as Production Manager you need a good Location Manager and location team to ensure the logistics of the set are taken care of on location.

LOCATION SCOUT vs. LOCATION MANAGER

The Location Scout or Manager is the liaison between the film company and the public. A Scout is generally new to the industry and, as expected, is hired to scout out possible locations for use on the production. A Location Manager should have many more years of experience not only looking for possible locations, but also managing the logistics of them — all the way through the production process, including managing the departmental location budget. For affordability, you may hire a Scout early for location research, then when the Location Manager of your choice is available, bring that person on to take over.

Choosing initial possibilities for locations is both a hugely creative and hugely logistical endeavor. The Location Scout or Manager has the responsibility for finding and presenting possibilities for the entire backdrop for the film by their choice of locations. In essence, they are painting the background. Is this person capable of finding the choices that are along the same lines as the Director's and Production Designer's creative vision? Balanced with that creativity, does the Scout or the LM consider logistical shooting issues when presenting the location choices?

The Location Scout or Manager will be seeking out possible locations from industry libraries, from discussions with other industry contacts, and will be finding locations on her own. She will be making cold calls to the public introducing them to the production company, and may have to deal with members of the public who have had bad experiences with other film crews — because you may want to repair this burned bridge to allow production access to a particular (perfect) location. Without a doubt, you need someone who is unwaveringly professional to provide this first impression of the production company. Choose wisely.

WHERE TO FIND LOCATIONS

There are a number of sources to seek out locations for the script. Government Liaison offices typically have a location library (often online) as a first stop for initial location research. These are picture files with further logistical information on them to aid Scouts and LMs in finding locations that have either had a film shoot there before, or who are interested in having a film shoot. You can use a Chamber of Commerce in a smaller town where there is no Government Liaison office. Real Estate companies are also of help. You will also consider previous locations from previous shoots, and the Scout or the LM may also contact co-Scouts and co-LMs on other productions. Naturally, Scouts and LMs spend a lot of time driving around too, because they may find a location that will work for the script close to another location that you have already chosen. Proximity of locations is a good thing to reduce the time it takes for company move. You want to spend more of the shooting day shooting film, not moving the unit.

WHAT TO LOOK FOR IN A LOCATION

When initially looking for a location, there are a number of issues to consider beyond the site's match to the creative vision. Here is a look at the logistical needs of potential locations. You want the Scout or the LM to consider these items, but if you are on a budget that is low enough, as Production Manager you may be heading up these considerations yourself.

PRIOR TO LOCATION SCOUTS & SURVEYS

Before even showing up to have a first preliminary look around the location, be sure the owners of the property (not just the renters) are willing to give permission to a film shoot at their place. Renters may be thrilled to learn of a film crew coming to shoot and may think they will be receiving the site rental money, but they do not own the property and do not have the right to allow a film crew such permission. Find out who the owners are.

While having initial conversations with the owners, fill them in with a nutshell explanation of film production. Tell them exactly what you intend to shoot at their property, and if you are considering redecoration (like repainting walls). Explain this process to the owners, assuring them that the crew will redecorate the property back to its original form on the production's departure. Find out how interested the owners are in allowing a film shoot, and what the owners might know or think they know about film shoots. There may be a lot of myths you will have to set straight about what a film crew is like on a location.

Consider, too, how big the unit is, how many vehicles. Is there enough space in the neighborhood to park all the vehicles and still provide access to the location? Is there space for the crew to set up? Is there space for a Cast and an Extras holding area? Where might you set up for the cast and crew lunch?

ON THE LOCATION SCOUT

Once you have preliminary permission, scout the potential location, considering all the departmental questions that may come up when you get back to the office. You have to think for both the crew and the owners of the property. You are indeed a liaison between the two.

When you speak with the owners and ask them a myriad of questions, ease their worries by telling them that your questions are all preliminary, not committed questions. You are scouting the potential of this property to fit into a series of locations and sets that make up the film shoot, and this location may or may not be chosen for many reasons that have nothing to do with the location's beauty. Explain the location research process: You scout the location and take pictures, asking preliminary questions about the location; then the crew narrows down the choice of locations in the office for various reasons; then the crew needs to come and survey the location for themselves to prepare for the logistics of a film set — those surveys often consisting of a few people at a time for a few visits, then a big survey of everyone just before shooting. Reassure them that production will arrange for insurance coverage should anything go wrong, and you will minimize the location surveys as much as possible. Respect the owners. If they are entering new territory entertaining the idea of a film shoot at their property, it is your job to help them understand what it means to have a film crew shoot here.

LOCATION SCOUT CONSIDERATIONS

When scouting a potential location or studio (or considering a potential one that the Scout presents), you have to think for all the departments: the Director, Camera, Sound, Art, Transportation, Catering, and so on.

LOCATION PHOTOGRAPHS & FILES

Location Scouts or the LM use a good camera to take photographs of all locations visited. Some locations can be captured with single pictures taken with a wide-angle lens, whereas other locations require full panorama coverage to properly evaluate them afterward. To take a panorama photograph (on a camera without a stitch function), stand in one spot and take photographs from left to right (or vice versa), ensuring you overlap the pictures a little. Afterward, stitch the photos together using photo manipulation software, or print out the photos and overlap and tape them together, pasting them into a file folder for presentation — the method to use will depend if the production team prefers to review the pictures electronically or in hard copy. Jot down the address, the owner name, and other logistical restrictions regarding each photographed location in an accompanying document, or in the file folder next to the actual photos. It is also good to note the date and the time of day so that the DP can consider the direction of the light.

Some crews capture video of the location along with the stills to further preview the look of a particular location. Still pictures are best because you can lay two locations side by side on a table to see how they match (or not) for the story and preview the visual edit between them.

LOOK OF LOCATION & REDECORATION

The look of the location will be the first and most obvious consideration. Can, however, the walls be repainted? Are there other redecorations that might need to be done to make this location work alongside other sets and locations? Might you need construction to bring in a flying wall from the set to match the exterior location here to an interior set at the studio? Have these types of temporary changes been considered in the budget? Will the owners allow redecoration, remembering that you have to redecorate back after the shoot is done?

COST OF LOCATION

To properly negotiate the cost of the location, you have to ask yourself and the owners a number of questions. How much access is needed: how much of the property and for how long? Do you need to move owners out of their property into a hotel for the duration of the shoot? Do you need to compensate the owner for loss of business during those days? Also consider the costs of permits, parking lots in the neighborhood, and compensation to other neighbors for disturbing access to their properties.

THE LOCATION & THE SCHEDULE

Are there any restrictions regarding the availability of the location? Are there other bookings already to work around? Are the other bookings temporary and are you able to offer a confirmed booking soon?

PERMITS, RESTRICTIONS & SENSITIVE ISSUES

Consider the permits you need and the time frame required to arrange for them. Also consider what restrictions the owner imposes, or sensitive issues the owner has about the property — like no smoking inside, reduced light level in certain rooms to preserve expensive paintings, no allowances for redecoration, and so on.

INSURANCE

What are the insurance needs for this location? Does the owner need to be listed as an additional insured on the production's policy? What is the minimum coverage required?

TIME OF SHOOT

How much access to sun does this particular location really receive? What direction is it facing? Consider the sunrise and set times, the tide schedule, or the traffic patterns and how any of these issues may affect the shoot on the day.

WEATHER

What is the weather like at this location? Is it predictable or not? Is it at the base of a mountain during rainy season, where it is likely you will have rain every day? Is it a waterfall that is trickling now, but with spring runoff will be blasting water off the rock within a few weeks? If you have to move to weather cover on the day, is there the potential for an interior location nearby?

NOISE OF THE LOCATION

Do not forget sound. If you want to use the location sound that is being recorded, consider if you are under an airplane landing path at this location. Is there an active railway track nearby? Do the pipes clank and crack when the heating in the building is on? Take a moment to really listen to the location.

POWER AT LOCATION

Production probably has a generator already, but if your budget is so low, you may be looking for locations where you can tie-in to existing power and pay the owner's power bill later. Consider this. If you are looking at potential studios, what is the power at this stage? There are different phases of power at different stages, and you need to be sure the studio space can handle all the equipment production is planning to load in. If you are bringing equipment from other countries, there is another factor to consider: the electricity cycles are different, too.

COMBINING LOCATIONS

What other locations are nearby that production may be able to use? Is there a room in this house, for example, that can be used as an office set for elsewhere in the script while the rest of the house is the house set? Combining locations in one place removes the need for some company moves and saves production a huge amount of time that can be spent preparing and shooting actual shots instead of driving around.

CREW & UNIT PARKING

How long is the unit? How many feet of curb space do all the trucks take up? Consider the location of the unit trucks and crew parking. Where will the hair/makeup/wardrobe and dressing room trucks be (also known as the base camp or the circus)? Will you need to hire Drivers to shuttle the cast and the crew back and forth from base camp to set all day to minimize travel time walking? Think through the crew equipment load in. Are there accessible doors and elevators at the location to ease this job?

ACCESS TO LOCATION & THE ZONE

How accessible is this location to major roads and to bus lines for crew who do not have cars? Is it close to other potential locations? Is it close to equipment rental houses? Is it in the union "zone" where production does not have to pay for travel time, hotels, and per diems to the cast and the crew?

TRAFFIC PATTERNS

Do you need to close a road to shoot at this location, even temporarily? What might you need to do this? Most places require permits and off-duty police paid for by production to allow you this permission, with daily A.D.s assisting with directing traffic. Some small towns may even allow you to take two road-closed signs and off you go.

LUNCH LOCATION

Consider where you will have all the lunch tables and lunch truck set up. Is there space at this location for this?

SERVICES IN AREA

Note services in the area around this location: the closest hospital with emergency services, food services in case you break for second meal, hardware stores, photocopy stores, and fuel stations.

OTHER ISSUES & EXTRA COSTS

Consider dressing space, equipment space, storage space, bathrooms, and security issues too. Can you lock up and have security here overnight, or do you have to return the equipment to your secured studio every night? What extras are being charged? Studios may charge you for the stage rental, but add on costs for use of the telephone, dressing rooms, and so on. Also consider hidden costs, like the need to rent a parking lot near the location because there is no access to parking at the location of choice.

PREP & WRAP TIME

How much prep and wrap time does the Art Department and technical departments need beyond the shooting time you need at this location? Negotiate a lower daily location fee on prep and wrap days. Who of the crew really needs to survey the location, so you can minimize multiple surveys and possibly annoy the owners? Are the owners informed of all the access requirements of production?

NEIGHBORS & THE COMMUNITY

What is the history of filming in this neighborhood? The Government Liaison office will know. Has production considered how to "give something to the community," as well as the location fee to the owner? Is there a greening project that the film company can take on to demonstrate to the community that the film industry is concerned about the environment and is grateful for their support in the making of this film? A film shoot is a huge endeavor, and the neighbors are being very gracious putting up with the inconvenience of your being there. Think about how to thank them for it, to leave a good feeling behind when you depart.

CREW MEETINGS ABOUT LOCATIONS

The Location Scout or Manager needs to present location choices, not location decisions, at these meetings. She will present the photographs and the comments about the issues that have been thought through so far about each location. Certainly list any restrictions and sensitive issues immediately. She has been anticipating the crew's questions, but there will be more. Write the questions down and collect them. You do not want to telephone the owners every few hours with another question; you want to contact them a few times, and be professional each time.

LOCATION SURVEYS

Mini-surveys happen during preproduction when the locations become confirmed and certain crew need to visit the location to design logistically how to capture the story on film at this place. The Production Manager needs to attend as many of these mini-surveys as possible, because many story changes happen and many "ideas" (read "costs") are created during these mini-surveys.

If the owners follow the crew around during the mini-surveys, the Location Manager needs to be the liaison. Crew will ask all sorts of questions about what they can and cannot do at this location. These questions can easily scare the owner from having the crew there at all. The Location Manager has to deal with this process. Many of the crew questions at this stage are ideas, and not solid decisions. The owner always has a say in access and use of the property.

The big location survey is done during the week before the shoot. All department heads go on this survey, and production will need a mini-van or two to drive them all around to see all the possible locations of the shoot. This survey is to confirm the decisions made during preproduction, and to refresh everyone's memory about what is going to happen on set. If big decisions are changed during this survey, there is much to worry about. Discuss your concerns with the Producer immediately. Big changes at this stage cost lots of money. Can production afford these changes?

PREPARING FOR THE SHOOT

During the location decision process, the Location Manager needs to arrange for all those permits and permissions and road closures and location contracts and insurances. There will be much to follow up on from all the crew meetings and from liaising with the owners of potential locations used and not. Always follow up with the property owners, whether production chooses their location or not. Send a thank-you note to all who you considered but did not use.

There is a generic location release on page 489 that you can use as a starting base for a more detailed location agreement, but remember it is most wise to consult Legal Counsel when finalizing any and all agreements for your production.

The LM also has hired a Location Assistant team to help with the logistical management of the location on the day. She has to inform the neighbors that a film shoot will be happening in the area (see a sample letter on page 490), and will have a Location P.A. deliver the letters by hand to each neighbor.

Location maps must also be completed to attach to the call sheet, including how to find location both in pictures and in words, noting the closest hospital, too, on the map. There is more on creating location maps in Chapter 13.

LOCATION MANAGEMENT DURING THE SHOOT

Briefly, the Location Department ensures the prep team has access to the location to prepare for shooting. They also make certain there are signs to the location on the shoot day, prior to the crew's arrival, to aid in their finding the place and where to park. They assist transportation in parking the unit because they know the parking plan. They liaise with the owners and deal with any of their fears or worries. They ensure there are garbage cans and other cleaning materials available for the crew's use so the location is protected. They make sure the lunchroom is set up and ready on time for use. They ensure the place is clean at wrap and looks better than when the crew arrived that morning, and they make certain the wrap team coming in tomorrow has access and also leaves the place looking better than they found it. They may even have to shovel snow off the outdoor set because it was supposed to be spring, and it happened to snow last night. What a team!

BURNED LOCATIONS

Have respect for each location where you film. Never burn a location (leave such a bad feeling with the owners that they will never again rent their property to any film production). Your shoot may be short in duration, but if you treat a location or an owner badly, you have burned that location not just for you personally, but for all future film productions. No matter how small a production you are, you are representing the entire film industry whenever you shoot somewhere. Consider yourself a guest at the location no matter how much or little you are paying to be there. Be sure the crew that you hire has the same respect toward each location.

—⁂—

Dealing with the logistics on set of all the vehicles, the equipment, the crew, the cast, the owners of the property and the public… it is no wonder that many Location Managers become Production Managers.

WE WERE SO COVERED – OR WERE WE?

We purchased all the right insurance. We reviewed all possible coverages with the Insurance Broker and were sure we were covered for any emergency or accident. We bought coverage...

... if the air conditioning leaked onto the set causing water damage

... if a tree fell on the studio causing damage and a power outage

... if a key cast member or the Director happened to die during production

... if someone in the lab turned the light on during negative processing, fogging all the footage

... if our production office was burgled and all the props and office contents were stolen

... if the generator just blew up for no particular reason

... if anything.

We were so covered.

Then an election happened in a foreign country wherein the sure-winner incumbent was defeated by a long shot candidate and the new government immediately canceled the event wherein our film would be shown. Four days before principal photography, our funding was cut.

Now, why didn't we think of that? I wonder if you can buy foreign-election-that-directly-affects-your-funding insurance...

PRODUCTION INSURANCE

17

Insurance is something you hope you never have to use — on a film production more than anything. But the longer you are in this business, the chances grow that someday you will exercise one of the policies. This chapter introduces you to the myriad of insurances that you need to purchase for a film production, and why.

BUYING PRODUCTION INSURANCE

You buy insurance from a Broker who specializes in the film industry. The Broker will shop around from insurance company to insurance company to win good rates for you. Choose a Broker you trust, who provides you with good service, and whose rates are competitive. Do not be afraid to shop around. You will bring this Broker with you from production to production if you are happy with their service, so choose wisely the first time.

There are four basic policies you need to purchase for a film production: (1&2) Comprehensive General Liability Insurance & Worker's Compensation Insurance, (3) The Entertainment Package (or Production Package), and (4) E & O (Producer's Errors and Omissions) Insurance.

(1&2) COMPREHENSIVE GENERAL LIABILITY & WORKER'S COMPENSATION

Simply put, these policies are used if someone is injured on the set or if you damage someone's property. They are truly, utterly, essential insurance for any and all film productions. Some Financiers will require a minimum amount for your Comprehensive General Liability coverage (anywhere from $3M to $10M). Most locations you shoot at will require minimum coverage, too. The law may require

Worker's Compensation Insurance, so that you protect the cast and the crew working on the production against work-related injuries. In some jurisdictions, you may only be able to purchase this insurance through the Worker's Compensation Board itself.

(3) THE ENTERTAINMENT PACKAGE

The Entertainment Package (or Production Package) is a collection of several specific insurance policies that cover you during principal photography. You can negotiate which specific coverages, but as this is the most common collection, you will likely end up purchasing the entire package:

CAST COVERAGE

You need insurance should the critical lead cast (or critical lead crew, like Director) falls ill or is injured by accident during the shoot and you need to suspend production for her recovery. This coverage, you see, is not just for cast as the name may imply. Usually eight to ten cast (or crew) members can be covered. Choose the most important Performers, the Director, and maybe also the DP. Should one of these people covered fall so ill as to be unable to finish the film (or to die), this coverage also kicks in to give you the money to redo the film (or parts of it) with someone else. This coverage, therefore, must equal the size of your budget. The deductible is hefty, but if you ever have to use this coverage, it will be worth it. As soon as you call the insurance company with the names of people you wish to be insured, they will be covered under accident coverage immediately. Send each person for a medical (by an insurance-approved doctor) right away, because by forwarding the medical to the insurance company, each person will now fall under full coverage (both accident and illness coverage). The Production Coordinator can arrange for speedy medicals.

FAMILY BEREAVEMENT COVERAGE

Imagine if one of the key cast has a family member die, and you find you have to suspend production for a day to reschedule around the funeral. You need this insurance. It covers the costs associated with that type of interruption. You cannot claim the full budget price.

FAULTY STOCK, CAMERA & PROCESSING

For film negative, imagine the light going on in the lab during processing. It can happen. It has happened. Hope it does not happen to you. If the raw production media (film stock, tape stock, digital capture stock), camera equipment, or the processing/transferring is faulty, you may need to re-shoot up to the entire film. Again, this coverage needs to be equal to the size of your budget. In order for the coverage to be effective, it is required that the Camera Department shoot, process and/or transfer, and view a camera test using the equipment they will be shooting with during the shoot. You cannot just pick up a camera, shoot with it, and then complain to the insurance company it is not working properly if you have not taken the time and the effort to check the equipment prior to renting.

NEGATIVE FILM/VIDEOTAPE (THE "PRODUCTION MEDIA")

This coverage works basically in tandem with the Faulty Stock, Camera & Processing coverage, and is a more general coverage for problems with the production media (which could be the digital original once image is captured, the original sound elements, or the original negative or videotape, for example). Exclusions from this coverage are the reason that Faulty Stock, Camera & Processing coverage was created.

PROPS, SETS, WARDROBE

Be sure this coverage exceeds the entire cost of your props, sets, and wardrobe rentals put together. Some set rentals, props rentals, and wardrobe rentals are so pricey on their own that the company you are renting from will require proof that your insurance coverage is adequate for them to allow the rental. In these cases, you need to call your Broker after the coverage is in place to arrange for a separate, personalized certificate of insurance proof.

PHYSICAL DAMAGE TO VEHICLES

When you set up a rental vehicle company account, you need to insure all the vehicles you are renting. Using the vehicle rental company's daily or weekly rental rates may be higher than this insurance, which you can arrange separately. Again, you will need to arrange with the Broker for a separate, personalized certificate of insurance proof for the rental company. With a mere telephone call, you can arrange this.

MISCELLANEOUS EQUIPMENT

"Miscellaneous equipment" is all the equipment you are renting, including the camera equipment. You will not be able to rent any camera, grip, electric and sound equipment without this coverage. Note, too, that office equipment for the production office is not considered "miscellaneous" and shows up on another coverage further down the list.

PROPERTY DAMAGE LIABILITY

When you rent a location or a studio, you may be taking "care, custody, and control" of that location or studio. Imagine renting Studio #1. The comprehensive general liability insurance you have already purchased covers damages and injuries to property and people outside the building and in the hallways of the studio space, but inside Studio #1 itself you need this coverage — because the comprehensive general liability is not in effect inside Studio #1 due to your having "care, custody and control" of this space. Every location where you shoot you may be assuming "care, custody and control" of at least a portion of it, so you will need this insurance. Either you call your Broker for each location you contract, or your Broker will set you up with blank "location certificates" to fill out the location name, the address, the owner's name, and the shooting dates to arrange for speedy personalized certificates to prove coverage. Do not forget to send a copy of all the completed certificates to the Insurance Broker, along with the owner of the location.

EXTRA EXPENSE

This coverage works in conjunction with other coverages. If the miscellaneous equipment coverage ends up paying for the replacement of a piece of rented equipment, it will not pay for the flight or the ferry ride for the replacement equipment's trip to the set, nor the downtime or the overtime to production waiting for the replacement equipment. Extra expense coverage will take care of this.

CIVIL AUTHORITY

This coverage kicks in, for example, when a civil authority declares a hazard in the area or in the building, and you are prevented from filming because of that declaration.

DISRUPTION OF OUTSIDE POWER

This coverage kicks in when there is a disruption of power beyond your location's local control. Imagine the city generator breaking down, creating a power outage that lasts long enough for you to need to re-shoot the day's work. This is one example of when you may trigger this coverage.

MECHANICAL BREAKDOWN

This coverage is another one that works in conjunction with other policies, especially the miscellaneous equipment coverage, to ensure full coverage when equipment breaks down.

OFFICE CONTENTS

Office contents include computers being rented, furniture, office televisions, and playback machines. All these are covered with this insurance. This coverage is useful to replace equipment when someone breaks into the production office and steals it all, but remember that in a few days all the equipment will be brand new, so the thief may return for a second visit. Such dual robberies are not uncommon. It goes without saying that you will need an office security system to minimize using this coverage, because even a few days without equipment in the office is horrific.

IMPAIRMENT OF COMPUTER SERVICES - MALICIOUS PROGRAMMING

Since reliance on computers is so acute for the entire production and postproduction process, this coverage is essential. It kicks in when your production is actually impaired by electronic data recovery costs and production loss due to malicious programming by either an insider or outsider.

MONEY & SECURITIES

As long as the petty cash in the production office is locked in a safe and the safe is broken into — and you can prove without a doubt how much money was in there — then you can make a claim on this coverage.

ANIMAL MORTALITY

If you are renting animals and one of them happens to die, you will have to pay the rental company (or wrangler) for the value of that animal, plus look for another that looks exactly the same to "re-cast" and re-shoot accordingly. Use this coverage to ease the financial burden. Note though, that this coverage does not cover your mistreatment or negligent use of any animals. It is even possible to include a particular animal on your cast coverage if the animal is very difficult to replace.

STUNTS, SPECIAL EFFECTS & OTHER COVERAGES

Discuss with your Broker other coverages that you may need or are available for your production. You can basically dream up anything else that could cost you money if it goes wrong, and you can buy insurance for it. The world of insurance is wide open.

(4) E & O INSURANCE (PRODUCER'S ERRORS & OMISSIONS INSURANCE)

The above three policies help you through production, but you will likely need limited E & O insurance during production, and definitely a complete E & O policy prior to releasing or airing the completed project. Your exposure to the risks of E & O increases as you exhibit the production to a wide audience.

We all know of lawsuits when someone sues a Producer or a Writer, saying that the Producer or the Writer stole his idea. This is a job for E & O Insurance. Errors & Omissions Insurance, once you have the coverage in place, says that you — the Producer — have done all the research necessary to prove that this idea was original (or purchased rightfully from the Creator), that these fictional locations as portrayed on screen truly do not exist, that the fictional character names are indeed fictional, that the music you hear on the soundtrack is original or courtesy of written permissions, and so on… but there is a chance the Producer made an error or an omission during all that research, and one of the legally "clear" items is not actually clear at all. E & O Insurance is a kind of "Producer malpractice" insurance.

Now you cannot refrain from doing all the research, and then purchase E & O insurance to protect yourself against lawsuits. No one sells "Stupidity" insurance. You have to do the research and the preparation in order to qualify to buy E & O coverage. You have to buy all the necessary music rights. Also, for example, you have to research to be sure there is not an actual dentist called John Smith in the "script" city — because your production depicts the murderer as a dentist called John Smith from a particular city, and this inclusion alone insinuates that the real John Smith is a murderer and you are labeling him so, whether you intend to or not. The real John Smith probably will not like your portrayal of him on film, and you will have to do a name change on the character. Be sure to acquire all the written permissions for all the product names you show on screen, or "greek" all the product names so that no one can read them. All this work makes sure your film is "clear." Once clear, then you will qualify to buy E & O insurance. There are research companies to help you with all this research work (see Chapter 33), but you will also need a professional team in the Art Department to be mindful of "clear" and "not clear" logos all over the screen before the images are committed to a shot.

The reason why you do all the research and work and then buy the E & O policy is because no Broadcaster wants to air your show and no Festival wants to show your film and no Distributor wants to sell your film without legal proof that it is "clear." If they do distribute or exhibit your film, and you do have questionable or unresearched legal clearance issues in it, not only you, but the Broadcaster, the Festival, and/or the Distributor can also be sued. People looking to sue in these cases are looking for companies with money, and they usually end up suing several people and companies at the same time to maximize the possibility of a settlement. You may be a poor Producer, but the rich Broadcaster or Distributor will also be a target. So do not think that because you have little to no money that you are above being sued and therefore do not need to do the research of a Producer with more money. In this case, you will have a hard time trying to sell your film without E & O coverage. Most companies who participate in the distribution of your film will need to be added as an Additional Insured on your policy to further secure their coverage.

During production you will have done some of the research, like script clearances, but not all of the research —because the music has not been added in postproduction yet, and filming is not yet complete, so logos showing up on screen in the final cut are still uncertain. You can still buy the E & O policy during production. It will be a policy with exclusions (especially exclusions for music rights), and some Financiers may require such a limited policy in place during the shoot. Once the production is completed and just before delivery, the policy can be amended to remove the exclusions when you supply the rest of the research to your Legal Counsel, who will report to your insurance company. Since Legal Counsel is involved, talk to them early about clearance issues.

CORPORATE POLICIES

If a company is planning to shoot several productions within the year, it may be cheaper to insure the parent company rather than buy separate policies for each production. Your Insurance Broker will be more than happy to discuss insuring several or future projects for you or the parent company.

ADDITIONAL INSUREDS

The production company is not the only one at risk in the making of a film. As you know, when it comes to lawsuits, "they" always look for the entity with money to sue, and "they" often end up suing several people or companies at the same time. If George Lucas is your Executive Producer, you can bet anyone suing you will also be suing your Executive Producer. Therefore, all the Financiers, Distributors, Broadcasters, Executives and their personal companies, and the Director and his personal company will ask to be named as "Additional Insureds" on the production and E & O policies. These people and companies need assurance that if you are sued along with them, it is not their own private insurance policy that takes effect, but the Production policies that you bought for this particular film. Certain locations owned by large companies and other big suppliers may also ask to be added as an Additional Insured to the entire policy. The Broker and the insurance company will expect this process, so you will find there is no extra charge to create these certificates.

INSURING MICRO-LOW-BUDGET SHOOTS

Micro-budget films cannot afford a full insurance package. If you only have $40,000 cash to get your film in the can (shot and transferred or processed), paying for a full insurance package will ensure you will not have enough money to make the film at all. You will have to manage most of the risks of production on your own. Which insurance coverages, however, will you really need for a micro-budget shoot?

Equipment Insurance: You will need insurance on the equipment you are borrowing instead of renting, because at the budget range you are working in, you cannot afford to replace any of the equipment should something befall it. Find out the current replacement value for even one of your studio lights. The cost is huge. No equipment house will let you borrow equipment, even on a favor, without insurance coverage.

Liability Insurance & Worker's Compensation: In case someone sues you, or in case an injury happens on set and someone sues you, you cannot afford to be without these coverages.

E & O Insurance: Do all your research to ensure a "clear" film, and purchase E & O insurance so that you can sell, distribute, and showcase your film after it is completed. This is an industry. You are not making films only to show your friends in your basement.

INSURANCE CLAIMS

Hoping you never have an insurance claim will not help you prepare if you do have one. Insurance policies are for when something is out of your control; you may have to file a claim some day. In short: Be honest, be clear, and be organized.

RESEARCH IT AND ACT ON IT

When an event that causes a possible insurance claim happens, the first thing you need to do is research it with the Producer and whoever else is required for the particular event. How much damage is caused? What is the nature of the damage? What will it take to repair the damage? When can you reschedule? Can you shoot around some of the damage? Set must continue working at the fast pace of principal photography, and you will find that you have to put into effect the repair plan long before the insurance claim is completed, and likely before the insurance filing is completed. Research, decide on a course of action, and set it into motion. You have to finish the film.

REPORT IT

Report the "accident" to the Insurance Broker as soon as possible — even if you are not sure if this will be a true insurance claim or not. Soon the insurance company will need a full report of the accident event and damage. You are already completing production reports daily. The DPR notes need to summarize the accident concisely. Get supplementary written reports from all people related to the accident. The insurance company will need these too. The insurance company needs to do research on the entire incident. The more you prevent information from getting to them, the more time they will take to conduct their research.

COST IT OUT

You need to account immediately what the costs were associated with the accident. How much will it take to repair the damage? Have you already rescheduled the lost day? The insurance company will analyze what the day cost that you lost, and give you that monetary amount to redo the day. They will not replace a lost cheap day with the cost of a new expensive day. You have to prove beyond a shadow of a doubt how much money you lost with the incident. You will probably have to assign a person to just do this and report this. Be sure the accounting report is clear to read and understand. Some people think they are being smart by padding an insurance claim by 60%, expecting the insurance company to slap on a "standard" deduction and maybe coming out ahead. Well, insurance companies will only discount questionable or unproven costs; if they discover you have padded the insurance claim budget, they will (rightfully) treat you with much less respect, and you may find your insurance claim takes an extraordinary amount of time to be evaluated (as they evaluate which costs may indeed be fraudulent). It pays to be accurate and honest.

The deductible you pay to the insurance company will automatically reduce the contingency in the budget, of course. When you have estimated the cost of the claim, you can create a new line in the cost report, near the insurance line, to track the monies due from the insurance company to pay for the overages associated with the claim.

SUMMARIZE IT

Put together a package for the insurance company of all the documentation they need, including production reports, call sheets, and summary of costs related to the accident. The adjuster will have a list of documentation she needs to review, so include this information in an easy-to-read package to help speed up her review of your file.

CASH FLOW IT

Insurance companies will work as fast as they can, but they have a different set of work hours than those on a film set. Insurance claims take time. The larger the claim, the more due diligence the insurance company has to undertake during their research. You will have to cash flow all the overages (front the money) associated with the accident out of production as it is now. Meet with the Accountant and the Producer to discuss a strategy for cash flowing production through the insurance claim wait. The insurance deductible will be deducted off the amount the insurance company pays you on settlement, so at least you do not have to write a check!

FOLLOW UP ON IT

It is essential you follow up with the insurance company. You are working for a production company that has an end date or a wrap date close in sight. Insurance companies have no contractual end dates, so their linear working priorities differ from yours dramatically. You have to keep the claim alive to see it to resolution as soon as possible.

—⁓—

You are now insured. You are now covered. The myriad of policies is not such a mystery to you anymore. All you need do now is hope you never have to use any of them. Still, you can rest at night anyway, because you are prepared if you have to make a claim.

THE GUY FROM THE BOND

There was a day when the crew was most tired, and the indecision between the key creative personnel was most high. Shooting inched along and there was no end in sight. This was the day that would not end. This was the day the Guy From The Bond came to set. It was a fateful day.

We all knew that Bonders only really visit a set when there is a serious problem. He must be questioning if the production was going over-budget or may not be finished on time. Still, we put aside our initial worries and said to ourselves he must have been in the neighborhood and just dropped by for a visit. So what if the set was a mere 4-hour drive from the Bonder's office?

But then he came back the next day. That is when the worry really set it. You have to give credit to the whole crew, though. We bonded together in worry and worry we did. Nerves were taut. Tension was thick in the air. I mean we knew all about the Guys From The Bond. They were wicked, evil people, who take over film productions and fire everyone from the Producer on down whenever they feel like it. They would fire you if you so much as blinked in their presence. They ate ground glass for breakfast, and they pulled wings off of butterflies for pleasure. They were certainly not anyone you dare cross.

This Guy From The Bond had to be particularly evil because he wore the guise of a nice guy. He smiled all the time. He hung out and chatted with crew. He was friendly. He had good jokes and a great sense of humor. But we were not taken in. He had to be evil. We knew he was the Guy From The Bond and we knew why he was here. But, who would be first to go?

Daily he showed up on set. Nerves stayed as tight as bowstrings. Sweated brows were rampant, with the key creative personnel leading the sweating contest. Still, we kept on shooting and waiting for the Guy From The Bond's move. He kept on hanging out with us and telling us stories of his days on set when he was in production. Days turned into weeks. The last day of shooting was coming ever closer.

Sighting distance from the end of production it finally happened.

One of the crew whispered to another, "You know, I think that Guy From The Bond really is a nice guy." There was a pause. A thought. Another whisper. And another. Word started to go around. This Guy From The Bond was not here to fire an entire crew. He was here to lend his production expertise to the key creative personnel to make sure the film would be finished on time. He used to work in production. We knew all his stories. Maybe we should give him a chance.

The Guy From The Bond stayed with us to the end of shooting, and we said our goodbyes to him as if he were part of the crew just like us, which in a way he was. His presence alone was the pressure that made the key creative personnel decisive enough to finish the film on time. And we were saved from the production that would never end. What a nice guy!

COMPLETION BONDS | 18

Financiers, Distributors, and Broadcasters through equity investments, advances, or presales have given you lots of money to make your film. But they are not in the business of funding production companies for the fun of funding production companies. They are buying into a finished film product, even though prior to delivery of the film, the "product" does not even exist yet. This makes their investment hugely risky; therefore they will want insurance on their investment that you are indeed going to finish the film, so they will have a product to distribute and sell to make their investment back and put them into profit. You need "completion insurance." This type of insurance is very specialized and is called a completion bond or a completion guarantee.

Now, there are a ton of things that can go wrong from preproduction to post and prevent you from finishing the film. You cannot just go back to the Financiers and say, "Sorry, we didn't do it." If you do not finish the film, the Financiers will want all their money back, and no doubt you will have spent a fair chunk of it prior to abandoning the project. Completion Guarantors (or Bonders) promise the investors that there will be a finished film on delivery, and that the project will not go over-budget. If the Producer cannot finish the film, the Bonder will step in, take over the production from the Producer, and finish it. There will be a finished film on delivery. This is a lot of comfort to Financiers.

WHEN YOU NEED (OR MIGHT NOT NEED) A BOND

Your Financiers will tell you if you need a bond. It will be a requirement noted in their investment agreements.

Micro-budget films rarely have completion bonds because realistically they cannot afford to buy one, and the budget on a micro-budget film is bound to be so low that the Bonder would look at the budget and say, "Heck, we could never finish the film for that little money!"

And, of course, if you are personally funding most of the money yourself, then you do not need any insurance to assure yourself you will finish the project. It is in your best interest to finish it.

Studios rarely have bonds too, because if the show is going over-budget, they have the buying power to raise the budget and flow extra money to production to finish it — therefore never going over budget at all. Raising the budget is not an automatic reaction by any means, of course. The studio will have to consider if raising the budget means they may still recoup the original budget plus the overage when the show is in distribution.

WHO DEALS WITH OR READS A BOND

The Producer will primarily deal with the details of reading the drafts and acquiring the bond, but the Production Manager will end up involved to a point too, as money transactions are critical to the bond coming into place, and some documentation needs signatures that you and the Production Coordinator can arrange. Some Production Managers will be more involved in arranging for the bond due to their experience dealing with the bonding company. In any case, it is good to read the bond and understand its demands and requirements.

HOW MUCH PAPER MAKES UP A BOND?

A completion bond is made up of a veritable ton of legal documentation, because the promise the Bonder is giving to the investors is hugely complex. Various bonding companies differ on the actual required documents, but this guide will help you to understand why so much documentation is necessary and what the various documents mean, some of which you will arrange to have signed.

VARIOUS REFERENCE DOCUMENTATION

Bonders need a full and ongoing picture of the production. If they have the ability to take over your production at any time, they must be kept informed of all facets of the production as it proceeds. You need to furnish them with: incorporation documents, scripts, cost reports, cash flows, production reports, insurance certificate, all financing agreements, interim financing agreement, co-production agreements, Broadcaster agreements, distribution agreements, chain of title, bank account information, cast contracts, key creative crew contracts, key location or studio contracts, prep schedule, shooting schedules, and post schedules. The Coordinator usually keeps the Bonders in the loop of ongoing paperwork, while the Production Manager takes care of the more confidential financing documentation.

"THE BOND"

The document one can call "The Bond" is an agreement between the Bonder and all the Equity Financiers being insured. It is a thick document that spells out the terms of the bond, how to call in the bond, what specific items the Bonder will deliver for the Financiers to the Distributor and/or the Broadcaster(s) if they have to take over the production, and other details. It is worth reading this document. Each Bonder has a standard template, but each Bonder's is different. To clearly identify the deliverables being promised, the Bonder will mark up the pages in all distribution, broadcasting, and investment agreements that note what deliverables are required, stating exactly what items are physically being promised. If the agreement says the Producer promised one viewing copy to a certain investor in their agreement, the Bonder will promise that delivery. If the Producer promised an EPK (Electronic Press Kit), if available, and fifty promotional slides to a Broadcaster in their agreement, the Bonder will promise delivery of the fifty slides. The fifty slides is a firm and specific promise, the EPK is not.

PRODUCER-BONDER AGREEMENT

This agreement spells out the terms of the bond for the Producer's perspective, what is expected of the Producer, the cost of the bond, and what happens if the Bonder takes over.

PRODUCER CONTROL LETTER OR OBLIGATION LETTER

This letter basically gives control of the production from the Producer to the Bonder "right now." The Producer signs this letter, and the Bonder files it away and only produces it again on the day the Bonder walks in to take over the production from the Producer.

BANK-BOND AGREEMENT

Presuming the Bank is also the Interim Financier on the production — and therefore loaning the production money to meet its cash flow needs — the Bank and the Bonder have an agreement that spells out the terms of access to money, taking the interim financing agreement into consideration. The Bank, the Producer, and the Bonder also sign this agreement.

BANK LETTER

The Bank, the Producer, and the Bonder sign this letter. It grants the Bonder access to the production bank account and all the production funds in it in order to complete the film.

POST FACILITY/LAB ACCESS LETTER

The post transfer facility (or production lab), the Producer, and the Bonder sign this agreement giving the Bonder access to the digital original or negative of the film (the "production media") at the post facility in order to complete the film for the Financiers. The Producer retains ownership of the digital original or negative, but grants the Bonder access to it, just as he grants such rights with distribution agreements. The Producer should never give up ownership of the digital original or negative.

DIRECTOR LETTER

The Director of the production has to sign a letter confirming that she believes that this production can be produced with the budget and the shooting schedule provided.

FIRST A.D. LETTER

Depending on the bond, the First A.D. may also be required to sign a letter confirming that the shooting schedule is adequate for this film to be completed on time.

If the Director or the First A.D. does not want to sign this letter, you have a problem. Do they really believe there is not enough time or money to complete this project? It is best you know this now. Make changes to the schedule or the budget, or replace the crew with people who believe there is enough time and money to complete the project. You cannot afford to start making a film with key crew members already planning to shoot over-budget and add extras days to the shooting schedule prior to your shooting the first frame of film.

WHAT IS THE STRIKE PRICE?

No Bonder will take over the production until the strike price is met. But what exactly is a strike price? The strike price is calculated as the entire budget minus all deferrals. The bonder is an insurance company. They do not put any money at risk. If they take over production, they have to have all the money of the budget to complete the film, and cannot afford for a Financier to be so upset the Producer is not finishing the film that the Financier decides to stop flowing money to production. The Bonder tallies what monies have been forwarded from the Financiers to the Producer so far, and deducts them from the full budget price, along with any production deferrals. Then they look at the amounts not yet paid by the Financiers. They will take over production (only if needed) when the Financiers have given their entire investment, or the Interim Financier has given the equivalent as an interim loan, to the production bank account. This procedure ensures the Bonder only has to pay the over budget costs in order to complete the production.

REBATE BONDS vs. REGULAR BONDS

Completion bonds can be structured two different ways. Each affects the production's cash flow differently and dramatically. Most Bonders offer both types of bonds.

Rebate bonds charge a high fee in preproduction (the gross bond fee); if the Producer finishes the film on time and on budget, the Bonder gives back a pre-determined rebate on the cost of the bond. Financiers often let the Producer keep this rebate as a bonus for finishing the production on time and on budget, instead of requiring it be considered production revenue and therefore payable to them to recoup their investment. The downside to rebate bonds is that you must have the cash up front to pay for the hefty fee, and this strains your cash flow.

Regular bonds charge a lower fee up front, but there is no rebate on delivery. This type of bond is easier on the cash flow, as you require less cash in preproduction to pay for it. As the Producer shoots more and more productions on time and on budget, the fee for the regular bond slowly decreases as added incentive for finishing on time and on budget.

If you and the producing team are relatively new, a rebate bond may be your only choice — as you will be a high risk to the Bonder, since your team does not yet have a track record completing productions on your own on time and on budget. A rebate bond may also be required in cases where the production has an excessive list of complexities, including: visual effects, water, stunts, remote locations, and so on.

WHAT HAPPENS WHEN THE BOND IS CALLED IN

The Equity Financiers that signed "The Bond" are the only ones who can call in the bond. The Producer cannot decide someday that production is going badly and call in the bond himself. The Financiers have to basically lose confidence in the Producer.

Now, Bonders do not want to take over a show. They are insurance people. They do not want to produce movies. They want to collect premiums. But many of them are ex-Production Managers and ex-Production Accountants. They do know a thing or two about making films. They can finish the film for you. They have also been reading your production reports and cost reports regularly. They are not stupid, and they will recognize when you are in trouble. If you fail to give them timely production and/or cost reports, they will become concerned. Are you hiding something? You could be hiding what you think is only inexperience or a mild case of incompetence. Well, inexperience might muddle through and go over-budget and incompetence may not finish the film at all.

Before the Bonder takes over the production, they will visit your set… often. They will be checking out the problems they may have to inherit and strategizing how to fix them. On these visits they will likely put pressure on the weak links of the production to work harder to finish on time and on budget. Remember, though, that when a Bonder comes on board, they are looking to make big changes. They will not be looking to replace the Third Grip, but they will consider what to do with the key creative personnel: the Director, the First A.D., the DP, the Producers. They may even consider changing the Production Manager and the Production Accountant. These are the people that sweat when the Bonder comes to visit the set.

When the takeover happens, the Bonder will most likely restructure quickly. They have already visited the set a number of times, so they have notes on where the weak links are, and they have already planned how to fix those links. Any or all of the First A.D., the Director, the DP, or the Production Manager may be replaced. The Producer is technically already gone because the Bonder has used the Producer Control Letter on the day of the takeover. Rarely will any of the rest of the crew be replaced. The Bonder needs the crew to complete the film. After such a radical change, the film carries on and will be completed. The Bonder will pay for anything over-budget that is required to finish the film, and finish it they will.

The Producer will have a hard time finding another Bonder to bond her future productions, so will probably have to produce shows small enough to require no bond at all for a few years or so — until trust can be built up again that this Producer can finish projects on time and on budget.

It may not be the end of the world, but needless to say, you do not want your production to be taken over by the Bond. Do what you can to finish the production on time and on budget. As a Production Manager, that is why you have been hired.

THE PM'S RELATIONSHIP WITH THE BOND

Remembering that Bonders are often ex-Production Accountants or ex-Production Managers, and knowing that Producers can and do call them for advice when hiring Production Managers, it behooves you to get to know the Bonder well, and keep them informed. Let the Bonder know what is going on during production. Never, ever lie to them. They will figure it out, and they will remember you for it. You need to keep up a regular conversation with the Bonder.

ALTERNATIVES TO A BOND

Some Financiers on smaller productions allow these alternatives to your purchasing a completion bond:

FEES IN ESCROW

If the production is small enough and the budget is modest enough, but the Financier requires some sort of guarantee that the film will be finished, you may be instructed to put a negotiated amount of cash into a separate escrow account at the Bank until the Financier allows release of these funds on delivery or audit. It works a bit like a trust fund. Funds in escrow do not help your cash flow at all, because you need real cash in the Bank doing nothing, but when the funds are released, they go back to you instead of having to reduce the production costs to cover an insurance premium to the Bonder. If you get into trouble finishing the film, the Financiers will direct you to spend the escrow money on production over-budget costs (probably instructing you to reduce the Producer fees while doing so to minimize overages), and the escrow money goes to the production instead of returning to your bank account.

WITHHELD FEES

If you have a significant trust level with the Financiers, and the production is small enough and the budget is modest enough, you may be instructed to withhold fees in lieu of purchasing a completion bond. Fees that are targeted for being withheld are primarily Producer fees and Corporate Overhead. The Financier will decide on how much of the fees need withholding, and you need to draft an agreement or a promissory note that these fees will remain unpaid until the Financier directs you to pay them — usually on delivery. Withheld fees are kindest to your cash flow. You do not need to have cash up front to pay for a completion bond or to put into an escrow account. The Producer and head office company, however, have to survive with partially deferred fees until the production is completed and delivered. If the project gets into trouble and is in fear of not being delivered, or of going over-budget, the Financiers can instruct the Producer to funnel the withheld fees to production costs instead of to himself and the head office production company. The incentive to finish the project on budget and on time is huge.

—⁘—

Your production has a completion bond, and you have started to set up your relationship with the Bonder, helping with all the paperwork to be signed to complete the bond's requirements. If you are good at managing the budget and bringing in the show on time and on budget — everything from hiring the right team to managing the cash flow — the Bonder will recognize these skills and respect you for them. You will end up with the pride of completing a project on time and on budget, and you may also find that the Bonder has recommended you to be a Production Manager on future shows with other Producers, because it is in the Bonder's best interest for Producers to hire Production Managers like you who bring in productions on time and on budget. If you are good, word will get around. And it will probably start here at the Bonder's office.

COFFEE vs. TEA

Coffee people are more decisive than tea people, but they do love to complain a lot.

I mean, you can go to craft service and choose from a host of varieties of teas: peppermint, English breakfast, Earl Grey, chamomile, orange pekoe, Irish breakfast, black, raspberry, strawberry-kiwi, rosehip, orange spice... the list goes on and on. Whatever your tea fancy, it can be addressed and you walk away a satisfied tea-drinker.

But, if you want a cup of coffee, you can have coffee. There it is. In the pot. Coffee drinkers do not look for choice. They look for coffee. They rush to it in the morning as if it were a life-giving liquid. And then they complain about it. It tastes awful. But ask them to change brands, and they will have none of it. This is the best coffee on the market. This is their tried and true brand, and they are loyal.

Well, being a tea drinker myself, I decided that choice was what they needed. I purchase ordered a selection of coffees from the coffee supplier, and scheduled a blind taste test for the coffee drinkers. Four pots, four cups of coffee each. Let the discussion begin.

They were bit uncomfortable about all the fuss I was making about this coffee thing. They had a tried and true brand, so why fix something that is not broken? But they were all sports and participated... or at least humored me.

Coffee number one was hated by all, without question. It was too bitter and left a kind of dusty residue in the mouth. One swallow and they had become instant coffee connoisseurs. Mixed reviews came in on numbers two and three. There was serious discussion about which was watery and which was overpowering. But number four... number four. Wow! Now that was a coffee. It sang in their mouths. Just enough bite to wake you up. A balanced flavor. They all decided this one must be their tried and true brand. Next to more inferior coffees it shone its best. They regretted all the insulting they inflicted on this coffee daily. This was their coffee and they were sticking to it, for they were loyal coffee drinkers.

I had to tell them. They had been drinking number one for three years.

They switched brands instantly. By the second week, they were complaining about it already.

PETTY CASH & PURCHASE ORDERS

19

This chapter could be renamed "How To Spend Money." The Production Manager deals with money a lot, to say the very least. Monitoring money is your day-to-day activity while the rest of the crew is busy finding, buying, and making things. How do you keep track of all the crew spending and their spending promises (for a promise of money is the same as money spent)? Well, first of all, they are spending money two simple ways: with cash and with checks. No different from how you spend money at home, just on a much larger scale.

You trust the crew to spend money wisely, but you still have to monitor the outflow of money according to the budget. You discuss planned purchases with the crew. You approve all purchases they make, whether it be by cash or by check. Cash can be monitored one way: through petty cash; but checks can be monitored three ways: by direct checks, by purchase order, and by check requisition. Here is a look at all four ways that money is spent:

PETTY CASH

Checks are best for receipt proof for the audit, but sometimes items can only be purchased with cash — parking lots and parking meters, for instance. Some purchases require cash because the seller cannot wait for the time it takes for a check to be approved and written. Most stores will take cash or credit, not check, so cash is the way to go for many, many production purchases.

Petty cash is mentioned first, because it is far from petty. When floats go out to single crew members totaling four digits, you will realize the weight and the seriousness of petty-cash purchases.

Ensure that the Production Accountant and you generate an accounting procedures memo to the crew to inform them how to assemble their petty cash correctly. The crew must sign out the petty cash float assigned to them, then provide either cash and/or receipts for the full value of that float later. Crew should submit their petty cash as often as possible, first for them to stay current with a full float, and second for you and the Accountant to stay current on the costs being charged to production. You will grant a lot of trust to crew members by allowing them to spend money through petty cash, but it is a big freedom for them when spending. Wardrobe, Sets, and Props have the largest petty cash floats.

Once the petty cash report is submitted, you look it over and approve the costs being spent. Do read the reports when approving costs. Be sure they are detailed, itemizing the reason for each cost so that Accounting can code each cost easily to line items in the budget. Audits will review these reports for accuracy later. Do your due diligence now. Also, you may need to find certain receipts later. When you are trying to remember how much a certain prop item cost to purchase when you are selling it again in wrap, you need this information. When an item is being returned for being faulty, you need this information accessible, too. Take time to teach the crew early what you expect for completed petty cash reports. It will serve you well later.

Be sure the petty cash report form has space for each receipt to report the date, company name paid to, description of item, amount with and without tax, and accounting budget code space (for accounting's use only, of course). If you have ever coded a petty cash report and all its various costs to various budget line items, you will start grouping like-receipts, such as all parking receipts, for easier coding next time. Petty cash coding is a lot of work.

While you are approving the petty cash reports, you can monitor petty cash spending on the PM-Only cost report. Technically, you do not need to monitor the floats gone out to each crew member, but you do need to monitor the costs as they come in, and code them to the PM-Only cost report; however, crew do not always keep current submitting and reporting the status of their petty cash spends, and late in production you may find a crew member with a huge petty cash report that comes to you unexpectedly — only because they did not do regular (at least weekly) reports. For this reason, you need to at least note the floats and who has them (like tracking spends through purchase orders), then deduct from the float as the actual spends are reported in.

After your approval of the petty cash reports, Accounting will code each single cost on each report to line items on the cost report, then file each report alphabetically by crew member name. This process is another reason why detailed petty cash reports are essential: When looking for a specific receipt, you will have to remember first who paid for the item, so you can look up the report by his last name, then you have to remember approximately when the purchase was made to find the right report. Because of the wide variety of costs on a petty cash report, it is physically impossible to file by subject matter.

Encourage crew members to submit petty cash reports early and often. You and the Accountant need to keep current on the actual costs to production rather than just the outstanding departmental floats.

CHECKS

Checks are great receipt material for the audit. With checks you can monitor each cost separately and accurately. Using purchase orders, you can even monitor money spent by checks long before the invoices come in, and Accounting can put aside funds to cover the purchase orders to pay those bills.

DIRECT CHECKS

Direct checks are checks for bills that happen regularly, but do not have a purchase order or a check requisition as accounting backup proof for that check. This does not mean that accounting backup does not exist for these checks. All checks require backup as proof for the calculation of the expense.

Since payroll happens weekly or bi-weekly, you do not need a purchase order to requisition each payroll check. You know about it, so you can estimate its costs in advance. Accounting just prepares the actual checks when the time sheets come in. Payroll backup consists of both the time sheets and the crew deal memos.

Rent and telephone bills and other such regular bills are part of the direct checks that Accounting generates and that you approve. Note all expenses as you approve them on the PM-Only cost report.

Accounting will file each check with its backup (invoice or time sheet) alphabetically by company or crew name. Payroll files are kept separate from the other direct checks as labor costs are such a huge portion of the production's expenses, and you tend to refer to the labor costs separately from the other costs on a production. Separate payroll files let you address issues of tax forms during wrap to the calculation of tax credits based on labor at audit.

Crew members who do not write purchase orders nor check requisitions may still charge expenses to the production, surprising you and the Accountant with invoices (usually in wrap) for costs without any accounting backup. Insist on at least a check requisition to explain the cost for the audit. If you have set up and informed the crew of a clear accounting policy requiring purchase orders or check requisitions for purchases, you have the authority to refuse the cost; sometimes, of course, the expense is valid enough that you will have to pay for it anyway and take the surprise hit to the cash flow. In these cases, you will no doubt remember the crew member who regularly does not supply accounting backup to production costs when you are hiring crew for your next production. Film productions spend large sums of money quickly. There will be enough production surprises to deal with monetarily without your having to deal with surprise costs from lazy crew members who do not fill out basic accounting paperwork.

PURCHASE ORDERS (P.O.s)

You do not want everyone to have piles of cash on them to spend at will. You do not want to give blank signed checks to crew members either. Nor do you want to give them a credit card to charge expenses at will. You need to control costs. You need to approve purchases before they happen. You especially want to approve large purchases and purchases where the supplier will be invoicing production at a later date. With a warning of these invoices-to-come, you and the Accountant can set the money aside to be able to pay them when they do arrive. You want purchase orders.

Both the Production Manager and the Production Coordinator will become involved in issuing purchase orders.

WHAT IS A PURCHASE ORDER?

If invoices just came flying in through the mail and Accounting wrote checks for them all as they happened, the budget would be overspent in a hot second. You need to know about spends before they happen to ensure you have enough money in the bank account to cover the costs. No invoice should be a surprise. When an invoice arrives in the mail, the Accountant should be able to say: "Oh yeah, that."

A purchase order (when signed by the Production Manager) is a promise that the production will pay the price listed for the goods or the services ordered, even though no invoice has yet been created. Approved purchase order in hand, the Accountant can set aside the money promised and not spend it elsewhere. Treat purchase orders like contracts. Be detailed so that the Accountant can match the purchase order to the invoice when the invoice comes in days, weeks, or months later. The P.O. will form part of the backup to justify the cost in the accounting files.

FILLING OUT PURCHASE ORDERS

Ensure the crew is detailed in filling out the P.O.s. Have them include as much information as possible on the P.O. to prevent misunderstanding. Describe the item, the purchase or rental conditions, and the rental period. Mention if tax is or is not included. Note which department is initiating the purchase, and for which episode and/or set it is going to be used. If there is a work order number to refer to, use it. Any and all of this information will help the Accountant match the purchase order to the invoice when it arrives. Do not forget to note today's date. (See samples of P.O.s on pages 492–493.)

WHAT CAN YOU PURCHASE ORDER

You can purchase order pretty much anything: equipment rentals with a weekly rate, daily equipment rentals, water bottle delivery, props purchases, construction purchases, car rentals, location rentals, and so on. The list is endless. If you can promise to pay someone prior to their invoicing you, and you know (even approximately) what it is, you can purchase order it.

PURCHASE ORDER APPROVALS

As the Production Manager approves purchase orders, jot the information down on the PM-Only cost report to track spends before they happen. These costs may not be officially spent yet, but they are costs committed and that is as good as money spent.

TRACKING PURCHASE ORDERS: THE P.O. LOG

The Production Coordinator can track the P.O.s as they are written on a P.O. log form. Accounting can supply the Coordinator with a stack of numbered purchase orders and she can chart why each P.O. was used. This log form is terrific for keeping the Accountant and the PM informed of the costs as they happen, and it also doubles as a terrific inventory list for a quick and easy wrap. Log as much of that information as you can on your P.O. log form. (See a sample on page 494.) When you want to refer to a particular purchase or rental later, you will find that your P.O. log is much more efficient than sifting through the stacks and stacks of P.O.s.

SIGNING OUT PURCHASE ORDERS

The Coordinator can have crew members sign out pre-numbered purchase order forms and note who has which numbers on the P.O. log. Now you can track down any blank P.O.s with as much vigor as signed ones. A blank P.O. is pretty much as valuable as a blank check.

WHEN THE PRICE CHANGES

The objective of the purchase order is to prevent the supplier from invoicing at a higher price than what was originally agreed, but sometimes there are extenuating circumstances and price changes. If the Coordinator is tracking the purchase orders, she can find out about these situations before invoicing happens, then distribute a "canceled" version of the first purchase order, and create a new one with the correct price.

WHO NEEDS COPIES OF PURCHASE ORDERS

Once signed by the Production Manager, just like a contract, the Coordinator can distribute the P.O.: one copy to the supplier, one or two to Accounting, and one to the Coordinator's files. The P.O. log may be detailed, but you will still need a copy of the original for reference.

EXPLAIN HOW THE PURCHASE ORDER SYSTEM WORKS

The purchase order system is a great system, and it works. Use it no matter how small the production. Set up a policy that you will not pay invoices without a purchase order on it. Most suppliers will not invoice without a purchase order anyway. They know that crew rarely has the authority to authorize large purchases, and they want to be paid. Purchase orders ensure that the Production Manager has authorized the payment and production must pay when the invoice comes in.

Beyond setting up the policy, take the time to explain to the crew how P.O.s work. You may have to do this a few times, but you will find the effort worth it, and Accounting (and you) will be grateful. You do not want any surprise invoices.

CHECK REQUISITIONS

Sometimes a check needs writing immediately, like a location or a prop deposit, and you had no time to calculate an estimate of the cost prior to it happening. Since a P.O. is used to say "this invoice will be coming, look out for it," then writing a P.O. at the same time that you write the check is pointless. You still need accounting backup to explain the details of the purchase, so in this case you need a check requisition. Check requisitions give you the opportunity of explaining why the item needs to be purchased, and they give space for the Accountant to code that cost to a line in the cost report before the canceled check comes back with the bank statement. As the Production Manager, check requisitions give you the opportunity to approve checks before they are written, and to note the cost on the PM-Only cost report as it is being spent.

With a check requisition system in place, the Production Accountant will not write any checks without your approval. The crew will learn this procedure quickly.

The Production Accountant can ensure there is a supply of check requisitions available for the crew to fill out, either on the distribution table or in a wall envelope for easy access. (See a sample check requisition on page 495.)

A WORD ABOUT CREDIT CARDS

You may have noticed that I have not mentioned credit cards as a form of spending production funds. When it comes to credit cards… don't. You may be cornered into using credit cards on the odd occasion to hold a purchase until the check is cut, or to pay for the odd, difficult purchase — but use them only when you absolutely have to. Write a purchase order for each item charged to a credit card and note on the form that the purchase was paid for by credit card, so you will not be surprised when the credit card statement comes in. Pay the entire amount on the credit card when the statement comes in. Production cannot afford the interest rates on credit cards.

Some low budget films think that cash flowing the production using credit cards is the easiest way of accessing money while they hope for certain financing contracts to come through. Financing using credit cards is a superbly dangerous way of spending money. The interest rate on credit cards far exceeds any bank interim loan interest rate, so this is the most expensive money you can buy — plus the debt of credit cards follows you personally for as many years as it takes for you to pay it off, with minimum payments structured to keep you in debt forever.

If you use credit cards for holding an item until it can be paid, like for deposits, then I modify "don't" to "beware." Credit cards are dangerous in one's personal finances; in a company they turn corporate finances into personal problems.

— m —

The Auditor will be examining the accounting files for backup to all the costs spent on production. A check alone in a file is not enough information to justify a production cost. Now you are aware of several ways of justifying costs, allowing the PM to approve and track costs as they happen. Even the Coordinator delves into the land of Accounting through tracking purchase orders. Together you are beginning to keep on top of the flow of money on a production.

BUY! SELL!

Co-productions have to deal with currency exchange. A few points change in the currency exchange rate can mean hundreds or thousands of dollars in the exchange if you are receiving a large drawdown check.

In the special circumstances of one particular show, I was set up at the bank to "spot trade" the money as we received it. For spot trading, the money is held at the bank in the original currency until you telephone in and say: "Buy!" Though the bank exchange rate changes once a day, the spot rate changes as the market changes... every few minutes. You basically become a small time Trader at the market.

Since it was new territory, I leapt in with both feet. I surfed the Web for information to chart the history of the exchange rate. I researched sites that documented the history on a daily, weekly, and yearly basis, and predicted trends. I had a bookmark to the site at the bank to see what the (somewhat) latest spot rate was. I read the newspapers daily: the finance section. I discussed the financial news with Bank Officials and Professional Traders. I bored my co-workers with my own rhetoric about what I thought was happening to the market.

I was playing the market. Me. I was a player. Wow! My dad would have been proud.

Every now and then I would call the bank for the true latest spot rate. How is the rate? Is it up? Is it down? Can I live with it? How long can I play the market before I really need to trade the money? Do I have hours or days? How long can I handle the stress? How do Traders do this every day when no one ever really knows the future? Uh... uh... okay! Sell! I mean, buy! I'll take it! Trade the money!

We did fine on the exchange. I needed a massage and a holiday.

CASH FLOWS

20

Financiers give you money to make the film. But they never give you all the money up front. Since you have not even started the film, they are basically purchasing a product that does not exist yet. They are purchasing it based on trust that you will do what you say you will do, and the film will end up a fabulous, marketable film. They will, therefore, have a payment schedule for their investment: a drawdown schedule. When you make it to first day of principal photography, you can drawdown part of the investment. When you make it to the end of principal photography, you can drawdown some more. You will have drawdown triggers all the way through production and post to delivery and beyond. The question is how much are you spending on a weekly basis, and will the timing of monetary inflows match the outflows you will be spending? You need a cash flow.

The Production Accountant can help create a cash flow, or you as the Production Manager may create it.

CREATING A CASH FLOW

To create a cash flow, you will need: (1) the production schedule, (2) a list of all the Financiers and their drawdown schedules — which you can source from the financing contracts or from the Producer, and (3) the locked budget. Since cash flow creation is a lot of work, it makes sense to generate it based only on the locked budget if you can.

Just like a budget, the cash flow itself is made up of the detail pages and the summary page or top sheet. Each budget line is exploded into multiple columns for you to allocate in which week(s) or month(s) each particular cost will be spent. So open up your spreadsheet program, like Excel, because it is time to start. (A sample of part of a cash flow is on pages 496 & 497 to help visually explain the document.)

CASH FLOW DETAIL

On a spreadsheet, enter the budget down the left side in the first column (or three to ensure you include a column for accounting codes and another one for descriptions of costs). Next, enter the production schedule across the top, a different week for each column during prep, also weekly during production, and monthly during postproduction. Yes, this will be a very big form. You will, by the way, be publishing cost reports along this same pattern: weekly during production and monthly during post.

EVALUATE AND BREAKDOWN EACH LINE

Now for the bulk of the work: Regard each budget line item, and break it down to allocate it to the appropriate week(s) or month(s) in the production schedule columns. This process takes a lot of time, but the thought and the effort you put in at this stage will be worth it for a valuable, considered cash flow.

ENTER COSTS WHEN THEY ARE INCURRED

Enter the costs in the time slots in which the costs are incurred. Your cast members may not need to have their checks for week #1 actually cut until fifteen days later, but once they have finished working in week #1, the cost is already incurred. It will be like you have written a purchase order for their check, and you know that purchase-ordered money is as good as spent; therefore, note their cost during week #1 on the cash flow in the column for week #1.

DIVIDE ALL LINES

Divide fringes into the appropriate categories. Divide contingency between production weeks and post weeks at a reasonable balance. Leave nothing unspent by the end.

DEFERRALS

If someone is deferring fees, enter those fees in the last possible column. Producers may defer some of their fees to cover certain financing restrictions. Find out what any deferrals and restrictions are from the Producer.

SPREADSHEET FORMULAS & REVISIONS

If you are good with using Excel formulas, use equations regarding and references to the budget column numbers to enter all the "scheduled" costs on the cash flow. If you can do this, then you will have the ability to modify the budget, and the cash flow will automatically modify itself through the spreadsheet's references. If you do not know how to use equations and references, do not attempt to do this.

The extra work copying and typing the numbers yourself will ensure the integrity of the information in the document. Due to the complexity involved with formulas on a cash flow on spreadsheet programs, it is easy for novices to miscopy formulas and end up with a cash flow that does not add up right. Sometimes you may catch the problem, and other times not. It is not worth the mistake, visible or not.

REFUNDABLE DEPOSITS & BONDS

At the bottom of the budget and cash flow, add a few budget lines each totaling "0" and use these lines to add location deposits, union bonds, and refundable tax outlays. These are the costs you will be outlaying early in production but expecting to collect back later in postproduction, so in effect their budget total is "0." They do, however, severely affect your cash flow and bank balance. Be ready for these costs.

TOTALS

Now you can total each column of the cash flow detail for each period (week or month) for the entire production, and know how much you are spending and when.

CASH FLOW SUMMARY PAGE

The summary page or top sheet summarizes all inflows and compares them to the outflows. You can do this on one page or two depending how many columns you have for the spending schedule.

You have already summarized the outflows on the last line of the cash flow detail. Bring those totals forward onto this page.

Make a new line in the left column(s) for each funding source separately. You could have very few financing sources, or you could have upwards of fourteen. It depends on the complexity of your production. Enter the amounts they pay out on the trigger dates in the cash flow in the various production schedule columns. Total them per period (week or month). This summarizes the inflows.

Now you can find out the difference between inflows and outflows. Subtract the inflows from the outflows on a weekly basis, but remember to keep a "running bank balance" as you calculate. If you have a positive or a negative balance remaining after the first period, you must bring this balance forward into your calculations for the next period. You need to do this so you can see if and when your bank balance is predicted to drop below "0." Once you can identify the week with the most negative bank balance, you will know how much money you will need to borrow from a bank or Interim Financier in order to finance the cash flow of the project.

Leave a line on this summary sheet to include and summarize the inflow and the outflow of the interim financing loan, so you can see where it needs to drawdown, and when you have to pay it back. (See more on interim financing in Chapter 21.)

CO-PRODUCTION CASH FLOWS

For co-productions, cash flows can be twice the work. You need a separate cash flow for each co-production partner. Of course, once you have both locked which budget lines each company will be accounting and reporting, each company will be responsible for their appropriate cash flow.

AMORTIZATION & PATTERN BUDGET CASH FLOWS

As you know, the amort budget will be made up primarily of preproduction, hiatus, and post costs, whereas the pattern budget will be the repetitive episodic costs. You can create a consolidated cash flow including both pattern and amort costs, since each period during episodic shooting the pattern budget is pretty much already the cash flow itself. This makes for relatively easy cash flow detail breakdown. Be sure to note the two different budgets (amort and pattern) in two separate columns on the left of the spreadsheet.

MICRO-BUDGET CASH FLOWS

Even on micro-budget productions, creating a cash flow is worth it. How much will you really need in the bank next week? In the land of micro-budgets, you have to be superbly tight with money. Since your budget is smaller (less line items) and your shooting schedule faster (less cash flow columns), creating a cash flow will be less work anyway.

—⁂—

Now you are clear on when you are going to spend the money and when you are going to receive the money. But what are you going to do about that cash flow deficit? Read the next chapter, then call the Bank or the Interim Lender.

BANKERS & FINANCIERS AT A PARTY

We have an image of Bankers and Financiers. They wear business suits to work. They deal with serious matters and are serious people. The parties they frequent are at glorious mansions overlooking the sparkling lights of the city. They attend these parties in their business suits and, holding a glass of fine wine in one hand (they have the knowledge to choose the best one at the party) and a tantalizing hors d'oeuvre in the other, they discuss matters of great importance with the other guests. All is beautiful. All is serene.

I remember one of these parties. The conversation centered around the food, the wine, the weather, and the view out the window. They were all beautiful, and once we had exhausted trading synonyms to describe them, the conversation dwindled. I found everyone to be surprisingly uncomfortable to be there. No one seemed to know what to say to each other. Boy, we needed an icebreaker.

Well, that was until the goat cheese hors d'oeuvres started to burn in the oven...

whose smoke happened to set off the fire alarm in the house...

whose system happened to be patched directly into the fire department for immediate attention...

and whose sound happened to wake the sleeping baby in the bedroom.

It was mayhem.

But somehow it was good. Every member of the party got involved. Some people rescued the now charcoal hors d'oeuvres from the oven. Another (the mother) attended to the screaming baby. Another was on the telephone to try to stop the fire department's imminent arrival. Others ran to open doors and windows for better airflow. And a cluster of Financiers and Bankers grabbed a chair and took makeshift tools to the fire alarm itself, on the ceiling, to try to dismantle it.

It was obvious not one of them knew how it worked. They tried to discuss matters over the screams of the baby. What a feat. They had to remove their jackets to allow freer movement of their arms working over their heads. And no matter how many parts they removed of the alarm, it continued with its ear piercing shriek... or am I thinking of the baby's screams?

Anyway, finally enough parts were removed and pried off with cheese knives, spoons, and penknives that the alarm was silenced. Soon, too, the baby followed suit and was put back to bed.

We all enjoyed the silence for a moment and then it was over. Conversation struck up and flowed freely now. All jackets were off. No one was uncomfortable to be there anymore. No more discussion of the food, the wine, the weather, or the view. We had just had one heck of an icebreaker, and the party really started.

No wonder the fire department showed up anyway.

INTERIM FINANCING 21

You have a cash flow that tells you that the production bank account will be in the negative by the time you make it to the second week of shooting. You will be receiving enough money to pay for the entire budget by the very end, but you need the money now — before the film is completed, delivered, and audited. You need a Bank or lending institution to loan you money to interim finance the cash flow.

The Production Manager and the Producer deal with the details of interim financing, though the Production Coordinator should be aware of how it works, because it is the production office that keeps the interim lender informed of the goings-on of production.

WHO ARE INTERIM LENDERS?

Banks, as well as specialized financing companies, provide interim financing for film productions, but for simplicity, I will call all interim lenders by the term "Lender".

HOW LENDERS FINANCE YOUR PRODUCTION

They don't. Lenders do not invest in film productions. They do not provide equity. They do not give grants. They do not provide you interest-free advances against future sales of your production. Lenders are, however, in the business of lending money. Though they do not finance your production, they do finance your cash flow if you can prove that 100% of the production budget is covered by "bankable" paper. This is why it is probably better to use the term interim "Lender" instead of "Bank" or interim "Financier".

HOW AN INTERIM LOAN WORKS OR HOW MUCH CAN I BORROW?

Basically, you look at your cash flow and determine in which period (week or month) your bank account balance is at its most negative. When this happens depends widely on your financing sources and their drawdown schedules. For example, you may find that you go into the hole somewhat in the third week in shooting, but you recover a positive bank balance at wrap and go into a deeper hole just prior to the fine cut. You must look at the most negative number. This is the minimum amount you need to borrow. Now look at the list of final drawdowns from your financing sources. These drawdowns will likely be triggered on delivery and/or the completion of the audit of production after delivery. Choose a collection of these drawdowns to accelerate. For example, choose the "paid on audit" drawdown from three financing sources. If these Financiers are considered bankable, the Lender will basically buy these drawdowns from you and loan you the money now. Then, when you reach the audit, these three Financiers pay the Lender, not you, the "paid on audit" money. Your interim loan is paid back, and you stop paying interest on the amount loaned.

HOW THE LENDER IS PAID

The Lender will charge you a bank or financing fee (the "set up fee"), legal fees, and interest for the privilege of your receiving certain drawdowns in advance. When you are determining the size of interim loan you require on the cash flow, be sure that the Lender's many fees are noted in the cash flow when you expect to pay them. The set up fee and the legal fees are paid up front. The interest is somewhat paid up front. The Lender will take an "interest reserve" from you and hold it aside so that when the interest is payable on a monthly basis, they have a pool of your money already from which to deduct the interest amount. Remember that Lender is not in the business of risk, and you have not made the film yet, so technically you have no collateral besides cash in the bank. Therefore, you will have to pay all the interest (called "the interest reserve") up front with all the interim fees.

WHAT IS "BANKABLE PAPER?"

Lenders are not interested in high-risk loans. Even you do not want them to be: When you put your personal money into a savings account at the bank, for example, you are not looking for a high-risk investment — you want guaranteed interest income. Therefore, when you buy a house and the bank loans you money through a mortgage, you have the value of the house as collateral to borrow against. When you apply for a personal loan, you have to provide at least equivalent collateral to borrow against. During production, the film has not yet been completed, of course, so a film production technically has no collateral to borrow against.

To provide comfort to the Lender that the interim loan is going to be repaid, you need signed agreements from all your Financiers to make up 100% of your financing. This is not an easy feat. The Producer, or an Executive, will be doing most of the work to close financing. To help, you can find out what issues might be holding up the signed agreements, and if draft agreements are acceptable to the Lender to begin the legal paperwork process to speed up the interim financing close.

Lenders will evaluate the financing sources of your production and will consider some Financiers as "bankable." Government agreements of your country will no doubt be bankable. The Lender is confident that the government will forward the money required to repay the interim loan later in the process when the production triggers dictate it. Foreign television stations from small countries that this Lender has never dealt with before are likely not going to be bankable. If you want any of their drawdowns accelerated, you will have to find another interim lender to take the higher risk, or the production company must take the interim burden onto itself somehow.

If you borrow against expected receivables, like tax credits, use the budget and rules of the tax credit to calculate an estimate of how much you expect to receive. The Lender will typically require a third party opinion of the calculation to determine if it is a reasonable estimation. They will also discount your estimate, loaning you a portion (typically 75% or 85%) because we all know that much can happen between preproduction plans and the accounting of final, actual costs. Depending on how you spend the money, you may not receive the entire expected amount and the Lender will want to be in a position of little to no risk when it comes to being paid back.

WHAT PAPERWORK MAKES UP AN INTERIM LOAN

Just like the bond, a Lender requires a veritable ton of paper — agreements and other documentation — to close an interim loan. It takes time to assemble all of this paperwork, so assemble it as soon as you have locked the cash flow and know how much of a loan you require and when. You will likely need the money quickly. The Producer, or an Executive, will probably deal with arranging for all this paperwork, but do be aware of the documentation required and what it means.

INTERIM LOAN & SECURITY AGREEMENT

This is the agreement between the Lender and the Producer. It sets out the terms of the interim loan, including the interest rate, the bank fee, and the legal fees. The "security" part of this agreement is the Producer's promise to pay back the interim loan no matter what.

ASSIGNMENT OF ACCOUNTS RECEIVABLE (OR OF BOOK DEBTS)

This agreement works in conjunction with the Assignment & Directions noted below. As you are basically selling drawdowns from certain financing agreements you have with third parties, the Producer has to assign these "accounts receivable" or third party payments to the Lender.

COPYRIGHT MORTGAGE

Since there is technically no collateral, as you have not completed the film yet, the Bank will take a mortgage on the copyright of the production — the only thing the Producer owns about the film — as part of the collateral. This includes a security interest against all the "intellectual property," against all the contractual agreements (with all suppliers, performers, crew, and so on), and against all the physical elements of the production as they come into being (like the original image capture or negative, and the original sound elements as they are produced). The "bankable" signed financing agreements make up the rest of the collateral.

SECURITY AGREEMENT (OF THE PARENT COMPANY)

Since most production companies are single-purpose companies set up and owned 100% by parent companies to produce one film, the production company itself does not own much to use as collateral against the interim loan. The parent company, then, must promise to abide by the terms of the interim loan agreement alongside the production company, and if the production company cannot pay back the loan, the parent company will, no matter what. Because of this corporate structure, the parent company signs a security agreement with the Lender also.

In certain circumstances where there is no parent company, the Lender may require the individual shareholders to put up a personal guarantee in order to give the Lender sufficient collateral against the loan to give them comfort that it will be paid back. A personal guarantee could mean that the individual shareholders will have to use their own personal houses as the additional collateral.

CERTIFICATE OF OFFICERS

This certificate is primarily a statement of facts about the status of the company, and includes a certification that the company is what is says it is, has no suits against it, and will abide by the terms of the interim loan agreement.

RESOLUTION OF THE DIRECTORS

The Directors of the production company certify in a resolution that they approve the production company's entering into a financial obligation to the Lender.

INCUMBENCY CERTIFICATE

This document is simply a statement of facts about who the Directors and the Officers of the production company are.

LAB PLEDGEHOLDER AGREEMENT

If the interim loan is not paid back for some reason, the Lender would have the right to take the "security" that is held against the loan (for example, to take all the elements that make up the film including the original image capture or negative and the original sound elements). Since the post facility (the "lab") has these physical elements in its possession, this agreement is the lab's promise to keep the elements safe for the Lender, and gives the Lender access to the elements at the lab. The lab cannot release these elements to the Producer until the Lender gives their permission.

SUBORDINATION OR STEP-BACK LETTERS

The production company or the parent company may have loans that are still outstanding with other institutions. If so, remember that the Producer, the parent company, and the shareholders have just guaranteed the interim financing Lender that this interim financing loan will be paid back no matter what. The interim financing Lender takes a general security interest in the project. If the other Lenders also have a general security interest that includes the project somehow, there will be a conflict. First, you need to identify what is the primary security of the interim financing loan — it is the specific drawdown payments from the various financing contracts that you are cash flowing with this interim financing loan. Next, you need to have the other Lenders "step back" from that primary security to allow first position repayment of the interim financing loan as soon as each of those drawdown payments is triggered and the money received.

ASSIGNMENT & DIRECTION AGREEMENTS (A&D'S)

As mentioned above, for an interim loan, you have technically sold some of the Financiers' drawdowns to the Lender to receive the equivalent money up front. But the Financier agreements bind the Financier to write all checks to your production company. The Lender requires an A&D from each Financier in order to be released from addressing the check directly to the production company. You are basically "assigning" certain drawdowns to the Lender, and "directing" the Financier to pay the Lender instead of you. Some Lenders prefer to assign all the drawdowns to the Lender, and the Lender will affect all the cash flow drawdowns to the company. Other Lenders will A&D only certain drawdowns.

INTERIM DRAW REQUEST

The Lender does not automatically start sending you money. You have to officially request the loan on paper, accompanied by a cost report. You may arrange with the Lender to have two or three draw requests, so that you are not paying interest on the entire amount starting in the middle of shooting — when you need only some of it now, and the balance of it closer to fine cut. Minimize interest payable if you can.

INTERPARTY AGREEMENT

Interparty agreements generally happen on international co-productions where some of the international Financiers may participate in the interim financing and others may not. To minimize risk, the Lender needs assurance that to complete the film, all sources of financing will indeed pay per the drawdown schedule they are contracted to honor. This is where the interparty agreement comes in. It covers the agreement of terms between the Lender, the Producer, the Co-Producer, and the Financier(s) not participating in the interim financing. It is a complex document that requires all four parties (minimum) involved in the discussions, and all of them have legal fees associated with drafting up the agreement. Enough said.

ADD THE LENDER TO THE BOND & INSURANCE

The Lender must now be added to the Bond and to both the production and E & O insurance. They are considered a Financier of the production even though they are only financing the cash flow. The Bond provides them assurance that the project will be completed, and being an additional insured on the insurance policies protects them from lawsuit.

MINIMIZING THE INTERIM LOAN AMOUNT

The more money you borrow, the less money you have to produce the film. The higher the interim loan amount, the more fees and interest you need to pay. There are several ways to minimize the interim loan costs payable by the production budget.

First, review the cash flow. Are there any costs that can be pushed to later in production?

The Producer may defer some of the Producer fees or corporate overhead to minimize the interim loan required. On the Producer's instruction, move these costs to the end of the cash flow schedule.

Also, though you may not be able to minimize the loan amount, you may be able to reduce interest payable if you negotiate with the Lender to receive the interim loan in installments, instead of all up front generating interest on the entire amount immediately.

Another way to minimize interest payable is to ensure the Lender receives timely drawdowns from the Financiers to pay off the loan. To do this, you have to be sure the Financiers receive all their trigger deliverables and documentation, including up-to-date cost reports, from you, the Production Manager. Check each Financier for unique details. A number of Financiers, for example, require an invoice to effect release of a drawdown payment — even though all the deliverables are received, the payment is clearly due, and the financing contract does not mention the need for an invoice. Be proactive to help minimize any waiting.

—❦—

Sometimes you will use two different interim lenders to make up the amount you need to borrow. With more players involved, the level of complexity increases. Hopefully you will not have to deal with much of this paperwork, but it is essential for you to be informed, because interim financing directly affects your day-to-day cash flow.

THE LARGEST GREEN-SCREEN SHOT

The CGI Company needed a green-screen shot of Extras walking around to insert them into an animated background to bring that background to life. It was the "sell shot." In this shot, the existence of real people would make the audience believe that the animated background was a real location, even though it depicted a city in space. The shot was only eight seconds long. What a simple shot... no?

The CGI Company told us the directions for camera perspective on the people: about twenty feet back and twenty feet up. We could rent a big studio. We could paint the floor green. No problem. We started the arrangements.

The CGI Company called us again. Hang on.

The perspective would work better if the camera were back about forty feet and up about forty feet, too. Well, that would mean scaffolding. Perhaps we could choose an overcast day for the even lighting, then lay down a huge tarp we could paint green. Wow. That would be a lot more work and a bigger crew, and the weather would add an element of unpredictability. Not good. We started to make arrangements while we continued to think of other ways of achieving the shot.

Then the CGI Company called again. Hang on.

The perspective on the Extras would still be too close. They would prefer if we could get the shot from about seventy-five feet back and about seventy-five feet up or more. Could we do it? Oh yeah. Sure. Snap our fingers. We can do that. We were stumped. Then it came to us... the outfield at the local dome stadium has a wonderfully flat-lit green outfield... we could rent the dome stadium!

Hang on. Rent the dome stadium for an 8-second shot? Were we crazy?

With the camera up on the 200 level for the right perspective, and the perfectly even lighting courtesy of the flip of a switch, and a bunch of A.D.s and a couple of Wardrobe people on the field with walkie-talkies to direct the Extras, it would be perfect and simple!

And it was. What a "sell shot" it turned out to be... especially for the few who were there that night!

OFFICIAL & PM-ONLY COST REPORTS

22

The cash flow predicts the future when it comes to cost spending: When are we going to spend it? The official cost report reports the past: This is what happened last week. The "PM-Only" cost report is all about the present: What is happening today? What may happen tomorrow that will affect my decisions today?

THE OFFICIAL COST REPORT

The official cost report is a valuable reference to many, since it details weekly the actual spending status of the production, including all actual costs to date, costs promised (or purchase ordered), and all estimated costs yet to happen to finish production. Cost reports are key to triggering drawdowns from Financiers. You, as the Production Manager, need to know how to report costs accurately and efficiently to trigger those drawdowns quickly.

THE DOCUMENTS OF AN OFFICIAL COST REPORT

The cost report is actually made up of three documents: (1) the cost report, (2) the trial balance, and (3) the explanation top sheet. Some Financiers may not require the trial balance unless requested, but that is the exception rather than the rule.

THE COST REPORT OR THE OFFICIAL COST REPORT

Always track costs compared to the locked budget allocations. The accounting software package that comes with the payroll company will generate this document; if you do not have a payroll company, you need to know the cost report's structure to generate the document yourself on spreadsheet software, like Excel. Itemize the locked budget accounting codes and descriptions down the left side, and then add more columns moving across the page to the right to include columns for:

> **Costs This Period**: This column shows only the actual costs paid this last week or month, depending on the length of the period. This column is useful reference to see what costs have been happening lately on production.

> **Costs To Date**: This column shows a grand total of all actual spends to date. To start the audit review, many Financiers require this column to reach a minimum spend of 95% of the budget. Once a cost reaches this column (or the Costs This Period column), you cannot change that cost. It is money out of the bank and is spent and coded. You need to do ledger entries for any costs in these columns you happened to have coded to the wrong budget line, in order to create an accounting trail for the Auditor to understand later.

> **Purchase Orders**: This column also can be called "committed costs" or just "committed." Here you can report all costs promised by purchase order for which checks have not yet been written. As you know, if the purchase order is completed, the cost is as good as spent. On the cost report, you can separate out these "promised" costs — since the money has not left your bank yet, and because the check is not written yet, the cost may fluctuate a little; therefore costs in this column may be modified, unlike costs in the actual columns. This is a valuable column for cost tracking, and it is essential you use it. If the Accountant is not taking advantage of this column, you will never have a true picture of what costs are promised and pending. You do not want to be in the dark about purchase ordered costs.

> **Total Costs**: This column is the sum of Costs To Date plus Purchase Orders.

> **Estimate To Complete**: This column may also be called simply: "ETC." Here you can note and revise what you expect to spend to complete the film for each budget line item.

> **Estimated Final Costs**: This column is the sum of Total Costs plus ETC. This column may also be called "EFC."

> **Budget**: In this column you transpose the locked budget line items for comparison to the actual costs.

> **Variance**: This column shows the difference between the Budget and the Estimated Total Costs. Negative numbers (costs over budget) should be shown in brackets, since minus signs are hard to read on a document with this many columns.

See a sample cost report page on page 498.

TRIAL BALANCE

The accounting software of the production will generate this document. A trial balance is a list of the actual bank transactions as entered into the computer ledger. It is not balanced to the bank statement, because the bank statement has not yet arrived in the mail. This is why it is called the "trial" balance. This is a good document for seeing to whom the actual checks are being written. It has more specific information than the cost report, but there is no reference between this document and the budget, and there is no detail regarding what the checks reference. That is why these two documents work together. Since this document can also go to Financiers, consider what the trial balance may say to the Financiers if the last ten checks written are all payable to the head office of the production company.

COST REPORT EXPLANATION MEMO

Always have an explanation memo accompany the cost report. You will no doubt have overages and savings that will generate questions to whoever will read the cost report. You want to minimize their questions to speed up the drawdown process and also keep the Financiers informed. Make a memo of the items that you think might cause concern or raise questions, addressing the reasons for the overages and the savings on the memo's top page. Doing this regularly will generate a lot of comfort in your cost reporting and will serve you well in dealing with the Financiers on this production and throughout your career.

PREPARING THE COST REPORT

The Production Accountant generates the cost report out of the accounting software (like Vista, or Cast & Crew) from the payroll company, or on spreadsheet software (like Excel). The Accountant will collect information from actual costs and from purchase orders from the accounting files, and will consult with you, the Production Manager, to iron out the amounts for the ETC column.

DESIGN AND PREPARE FOR AUDIT

Remember as you set up for the first cost report, you need to keep in mind that the final cost report is to be audited or reviewed somehow. You must design an accounting report system with the audit in mind. Speak to the planned Auditor in preproduction to discuss your accounting and reporting procedures. Ensure that the Accountant (or you) collects the various information needed for the audit, including copies of all agreements, copies of all DPRs and call sheets, accurate cost reports and explanation pages, list of Financiers, their investment amounts and contact information, citizenship lists, residency lists, plot synopsis, and so on. Make an audit file now to collect this paperwork. Read Chapter 36 for more information on audit preparation.

THE COST REPORT SCHEDULE

Meet with the Production Accountant and the Producer to discuss the cost report schedule. How soon can Accounting output the first draft cost report, including both the costs of payroll from last week and other less weekend-related costs? The sooner you can generate the first draft, discuss it, hone it, and publish it, the sooner you can keep the Financiers informed of production's progress, and the less they will worry about the production. The faster the cost report, the faster you can address any financial problem you have — because you will know how much production is costing, not just estimating how much it is costing.

As a suggested schedule: Perhaps the Accountant can work on the cost report on Monday and publish the first (internal) draft by Tuesday afternoon, when you two meet to review it. On Wednesday morning you, the Accountant, and the Producer meet to discuss the draft including your input. The Producer may know of places in the estimates-to-complete to be tightened or that need more money allocated to them for further spending. Then the report is finalized and published as official by Wednesday afternoon. Set up a schedule and approval system that works for your producing team.

THE COST REPORT & PRODUCER MEETINGS

Meet with the Producer, and also with the Accountant, at least weekly to discuss costs. You will be meeting them anyway regarding the cost report, so discuss the progress of production then, too.

When you meet with the Producer regarding the cost report, bring questions to this meeting. You will use notes from these discussions with the Producer as notes on the explanation sheet that accompanies the cost report. This is also your opportunity to discuss and strategize with the Producer how to keep production functioning on budget — or bring it back on budget. Discuss how to deal with costs that appear to be going out of control. Are you on budget? Are you over, and if you are, why are you over? Are the circumstances out of the Producer's control? What are they? How can you bring the production back on budget? Can you wrap an hour early today or tomorrow to help? These are questions that may run through the minds of Financiers reading your cost reports. Address the questions and the issues before they ask you for explanations and your plans to deal with the issues.

Address all over-budget issues immediately. Waiting before acting costs you money that you cannot afford. If you spend money too quickly on production and do not pull back on costs, the crew may feel a false sense that you have money to burn and continue to spend accordingly. The crew does not have the budget in their hands and they cannot tell how much there is to spend unless you tell them.

ESTIMATES TO COMPLETE

In the ETC column of the cost report, you will have the chance to re-budget and re-budget as production moves forward. As you adjust the estimates to complete, you will create overages and will have to take equivalent savings in other budget lines to balance the movement and keep the cost report total matching the locked budget total. You want to be minimal in moving costs around from line to line, because each movement of budgeted costs will generate overages and savings that will generate questions of "why" by Financiers and that you will have to explain. The more movements you have early in production the less confidence there will be in the accuracy or the integrity of the original budget. See more below in "Dealing with Overages & Savings."

CO-PRODUCTION COST REPORTS

If you are creating cost reports for a co-production, you will have to generate three (not two) cost reports: one covers this country's costs; one shows the other country's costs; and one is a consolidated cost report including both country's costs. Because of this situation, you have to report costs in one currency.

The accounting ledger, however, is divided into five accounts; and yes, the complexity is like a five-episode series shooting simultaneously. The accounts will cover separately: (1) country #1 costs that occurred in country #1; (2) country #1 costs that occurred in country #2; (3) country #2 costs that occurred in country #1; (4) country #2 costs that occurred in country #2; and (5) the consolidated costs. You can then use a transfer account on the trial balance to move the costs from country to country for clean audit tracking.

The reason for this complexity is that there is bound to be overlap in the expenses no matter how you try to keep the two Co-Producer's responsibilities and portions of the budget apart. Technically you can "sell actual receipts" from one country to the other. If you have only three of seventy-five crew members (due to citizenship) being costed to the other country's budget, you do not want the checks to come directly from the other country, leaving them to calculate the nuances of crew payroll while you have a payroll company taking care of the rest of the crew. You will end up transferring costs on the accounting books and will need to generate the necessary three cost reports using five ledger accounts.

Using this system, each Co-Producer supplies the other with weekly local cost reports to enter into their respective accounting system (unless you can link the systems by a network) to generate the information for both audits. Yes, you will need to do separate audits for each country.

Though this system may seem a bit excessive for cost tracking, it is not excessive at all. It is essential that you know what the costs of production are at all times.

SERIES (AMORT & PATTERN) COST REPORTS

If you have a thirteen-episode series, you will be creating fourteen cost reports. One will be the amortization cost report and the rest will be the thirteen episodic cost reports. This system, which began with the budget structure, allows you to compare costs from episode to episode. When you save money on one episode, you can apply it to the overage on another episode. The further you move into production the more cost reports you have to print weekly to look at the costs. By the time you are shooting episode #10, you have to print out eleven cost reports to review, because no doubt you will be adding a few costs to previous episodes as you go. You will not necessarily have locked out the costs in episode #2 because it is still in postproduction. If you fail to review all the cost reports regularly, you may not notice the few added costs here and there that happen and eat into your projected savings or increase your projected overages that you were planning to address on later episodes. You may be more over-budget than you thought you were.

Also note, that only when production is over, can you complete and lock out the costs in the amortization (amort) cost report and divide its total across the entire series of cost reports. Though the amort cost report details costs from preproduction, it also covers costs for wrap and postproduction, and these costs remain unspent, and therefore unknown, for some time yet.

THE PM-ONLY COST REPORT

The official cost report only comes out weekly. As the Production Manager, you need to know how to track cost spending for yourself during production, and prior to issuing the weekly official cost report. The day-to-day spending of production will affect your day-to-day decisions and recommendations regarding issues that come up. You need to consider, and keep updated, pessimistic and optimistic cost estimates to finish production. For this, you need a system like the PM-Only cost report.

COLLECTING INFORMATION FOR THE PM-ONLY COST REPORT

How do you collect and remember all the veritable ton of information from set and office that will update the many lines of the cost report for you to have current ETCs? Think simply. You have to write it down somehow. There is no way you can remember ever-changing numbers without writing them down.

Basically you need to track estimated actual costs, and estimated promised or purchase ordered costs. Exact actual costs and purchase orders are in the domain of the Production Accountant. Of course, this does not mean you can estimate your numbers badly, it means you can allow yourself more leeway regarding accuracy, because your document is not official.

When you make deals, or you learn information at meetings, or you discuss information on set, note cost details on sticky notes like Post-its. You can later transpose and gather these bits of information onto the PM-Only cost report.

If you have to give priority to some costs over others, target the bigger costs. It is likely that payroll is your largest weekly cost. How much did Accounting spend on payroll last week? Make a notation.

Also target questionable areas. Special effects and stunt costs may not happen daily on your production, but when they do happen, they are significant and many circumstances can increase their cost on the day of shooting to get it right for the camera. You need to track these. You will know by the end of preproduction which costs are going to be in the questionable category for you.

Finally, target areas of the cost report that domino into others. For film, it is easy to see that the more film stock you buy and use on set, the higher your processing and printing or transfer costs will be; that dominoes into more editing time. For digital, it is effortless to capture more and longer takes than with film; however, this behavior also dominoes into increased editing time, raising both edit labor fees and equipment and suite rental costs. It is therefore good to track the cost from as close to inception as possible: from the purchase of picture stock or the amount of footage used in a day.

Review again the areas of the budget you targeted as expensive: large locations lead to vista shots which may in turn lead to more Extras, A.D.s, Hair, Makeup and Wardrobe, which in turn leads to more supplies for those departments, and so on.

Now that you have collected information regarding costs and promises, here are a number of ways of tracking them on paper for reference. Samples are on pages 499–502.

THE PM-ONLY COST REPORT #1 – SPREADSHEET FROM ACCOUNTING

If the Production Accountant outputs the official cost report on a spreadsheet form (like Excel), you can nab a copy of this file and put it on your computer for personal manipulation.

Insert a column for PM-Estimated Costs prior to Total Costs column and include these PM-estimated costs in the totals. It is also wise to insert a line each time you need to explain the estimate or the reality of the cost in the new column for your personal future reference. Do not rely solely on your memory. There are a lot of budget lines to track and a lot of overages and savings!

It is time to start entering all those costs and promises you collected as information until now. For example, you sign a purchase order for the daily rental of a special piece of equipment for $1,000. Note the $1,000 in the PM-Estimate column in the appropriate line of the PM-Only cost report. Insert a line below to describe that $1,000 was for the special piece of equipment. Later in the same week you sign a purchase order for the daily rental for another piece of equipment for $1,000. If you had not made the notation under the line in the PM-Only cost report, you may be confused if you had already entered this new piece of equipment since the cost happens to match. Now you can add the second $1,000 to this line, and insert another line describing the second piece of equipment. Next week review the official cost report to see if these items are now in the official purchase order column. You will not need to track them anymore. The Accountant is tracking them.

The "under line" notations are also good in case you happen to track a cost that the Accountant has already included in the Total Costs. If the notation is there in wording, together you will discover the duplication and correct the error.

The beauty of this system is that the PM-Only cost report is the same format as the official cost report, so comparing the two documents side by side is incredibly easy. The drawback of this system is that you have to reformat the document each week (or accounting period) to insert the PM-Estimate column and insert costs and explanation lines that did not make it to the official cost each week.

THE PM-ONLY COST REPORT #2 – SPREADSHEET MADE BY PM

If the Production Accountant does not work on the same spreadsheet program as you do, but you still like the format of the cost report for notations, and you enjoy taking advantage of the computer's ability to calculate on spreadsheet programs, you can still create a working cost report for yourself. Whatever the accounting software is, the Production Accountant will likely be able to output a copy of the official cost report to an overall spreadsheet program (like Excel). This procedure will help you start. The columns you will need to create and/or save are:

> **Total (Actual) Costs**: Transpose or computer-translate these totals from the latest official cost report.

> **PM-Estimated Costs**: You will be inserting costs and cost promises in this column, and look to see these costs are included on the next official cost report.

> **ETC**: Transpose or computer-translate these totals from the latest official cost report. You will be manipulating these costs, too, taking into account the PM-estimates of the future.

> **Estimated Final Costs**: The column should have formulas in it to add the Total Costs to the PM-Estimated Costs and the ETC Costs.

> **Budget**: Again, this column can be transposed from the official cost report, and since it remains unchanged, you only need do this once.

> **Variance**: Ensure this column is the spreadsheet formula showing the difference between the Budget and the Estimated Final Costs.

You enter costs and cost promises the same way as in the previous spreadsheet system. Insert the PM-estimate totals on the line to be included in the final calculations, and then insert lines to make explanation notations for the costs you have mentioned.

You can modify this working document to add all the labor costs into one line, if you would like — and if the budget line items permit by their structure — but this is not advisable. The further you modify this document from the original format of the official cost report and all its specific lines, the more you will have to double-check your calculations because errors may be there. You will need to refer to the official cost report alongside the PM-only cost report for the most accuracy. Also, by looking at generalities (like all the payroll on one line) you will lose the specifics of where in the payroll you are going over and need to pull back.

Each week (or period) you will need to update the Total Costs and ETC costs from the official report. Once you create the document, you will be adding lines to the cost report, so you will no longer be able to insert sections of the official cost report by computer. You will have to enter the updated numbers manually. Still, it is good to become fully familiar with the lines of the cost report. Just as you expect the First A.D., for example, to know the script and the schedule inside and out, you are expected to know the costs of the budget inside and out. It takes working with these numbers and the constantly changing cost report over and over again to assimilate this information. The time you put in will be well spent.

The beauty of this system is that you spend enough time on this document that you become fluent in the cost report's contents. The drawback is that it does take a good amount of time to keep this document updated and current.

THE PM-ONLY COST REPORT #3 – BUDGET FORM

If you are more comfortable working with and manipulating budget software than you are spreadsheet software, you can create a PM-only cost report in the budget program. Instead of creating a column for the PM-estimates, you add new PM cost estimates only for projected overages and negative estimates for projected savings in each appropriate detail line of the budget.

This is a good system for tracking crew overtime. If the Production Accountant, for example, tells you how much overtime was spent on each crew member this week — or you estimate the costs from the production reports if it is critical you know sooner than by the end of the week — you can add the estimated overages for each crew member in their labor lines in the budget, noting the extra cost was for "overtime week #1," or whatever week it is. Then you can use the subgroup feature of the budgeting program to associate all the labor overtime costs to one subgroup for each week. This way you can see the total of all crew overtime spent in each single week and predict overtime for the following week, or decide how much overtime needs to be cut back to return to budget.

The beauty of this system is that the costs estimates remain on the budget program, a program with which you are most likely familiar, and you can use the features of the budget program to group cost overages to aid in your predictions for future cost spending. The downside of this system is that the budget format does not match the cost report format, so it may be difficult for you to compare the two very different documents to check the integrity of the overage and saving projections.

THE PM-ONLY COST REPORT #4 – PENCIL COPY

Okay, if you are bad working on computers or you particularly like pencils' portability and "erasability," this system may work for you. With this system you work on a photocopy of the official cost report, penciling overage and saving estimates and notations in any space available around the lists of numbers.

Though you can always see what actual costs have been spent, this system does not allow you to accurately predict the costs that are remaining (especially high budget costs like labor). It is therefore wise to set up a spreadsheet file alongside this system to detail and total labor costs, hours, and overtime. Show each week's overtime costs in a separate column for more detailed analysis.

You need to transpose all your notes weekly from the old cost report to the new official cost report. While doing so, question each notation. Is it still valid, or is it addressed by the new cost report? Through the transposing, the information of the cost report will be reinforced, and you will be reminded of how much — or how little — money is left in each category. You will stay current.

The beauty of this system is that your notations regarding costs are easy to add and to erase to the exact document that the Production Accountant uses, so document comparison and updating is the fastest. The downside to this system is that you still need some sort of spreadsheet file to track costs like labor costs and overtime, forcing you to have two documents to update instead of one. Also, all calculations have to be done manually, and if the official cost report prints out in tiny print, you will have to write very small to add all the information you need to add.

RECORDING PETTY CASH FLOATS ON THE PM-ONLY COST REPORT

Crew often receive petty cash floats, then later return receipts equivalent to the float, and ask for more money to top up their float or return the unused portion of it. You never know how much they have actually spent until they submit their petty cash reports. That is why you want them to submit reports often. If the Production Accountant is noting the floats on the purchase order column of the official cost report, you do not need to track these costs. If the Accountant is not tracking floats here, you can note the float that has gone out to crew members on the PM-only cost report on an appropriate line where you expect most of the receipts to be allocated. When the petty cash reports come in for approval, you can change the notation to report expenses instead of a petty cash float to that crew member. If the float is reimbursed, then you have to note a new line of a refreshed petty cash float to that person, too.

ESTIMATING THE FUTURE WITH THE PM-ONLY COST REPORT

As you can see, with the PM estimates and the adjustments you make to the ETC predictions, you are basically re-budgeting the production over and over again, becoming more and more precise as the costs move from predictions to actuals. Accountants report what actually happened. You need to consider and estimate what might happen for the remainder of the shoot in order to arrive at the end of production on budget. Remember that the PM-only cost report is not an official document. It is only an estimate of what might happen. Since the future is not written yet, you can estimate it either pessimistically or optimistically. Really, you need a balance between the two. You have to have some pessimistic projections so that when some things go wrong, you will have the money somewhere in the budget to cover the unexpected, but you do not want to be too pessimistic and end up with a surplus that never makes it to the screen. Use this tool to help you keep track of the ever-flowing costs and promises. Keeping on top of the costs as soon as they happen is the only way to look forward.

MANAGING CASH FLOW THROUGH PRODUCTION

What happens when the costs come in faster than the anticipated drawdowns and interim financing inflows come in to cover them? You are presented with the dilemma of who to pay first in your stack of accounts payable, and who might be able to wait a bit longer before you pay them.

Payroll can never wait and will always be your first priority. Never let the crew know there is a cash flow problem. Pay payroll. The "problem" is likely a slow drawdown or two that is due payable to you now anyway. It is not like you will not be receiving the money, it is only a question of when. The crew, though, has no other means of support other than their paychecks. They have worked for you. You now owe them the money. Period. You never want your company to be known for not paying crew. This label is hard, if ever, to erase, and may even prevent you from hiring crew on all productions in the future.

If cash flow is critical, calculate how critical. Some suppliers may help you at these times. Many of them have given you thirty days to pay their bills already anyway. Discuss realistic payment terms with them, and keep them updated if they are helping you through a cash flow crunch. And though this may sound obvious, never promise the same money inflows to several suppliers.

DEALING WITH OVERAGES & SAVINGS

When you were budgeting in the first place, you wanted to be sure there was some "room to breathe" in the budget. Of course, there is a contingency, but you could not predict with exact accuracy every cost yet to come; some of your specific line item estimates were optimistic and some had to be pessimistic to create a working balance. As mentioned, the closer to end of production, the closer you move to actual costs from estimates. Though you will want to preserve some of these pessimistic predictions, you have to let go of more and more of them every week, or you will end up "surprisingly" under-budget by the end of shooting. Your margin for estimates narrows weekly as wrap approaches. The line between pessimistic versus optimistic predictions is a fine line to balance.

You are bound to have savings and overages in the cost report. No one can possibly budget a production and be exactly right in cost predictions for each budget line. You will end up having to move savings from one part of the cost report to cover overages elsewhere.

When you have an overage in a category, increase the ETC in the needy category and decrease the ETC in another category somewhere else in the cost report. Never allocate costs directly to the contingency line. Contingency is not a spending category... it is simply a contingency. If you go over-budget in a category where you want to take costs from contingency, increase the ETC in the needy category and decrease the ETC in the contingency line.

Every time you move costs, make a notation of what you are moving and why. You may need notes when completing the explanation memo, or when you are moving costs in the future, and forget why you added money to a particular category.

When moving costs, try to move them to and from similar or logical categories. For example, if you expect to go over $5,000 in studio costs, but you expect a significant savings in location rentals, you can take the $5,000 from location rentals to balance. Or, you are expecting to go over $1,500 in construction labor, but the Construction Manager expects at least at $1,500 savings in construction supplies. This movement is also logical.

OVERAGES BEYOND THE CONTINGENCY

They should not be there yet, but if overages are increasing to the point where all the pessimistic predictions you had in the budget and the contingency are not going to cover them, you and the Producer, and likely the Executives, must address this problem immediately.

Discuss the growing problem with the Producer(s) and come up with a plan to stop the excess spending as soon as humanly possible. Meet over the official cost report immediately and bring all your PM-Only notes. Draft new official cost reports as soon as possible to keep you current on the outflow of money. You have to know how much production is costing in reality. Where is source of the hemorrhaging? Review the production reports. Talk with the First A.D. and the Producer. If you do not stop the spending now, someone else will… and that could involve replacing you. You may have to suggest to the Producer that someone needs to be fired to effect a real reduction in spending. Do not be afraid of advising radical changes. Just reason it out first. You may have to restructure how to shoot the rest of the production. Are you going to combine locations in a quick re-write to save on a unit move? The Producer may act, or not, on your advice. "Over contingency" decisions are weighty ones, and you need to do what you can to help the Producer make informed decisions.

If you do go beyond contingency in going over-budget, the Producer may decide to ask the Financiers for more money to finish the film, based on extenuating circumstances. Or the Producer may decide to cover the entire overage himself and recoup that over-budget coverage after all the equity investors have made their money back when the project is sold around the world. The Financiers, however, may decide to call in the completion bond to finish the production and remove the Producer from the picture. Basically, you want to address any potential budget overages before you end up in this position.

Some completion bonds require less than 50% of the contingency spent by 50% through shooting, some require less than 60% of it spent prior to wrap. Even if the Bonder does not commit you to this type of promise in writing, either system is a good guideline. You will need to reserve a good portion of contingency for postproduction.

DEALING WITH SAVINGS

If you are significantly under-budget, you want to know this as soon as possible, too. If, at the end of production, delivery, and audit, you come in under-budget, the Producer will likely have to pay back to the Financiers all the money that was not spent. Now, who wants to do that? You want to spend the money on the screen. If you expect significant savings, and know enough in advance, you can augment parts of your budget, adding more special effects or publicity or whatever else to make a better film. You may have to inform the Financiers of your request to apply savings in this manner depending on the amount you are expecting, but if you come up with a good case to spend the money making a better film, they are likely to support you in it. They have, after all, invested in this film and want it to be the best it can be.

Do not wait until the very end and then spend all the savings at once on capital items the head office company may want to keep. This is not spending it on the screen. You must spend production money on valid production costs. Financiers have the right to refuse costs at the audit stage, and the Producer could end up with a bill instead of the final drawdown check.

Some Production Manager's deals let the PM keep any production savings at the end as a bonus. This deal, however, tempts Production Managers to be extraordinarily cheap in order to line their own pockets, so it not a good idea. If you regularly bring in productions on time and on budget, good word about you will spread around, and your management career will flourish without these bonuses.

NEW BUDGET LINES

You can add new budget lines to the cost report when costs come in that do not fit into any of the existing categories. The budget column on the cost report will read zero for these new items since they are items that you have not budgeted for at all. If there are a number of newly created budget lines, anyone reading the cost report (including Financiers) will become rightfully concerned. Why did you fail to budget for an entire item such as this? Address newly budgeted items, with reasons why, on the explanation memo that accompanies the official cost report.

NO NEGATIVE ETCs

No cost report should have a negative number in the ETC column… well, unless you are truly expecting a check to come as income for this budget line. Income on an expense line is very, very unlikely. When reviewing the official cost report, ensure the ETC column shows no negatives. Adjust the Estimated Final Costs to consider the overage and bring the ETC line back to zero or to a positive number. If you do not correct this, you will gain a false sense of being on or under-budget when reading the cost report.

RELATED PARTY EXPENSES (RPTs) & LOCKED EXPENSES

The Producer may have had to report a list of related party expenses to the Financiers. These are expenses paid to non–arm's length companies or people: all costs paid to all Producers, to their families, to companies related to the production company and/or head office. Find out if there is such a declaration. If so, these costs will be locked, and you will not be allowed to spend any overages in these categories without that Financier's approval. Obviously you need to know this information at the start of production prior to monitoring even the first cost report.

ABOUT SPECIFIC COST REPORTS

Since cost reports happen at funding trigger dates during production, there are certain expenses you expect at different times.

END OF PREP / FIRST WEEK OF PRINCIPAL PHOTOGRAPHY COST REPORT

On the first day of shooting, development is officially over. The project is now a film. You have to pay back all the development loans. Since the development loans are paid back on first day of shooting, you must have these costs paid for on the first shooting week's cost report. You will not see these as expenses yet on the last week of preproduction's cost report.

If you have arranged a "check swap" with the funding company (swapping your paid-back development check with the first day of principal photography's drawdown from the same company), you can at least purchase order the development expenses on the cost report until the actual day the swap happens. Since the first day of principal photography drawdown will also be triggered by other deliverables like this cost report and perhaps other documents, you may not receive this money from the Financier exactly on the first day of shooting. This is why you can purchase order the development expenses.

During preproduction be sure the Production Accountant acquires from head office, or from the person who has the receipts, complete "auditable" backup for all the development costs that you have to expense to the cost report this week. The Accountant cannot list expenses on the cost report for which there are no official, valid receipts.

Refer to the cash flow to check how you are doing on costs that you expected to be spent by now. Other costs you should expect to have paid include: bonding fees or fees being held in escrow, story rights, deposits for various departments, bonds for various unions, and checks for any crew due payable on first day, like the Director, and so on.

Since this cost report will trigger a lot of financial drawdowns, ensure it is created quickly and accurately, and is published immediately. You will need the inflow of money, because now that the camera is rolling, you are spending money faster than ever.

COST REPORTS THROUGHOUT PRODUCTON

Review again the section above on managing cash flow through production for addressing cost report issues.

The first week of principal photography tends to generate a lot of overages, especially overtime. It is often a wake-up call to the producing team who has to bring the costs back on line. Deal with these circumstances now and bring costs back on line. Consider, first, that you are all new to this set including this working team, so production often is somewhat slow to get up to speed that first week. Once on set, you may discover that you have scheduled too much to accomplish in this first week, or that the set you hoped for is not quite ready yet. The crew, too, may find the week #1 to be a wake-up call to get on track. Capitalize on the eagerness and the energy of the crew in that first week, but do not burn them out. Excessive, repetitive overtime will tire a crew, causing less energy as the shoot progresses, which will show up in set delays and accidents. You cannot afford this situation.

As production proceeds, you may find that overages begin to generate in categories such as travel, transportation, construction, the various Art Departments, or any others. Valid overages can happen for any number of unforeseeable reasons. Construction overages, for example, can happen because you have budgeted for certain sets, then when you are on location surveys you find the construction team has to do some modifications to various locations, too, in order to make the locations match the sets. Anticipate what you can, and be ready to address what becomes excessive.

FIRST WEEK OF WRAP COST REPORT & THE PM'S LAST COST REPORT

As Production Manager, you will be around for a few weeks of wrap, so will generate more than one cost report after shooting has ended.

Be sure you are leaving contingency for postproduction, too. In the last "production" cost reports, most of the shooting ETCs should be minimal to cover the invoices expected shortly, or zeroed out because that category is completed. The set crew, for example, no longer comes to work. A few people are here in wrap, but you can leave a little money in their ETCs to cover the final anticipated payroll. As you zero out accounts, you may discover more savings to re-allocate. Is there enough money aside for looping during postproduction? Is the publicity budget in need of a few extra dollars? Find logical places to reallocate the little savings you may have left.

You will be handing your final cost report over to the Postproduction Supervisor, and the Production Accountant may be handing the accounting files over to a Postproduction Accountant. Beyond giving them the cost report and the regular explanation memo, you need to give them as much history about the budget and the cost report as you can, especially if you have moved any budget accounts around related to postproduction. For every ETC cost that is not in the postproduction section of the cost report, make a note of explanation for the person(s) to whom you are handing the responsibility. They need to know if and when they can spend any ETC that never receives an invoice in the future. The more detail you supply now, the less chance you will be bothered at home with questions about your unfinished business. You have been hired to track the spending, but you must hand over the cost report responsibly in postproduction.

—◠—

You have made it through production — tracking the ever-flowing expenses, predicting the future, and then finding out what the future indeed did bring. This chapter has supplied an overview of the accounting issues in which the Production Manager immerses herself, but this does not end the responsibilities of the job. Even though you are not a lawyer, it is time to move onto business affairs issues that involve you.

MORE CONTRACTING ISSUES | V

Cover yourself! (Get it in writing)

PAID HOLIDAYS

Film shoots often work weekends and holidays to take advantage of location access and traffic patterns. Otherwise, they go on hiatus to avoid holidays. I can't remember the last time I was actually paid for a Christmas holiday. But there is one holiday-type day I do remember.

The Director of the film was thrilled to find out I was a sailor with my own boat. One of the scenes was in front of the water, and he wanted a boat anchored in the background of the shot. He asked me to do the honors.

Sporting a bikini, I went to work with cell phone and walkie-talkie on board and another sailor to give me a hand. We anchored the boat as instructed on the walkie-talkie to create optimal angle of the boat to the camera. Then settled in for a day's relaxation. I didn't know what my orange bikini would look like from shore until the Director's voice came over the walkie: "Uh... Deb, are you wearing anything out there?" I must have looked naked. Oh boy. I quickly came back over the walkie: "Gee, was I supposed to?" And they all laughed. It was obviously not an issue, since the boat would be so far in the background.

So, for the day, I lounged aboard my sailboat, the sun shining, a sailor to bring me drinks and... getting paid. Then I wondered, how does one declare this on a time sheet?

DEAL MEMOS & LONG FORMS

23

You have delved into the land of accounting many times. Now that you have mastered dealing with purchase orders, cash flows, and cost reports, you will have no problem with various contracts.

CREW DEAL MEMOS

As Production Manager, your mandate is to sign on the crew as soon as you can, to start them working on the production. For the Production Coordinator, one of the active file folders atop your desk is the "Crew Deal Memos" folder; the faster the crew has signed deal memos, the faster you can create an official crew list and know that production is underway.

THE PM MAKES THE DEALS, THE PC TRACKS THEM

The Production Manager talks to the crew one by one to strike a deal with them. Making the deal was covered in a previous chapter. Remember to note the deals and revise the PM-only cost report with the actual numbers instead of the budgeted numbers. How do these deals affect the bottom line of the production costs?

The Coordinator can keep track of the deal memos being signed. Ask the PM daily who is on board and needs a deal memo. Not all crew know where to find deal memo forms.

THE START PACK

The deal memo form itself is only one of the documents you will need to have crew members fill out when they start work. There can be quite a number of forms to complete, so the Coordinator can assemble all the appropriate forms and create a "start pack." Discuss with the PM and the Accountant which forms you may need to include in the start pack for this production:

> **Union or non-union deal memo**: Unions will supply their forms on request. See a sample non-union form on page 503.

> **Crew I.D. form from payroll company**: The payroll company will supply this form; the information may duplicate much of deal memo information.

> **Tax form for employees**: This form is for Accounting or the payroll company to calculate the tax to be deducted from each person's paycheck.

> **Corporate form in lieu of the tax form for employees**: On this form the Corporation promises to be responsible for payment of all applicable taxes.

> **Corporate declaration of tax number**: If the Corporation has to charge tax to the production company, it must supply a tax number.

> **Copy of incorporation certificate**: Actually, the Corporation supplies this form, but a notation in the start pack reminding the crew member is useful.

> **Citizenship form for tax credit**: You may need each crew member to declare his citizenship for tax purposes later. Do it now.

> **Dual Citizenship form declaring citizenship for the other country on a co-production**: This declaration allows the Producer to later choose to which country's budget this person's pay is allocated.

> **Residency form for tax credit**: Again, residency forms may be needed for tax purposes later.

> **Permittee form**: If this crew member is not a member of the union to which you are signatory, you have to ensure she arranges for a permit to work on the production. Since permittees are new to working on union productions, they often forget to fill out this form. Help them to remember. Production will not pay for the permit but there is often a form to complete to allow production to deduct the permit fee from the crew member's paycheck.

The start pack becomes quite the package of paper, doesn't it? If it is all assembled for completing at once, then you will not have to chase down the entire crew multiple times to have them fill out all the necessary forms during production. You will save yourself loads of time. Do it now.

Also, as you can see, you may need to make at least two different start packs: one for Employees and one for Corporations.

CORPORATIONS vs. EMPLOYEES

As employees, we are all familiar with source deductions. Taxes and pension fees are deducted from our paychecks at source, giving us a net fee on the paycheck. Corporations are not employees, and are responsible for source deductions themselves, so they invoice production for the gross fee. Some crew members will come to production as incorporated businesses; some will not, but would like to invoice production instead of joining on as an employee, so they do not have taxes and other source deductions removed from their paycheck at the source.

WHEN THE CREW MEMBER IS A CORPORATION

Since crew members travel from production to production, contract to contract, throughout the year, they are basically freelance and running their own companies. They can incorporate as a business. An official corporation means that the crew member has a company name that ends a designation like: Inc., Incorporation, Corp., Corporation, Ltd., Limited, Unlimited, or other choices that vary by country. Accounting will need a copy of the incorporation certificate from the government as proof of the company's existence, and likely will have another form or two to complete. Incorporated, the corporation takes on the responsibility of paying for all applicable taxes and other source deductions (like pension and employment insurance, etc.) due from the production company.

WHEN THE CREW MEMBER IS AN EMPLOYEE

Employee status means that Accounting will be making source deductions from the crew member's paycheck at the production company. The production company is the crew member's employer. If the crew member is not a corporation, then he is an employee. Obtain plenty of tax forms from the nearest tax office to include in the start pack, as mentioned above. Filled out, these forms tell Accounting which tax category to use for each employee.

WHEN THE CREW MEMBER IS NOT A CORPORATION

In nearly all cases, if crew members are not incorporated, they must be treated like employees. They cannot invoice like companies. Non-payment of taxes is a serious offence to say the least, and the production company will not want to be party to this by paying employees who invoice. The Production Accountant can explain in detail the tax reasons to crew members who insist on being "employees who invoice."

WHEN THE COMPANY IS REGISTERED

The process of incorporation creates a separate legal entity from the employee. It creates a corporation, and there are a lot of legal and accounting requirements to keep a corporation in business. The process of registration and the nominal fee it takes to register a company is not the same. A registered company is still very much legally attached to and part of the employee. For this reason, registered companies must be treated like employees and are subject to source deductions.

LONG FORM AGREEMENTS

Some crew will have long form agreements alongside their union deal memo. These people may include the Director, the DP, the Line Producer, and the Production Manager. Long form agreements spell out many more specific terms of their engagement. The Production Manager should handle drafting all the deal points for Legal Counsel to draft the official, legal document. Remember, though, that each of these people will have to complete a start pack, too, to accompany the long form.

HANDLING SIGNED CREW DEAL MEMOS

Just another reminder: Signed deal memos are confidential. Never forget this fact. Treat them accordingly.

THE PC OR ACCOUNTING TRACKS CREW SIGNING DEAL MEMOS

On some productions the Coordinator tracks the signing of all crew deal memos, on others it is the Accounting Department that does so. Find out and set up a system to ensure all deal memos are completed fully.

Some crew will forget to sign their own deal memos. When they do forget, they somehow think they will be paid on schedule anyway, even though they have supplied production with no personal information about themselves. Go figure. The Coordinator can use a crew list as a top sheet to track whose deal memo you have and whose has yet to be completed. Note that some crew will take their deal memo straight to Accounting, or leave it in the Production Manager's office. Collect them all for the production files, in order to see that they all are completed. Keep copies for your files, signed and unsigned, in case any are lost in the flow from your desk to Production Manager's signature to Accountant's files.

DEAL MEMOS ARE CONFIDENTIAL

Some crew will not want the Production Coordinator to see their deal memos, even though the Coordinator is in charge of coordinating and distributing them all to the appropriate departments and unions. If so, be patient and obtain a copy of the deal memo from the Accountant later, if need be.

THE PC DOUBLE-CHECKS DEAL MEMOS ARE COMPLETE

Before you have the Production Manager sign the deal memos, check them over for completeness. Be sure the crew member has actually signed the forms, the rates are noted, and the proper permit papers are attached, if applicable. Some crew may even fill in the wrong union's deal memo form and not notice. Determine a crew rate sheet from the Production Manager, and keep one at your desk for easy reference.

SIGN DEAL MEMOS IN BUNCHES

Of course the PM can sign the deal memos one at a time, but it is more time-efficient to have the Coordinator collect several; then you can sign them a bunch at a time at your daily meetings. It is your choice. The Accountant may be waiting desperately for one particular deal memo, so keep her in the loop about which deal memos are ready for signature. In either case, do not leave the signing of deal memos too long. It can be wise to copy the unsigned deal memos to Accounting immediately, and follow up with signed ones later.

WHO NEEDS COPIES OF DEAL MEMOS

The Coordinator can copy and distribute the signed deal memos. Treat deal memos with the confidentiality of any other contract. Send copies to Accounting, the appropriate union, the crew member, and file a copy in the production files. Ask Legal Counsel if he needs a copy. He will probably want a copy of contracts only for selected key crew. When sending the copy to the crew member, place it in an addressed, sealed envelope, including the word "confidential" clearly on the front of the envelope. The crew will appreciate your care.

HOW TO FILE DEAL MEMOS

As production continues, you will be handling numerous deal memos, for even daily crew who work for a single day need one. Highlight the crew member's last name (not the corporation name) and file the memos alphabetically. If anyone ends up with a deal memo in two different departments, you will find both deal memos together in an alphabetical set up. Note on your crew list cover sheet which deal memos are completed. Though the Production Accountant has a set of deal memos, they are being prepared and filed for the audit. The Coordinator's production files will be referred to more often by head office after production is completed, and when all the accounting boxes are sitting in the auditor's office.

TRACKING DAILY CREW

Keep a log of all daily crew, their jobs, and their telephone and cell numbers. You can attach a sheet to the back of your crew list with this information. Copy it for the A.D.s and for the Production Accountant, too. Daily crew work so briefly that they can easily be forgotten in the flow of paper and not be paid. The list of names and telephone numbers will also jog your, the PM's, and the A.D.'s memories of good daily crew for future reference.

WRAP DEAL MEMOS AT THE VERY END

At some time during production you will have all the deal memos of all the main crew, and you will feel comfortable enough to file this desk folder into the cabinet. Do not remove it from your desk so hastily. Production will be hiring dailies (daily crew) right up to and including wrap. Even you will probably be hiring a daily P.A. to help set up the wrap party.

—⁓—

Daily crew will keep you current on signing deal memos long after you thought you had arranged for the last deal memo, but basically you have now contracted the crew and they are working. Cast have their own issues to deal with, so it is time to consider them next.

ONE MIRACLE, PLEASE

Set called in a panic. They needed to change call time for a particular actor to two hours earlier. Today. The actor lived out of town, was no longer at home, and had no cell phone. He was somewhere in the city. I had to find him wherever he was and get him to set immediately. What am I, a miracle worker?

Think, think. Where could he be? I didn't know any of his friends. I didn't know what he likes to do on his time off. How does one go about finding someone who's just visiting a big city? Where was my crystal ball?

I went over any casual conversation I'd had with him. Any conversation I'd overheard him have with someone else. Topics included: acting, script revisions, the schedule, the weather. I needed something more personal. Sitting next to him at lunch one day, he had talked about getting into acting. About his home town. About a bar where he used to work in his home town. The bar was part of a chain. It was a long shot.

I got out the white pages. There were eight of these bars in town. Bar number one thought I was absolutely crazy to try to find him this way. I continued, anyway. Bar number two thought I was crazy also... but the staff, surprised, actually found him there and brought him to the telephone.

When the actor got on the line, he obviously thought the bar was playing a joke on him. When I confirmed his identity and mine, and why I was calling, he was stunned to the point of near speechlessness. He would go to set immediately.

I hung up the phone, then contacted the set to report the news. Then I sat back, a little stunned myself.

CAST CONTRACTS & IMMIGRATION

24

For the Production Manager, casting primarily happens under the Producer's supervision, not yours. You need to be involved, though, when it comes to what the deal is in all its costly details. You also may be more involved in casting arrangements for the supporting cast and the extras.

For the Production Coordinator, one of the file folders on your desk is labeled "cast contracts." It was a handy file to keep you abreast of the casting status as it happened, but now that contracting is near, you may be the one striking the actual contracts. You will also be involved in immigration issues should the Performer need a permit to come and shoot on your production.

AUDITIONS

The Casting Director and her company usually set up the auditions. Sometimes, however, the job, or part of it, falls to the Coordinator. The Production Coordinator will be more involved in audition arrangements than the Production Manager. But then again, the PM is probably dealing more with locations issues than the Coordinator.

SET UP THE AUDITION SESSION

Arrange for a room or a casting facility, a video camera, a monitor, digital picture stock, and a person to operate the camera. The Casting Director will supply you a list of attendees, what parts they are reading for, and times they are coming. Copy this schedule for the Director, the Producer, the Casting Director, the Camera Operator, the Receptionist, and whoever else is going to be involved with the session. Keep a spare for the production files.

MAKE AUDITION SIDES

Audition sides, like script sides, are selections of the script for reading during the audition. The Casting Director will choose which scenes are for which character. Make copies, marking the character name boldly on the front page for all the appropriate Performers, for all the crew attending the session, and for a few spares. Do not reduce photocopy audition sides, and be careful in selecting the pages. For example, if a scene starts on a page before the character's lines start, you will likely need to copy the preceding page or two to give the Performer as much information as possible about his character for the audition. Performers are rarely allowed access to the entire script before auditioning. Give them what help you can.

DISTRIBUTE AUDITION SIDES

Once the sides are made, inform the Casting Director. She will arrange for Performers to come into the office to pick them up. Some agents will ask you to send the sides to their office. Make absolutely sure that you give each Performer the sides for the correct character.

CAST CONTRACTS

You have a copy of the Performers' union agreement. Read it. It may be dry reading, but it is essential that you are familiar with it. Since the Coordinator may be preparing the cast contracts from the deal memos supplied by the Casting Director, it is imperative that you understand the union agreement as well as the Production Manager does. Attend any union/A.D. meeting in preproduction to meet the union representative. Let the Production Manager shepherd the long form agreements or addendum to the cast contracts with Legal Counsel.

DRAFTING THE CAST CONTRACT

The Casting Director will send you a copy of each Performer's deal memo. Prepare a draft cast contract for each one on a union contract template. Show both the deal memo and the contract to the PM, who can check it for accuracy and approve the deal. The PM can also note the cost of the deal points on the PM-Only cost report. The Coordinator then prepares the original agreement and arranges for signatures. Be aware that cast contracts incorrectly completed can cost the production unnecessarily large sums of money. Write them up extremely carefully. Double-check your work. Let the PM triple-check it.

STAR LONG FORM CONTRACTS

Star long form contracts are primarily created by lawyers, but sometimes are generated from you or the PM as addendums to the union agreement, with the lawyer just checking them over. Stars are considered Principal Actors by the union, but their rates are naturally above scale rates. Carefully read the deal memo provided by the Casting Director, then be very clear and very simple completing the draft "pencil" version of the contract. Let the lawyers use legalese. Note on the union form all the information that relates to the A.D.s (like private dressing room provided), to Transportation (like transport to/from set), and to postproduction (one looping session included, HD viewing copy of finished film provided). Do not note any fees on this form — detail the fees on the addendum. Addendums assure privacy of information. You can then copy the union form to the A.D.s, showing the promises but not the money, and copy the whole, more confidential contract with addendum, only to those who need to read the whole deal.

NON-UNION CAST CONTRACTS

Most of the advice for completing union cast contracts still applies to non-union cast contracts, but the form will be of your own making. If Legal Counsel does not make the agreement for you, know that there are two separate items that you must buy from the Performer: the Performer's time on the work day, and the right to use the Performer's recorded images and sounds afterward in the distribution of the production. If you do not specifically note that the fee includes the right for you to use the Performer's images and sounds, then, technically, you do not have the right to sell or show the finished film anywhere. Have Legal Counsel review your form before use.

EXTRAS VOUCHERS

General Extras (or "Background Performers"), Special Skills Extras, and Stand-Ins are cast by an Extras Casting Director and fill in extra vouchers on set from the A.D.s as their contracts. Sometimes you will be involved in finding Extras with specific special skills. Make sure the A.D.s have enough vouchers for use on set. If you are working non-union, you must ensure all Extras have signed an extras release form allowing production the permission to use their images and group sounds in the film, so the Producer can show and sell the finished product. (See a sample extras release on page 504, but remember to consult Legal Counsel whenever finalizing agreements such as these.)

ENSURE CORRECT NAME SPELLINGS

Some Assistants in casting offices do not spell Performers' names correctly. Double-check the exact spelling of the Performer's name with each Performer's Agent. Make sure the contract reads correctly. You will be referring to the contract when drafting up the credits. Nothing is more embarrassing that misspelling a Performer's name when the world can read it.

LIST OF TALENT AGENTS

The union will have a list of talent agents. Obtain a copy. Cast contracts are almost always "care of" an agency address, telephone number, email address and fax number. If the cast deal memos do not have complete talent agency information on them, then the list you acquired will help you.

AGENT vs. MANAGER

Some Performers have Talent Agents plus Personal Managers. Talk to both. Find out where their jurisdictions lie. One may be in charge of contracts, the other publicity. When you have a question, find out to whom you should speak first. Inform the PM.

DECLARE RATES TWICE

Keyboarding numbers are difficult. You do not have the luxury of spell check. Always include the Performer's rate twice on a contract: once in numbers and once describing the calculation. A daily rate written as: "$980.00 (Scale Plus 50%)" and an hourly rate as: "$85.00 (Scale)" makes your intentions doubly clear, just in case you make a mistake when keyboarding the numbers.

WORK PERMITS

All non-union Performers working on a union production need work permits from the union. New Performers will pay for the permits themselves; established Stars will likely have negotiated for production to pay for them.

CAST CONTRACT SIGNATURES

Either the Production Manager or the Producer signs the cast contracts on behalf of the production company. As PM, decide with the Producer who is going to be signatory. It should be the person who can double-check the accuracy of all the deal points. A signed cast contract that has not been checked for accuracy to the deal points can easily reveal a very expensive or very insulting mistake. Conduct due diligence.

DISTRIBUTE CAST CONTRACTS

Typically, three originals are struck for: the Performer, the production company accounting office, and the union office. Make sure that both Legal Counsel and you also receive copies. Assistant Directors often ask for copies to keep up with contracted promises. Mask the rates section to keep confidentiality.

PICTURES AND RESUMES

Ask each agent for pictures and resumes for each cast member on production. Publicity, Wardrobe, Hair and Makeup will be appreciative. Post your copies of the photographs in the production office with character names added at the bottom. For Stars, you may need extra copies for autographs. Discuss the Performer's attitude toward autographs with the Agent.

"CHANGE OF DATE(S)" MEMOS

If the dates as listed on the contract change, note the time and the date you spoke with, and received confirmation from, the Agent or the Performer. Draft a memo detailing this confirmation and refer to the contract number (if applicable). Then copy the memo to all the people who receive the cast contract. The union agreement specifies how many hours notice is required for various changes and cancellations without penalty. Consider this memo to be a new addendum to the contract. By noting the time and the date you spoke to the person, the memo becomes very useful to Accounting in determining if a Performer has to be paid for the day canceled or changed. (See a copy of a Change of Date form on page 505.)

IMMIGRATION & TRAVELING STARS

The Production Coordinator handles the logistics of immigration for cast and crew, since immigration permits can of course apply to both. The Production Manager needs to note and track the costs associated with the immigration process.

ARRANGING FOR AN IMMIGRATION PERMIT

Following are procedures for bringing a Star across borders. If you are traveling a crew member, adapt the information below.

INFORM THE IMMIGRATION OFFICE

Warn the immigration office as soon as you know that a non-national worker will be coming to work on the production. Give them the opportunity to be prepared in case production decides on a particular Performer very shortly before filming begins. Discuss the latest procedures.

COLLECT IMMIGRATION INFORMATION

Collect this information from the Agent, the Performer, or from yourself:

> Complete Legal Name (some performers have stage names)
> Permanent Home Address
> Home Telephone Number (immigration may/may not need this)
> Agent's Address (for the union work permit)
> Agent's Telephone Number (for the union work permit)
> Date of Birth

> Country of Birth
> Citizenship
> Union Work Permit (to prove union's permission)
> Job Description (character name and film title)
> Arrival Travel Date
> Flight Company, Flight Number, Arrival Time & Air Terminal
> Departure Travel Date★

★ Add at least two months onto the departure date in case of emergency. If production shoots an extra day or two and the permit has expired, you will have to take the Performer across the nearest border to arrange and pay for another permit.

PAY FOR THE PERMIT

In some countries, you have to arrange for the Performer to pick up and pay for the permit at the local embassy or consulate. In other countries you can meet the Performer at the airport and pay for the permit on arrival.

MEET PERFORMER AT AIRPORT

Whether the Performer has the permit in hand or not, always have a representative of the production company to meet him at the airport. Be there for emergencies, be there for hospitality, and be there for professionalism. Often the Transportation Coordinator or the Star Driver will be that person of contact.

MORE ABOUT TRAVELING STARS

While the Coordinator asks questions of the Star for immigration purposes, she can also find out his various preferences. You are probably the first person the Performer will be dealing with on the production, so now is the time to make a good first impression.

RESEARCH PLACES TO STAY

The Production Manager knows how many people will require a hotel for production. Research the places people can stay so you can strike a deal with one hotel to house them all. Does the hotel you choose have both rooms and suites to match all the deals you are making regarding travel and living? Who is paying for the incidental costs, like telephone, in-room movies, and internet access? Is the stay long enough to warrant renting a furnished apartment instead of a hotel room? Go and see these places, or ensure the Coordinator goes and sees them and photographs them, not unlike a location scout. You want to know what the visiting cast or crew is going to experience before you ask them to stay there.

HOTEL ROOM PREFERENCES

The Coordinator can ask the Performer about the hotel room preferences. Does the Performer like lots of or little sun exposure? Does he need a pool, fitness facility, or smoking/non-smoking room? Would he like to be in a particular area of town? Know your options before calling and promising the world.

AIRPLANE PREFERENCES

Does the Performer want a bulkhead, aisle, or window seat? If inflight food is included, does the Performer have a specific meal requirement? Is there a frequent flyer number to attach to the ticket sale?

FOOD PREFERENCES & ALLERGIES

For Craft Service and Catering, ask about food preferences and allergies. Does the Performer want lots of fresh food, or does he have a penchant for dark chocolate? Are there any food allergies?

AUTOGRAPH PREFERENCES

If you have not already discussed how the Performer likes to deal with autographs, discuss this now. You may be asked to store the names of people who wish autographs, so that the Performer can sign them all at once at the end of the shoot.

SEND SCRIPT PACKAGE

As with any cast member, as soon as a Star is on board, send him a script package with all the latest in paperwork from scripts to crew list to cast list. Include a personal letter of welcome, and if he has not traveled to your city before, include some travel information.

MEDICAL

Likely you will need to arrange for the Star to have a medical in his town in order to add him to the production's insurance policy. Arrange for this right away. (See more on Insurance in Chapter 17.)

ADR SESSIONS & CONTRACTS

ADR stands for "Additional Dialogue Recording," and is the recording of voices to match picture during postproduction. ADR is also known as "Looping." Since ADR usually happens after wrap, you may not have to deal with it, but if you are working on a series, you will.

ARRANGING FOR ADR

The Post Supervisor or the Post Coordinator will handle most of these booking arrangements with assistance from the Production Coordinator. The Production Manager needs to note the appropriate costs involved, as some ADR sessions will be covered by inclusive deals on the cast contract. The Production Coordinator not only needs to check that the paperwork is completed to ensure the Performer will be paid for the session, but also needs to report the session on the DPR.

BOOK & CONTRACT PERFORMERS

The Post Supervisor or the Post Coordinator usually arranges for the ADR studio, while the Production Coordinator arranges for the Performers' attendance. Make sure there is a signed contract for each Performer who is going to be recorded. Performers who have performed on set already have contracts. New voices may be added during postproduction. Generate these voice-only contracts as you would cast contracts. Refer to your union agreement, if applicable.

PERFORMER WORK REPORTS

As the A.Ds fill out work reports daily for the Performers on set to report what hours the talent worked, someone at the ADR session must fill out the form for each session. Send a blank report to the session. You can help by filling in the production company name, title, date, and Performers booked.

MAKE A MEMO ANNOUNCING THE ADR SESSION

Send a memo confirming the details of the ADR session to Postproduction, Accounting, Producer, and Production Manager. Accounting, now aware of the session, can track down the work report if it does not come back from the recording session speedily.

KEEP A COPY OF ALL INFORMATION

Keep a copy of all the information about the ADR session in your desk file folder in case you have to track down anything, like missing work reports. Send a copy of all appropriate information to the Performers' union office.

—⁓—

Cast contracts seem overpowering when you first start working with them. They are legally binding and do promise a lot of the production. When you have contracted your final cast member, you may find that Stunt contracts, being under the same union jurisdiction, keep the Coordinator busy making new contracts all the way through production. To prevent costly mistakes, accuracy is key in the completion of any and all cast contracts. If the Production Manager has to spend time with the Coordinator to ensure she is up to speed on the intricacies of cast contracts, it will be time well spent and money well controlled.

SET FOOD EXTRAVAGANCE

- -

You know you work in the film industry when...

You sit down to a lunch in the middle of a field in the middle of nowhere to dine on roast beef and Yorkshire pudding, and you have a choice of at least two salads and at least two desserts.

It's four o'clock in the morning, and it's time for lunch.

You get tired of having grilled salmon... again.

The milk in your fridge at home expired in June... and it is now August.

SUPPLIER AGREEMENTS

25

Anytime you make an agreement with a supplier, whether you are the Production Manager or Coordinator, you should commit to the deal on paper and have it signed by both parties as soon as possible. Writing commits both you and the supplier to the terms of the deal. The Accountant, too, will have excellent reference and backup for when she is calculating and writing the appropriate checks.

SUPPLIER LETTERS OF AGREEMENT

When the Production Manager makes a verbal deal with a supplier (like the Caterer or the Casting Director), make a letter of agreement up immediately to confirm the details. If you relate the details of the deal to the Production Coordinator, the Coordinator can create the first draft letter or agreement. You can then tweak the document both as a second set of eyes for accuracy to the deal points, and to approve the document. Being the signing authority, all letters of agreement should come from the Production Manager.

HOW TO MAKE A LETTER OF AGREEMENT

Since you are not a lawyer, do not try to write the way you think a lawyer sounds. Be simple and direct. Use letterhead to type a letter to the supplier, including their name, address, telephone and fax numbers. Address the letter to the person signing the agreement. Start the letter with: "This letter confirms the following:", then proceed to explain very plainly what the details of the agreement are, what the production company is promising, and what the supplier is promising. End with: "Your signature below indicates your agreement to the above," and mark spaces for the Production Manager and the supplier's representative to sign. Ensure copies of these letters go to the Production Accountant, the supplier, the Legal Counsel, and to the production files with the Production Coordinator. (See a sample Catering letter agreement on page 506.)

WHEN TO USE LETTERS OF AGREEMENT

Letters of agreement can be for Caterers, Casting Directors, Animal Handlers, someone giving permission to use his name in the script, or even non-union crew members. The options are endless.

PM & LEGAL APPROVES WORDING

The Production Manager should review all letters of agreement before sending them out for signature. Since you are signing them all, this procedure will be easy to accomplish. Depending on how complex the letter is, you may elect to forward it to Legal Counsel for re-wording. The simple, direct phrases presented will be a terrific start for a more formal contract. Collect the wordings of successful simple letters of agreement for reference on future productions.

WHERE TO FILE LETTERS OF AGREEMENT

If these letters are with crew members, file with the crew deal memos. If they concern clearances or the contact list, file them with the clearances or the contact lists, respectively. Use logic. File catering agreements in the catering file. Since the Production Accountant will file these letters by alphabetical order, the Coordinator can afford to file them by subject matter. When head office looks through the files later, they may not know the specific company names, but they will be able to look up agreements filed under "catering," "equipment house," "casting director," and "animal handler."

—⁂—

Committing to agreements assures how much is being spent, and what the deal terms are. Since nearly everything related to production has a price tag attached to it, once these deal letters are signed, you will have comfort to move forward. The deal has been made and agreed to.

AUDIENCE FOR A FALL

- -

I came to set one day just before lunch. We were filming in a generating station. Lots of pipes, large machinery, tall metal staircases, and cement floors. The place was laced with atmosphere. It was a perfect place to film this scene.

The crew was hard at work preparing for the shot. Tension was high. Concentration was focused. The Assistant Directors called for the set to be locked up. Silence fell and all eyes turned to the shot. The sound rolled. The camera rolled. "Action."

There was a scuffle at the top of the stairs. A cast member slipped and fell onto the stairs. But he did not fall down just one step. He fell down more. Two, three, ten, twenty, thirty. Smack, crunch, thunk, he seemed to hit every stair on the way down with sickening crunches. Thunk, crunch, wham, smack, splat. He landed on the cement floor face down. He did not move a muscle. The crew stared on in anticipation; it was a painful fall to watch. The camera kept rolling. "Cut."

A sigh of relief, and the crew broke into applause for the man in the crumpled heap at the base of the staircase. Then the Assistant Director called out, "That'll be lunch, one hour!" And everyone left.

At the sound of lunch, the stunt man stood up and headed off with the crew. Not a scratch on him, though, heaven knows why.

THE SPECIAL DEPARTMENTS

26

The special departments, like special effects, CGI, stunts, and shots starring children and animals, are often the "sell" shots of the film. We love to talk about them. We impress ourselves with how inventively we made movie magic become reality on the screen. Anything is possible… for a price. I will not discuss how much certain shots cost, because the world of imagination is open, and you might as well ask how long is a piece of string. You do need to consider, however, the following issues when dealing with the special departments.

PREVIS – 3D or 2D PREVISUALIZATION

Preparation is unmistakably key to successful special shots. By the time you go to camera, you and the crew should be so familiar with what is about to happen that you feel like you have already completed the shot.

When you realize how much prep time and cost is required for each special shot, you do not want to shoot footage that will end up on the cutting room floor. Depending on the planned complexity of the Director's vision and the limitations of your budget, you can storyboard the sequences, have the art department build a model, or hire a previs company to work with key crew to build the sequences in dynamic 3D. At minimum, you want to cover the sequences with action or special effects, but you can also previsualize the entire production. For some sequences it will always be faster to draw a few storyboard panels, but for others a previs pass using computer animation will be faster, more manipulative, and easier to understand visually. The previs has the added benefit of translating well into production. You may therefore find yourself in need of both a Storyboard Artist and a Previs team.

The Previs team facilitates the Director, DP, and Picture Editor coming together to test the creative vision of certain sequences and/or the script as a whole. Beyond these key crew forging their collaborative relationship early in preproduction, there are a number of other benefits to previs. For the DP, a rough computerized model of chosen locations can be built to explore and find out if the desired camera angles, staging, and lighting are even physically possible at those locations. It also provides a platform for testing out various scenarios cheaply and quickly. After the shot and lighting are designed in the computer, the Previs team can do a technical breakdown to output set, camera, and lighting specifications as well as diagrams to streamline activities on the shoot day. Also, the computer assets that are built can be used as a foundation for production CGI shots and other cross media uses (the website, bonus features, video game development, etc.).

Since the Previs team is basically supporting the definition of the Director's vision during preproduction, typically it phases out from production once principal photography begins. If, however, the vision is complex enough, the Previs team may attend set as a resource to re-test modified sequences on the fly.

FINDING THE SUPPLIER FOR SPECIAL SHOTS

RESEARCH SUPPLIERS

Carefully research potential suppliers for the special shots prior to committing to one. For this, you need to know without a doubt what production needs from the supplier for the "sell" shots. The previs or storyboard plans will help you in discussions. Be specific when interviewing suppliers. What is their track record? What special shots have they done for other films that may be related to what you need? You do not want to be a training ground for these suppliers. What exactly have they done for the shots on their show reel, and which of those shots have been done partially by them with another supplier embellishing the effect somehow? Know what you are buying before you commit.

SAFETY

In all cases, safety issues come first. The suppliers should be well aware of safety issues, so discuss safety with them. The Worker's Compensation Board is another source for safety preparation, but you may find the crew unions are more up on the specific safety requirements for film-related safety — even publishing safety requirements for certain special shots — because this is a very specialized industry. Be sure all safety precautions being taken are clearly identified and explained to the crew, both verbally at a meeting and detailed on the call sheet for their reference. Again, safety is a first priority. You want to see "special" on set, not "surprise."

PREP TIME FOR SUPPLIERS

There is no such thing as a "spur of the moment" special shot. If the supplier thinks he can promise you this, find another supplier. Of course, this means that you are responsible to commit to the supplier early enough in preproduction to allow the supplier enough prep time to prepare and practice for the special shots. Animals need time to train; they cannot "cram for exams." Special effects suppliers need time to test their explosions so they know ahead of time how big the blast will be, and how much smoke it might generate at the location chosen. You will also need time to arrange for the permits required for certain special shots.

SPFX – SPECIAL EFFECTS

Special effects are on-set flash. They can range from the use of dry ice, steam, or smoke as atmosphere, to the creation of a waterfall, snowfall, rainfall, wind, blazing fire, or explosions on set. Some special effects may be simple enough for the Props Department to handle, but as the complications increase, you will need a reliable, experienced supplier: a special effects company.

Most of their equipment has some kind of motor that will blot out your sound. Sound will record guide track anyway during the take, and should record wild lines of the Performers running their lines in the same sound atmosphere of the set — without the camera and the special effects equipment running. The Editors may be able to match the wild sound enough with the picture in post using the guide track as, obviously, a guide. Be prepared to pay for an ADR or looping session later for the Cast anyway.

For special effects, the Production Manager needs to liaise often with the SPFX Supervisor. The Supervisor is the key person for design and preparation of the shot, so he will know if the costs are increasing to achieve the result wished for by the storyboard. Complications during preproduction, and redesigning of the storyboard sequences can easily increase the costs of these special shots. This person is also the key safety person on the day.

POSTVIS

Very much like previs, and typically using the same team, postvis (postvisualization) takes the production footage as it is shot and does a previsualization pass on the effects before a CGI company bids or works on the production. Again, it is a low-cost visual testing ground for the Director's vision, but in this case, later on in production. This type of preparatory work can save considerable time and money in postproduction because you know exactly what you want and need to complete the CGI effects. You can also screen postvis sequences for test audiences who will be able to provide much better feedback than if they saw the same sequence interrupted by visual slugs that stand in for missing CGI shots.

CGI – COMPUTER ANIMATED EFFECTS

CGI actually stands for "computer generated image" or "computer graphic imagery." Some may be 2D computer effects — like painting in smoke and painting out animal tethers — while others may be 3D computer effects, like painting in a solid object — like a car falling off a cliff. If you have complicated CGI on your production, you may even have two separate departments, one for 2D effects and one for 3D effects, and if you have a huge number of effects on the production, you may even have two or three different CGI suppliers to deal with the workload in time to complete the film.

When one first mentions CGI, you tend to think of making animals talk and creating computerized mechanical characters to star alongside the Cast. You do not often think of enhancing an explosion that the SPFX team has already made on set, or of painting out animal tethers, or of removing the sound boom from the shot. Well, these are CGI shots, too, even though they appear "invisible" when the final film is done — and they are just as expensive as other fancy "visible" CGI shots. Try to minimize the invisible CGI fixes to ensure the CGI money in the budget goes toward the most dynamic effects shots.

As mentioned before: Beware! When the crew knows you have a CGI supplier on board, they may become lazy when shooting the set special effects and when working with animals. To increase shooting speed and do less preparation themselves, they may leave all sorts of tethers and other visual items in the shot, figuring you can "fit it in post." Remember CGI fixes are the most expensive way you can fix problems. The few minutes saved on set doing a proper rehearsal may cost you hours and tons of money in post to fix.

For this reason, CGI shots must be storyboarded and/or previsualized. Shooting extra footage that ends up being cut out of the film is certainly expensive, but animating extra footage is unthinkably expensive. The bonus about previs of animated sequences is that assets built for previs often can be used in or contribute to the final animation, putting you ahead of the game.

Again, the Production Manager needs to liaise often with the CGI Supervisor. Find out if the crew is adding shots to the CGI list on an ongoing basis. This person should also be the one on set supervising the shots that are going to be combined with the CGI animation.

If you are setting up the CGI room for the animation team, ensure you have enough air conditioning and airflow in the room. This much computer equipment in a small space generates an awful lot of heat.

MOTION CONTROL

Motion control is related to CGI animation, as motion control shots involve synching the camera action with animation to be painted on afterward. If the camera is stationary, animation is easy to paint onto the shot, because neither the shot nor the drawing board (computer screen) is moving. Once camera movement is involved, the animation has to move at exactly the same rate that the camera does, so the animation does not "slip or slide" across the screen. For example, if you dolly toward a Performer who is holding a CGI-animated snow globe, you need motion control to ensure the snow stays inside the globe. Motion control shots can be truly dynamic indeed.

Your first question with motion control should be: Does the camera really need to move? If camera movement on this shot is not critical to the story, it is much, much more affordable to animate the shot without adding the complexity of motion control. Is this really the best place to spend a good chunk of production's budget? Of course, if all the shots of the film are moving camera, and every single time you cut to an effects shot the camera becomes static, this will look terribly obvious and certainly not so good. Be sure the style of shooting and effects match the size of budget you have.

The Motion Control Supervisor will be key in planning all the various elements required for the shot using motion control. On the day, the motion control team will hook up a computer to the camera to record and program in the camera movement for repetitive playback both on set, and later on the computer screen for the animation. As for elements, the Supervisor may need a shot of the action complete with Performers on the set; a separate shot of the set using the camera movement, but seeing no Performers (a background plate); and a separate shot of the Performers doing the action against a blue or a green screen using the camera movement but not seeing any background. Because of this level of technical complexity, on the day, the Motion Control Supervisor may need to direct the shot instead of the Director. Placement of every element and Performer in the screen, including the camera movement, is critical to the success of the blending in of the animation into the shot in postproduction. This need for exacting technical accuracy, however, may result in somewhat stale screen performances, as the Performers are asked to act in a hugely sterile, technical-first environment.

BLUE SCREEN OR GREEN SCREEN

Blue screen or green screen is an old effects process, but it is still used. Since skin color is so far opposite the blue or the green you use on these screens, you can "key-out" the flat blue or green from behind Performers to insert a background, like a fantastic planet, behind them — to give the audience the illusion that these Performers are actually on that planet you have pasted behind them. This process is sometimes still called "chroma key"; its colors are chroma key blue and chroma key green. Old chroma keys used to leave a blue (or green) halo around the Performers — especially around their hair where the line between action and background is uneven; since technology has advanced, blue screen shots can be pretty much invisible.

Of course, using blue screen, the Performers may not wear any blue in their wardrobe, or if using green screen, they cannot wear any green. If they do, the blue or the green color will also be "keyed-out," and the background will be inserted where their blue jeans or green sweater was, too. More advanced technology allows the ability to key out only certain shades of blue or of green, but there is a limitation. For this reason, ensure that the Wardrobe Designer is involved in conversations about blue screen or green screen shots. Be sure that the costume design and shooting schedule does not have you painting the screen from blue to green to blue to green every other day.

Painting an even color of the blue paint or the green paint is critical to being able to key out all the color in postproduction. Be sure the screen is painted early enough in advance in case there is streaking and you have to have it painted again. It goes without saying that you need to hire professionals to paint these screens. Even lighting is also critical to a successful key. Arrange for a pre-light to give the crew the time to get it right without the shooting crew waiting around to watch them work.

WORKING WITH ANIMALS

We love animals, and we remember fondly many shots with animals from various films. The script calls for a fox, dog, cat, owl, rat, spider, horse, rabbit, ferret, squirrel, otter, ant, monkey, trout, chicken, goat, duck, pig, llama, alpaca, or whatever to do something specific or to be somewhere specific. You need a trained animal (or insect) and a Wrangler (or Trainer or Handler). Remember, though, that animals will be animals whether they are trained or not. It is in their nature.

Show the Wrangler the storyboard or previs plan. In your early meetings, professional Wranglers will tell you what a particular animal may or may not do on command. Ensure you commit to an Animal Wrangler early enough for them to complete the weeks of training they will need to train their animals to do the specific tasks you require in the script. Some animals are more trainable than others. Even within species, like dogs, some breeds are more trainable than others.

Just like with any of the special departments, be specific in what you need of this supplier. Negotiate a fee based on specifics. That is why you ensured a storyboard or previs plan was in place early.

Prepare, too, to schedule around the animals. They grow tired. They do not understand how important this film is to you, and will not work beyond their tiredness to complete the shot. When they tire, they tire and it shows. If they are transported a long distance, they need time to adapt to their new surroundings. They may need time on set in their new environment to become comfortable before performing. Ask the Wrangler.

Shooting multi-camera when animals are on set is helpful. Animals cannot repeat performances the way Performers can. Use a reduced second unit (or animal unit) to capture animal reaction shots. Why have the entire main unit crew standing around waiting for the animal to perform — or not — for the camera? Be sure the animal unit is scheduled to gather shots after main unit has captured the main action of the same scene. If the animals and main cast have to interact, you want the animal unit to capture shots to fit into main unit's shot plan, not have the animal unit shoot reaction shots first and dictate to main unit (and to the Director) how to film a certain scene.

Some animals are dangerous and may panic with lots of people around. Most animals are not used to the number of people required to be on a film set. This is another reason that second unit is helpful. If animals need to be on main unit, ensure that safety issues for the crew and for the animals is addressed, and ensure the crew is fully informed both verbally and on the call sheet. Remember that most animals have a more highly developed sense of smell than people, so certain smells in the location's environment will affect them and therefore their performance. As I said, animals will be animals. Research and be prepared.

STUNTS

Stunt Performers are more predictable than animals, to say the very least. But the stunts themselves are filled with uncertainties no matter how well you plan for them. Weather may even play a factor. Imagine the stunt over the raging river, and when you arrive at the river, it is covered in ice, and the fellow could just walk across it instead of swinging over it. This is not a very exciting stunt anymore.

As Production Manager, when you know the details and the plans of the stunt, you will need to negotiate a stunt adjustment fee based on the danger level of the stunt, and the number of times you have asked the stunt to be performed. Since you have to pay for each take, and no two takes will look alike, you will undoubtedly need a second camera or two on the day.

Liaise with the Stunt Coordinator, and ensure they come to relevant preproduction meetings to keep in the loop of preparation for camera. To properly prepare, this person will need to walk through the locations where all stunts are going to be performed.

One last word about stunts: Never allow safety to be jeopardized to have more "flash." Be smart.

WORKING WITH CHILDREN

Working with children is not unlike working with animals. They are not the same, of course, because you can talk with children, but there are some distinct similarities between the two. Children tire. They do not have the attention span that adults have, so you cannot expect them to work effectively for hour after hour. They cannot duplicate a performance take after take, but will fade around take two.

On a film set, when children are performing, they are working. Yet in most places there are no laws to control the working conditions of children, because most governments simply state that employing children is illegal. Governments, however, are dealing with this dilemma, though some more quickly than others. You may find that on a co-production the two governments have directly conflicting laws governing the working conditions of children on a film set. Address this dilemma early.

If you are in an environment where there are no governing laws about hiring children, know that Performer unions have had very strict rules about working with children of different ages for a long time. The unions stipulate how long a day children are allowed for a work day, how much tutoring time is required each day, how many rest periods are required and for how long, and that no overtime is allowed. Typically when you hire children there are no governmental working conditions, so abide by the union rules, whether you are a union shoot or not. These rules were designed to protect the children. As you are technically hiring them illegally, you may need to prove that the working conditions you provided them were thoughtful and protective of them. Do not get yourself or the production into trouble when hiring children.

During the school season, you will have to hire a Tutor for children you have working on your set if you are shooting on school days. If the Child Performer has worked before, her parent may have a specific choice of Tutor. If you have a number of children of varying ages, you may have to hire more than one. Check the rules with the Performer union you are signatory to, or whose rules you choose to follow.

Always meet the Parents and/or Guardians. One of them is bound to be on set with the Child Performer anyway, but meet them ahead of time to give them comfort that this production is professional and thoughtful to the needs of children on set. Think about what you are going to do to be true to your word. Film sets are not child-friendly in general. There are many safety hazards for children all over, and the hurry-up-and-wait nature of a film set is very boring for children. Have you hired a crew that is child-friendly? How is the Director's patience with children?

As animals will be animals, so children will be children. Do not expect them to act or react like adults. They are children and act accordingly. Allow them their childhood. You are only a child once.

OTHER SPECIAL DEPARTMENTS

Other special departments can include: television synch (since you need special equipment to synch the television 30 frames per second motion to the film 24 frames per second capture, though tweaking camera settings can suffice when shooting digital), helicopter flying shots, shots from boats, and so on. The issues are the same as for the departments noted above. Plan. Research. Hire professionals. Safety comes first.

—⚏—

When it comes to special shots or "sell" shots, think simple, even if you are using a special department. Simple can be well done. For example, a wire being pulled off screen can move objects as well as CGI can in postproduction, but is much cheaper. Faking outdoor movement in a studio space in front of a rear projected moving image and using a fan (known as Poor Man's Process or PMP) may suffice in place of a complex on-location traveling shot or even in place of a time and labor consuming blue screen shot. This is a creative industry. Be creative in problem solving to creating the magic. Use the special departments when you have exhausted the simple effects and want to spend the money on something spectacular. That will be using the budget wisely and putting the money where it belongs: on the screen.

MORE PRODUCTION & COORDINATION ISSUES | VI

Fast, good, cheap… pick any two.

I WON'T GO BACK TO WHITE

When it comes to revising a script, I hate going back to white. I will search high and low for every pastel-colored paper on the market to postpone the inevitable "return to white."

It was very close to end of production, and I was happy that we had never had to return to white. We had survived numerous script changes and I was certain the revisions were at an end. We had been from white to pink to blue to green to yellow. The standards. Then on to buff to salmon to gray to goldenrod to sand and at last to lavender.

Then one more revision came in. It was a short two-pager. I couldn't bear the thought of going back to white for such a short revision. But we had exhausted every pastel paper on the market. So, I got out red and green highlighters, and with the help of the office staff drew a pattern on each page to publish... the plaid revisions.

SCRIPT FORMAT & REVISIONS 27

Script revisions happen for many reasons. When evaluating a scene in the editing room, it is decided that more dialogue needs to be added to a previous scene to explain this scene's reason for being. Another scene ended up longer than planned in screen time, so the solution is to shorten a different scene that hasn't been shot yet. The list goes on.

THE PRODUCTION MANAGER & SCRIPT REVISIONS

Some script revisions affect the budget with the addition of locations or props or whatever, others save the budget money, and others again have no affect at all on the budget. As the Production Manager, you are probably already in the loop concerning what revisions are about to happen so have anticipated the costs or savings associated with the script revisions yet to come. When the revisions are published, read them immediately. Do the changes really reflect what you expected, or are there other surprises there for you and the budget? There may be…

THE PRODUCTION COORDINATOR & SCRIPT REVISIONS

The Coordinator is responsible for the typing up and publishing of accurate script revisions, though the Assistant Coordinator may be the person assigned to the actual keyboarding. What the Coordinator needs to know inside and out is script format and how to manipulate it.

FORMATTING THE EARLY DRAFTS

There are many wonderful books on the market that can explain script formatting in great detail. There are also many lovely programs (like Final Draft and Screenwriter) that help Writers format scripts as they write. This chapter will not attempt to replace them, but will present you with a nutshell version of what you need to know about script format and give you the information to manually format a script. Because, even if you use script-formatting software, you still have to understand script format to generate what you need for the shooting set. In many cases, though the script was created in scriptwriting software, the shooting script is transferred to word processing software for publication and shooting-stage revisions. As the Production Coordinator, you must know script format better than even the Writing Department. A well-formatted script is essential to clearly and easily explain the story to the crew for filming.

CHOOSE A SCRIPT FORMAT

Of the several formats used, and endless versions on those formats by Writers and Producers, choose between two of the basic kinds: feature film format and comedy format. Seek the Writing Department's and the Producer's approval in choosing a script format.

FONT

Always use courier font, as each character of the typeface has the same spacing. You need this consistency for the written word so that the script is entirely legible, and so that one script page will equal about one minute of screen time for every script.

WHO TYPES THE SCRIPT

The fastest keyboardist in the office should type scripts on condition that is also the person who best knows script format. Re-formatting pre-typed pages takes almost as long as re-typing an entire script.

MAKE THE FORMAT & LABELLING CONSISTENT

Be consistent about labeling scene locations, about identifying character names, about everything. This advice cannot be repeated too many times. The reason: If a script notes Ken's living room as: "KEN'S LIVING ROOM," "LIVING ROOM," "INTERIOR KEN'S HOUSE," and as "THE ELLIOTT LIVING ROOM," the crew will be confused over how many locations the script actually needs. Script formatting software will consider this one location as four separate locations because each of the names is slightly different.

INFORM THE PM & CREW OF CHANGES WHILE TYPING

When you type the script, you are reading it word for word. You are bound to notice that, for example, seven new props have been added to a certain scene. Note this down and talk to the Props Department soon to find out if they are aware of the forthcoming change. Mention it also to the Production Manager. Since the script itself will take a few more hours to type, print, copy, and distribute, informing the crew as you keyboard it in can give them added time to address the new changes.

WHAT TO LOOK FOR	WHOM TO TELL
Changes that affect today	Appropriate department(s)
Changes that affect tomorrow	Appropriate department(s)
New characters	Producer/Casting Department
Changed character names	Clearance company/Legal Counsel
Changed location names	Clearance company/Legal Counsel
New locations	Locations Department
New props	Props Department
New wardrobe	Wardrobe Department
New action (stunts, effects)	Appropriate Department(s)
Changed dialogue	Performers affected

IF THE PC IS NOT THE KEYBOARDIST

If you choose a keyboardist other than yourself, have a copy of the source file (or handwritten script pages) to read as the typing is happening. Keep atop the revisions. Make notes. Inform the crew.

TYPING FROM VARIOUS FORMATS

Writers will give you scripts on anything from electronic format to handwritten sheets of paper torn from a binder. Especially on a series, it is your job to make each script format the same.

> **Formatting From Electronic Version**: If the script is given to you electronically, the Writer's word processing program or script writing software may not be the same as yours. On translating the file into your word processor, you will either find yourself re-formatting the entire script or, at worst, needing to re-type every word. Whichever you do, print out a copy for the Producer and the PM first, then read the script as you work to be sure correct scene breaks occur.

> **Formatting From A Plain Text File**: If the Writer and you do not have compatible computer programs, at the very least your computer can read an ASCII or plain text version of the file. Unfortunately, all document formatting is lost in the transfer, but the text is there. Print out a copy for the Producer to review as is, then begin the process of formatting the plain text into a legible script.

> > **Typing From Handwriting**: If the Writers give you script in handwritten form, you will learn to be very good at reading their individual handwriting. Most Writers are so fast to capture the idea on paper, that they may overlook proper spelling and grammar. In this case, do not always type word for word. Read the script as you type to determine if the "mistake" you are reading is an intentional style of writing or a typo. Proper scene breaks can be missing, too. Do not have characters walk from room to room or flash forward in time without breaking for a new scene heading.

WHEN NOT TO RE-FORMAT OR RE-TYPE

The Producer may suggest that you do not immediately re-format or re-type the first script that you have received from Writer. She may want to radically revise the script from its present state. Save yourself the work. Find out.

IF YOU NEED HELP FORMATTING

If you are worried about script format, or have a question about where to break a scene, or how to number a scene, go to the A.D.s. They have to schedule the script scene by scene, and so will be happy to advise you.

WHEN IS A DRAFT FINAL?

All early (pre-final) drafts should not have scene numbers. Only when the script is declared by the Producer to be a "Final Draft" should you number the scenes. This system ensures that the crew does not do heavy break downs of what they need for their department on a draft of the script that has yet to go through more major changes. Keep in touch with the Producer and the Writers about how close to "final" the script is.

WHO NUMBERS THE SCENES?

Some A.D.s like to number the scenes in the script themselves. Most expect the Coordinator to do the job. If you are unsure about how to number a sequence, ask the A.D.s. You have the knowledge of script formatting, and they have the knowledge of how they plan to shoot this collection of scenes.

SAVE AT LEAST TWO COPIES

The script in your computer is a long document. Save it, and a backup copy. If you do not, just imagine having to type the whole script over again from scratch.

TITLE PAGES

There are about as many versions of title pages as there are versions of script formats. Be clear. Be consistent.

TITLE & WRITING NAMES

Center the title and the Writer(s) names and place them about one-third the way down from the top of the page. The title is underlined or quoted. Identify all the Writers of the project as they are to be credited contractually, ensuring spelling and name order is correct. If in doubt, check with the Producer.

PRODUCTION COMPANY NAME, ADDRESS & TELEPHONE

To identify ownership of the property, note the production company name, address, and telephone number at the bottom right or the bottom left of the title page.

SCRIPT STATUS & DATE

Is the script a first, second, final draft, or pink revision? For early drafts, type which early draft and the date. For any script after the first final draft, list all the revisions and dates in a growing list. This list will remind crew of all the different parts they need to collect to make a single complete script. Place the list at the top right or the bottom right of the title page. Leave enough room for at least twelve different colored revisions.

COPYRIGHT AND/OR DISCLAIMER

Some production companies require a copyright notification and/or a disclaimer on the title page. Ask the Producer or the Legal Counsel. If you need one, place it at the bottom center of the page. If it is long, use small print.

SAMPLE TITLE PAGES

Since pictures can speak more than words, see two samples of title pages on pages 507 and 508. One is for a very revised single production script, and the other is an early draft of one episode of a comedy series.

FEATURE FILM SCRIPT FORMAT

This format can be used for feature films, Movies of the Week and any type of drama program. It can also be used in a series format, but for this case, presume that the production is solitary.

PAGE HEADER

For page one, center the title at the top of the page. Specify the color and the date of the latest revision at the top right. For all other pages, make a header at the top left that reads title, color, and date. The redundancy is especially important to identify pages when they are faxed, copied onto the wrong-colored paper, or found separate from the script.

PAGE NUMBERS

Scene numbers and page numbers can be similar or even identical, depending on the pace of the script. If you use a dash before and after page numbers, you will find it harder to mistake page numbers for a scene numbers (which are also on the right side of the page). You can also choose to have a period after all page numbers to differentiate them from scene numbers.

TAB SETTINGS

Listing them from left to right, these are the tab settings you will need:

> 0.5" left of left margin   Scene #
> Left margin   Scene Headings & Action
> 1" in from left margin   Dialogue
> 2" in from left margin   Parenthetical
> 2.5" in from left margin   Character Name
> 5" in from left margin   Transitions
> 0.5" in from right margin   Page #
> Flush Right   Scene #, Revision Marks

SCENE HEADINGS

Make scene headings bold and in capitals so that you and the crew can find them quickly. Scene headings are made up of three parts: inside/outside, where, when. Begin with "Int." (Interior) or "Ext." (Exterior), then describe the location, then use a dash, then end with "Day" or "Night." Always include all three parts. Read the script carefully, if need be, to gather the information for all three parts. Do not use more than one dash. Script formatting software tends to consider a dash as an indication that the location description is completed; the information after the dash will be considered the time of day. You do not want to have "Living Room" as your time of day description. Finally, be consistent about the location descriptions. Do not give one location more than one descriptive name.

SCENE NUMBERS

Place scene numbers far into the margins at both sides of the page for fast, double reference. You can precede the number with "Sc." if you like, so that crew will quickly differentiate between the scene and the page numbers.

ACTION

Description of action is generally very sparse in a script. Ensure you use hard returns at the end of each line instead of letting the computer do the line scrolling. This tactic will be useful when you come to revise the script line by line on a word processor.

WHEN TO CAPITALIZE IN ACTION

Character names, technical action, and sounds can be capitalized, but with action description being sparse, capitalizing words can get out of hand.

> **Character names:** Capitalize a character name only the first time it appears in a scene. This will help crew to determine who plays in the scene.

> **Technical Action (left margin):** Terms like Angle On:, Different Angle:, Music:, SFX (Sound Effects):, SPFX (Special Effects): are all capitalized and placed on the left margin for notice. These are specific requirements of Camera, Sound, and other technical departments.

> **Technical Action (within description):** When technical effects are not highlighted by placing them on the left margin and are written in the middle of a descriptive paragraph, capitalize the feature for notice. These include: BANG!, LIGHTS ON, and so on.

DIALOGUE

Dialogue margins are rather flexible. How wide or how narrow they are depends on the intended pace of the dialogue. Discuss this issue with the Producer or the Writing Department. As with the action, use hard returns at the end of each line so that you can revise each line individually later.

CHARACTER NAMES

Capitalize all character names and be consistent. The script may give a character several names throughout the course of the story, but you should let each character have only one name. If a character changes names during the script, keep using one name and add the new name in brackets beside the character name later. Do not center character names if you are using any formatting software, because the software relies on specific tab settings to find the character names.

PARENTHETICALS

You will see words in brackets beside character names and underneath character names. Parentheticals are the ones underneath. They are descriptions of how the dialogue is to be read, or what is to be acted simultaneously. These tend to be in lower case.

		MAX
>	How words are said	(whispers)
>	Who words are said to	(to computer screen)
>	Where words are said to	(to off screen)
>	Actions to be performed	(waves hand)
>	Laughter & sighs	(chuckles)

Directions in brackets beside the character name are production explanations, not directions for the Performer. These tend to be in uppercase.

>	The dialogue continues	MAX (CONT)
>	Location of the character	WOMAN (ON TV)
>	Speech is voice over or narration	MAN (V.O.)
>	Dialogue is heard from off screen	VOICE (O/S)
>	Alternate character name	PERSON WITH HAT (MAX)

TRANSITIONS

Transitions are editing commands that carry you to an entirely different scene. These include: Cut To:, Dissolve:, Swish Pan To:. Do not confuse these with on-set technical commands, like "Angle On," that instruct you to a new camera angle within the same scene.

CONTINUED

Note "continued" in brackets at the bottom and the top of each scene that continues onto the next page. This makes each page clear about whether the scene ends at the bottom of the page or not. When noting "continued" at the top of the next page, add the scene number for clarity.

SCRIPT PAGE SAMPLE

Review the two samples on pages 509 and 510. They show all the formatting notes mentioned above.

COMEDY SCRIPT FORMAT

This format can be used for comedy, sitcoms, or any fast-paced dialogue scripts. Since single episode productions have already been addressed, presume that the comedy script is for an episodic television series. Basically, use the same format as the feature film script format, incorporating a few changes.

PAGE HEADER

Add the episode number to the header. With a series, you will be handling revisions for many episodes at the same time, and will need to identify each page separately.

ACTION

Action is completely capitalized for this type of format.

DIALOGUE

Dialogue is still upper and lower case, but is double-spaced for easy, fast reading.

SCRIPT PAGE SAMPLE

Again review the sample script pages on pages 509-511 to see the differences between the feature film script format and the comedy script format.

SCRIPT REVISIONS

When you revise a script, you need to highlight to the crew exactly what has changed without asking them to re-read the entire script every single time. Here is a step-by-step process to keep atop the many revisions that flood the Coordinator's desk.

COLLECT SCRIPT REVISIONS IN DESK FILE FOLDER

You collect notes for script revisions from many sources. The Producer and the Writers give you marked-up copies of the script. You have taken notes during production meetings as future script changes are discussed. You have notes from the script clearance company about changes that need to be made. You have heard the A.Ds mention that a scene will be shot in a different way than what was originally written. Make a note about this, too. Store all your notes in the desk file folder labeled "Script Revisions." When you come to revise the script, all your notes will be in one place.

WHO APPROVES THE REVISIONS

Though revisions and requests for revisions come from far and wide, they must all be approved by the Producer. Review them with him.

WHEN TO REVISE A SCRIPT

Publish a new script or a new set of pages only when there are enough revisions to warrant their publishing, or when the change is drastic enough to require that you inform the crew immediately. Ask the Producer. If you have been informing the crew of changes before they happen, publishing the pages daily or hourly is not crucial.

WHY USE COLORED PAPER FOR REVISIONS?

Colored revisions are for instant and distant recognition. If a crew member shows up on set and sees everyone with a yellow script while hers is blue, she will be instantly aware there are script revisions to be had and will seek them out.

WHEN IS IT REVISED PAGES vs. REVISED SCRIPT

Consider the number of pages that you need to revise. If revised pages account for more than 70% of the script, you will do better to publish an entire new draft on the new paper color, re-formatting the pages as you go. You cannot, however, revise an entire script once shooting has begun. Continuity is already using the script to make notes to the editors, and is sending the script page by page to the editors as the film is being shot.

TYPING THE REVISIONS

When it is time to revise the script, here is how to tackle the job.

CHANGE THE TITLE PAGE

Add the new revised color and date to the list of revisions on the title page.

CHANGE THE PAGE HEADER

Change the header on each page to note the correct new color and date for the revision.

MAKE CHANGES AND MARK NEW REVISIONS

Every time you change a word in the script, mark the changed material with an asterisk (*) flush right on that line. There is no limit to the number of asterisks you can use on a page. With this system, crew can immediately see which lines to read on the revised page to look for the new material.

REVISING A REVISION – CLEAR OLD REVISION MARKS

Before revising a script that has been previously revised, erase all previous revision marks (asterisks). If not, you will find a build-up of asterisks, and finding the latest revision on the page becomes increasingly difficult.

SOFT RETURNS vs. HARD RETURNS

Because you revise the script one line at a time, you need hard returns at the end of each line to allow you to flush right and place the asterisks. If soft returns (automatic word wrapping) are still in the script at this point, search and replace them on the computer with hard returns.

A & B SCENES

Once a script is marked "final," the scene numbers cannot change. To insert new scenes in between two existing ones (like between scene 6 and 7), you must number the new scenes with A's and B's, ie: Sc.6, Sc.6A, Sc.6B, Sc.7. Hope you never have to insert a scene between scene 6A and 6B. If you do, try: Sc.6A, Sc.6AA, Sc.6B. If you have to insert a scene prior to scene 1, use: Sc.A1.

OMITTED SCENES

Once a scene is added to the script, it must always be listed, even if it is omitted. Like any scene header, note the scene number and "omitted" beside. Keep this notification in every revised draft that follows.

A & B PAGES

As the scene numbers remain fixed in a "final" draft script, so do the page numbers. If the revised page becomes shorter due to omissions, leave the rest of the page blank. If the revised page becomes longer, continue the revision on an "A" page. Your page numbers can therefore look like this: page 12, 13, 14, 14A, 14B, 14C, 15, 16, and so on.

OMITTED PAGES

When the new material has you removing one or several pages from the script, mark the span of pages numbers missing atop one of the revised pages. Your new page number sequence could, therefore, look like this: page 12, 13-14B, 14C, 15, and so on.

—w—

You will liken keeping up with script revisions to trying to catch a waterfall. As soon as you finish publishing one colored revision, another — or the plan for another — lies waiting in the wings. Be ready for the effect they have on the budget, and to distribute the information out to the crew as soon as possible. You can do it.-

WHAT MEANETH NINE TO FIVE

- -

There is nothing whatsoever nine to five about working in film — except, maybe, one thing.

Renting an ice rink in the middle of hockey season means that you have to travel to work at 2:30 in the morning with the radio in your car cheerfully saying, "And here's a song to get you home safely tonight."

When the boiler breaks in the production office at 3:00 a.m., you won't be able to get in touch with the landlord before 7 or 8. String all baseboard heaters into the smallest office you can, and gather any people in the office for that early morning huddle. Keep your parkas on for added warmth. Draw straws to find out who is the next person to walk down the icy hallway to make the next photocopy.

Then, think about it. Who is going to call the production office at 3:30 in the morning? The set. Go to the set with the Production Manager. It's an ice rink. It's bound to be warmer. Just remember to be back in time to arrange for the fixing of the boiler.

Have lunch at nine in the morning, and an afternoon snack around noon. Start fading about three, but the end of the workday is nearing. Be prepared for this. Driving home is one of the few times you get to mingle with all those nine-to-fivers. It's five o'clock rush hour.

PRODUCTION SCHEDULING

28

There are preproduction schedules, production schedules, one-line schedules, shooting schedules, and Second Unit schedules. The Production Manager and Coordinator need to be up to speed on all the types of schedules.

The PM especially needs to be able to read and review the schedule to evaluate its plausibility for the show's being able to be completed on time and on schedule.

The Coordinator may not need to type the schedule, only photocopy and distribute it, since the Assistant Directors typically generate all schedules with their scheduling software. If there is no access to this software, the Coordinator will have to be prepared to lend a hand.

PREPRODUCTION SCHEDULE

Pretty much every day in prep the Assistant Directors revise a list of the events that are scheduled to happen during preproduction. This list includes times of meetings, location surveys, and wardrobe fittings, and is usually drafted in the form of a memo.

The PM needs to know what meetings are being scheduled, and be involved in as many as possible. Who is meeting with whom? Are the special effects prep issues being addressed?

The Coordinator's job is to distribute the prep schedule to the crew daily. If the schedule is given to you handwritten, you are to type it up also.

PRODUCTION SCHEDULE

The Coordinator can make this schedule with input from the PM. Collect information from the PM, the Producer, and the A.D.s to generate a one-page week-by-week breakdown of the entire production's schedule. For each week note if the production is prepping, shooting, on hiatus, on holiday, or wrapping. Also note which days of the week are shoot days. At a glance the crew can now understand the entire schedule, even which weeks are non-Monday-to-Friday workweeks. Include dates for post events like the dates for rough cut, fine cut, delivery, and audit. When this schedule revises, copy it onto colored paper just like a script revision for notice. Long after production has completed, the Accounting, the Publicity, and the Legal Departments will be referring to this schedule. Be accurate. Here is an obviously hypothetical example for production dates only:

Mon.Sep.01	*Labor Day Holiday (off)*
Tue.Sep.02 - Fri.Sep.05	*Prep*
Sun.Sep.07 - Thu.Sep.11	**SHOOT EPISODE #1**
Mon.Sep.15 - Fri.Sep.19	*Hiatus*
Mon.Sep.22 - Fri.Sep.26	**SHOOT EPISODE #2**
Mon.Sep.29 - Fri.Oct.03	*Wrap*

PRODUCTION BOARD (STRIP BOARD OR THE BOARD)

The A.D.s create the shooting schedule by first making a production (or strip) board. The board is typically created on computer with software that emulates the look and interaction of the old physical board. The physical board is large and black, and when opened, displays many colored vertical strips coded with numbers and words. There is also a large white "header board" strip that displays the legend for the number codes. The entire board is written in pencil. On computer, the board looks just like an electronic version of the physical board — though there are many other display formats available to you at the click of a button. Become familiar with looking at and reading a board. (See a sample Strip Board on page 512.)

"DECODING" OR READING THE STRIP BOARD

Since the A.D.s are the ones that create the board, you do not need to know all the details of creating one yourself. But, since the board always depicts the schedule in its latest form, you should know some of the basics of the language and the codes of a strip board.

EACH STRIP IS A SCENE IN THE SCRIPT

Each colored strip on the board represents one scene of the script no matter how long each scene is. Though the information on each strip can vary from A.D. to A.D., you can read on each strip: the scene number, whether the scene is day or night and interior or exterior, a written description of the location, a micro synopsis of what happens in the scene, and a list of the characters needed for that scene (with each character represented by a number code).

THE HEADER BOARD

The header board is the first panel of the board and it tells you: the film title, the key crew names, the version of the script used for this schedule, and a legend of which character has been assigned to which character number. These character numbers are the same ones you use on the cast list and the call sheets.

WHY DIFFERENT COLORS FOR EACH STRIP

The colors of each strip tell you at a glance if the scene is day or night, interior or exterior. A legend that is often used:

White:	Exterior day	(think bright light, like the sun, appears white)
Yellow:	Interior day	(think the color of household lights are yellowish)
Blue:	Exterior night	(think films often light night scenes blue)
Green:	Interior night	(think yellow "interior" plus blue "night" equals green)

Black and red strips serve as borders between the days. Red identifies a weekend. Black strips usually have a white space to summarize the date and the total number of pages scheduled to be shot for that day.

WHY DIVIDE THE PAGES BY EIGHTHS?

You see the scene page counts are listed in eighths of pages and wonder why would anyone choose fractions that are difficult to add and subtract to use as numerical totals. Eighths are a good fraction for division. You can divide a page in half, and in half again, and in half again, and still have a readable fraction. Always list page counts in eighths (use 4/8 instead of 1/2) because, as you know, you can more readily add and subtract the fractions with a common denominator.

When the schedule changes, if a manual scheduling system is being used, the Coordinator should take the time to double check the daily page count totals. Sometimes these totals are forgotten when it comes to recalculation. Computer scheduling software removes the need to do this. Make your primary math teacher proud.

READING THE SCHEDULE

The A.D.s schedule a production taking into account many factors, so there is no "right" and "wrong" when it comes to scheduling, but there are a number of issues and questions you as Production Manager can address and discuss with the A.D.s to make some schedules more workable than others.

PERFORMER AVAILABILITY

Performer availability will be your first limitation for deciding which scenes you are filming and when. If you can only have your Star for the first three weeks of filming, then you will have to schedule all his scenes then. Period. For Child Performers and Animals, consider Performer availability issues to cover the length of the day they can be there without tiring out. You may even find that your first day of principal photography is based on the yet-to-be-announced wrap day of your lead Performer on another shoot. If this is the case, of course, keep in daily contact with the other shoot, and try to relax amid the stress.

LOCATION AVAILABILITY

Location availability is at the top of the limitation list, along with Performer availability, for dictating your schedule for you. It is logical, though, since you do not want to travel to one particular location three to four times during the shoot when you can shoot all the scenes at once, saving the unit company move and setup time.

TRAFFIC PATTERNS

Does the schedule take into account traffic patterns or work schedules? If you need a downtown office, do you need to shoot during a weekend day to gain access? If you are closing a street, do not plan to do it during rush hour on a weekday.

NUMBER OF SCENES PER DAY

How many scenes are you targeting to achieve daily on the set? Keep in mind the next two sections, because some scenes take longer to complete than others. Still, if you are planning a large number of small scenes, ensure that the schedule addresses all the required time needed for costume changes and set decoration changes to achieve all the scenes.

NUMBER OF SETUPS PER DAY

Consider the Director's shot list for each scene when planning for how many scenes to target each day. Some scenes can be covered in one setup, and others take plenty more. If the camera has to move a number of times to new positions on set during the day, remember that lighting too will have to change, and together preparation for these two take up a lot of set time. Crack television crews may achieve about 20-27 setups per day, and perhaps 40-45 setups if there is a second camera running, while new Directors may manage to complete only about 9-11 setups in the same time. IMAX 3D is so technically complicated that you may expect to achieve about only 4-5 setups per day.

NUMBER OF 1/8'S OF PAGES PER DAY

Make sure the schedule addresses a reasonable number of pages for you to achieve each day. Feature films may plan for about 2-3 pages per day, while television movies and series plan for about 7-10 pages per day. Dialogue scenes may be high on page count but not difficult to film, while other scenes that involve complicated special effects may be very low on page count, but will take you an enormous amount of time to capture. Remember the extenuating circumstances of various scenes when you determine a reasonable page count for the day.

WEATHER COVER

Weather issues have to be addressed by the schedule, even though weather is unpredictable. You can, however, predict tides, so you can be sure not to schedule a scene at the beach when the tide is so far out it would be a scene at the mud flats. For the unpredictable part of weather, how is weather cover being addressed? It is best to schedule exterior scenes early in the schedule so that if the weather is bad, you can reschedule them later and shoot some other scenes at an interior "weather cover" location. Is production prepared for weather cover, or is the set still being built, so there is nowhere to shoot if the weather is bad? Have a contingency plan all the way through the shoot.

SUNRISE & SUNSET

Sunrise and sunset is also somewhat predictable, as you can look up the times on a chart. The quality of that particular sunrise and set is, of course, the wild card. The further from the equator you shoot, the longer days you can shoot outside in natural light in the summer, and the shorter days in the winter. Be sure the schedule does not try to achieve too many scenes for the light available. No A.D. can hold the sunset for the Director.

TURNAROUND

If you are shooting nights, then want to flip back to days, you have turnaround issues to consider. Has the crew had enough time to go home, rest and return to work, or do you need to take a day off to give them enough turnaround time? For this reason it is best to schedule day scenes first, then night scenes later, if you can. That way, as you do an hour or two of overtime during the shoot, you will not be in danger of biting into turnaround time (very costly overtime) because you are planning on shooting later and later anyway as the schedule proceeds. Consider if any of the night scenes can be shot as day-for-night (D4N) in order to eliminate the need for night shoots altogether. This choice, however, must fit in with the creative look of the film as you balance both the business and creative sides of the industry.

COMPANY MOVES

Limit the number of company moves during your shoot days. You want to spend the prime portion of the shoot day shooting film, not paying for the crew to pack up, move to a new location, and unload over and over again.

DAILY TARGETS

Though the schedule plans certain scenes on certain days, should production happen to get ahead of itself, is there a plan for targeted scenes each day, so you do not have to wrap early and still pay the crew for a full day's work?

SCRIPT ORDER

Because of the cyclical nature of stories, where the first scene and the final scene are often in the same location, you will never shoot a film in script order. But you can address some internal script order if need be. Some scenes may need to be played before other scenes, and the Director may request certain scenes to be filmed before others to help the Performers with their characters' emotional arcs. It does help the cast (and the crew) to shoot the script in as close an approximation to story order as possible to develop their characters as the story develops. At the beginning of the shoot, the Cast is not very familiar with each other, so consider scheduling scenes where characters are unfamiliar with each other at the beginning of the schedule. Another reason why script order may need to be considered is: If someone needs a huge change in makeup from young to old, you cannot afford the set time to have the makeup applied, removed, applied, and removed again during the shoot.

FLEXIBILITY

Above all, the schedule needs to be flexible. The unexpected happens during a film shoot. The schedule needs to be able to change if circumstances dictate so when the cameras are rolling. How is the schedule flexible?

THE IDEAL SCHEDULE

You are blessed with shooting all the day exteriors first, then all the night exteriors next, then all the day interiors, and finally all the night interiors — staying in script order from beginning to end with no availability problems for Cast or locations. Well, we can all dream…

A.D. BREAKDOWN PAGES

In creating the schedule, the Assistant Directors breakdown the on set needs of each scene (from props to stunts to Background Performers to anything else), not just the list of characters. The scheduling software uses this breakdown information, together with the on-screen production board, to create a detailed schedule that includes scene requirements lists for each appropriate department. In this case, the Coordinator never sees the actual A.D. breakdowns; the breakdowns remain on the A.D.'s computer. When the schedule is created manually, the A.D.s need to generate one breakdown page per scene. Once the pages are placed into the schedule order to match the strip board, the Coordinator can create the detailed shooting schedule document. (See sample manual A.D. Breakdown Pages on page 513 and 514.)

ONE-LINE SCHEDULE

Scheduling software will output a one-line schedule for the A.D.s, and typically a printout of the strip board in horizontal format is used in place of the one-line schedule. If the Coordinator needs to create a manual "one-liner" instead, refer to the A.D. breakdown pages and remember that each line equals one scene. When you look at it later, it should remind you of a strip board typed up sideways.

WHAT INFORMATION TO INCLUDE ON A ONE-LINER

Think minimal information. For each scene on the one-liner, include: the scene number, scene location description, specify interior or exterior, day or night, the continuity day number, list of characters in that scene (by number code), page count, and the shooting location. Note Background Performers (Extras) by using an "X." If you have a number of scenes on one set, include a micro-short synopsis to differentiate the scenes from each other. Also include a legend to explain the number codes you used. Revise the schedule on colored paper, just like you would a script revision. (See a sample One-Liner on page 515.)

WHY MAKE A ONE-LINER

The one-line schedule is good to display the scene order (with minimum necessary description) of the entire shooting schedule in the shortest possible format. Because is it very short, more of the crew will likely read it and all its revisions in detail.

SHOOTING SCHEDULE

Again, scheduling software will output a shooting schedule for the A.D.s, but if the Coordinator needs to create one instead, combine all the information from the one-line schedule with all the breakdown information from the A.D. breakdown pages. Include the scene synopses, all the various departmental set requirements, and list the characters by name as well as by number. Depending on the detail of the A.D. breakdowns, the shooting schedule can easily become as thick or thicker than the script. Revise it using colored paper, like a script — even page by page if necessary. And since you will use all this information again on the call sheet, consider designing the shooting schedule to be in a similar format to the call sheet, so you can cut and paste the information daily, creating fast draft call sheets. Be sure, though, you design a schedule that suits both you and the A.D. team. (See a sample shooting schedule on page 516.)

SECOND UNIT

Second unit has its own shooting schedule separate from main unit, so clearly define it and print it on another colored paper for identification. Since second unit is often picking up shots that main unit did not achieve or that the Editor requests, the second unit schedule may change rapidly. They may stick to a simple format for their shooting schedule, or just have a long advanced schedule noted on their second unit call sheets to remind them of the ever-changing future.

SCHEDULING FOR LOW-BUDGET PRODUCTIONS

If the production is very low budget, you will not want to publish a revised, thick shooting schedule every time there is a small schedule order change. Instead, make a "shooting schedule" (complete with all the set requirements) in script order and call it the "script breakdown." Now you are free to revise the much shorter one-line schedule every time there is a schedule change, minimizing photocopying, and revising the script breakdown only when the set requirements change.

SPECIALITY BREAKDOWN MEMOS

The A.D.s will assemble a series of mini schedules directed toward specific departments, like a listing of all the stunts and on what day each stunt will be. If there is no scheduling software to generate these breakdown memos, the Coordinator can design the form as he pleases, keeping clarity in mind. A version of the one-line schedule is best for familiarity. Using a graphic or small drawing code at the top of each specialty breakdown will help to identify each breakdown at a glance. Here is a list of some of the specialty breakdowns you will use, and why:

> List of Background Performers (what scene they are in, what day they play)
> List of Stunts (who plays them, what day they play)
> List of Picture Vehicles (what day they play)
> List of... (whatever else the A.D.s think of!)

—⁊—

With your knowledge of schedules and how they work, you (the PM and the Coordinator) and the Assistant Directors are a team now. You can even add eighths of pages blindfolded. Better than that, you can see the plan for production ahead of you, and can now foresee finishing on time as well as on budget.

FOR THE CREW ONLY

Few Executives read all the credits in the memos you generate. They have very little time to worry about anything beyond the contractual and the financing credits. It's up to you to check most of the names and spellings on your own. That is until the credits hit the screen. I learned this when the Assistant Coordinator and I decided to put our nicknames on a very early draft of the credits.

Working on a French co-production, the Assistant Coordinator decided that hers and my name were not in keeping with the French flare of the show. We needed appropriate nicknames. We included these names on an early draft of the credits. The Production Manager and the Producer chuckled but didn't oppose the inclusion, so the credits went forward.

Executive Producers and financing companies on both sides of the Atlantic reviewed draft after draft of the credits. No one changed or deleted our "French" names. We were thrilled that all the Executives supported the little fun we injected into the credits.

Then came the first crew screening of the film. It was a heavy dramatic film. At its inevitable conclusion the credits began to roll. The crew was suitably depressed until the office staff credits rolled by. Chuckles and lightness filled the room. The Production Coordinator was credited as "Miss Paté" and the Assistant Coordinator as "Babette."

A memo came to the office from the Executives the next day to remove our nicknames from the credits. Well, at least we got to see them once on the big screen.

CREGITS 29

You start gathering information for them in prep, the Production Coordinator makes a first draft of them on first day of shooting for the PM's and the Producer's eyes only, and on your last day in wrap you are still trying to finalize them. They are the screen credits.

SCREEN CREDIT DESIGN

The Production Manager needs to discuss with the Producer the design for the credits — both head credits and tail credits. Sure, a company may be contracted for the design or the look of the credits, but you need to know which names are required in what order and which logos are to be included where, to satisfy all contracts, as well as ensure that the look of the credits works for the film.

HEAD & TAIL CREDITS vs. MAIN & END TITLES

Head credits (also known as opening titles) start at the beginning of the film before the first image fades in and typically end over the initial images of the story. The 20-second head credits in the film *Unforgiven* may be the shortest set of head credits ever seen, whereas *The Fugitive* may have one of the longest sets, lasting a good 15 minutes into the story.

Tail (or closing) credits are obviously the remaining credits at the end of the film, after the final shot fades out.

Main titles, however, can display during either head or tail credits, and they are treated with equal contractual importance to head credits. *Unforgiven* is a great example of the main titles being split between the company logos alone on display during the head credits, and the balance of the main titles (star cast, key crew names, etc.) displaying first up in the tail credits just before the end titles.

RESEARCH CREDIT PLACEMENT

Watch credits on TV or on rental features as research. What credits can you include realistically, especially for the tail credits? Does the production have limited allowable screen time, like on television series, where you only have enough time to display the heads of department's names, or is there enough time to display the entire crew and their Assistants? Is production a low-budget feature with so many donated items that you need to credit everyone's generosity? What logos need to be included and what union requirements dictate credit order and inclusion?

CREDIT ROLL LAYOUT vs. CARD LAYOUT

Credits on cards can display more names on the screen in less time than a credit roll or a crawl. Cards are also cheaper than a roll, though a credit roll is a standard credit format for feature films. When planning credit layout, consider television safe area even if the production is a feature film. Why not have legible credits without further manipulation in post, if and when, the production is sold to other markets? The most affordable credits you can buy use the existing fonts in the post facility's system. These credits can be superimposed over the film's images or displayed on a blank (typically black) screen. If you choose to download a custom font to the post system, make sure you own the rights to do so. Also ensure you choose an unmistakably readable font. At the end of the day, everyone wants to be able to read his name clearly.

Finally, know how much screen time you plan to have, or are restricted to, for both opening and closing credits.

THE PREVIEW DRAFTS

The Production Coordinator has been collecting notes and copies of pages of contracts in the desk file folder associated with credits. On or near day one of principal photography, make a preview draft of the credits to review with the Production Manager and the Producer only. The PM and the Producer need to provide their input before the draft is distributed to the many other people necessary for approvals, because credits are a very sensitive issue. It is all too easy to offend someone by omission, incorrect title and/or placement, and by incorrect spelling. By the Coordinator, the PM, and the Producer reviewing the draft and double-checking each other, the initial design ideas of credits can be ironed out, and an excellent first draft of the credits will be distributed as the first official draft. It may take a few preview drafts to get there, but that is to be expected.

THE PC COORDINATES THE PREVIEW DRAFTS

The Coordinator generates the actual drafts and gathers input from all sources to consolidate the credits.

MAKE A LIST OF CREDIT PROMISES

To begin the preview draft, consolidate your notes to make a list of who and what credits have been promised in all contracts, deal memos, and letters of agreement. Ask postproduction and the Legal Counsel for credit promises in contracts or agreements that you do not handle.

APPROVE A CREDIT LIST FORMAT OR DESIGN

The Producer may have a preferred format for the credits, or may want to choose from several formats that you present. When making a format, find out as much as possible from the Producer and the Production Manager. Which positions require a head credit? Are there a limited number of head credit cards? What positions begin the tail credits? Will the tail credits be a roll or on cards? Find out from postproduction how many lines can fit on a card where the names remain legible. Just like the PM, watch feature films and television movies and series to write down the template of their credits. You will find that productions vary greatly in style. (See two samples of credit styles on pages 517-523.)

INCLUDE CARD OR ROLL TIMINGS

When assembling any draft of the credits, include the screen timings of each card or of the duration of the roll. From this, those approving the credits can see instantly if there is a timing problem with all the people and the companies they would like to, or have to, credit. Find out any and all timing restrictions from the PM and the Producer.

CHECK SPELLING

Checking spelling cannot be stressed enough. Double-check! Triple-check! Be absolutely certain that every single name is spelled correctly. Call the Performers' Agents and confirm again how to spell each Performer's name if need be. There is no computer spell-check program that can check the spellings of names.

MAKE THE FIRST PREVIEW DRAFT

Combine the information and the format to create a first preview draft. The Production Manager and the Producer may revise this draft several times before allowing it to be called the "first" draft and present it to the countless Executives and companies involved for approvals. They are also relying on you to present the credits honoring all contracted promises. Note each contracted promise in the far right margin in brackets along with the card timing (if applicable). Since few will read all the contracts and deal memos you do, this will be a critical reference when they want to change certain credits. Here is an example:

Card #1	starring		0:03
	KEN ELLIOTT		("starring," single card)

Card #2	with		0:03
	LAURA SOUSA	("with," head credits, shared card)	
	RICHARD PATZ	("with," head credits, shared card)	

Card #3	and		0:03
	MO DANIELS		
	as "Spitfire Mo"	("and…as," last head credit, single card)	

REVIEWING THE PREVIEW DRAFTS

As Production Manager, review the preview drafts of the credits with the Producer. Is there enough screen time for all the credits at both head and tail? Is the design and the format acceptable at this stage? Do the credits as presented abide by the union rules for screen credits that stipulate who must be credited, and placement of certain credits? Double-check any spellings of which you are the slightest bit unsure. Carefully check the financing agreements; have you honored their credit requirements in wording, logo placement, and credit duration? Discuss, too, with the Producer if there is anyone else you need to have in the "preview" loop of credits to ensure credit completeness, like postproduction and the Legal Counsel.

After the Production Manager and Producer provide their input, the Coordinator may be up to the second or third preview draft. Be sure all preview drafts are marked clearly as such to avoid alarm if someone finds something missing that they find obvious.

THE EARLY DRAFTS

Now that the first round of information has been collected, make the first draft of the credits. These are not final drafts by any means, but you need to be sure you have considered all possible credits before paring down to the final, approved version.

THE PC COORDINATES THE EARLY DRAFTS

Again the Coordinator will generate and track each draft.

MAKE A COVER PAGE MEMO

Mark clearly on a cover page memo to whom these credits are going, and which draft it is. The cover page memo is designed to keep the confidentiality of the credits underneath, and to clearly keep track of who is providing input to these credits.

WHO GETS THE EARLY DRAFTS

The first and early drafts are sent to Executives and companies for approvals. The PM will know which companies will need to see the credits for approval. These people also include all Producers, the Legal Counsel, postproduction, and anyone else the PM and the Producer so deem. Guild and unions need to approve credits specific to their members. Though you may not want to send them an entire draft, you can lift appropriate sections of the credits to them with a letter announcing and describing the credit(s) being granted.

CALL FOR AND RECORD APPROVALS OR REQUESTS FOR CHANGES

Everyone on the cover page memo must respond to the credits with approvals or requests for changes. If some of them do not respond, call for the information. Note all changes on your copy of the credits, and code each request to the person requesting. Some requests will be in direct opposition to others. When the Producer reviews all these requests together, she can identify who is asking for what, and can deal with the conflict. Let the Producer handle all issues that come up regarding the credits.

WHEN PEOPLE CHANGE THE SPELLING OF THEIR OWN NAMES

Some people will ask for different spellings of their names to the ones contracted. If this occurs, confirm each new request in a letter or a memo to that person, with a copy sent to the Producer and the Legal Counsel. If that person changes his mind after the credits are completed, you (and Legal Counsel) will have written proof of the credit requested.

HOW MANY EARLY DRAFTS DOES IT TAKE?

It takes many, many drafts to approve credits. The more Executives, the more drafts it will take. This is why you need to start the credits process as early in production as possible. When it seems to you and the Producer that the credits are approved from all sources, you are ready to make the first of the "final" drafts.

THE FINAL DRAFTS

The heading reads "drafts" for a reason. As soon as you publish a final draft of the credits, someone is bound to call in with a change.

THE PC COORDINATES THE EARLY DRAFTS

Put off finalizing the credits until the last possible moment. Postproduction will be able to tell you the date the credits are typeset, then go to camera. Find out the last possible date from them.

WHO RECEIVES THE FINAL CREDITS

Final credits are sent to the same people as the earlier drafts, but are also sent to government agencies, Financiers, Publicity Departments, Distributors, Broadcasters, and to other people that the Producer or the Production Manager advises. (See a suggested list for the distribution of final credits in Chapter 30.)

DATE THE FINAL DRAFTS

Note the words "final draft" along with the date on the cover page memo and on the credits themselves. When there are several final drafts published, the date will be the only way to discern them from each other. If not, revised final drafts will have to be labeled creatively, like: "revised final draft," then "final and approved draft," then "very revised final draft."

KEEP POSTPRODUCTION INFORMED

Especially if there are several final drafts, keep in touch with postproduction. Make sure they typeset and go to camera with the latest of the final draft credits. Warn them, even by telephone, when you know changes are going to be made to the credits.

LOCKED CREDITS TRIGGER ISAN REGISTRATION

Once the final credits are locked, you can now register the ISAN number that was previously reserved for the production, or apply for one if a number has not yet been reserved. Since final postproduction names need to be included in locked credits, you will probably be around for the triggering event on a series, but not on a feature film. In any case, you can remind postproduction when to register the ISAN number. (See more information on the global, numerical ISAN identifier in Chapter 12.)

Your eyes will grow tired from looking at the same names over and over again. The Coordinator can still have an Assistant help by double-checking using her own fresh eyes. You will get no thanks for correctly spelling each person's name in the credits, but you will certainly hear about the one name you misspelled and forgot to check. Any oversight you make will be displayed brilliantly on the big (or little) screen. Do everything you can to be letter-perfect.

ROUTINE DOCUMENT DELIVERY?

It was the same routine every day: take the draft call sheet to set and review it with the Director-Executive Producer. Take a few moments to check on the status of today's filming and finalize the plan for tomorrow. But first, on arrival on set, find a spot and wait off to the side for the right moment, a break in the day's shoot – during lighting, for example – so that we could focus on the status report and planning at hand.

Every day I arrived on set, expecting the same ol' routine. One day I was uniquely surprised.

Timing was perfect. The crew had just started lighting, so we had time. The Director-Executive Producer was taking a break already. He was, however, not off set. Far from it, he was in the middle of set. And I do mean the very middle. There he was, lying flat on his back on the floor of the set, face up to the lighting grid. He looked like a man who really needed a break. And oddly enough, he looked rather comfy.

I did not want to disturb him, but it was time to discuss the call sheet. If I waited too long, lighting would be over, and he would be up and working again, the moment lost. Now was the time. So what could I do? I did the only option I thought was right for the moment. I lay down on the floor next to him, face up to the lighting grid, and held the call sheet over our heads for discussion. He smiled.

The meeting happened. The work got done. And we had a refreshing break from routine.

DOCUMENTATION DISTRIBUTION

30

The Production Manager may stand in awe of the Coordinator amid the wonder of flying documents and emails, and well you should, because the PC certainly knows how to generate and distribute documentation. But as for remembering who received which version of what production information, the Coordinator needs help. That is what this chapter is for. No one's memory can retain such ever-changing lists of information. This system will help the PC track all the documentation that needs to be circulated during production.

REDUCING PAPER USAGE

With the ability to digitally transfer production information, it is natural we should move toward a paperless system and be kind to the environment. Even with best efforts, however, it is true we are often required to continue distributing information on paper. Legal documents need wet signatures on original hard copy, even if the agreement was first signed electronically or by fax. The cast and crew on set do not carry computers in-hand. So, rather than shift into an entirely paperless environment, digital transfer of information has fragmented the channels we use to distribute information. Different people are on different computer, email, and smart phone systems that link only temporarily to make this production.

So how do you reduce paper usage? Be creative and involve the crew in coming up with "green" ideas. Set a policy for the production's support. Print and photocopy documents double-sided when you can. Production scripts must remain single-sided in order to insert pages as revisions demand; however, reuse retired scripts and revisions to photocopy other documentation, such as memos, note paper, telephone messages and such. Keep in mind that due to confidentiality, you will not be able to reuse much of the documentation that the Production Accountant generates. Individually address documents for distribution with the name of the recipient to ensure the right people receive the right documents. Doing so avoids the need to copy a slew of unlabeled spares because you are not sure if the essential folk actually received the information. At meetings, consider projecting an electronic copy of the reference material on a screen if possible, or make limited copies for people to share. When everyone participates in the ideas, everyone can be a proud part of the solution. Now that is teamwork!

TRACKING SYSTEM

Setting up a tracking system for documentation may seem insignificant at first, but as production proceeds, copious amounts of production information and revised documentation must be distributed to a growing list of recipients both on the crew and in offices around the world via a number of different communication methods. At any given time, you must be able to know who has what information. A tracking system is essential.

WHO KEEPS TRACK OF DISTRIBUTION

Though the job of keeping the records is often delegated to the Assistant Coordinator, the Coordinator is ultimately responsible for the working of the system. Work together.

MAKING A TRACKING SYSTEM

You need a system that is quick, simple to update, and easy to read. Following are some different systems that work well, but no one system can address all the ways you will distribute information. Combine tracking systems as needed, but make one of them dominant, and have it refer to the secondary one. For example, if you choose the physical distribution binder, include a page or two to reference all recipients of the digital distribution method, and identify the folder location of the digital portion of the tracking system.

THE DOCUMENT DISTRIBUTION BINDER OR FOLDER

Devote one binder to document distribution. Use divider tabs to mark the differing types of documentation (each episodic script, crew list, cast list, call sheet, etc.). In each section, create a chart that lists the names of the people or the companies to receive the specific document in the first column, and mark the rest of the columns for each revision of that document, labeling color and date. When distributing the actual document to each recipient, note in each appropriate box the date and method of sending. Codes work best to identify the method used, like "E" for emailed, "D" for delivered by hand or by crew member, "F" for faxed, and "C" for couriered. This system requires the tracking binder to be close at hand for several people to use. This system is good to keep all the information in one spot, but you cannot see each company's list of documentation without flipping many pages. (See a sample on page 524.)

If you have a shared drive for the production office, you could create this "binder" electronically in a shared folder; however, this would require computer access to the folder on the shared drive for everyone who updates the electronic "binder". Since this universal access is somewhat impractical, it is recommended to use the old fashioned, physical binder. The physical binder is wonderfully low-tech and happily portable around the office.

CHARTS ON THE WALL ENVELOPES

Since you have wall envelopes collecting documentation for various companies, you can create a chart to post on each one to use as your tracking system. List the documentation that each company requires in the first column, and mark the rest of the columns for each revision of that document, labeling color only. When delivering the contents of the envelopes, note the date in each appropriate box. Though this system shows you at a glance which document each company receives, not every company you will distribute to will have a wall envelope, since most external companies will expect to receive documents electronically. You will require a separate written log elsewhere for the electronic recipients. This system is good for showing each company's list of paperwork at a glance, but the information of all companies is spread out around the office. (See a sample on page 526.)

DIGITAL DISTRIBUTION OR DIGITAL HOLDING FOLDERS

Weekly updates to external companies, like financiers, work well if you are using wall envelopes to collect paper documents over the course of the week and deliver them at week's end. With electronic communication, it is easiest for you to send revised documentation immediately as it is generated. If, however, the external company requires updated documentation electronically on a weekly basis, create a set of folders on your hard drive to work as digital holding folders (or digital wall envelopes). Collect copies of the files you plan to send at week's end, and with an electronic reminder on your computer, you can send the information in bulk right on schedule every week. File a copy of the emails that you sent in a folder specific to document distribution to use as your tracking system. The challenge with this system is that, unless you are using a shared drive, the responsibility of document distribution to the affected companies falls to one crew member.

KEEP EXTRA COPIES OF DOCUMENTS ON STANDBY

You will discover very quickly that some people have a natural tendency to lose copies of documents over and over again. Other people will take the last copy from the distribution table and not inform you. Especially keep an extra copy or two of collated fully-colored scripts on standby (but not on the distribution table) for these purposes. You will welcome these standby copies when you are rushed and have to generate a collated seven-colored script for someone immediately.

TWO COLLATED SCRIPTS IN OFFICE FOR SIDES

Besides any standby copies of the script, keep two fully-collated scripts in the office for use when making the daily sides for the set. At the end of the production, these scripts, if well kept, can serve as master copies for any final scripts that you must photocopy for Executives and companies.

STORE LEFTOVER COPIES IN AN "ARCHIVE" BOX

As some people tend to lose documentation, so other people and companies will remember at a later date which documentation they require. Keep old versions of all documents in an "archive" box instead of throwing them out. Often people will be satisfied with an older copy of the script because they just want to have an idea of the plot.

STARTER DISTRIBUTION LISTS

The checklists that follow will jog your memory when distributing anything, document or otherwise. The Production Coordinator and the Production Manager should review these lists to jointly decide who needs to receive what.

DEPARTMENT HEADS

When you have something to go to all department heads, refer to this list. When creating your own distribution lists, review this list to be sure you address the entire crew.

- ☐ Producer (any and all)
- ☐ Director
- ☐ Story Editor
- ☐ Production Manager
- ☐ Production Coordinator
- ☐ Production Accountant
- ☐ 1st A.D.
- ☐ Location Manager

☐ Continuity Supervisor
☐ Casting Director
☐ Publicist
☐ Production Designer
☐ Art Director
☐ Set Decorator
☐ Props Master
☐ Wardrobe Designer
☐ Hair Stylist
☐ Makeup Artist
☐ Director of Photography
☐ Sound Mixer
☐ Gaffer
☐ Key Grip
☐ Special Effects Supervisor
☐ Stunt Coordinator
☐ Construction Manager
☐ Transportation Coordinator
☐ Postproduction Supervisor

OFFICE KEYS LIST

Okay, keys are not documents. But you do need to hand out many of them to the crew and need to monitor who has what. When the security code changes, for example, you need to know who to inform. Ensure the PC and the PM decide who really needs which key. Do not just copy tons of keys and hand them out. Use a key sign-out list. Know who will actually be using the office after hours. For the security system, make sure each person with a key knows how to use the alarm system properly. If the system requires an access card, never hand out door keys without matching access cards. Here is a starter list for discussion:

Producer
Production Manager
Production Coordinator
Assistant Coordinator
Office Production Assistant
1st A.D.
2nd A.D.
3rd A.D.
Location Manager

Location Scout
Production Designer
Art Director
Set Decorator
Props Master
Wardrobe Designer
Construction Manager
Transportation Coordinator
Driver Captain
Head Driver
Craft Service

THE JOY OF DOCUMENTATION DISTRIBUTION LISTS

It is time to move onto the majority of the documentation distribution lists that you will require. Again, the PM and the PC need to examine and fine-tune these lists to create your own "Joy of Distribution" lists. When completed, give copies of your lists to all the office staff, and to the A.D.s (for set-related distribution).

SCRIPT-RELATED DOCUMENTATION

Scripts are generally very long documents; therefore, keep an accurate list of who should receive each script to prevent over-photocopying.

SCRIPT – EARLY DRAFTS

If the draft is very early in preproduction, some of the people on this list may not be hired yet. Even though this list of names is large, check with the Producer to determine which of these people really requires the current early draft of the script.

Script Research Company
Executive Producer
Producer
Director
Story Editor
Casting Director
Director of Photography
Production Manager
Production Coordinator
Production Designer
1st A.D.
2nd A.D.

Location Manager
Art Director
Set Decorator
Props Master
Wardrobe Designer
Continuity Supervisor
Sound Mixer
Gaffer
Key Grip
Special Effects Coordinator
Stunt Coordinator
Transportation Coordinator

SCRIPT – MAJOR REVISIONS ONLY

This distribution list is for those who may not need every little revision of the script.

Publicist
Performer Unions
Government Agencies

SCRIPT – EVERY REVISION

At this point, it is too obvious to list the entire shooting crew on this list, so these are recipients BEYOND the set crew to consider.

Distributor or Broadcaster
Funding Agencies
Executive Producer & Head Office Personnel
Editors
Completion Bond Company

SCRIPT RESEARCH REPORT

The clearance company responds with notes of character names that must change, songs that must be cleared before singing on set, and warnings of any copyrights and trademarks that are being infringed. (See more on script clearances in Chapter 33.) Distribute this report to:

Executive Producer
Producer
Director
Story Editor / Story Department
Legal Counsel

Production Manager
Production Coordinator
Production Accountant
1st A.D.
Production Designer
Art Director
Set Decorator
Props Master
Wardrobe Designer
Continuity Supervisor

SCHEDULE-RELATED DOCUMENTATION

You are already familiar with numerous kinds of schedules. BEYOND the set crew, these are other people to keep informed. Call them first to confirm which document(s) they require.

CALL SHEET (SENT VIA EMAIL OR FAX DAILY)

Distributor or Broadcaster
Performer Unions
Crew Unions
Extras Casting Director
Funding Agencies
Government Agencies
Completion Bond Company

ONE-LINE SCHEDULE & PRODUCTION SCHEDULE

Executive Producer & Head Office
Editors
Publicist
Distributor or Broadcaster
Funding Agencies
Government Agencies
Completion Bond Company

SHOOTING SCHEDULE

Executive Producer & Head Office
Editors
Publicist
Performer Unions
Funding Agencies

Government Agencies
Completion Bond Company
Performers (who are not on set)

OTHER DOCUMENTATION

This section is made up of lists, contracts, and breakdowns. Since you, as the Coordinator, are responsible to disseminate information to those not on the crew, these lists cover those people and companies.

CREW LIST

Executive Producer & Head Office
Editors
Publicist
Distributor or Broadcaster
Crew Unions
Performer Unions
Funding Agencies
Government Agencies
Completion Bond Company

CAST LIST

Executive Producer & Head Office
Editors
Publicist
Distributor or Broadcaster
Performer Unions
Funding Agencies
Government Agencies
Completion Bond Company

PERFORMER CONTRACTS

Talent Agent for Performer
Production Accountant
Production Coordinator
Legal Counsel
A.D. (with pay rates masked)

PERFORMER PICTURES & RESUMES

Production Coordinator
Publicist

EXTRAS BREAKDOWN MEMO

> Performer Union
> Extras Casting Director
> Executive Producer & Head Office
> Production Coordinator

CREDIT LIST – FINAL

> Executive Producer & Head Office
> Producer
> Legal Counsel
> Production Manager
> Production Coordinator
> Production Accountant
> Publicist
> Postproduction Supervisor
> Distributor or Broadcaster
> Funding Agencies
> Government Agencies
> Completion Bond Company
> ISAN profile (a copy of the actual document is not necessary, just input the data online)

THE PRODUCTION REPORT & ALL ITS BACKUP DOCUMENTATION

As you know, the DPR is actually a compilation of reports from each of the departments. Each departmental report has its own set of recipients for distribution, as does the daily production report itself. Start with these distribution lists, and consult each department and the Production Manager to create your own set of report distribution lists for the production. Determine and note who keeps the original of each report.

PRODUCTION REPORT – DRAFT COPY

Be sure the Production Manager has approved even the draft copy before distributing this document.

> Production Accountant
> A.D. (who writes the report on set)
> Executive Producer
> Completion Bond Company
> Production Coordinator

PRODUCTION REPORT – TYPED AND SIGNED COPY

Now approved by all parties, the production report has a wider distribution. It remains a confidential report. Treat it as such.

Production Coordinator (keep the original)
Executive Producer
Producer
Production Manager
Production Accountant
1st A.D.
A.D. (who write the report on set)
Funding Agencies
Completion Bond Company

CONTINUITY TOP SHEET

This report is the Continuity Supervisor's summary of all scenes shot or not, and an update on the timing of the entire script. This is the form to refer to when completing the continuity section of the production report.

Continuity Supervisor
Editors
Executive Producer
Producer
Production Manager
Production Coordinator
Production Lab / Transfer Facility (copy may go straight from set)

OTHER CONTINUITY DOCUMENTATION

Shot reports, log forms, wild sound reports, and any other continuity paperwork detail even further all the information the Editors need to know for postproduction.

Continuity Supervisor
Editors
Production Coordinator
Production Lab / Transfer Facility (copy may go straight from set)

SOUND REPORT SHEETS

The Sound Department reports on the quality of the contents of each roll of sound stock they use. They usually use a two-part form that enables them to keep a copy of their paperwork upon sending you the editing copy. These are the forms you count when completing the "sound stock used" section of the production report.

Editors
Production Coordinator
Production Lab / Transfer Facility (copy may go straight from set)

CAMERA REPORTS

Just like the Sound Department, the Camera Department reports to the lab or transfer facility and to the Editors the contents of each disk, tape or film roll, and which take or takes to transfer or print.

Editors
Production Coordinator
Production Lab / Transfer Facility (copy will go straight from set)

DAILY PICTURE STOCK SUMMARY

The Camera Department also reports to production the amount of raw picture stock used to date, and the amount of unused stock on hand. This is the form to refer to when completing the "picture stock totals" or "film totals" section of the production report.

Production Coordinator

PERFORMER WORK REPORTS

Already discussed, this form is a time sheet for Performers. Refer to it when completing the Performer's section of the production report.

Production Accountant
Performer Union
Production Coordinator

EXTRAS VOUCHERS

These forms serve as both contracts for Background Performers and as time sheets. Refer to these when completing the Extras' section of the production report.

Production Accountant
Performer Union
Production Coordinator

DRIVER TIMES

Since the Transportation Department often wraps at the end of the day after the last A.D. does, they forward their daily work times into the production office later. Sometimes you have to call for this information. These timings will complete the crew attendance section on the production report.

Transportation Coordinator
Production Accountant
Production Coordinator

—⁂—

You have noticed that the Production Coordinator keeps a copy of every document that is distributed. Documentation is lost now and then. The production office needs to have the backup copy for anything the PC or the office handles. It is the Coordinator's production files (both electronic and physical) that end up going to head office as a complete record of what happened during production. With every piece of information and report you file now, and the record you have of everything that has been distributed in the office, you will be assembling that set from day one — with a little "joy" in the distribution, because you have a system that works to help you.

ONGOING SPECIAL ISSUES | VII

Find out how much "free" costs.

THE NAMING OF A REVOLUTIONARY

Once upon a time, in the early 1960s, the U.S. Military needed to devise a way to protect their computers should a nuclear attack take the systems out. It was, after all, the Cold War.

An employee of the RAND Corporation came up with a revolutionary design to network computers without a central authority. Messages between computers would be sent in "packets," each packet addressed separately, and would travel the network of computers through various "nodes" to be reassembled at the destination. There would be so many connections (nodes) that if one node were missing, the other nodes would do the job, and should the one packet be intercepted, the message would be incomprehensible alone. And so this unique network was born to four computers by 1969.

What it didn't have yet was a name.

Once the initial network was in place, education nodes were added, giving (mostly) science researchers access. Next on board, in the later 1970s and 1980s, came the public libraries, and finally commercial enterprises. Out of that development came a set of standards (protocols), including a set of technical standards called TCP/IP (Transmission Control Protocol/Internet Protocol) for sending, addressing, and receiving the information packets; and finally, a web browser language for display called "HyperText Transfer Protocol" (HTTP) was developed that allowed links between pages among its features. Now nearly everyone was sending and receiving information the same way.

With commerce on board, the network needed to be, not only standardized, but also user-friendly. Network (domain) addresses were (and still are) long-numbered names, such as: http://123.45.678.9. Imagine trying to remember every company's website address as these kinds of numbers... impossible. Out of need, the standard domain naming system (DNS) was born, and with it ".com", ".gov", ".net", ".org" and their "dot" cousins. The text names were applied on top of the actual website address, so consumers could remember destination addresses like "organizationname.org", more readily.

The network itself, however, still did not have a name. It was now the early 1990s.

Next, a British fellow in Switzerland led the creation of the "world wide web" (the "www" of web addresses). Browser software now display graphical web pages – pictures and text together, and we loved it. Use of the network exploded from about 300,000 nodes in 1990 to over 2,000,000 in just three years.

Names now jockeyed for position as the official label of this fast growing world wide network – names such as "Cybernet," "Information Highway," "The Web," and "Cyberweb." But with no central authority, and no one to ask, "What do we call it?," we had to wait for the people – the users – to assume the chosen name.

'Twas finally around 1992 that we finally named it... the "Internet" – over 20 years after its birth.

Nearly another 20 years later, the Internet continues to evolve, though we now have a hard time estimating how many nodes there are anymore. Last count, in 2006, pegged it at around 450 million, though we tend now to look at the number of users, which is closer to 1.5 billion today. High-speed broadband access is commonplace. Video/audio streaming and social networking opened up new methods of user interaction. And now there is wireless. Wireless – a word that was the name for "radio" way back when – is well on its way to revolutionizing Internet access and usage yet again. Shouldn't we – the users – assume a proper name for this new revolutionary or are we going to wait until at least 20 years after its birth?

PUBLICITY &
THE AUDIENCE

31

The audience can be well-connected to the production long before the film's premiere screening or first broadcast. Word-of-mouth publicity is enhanced through the production website, social networking, and the blogosphere, to name a few. Unit publicity can help the film to connect to its target audience. Messages will be shaped. Various communication formats will be optimized. Release of those messages will be timed. The goal is to help germinate that very valuable positive word-of-mouth publicity that drives audiences to seek out certain movies from the crowd.

As the PM or PC, you will not be much involved in the shaping of the entire publicity plan or the messages themselves, but you can assist the publicity team to collect the necessary elements during that fleeting and most interesting part of production: principal photography.

UNIT PUBLICITY vs. MARKETING

First up: unit publicity is not marketing. The goal of unit publicity is to reach the audience, to generate word of mouth. Whereas a marketing plan will include the purchase of ads and banners on television and in newspapers and magazines both on and offline; a unit publicity plan will seek to arrange interviews that become stories in those same on and offline places. In effect, unit publicity seeks out "free" coverage. Of course, with ads, you control the images and message portrayed; you are paying for it. With interviews, there is less control of the message and actual content, but you can at least shape that message with pre-interview discussion, sample questions in a press kit, orchestrating a newsworthy publicity event, and so on. The actual text will remain in the hands of the reporter or blogger.

Since we are talking about news articles, there is a requirement that your film has to somehow be newsworthy. The project does not have to be controversial, but it does have to have some sort of story behind the production that the audience wants to hear about, read about, talk about, and share. The goal is to have the public spread the word. The Unit Publicist is the professional to help find that story and that visual look that will generate, not only interest in the production, but more important, interest in seeing and buying the finished film.

UNIT PUBLICITY'S SCHEDULE & MAIN UNIT'S SCHEDULE

The unit publicity schedule is very much parallel to that of production's. The unit publicity plan is formed during preproduction (by the Producer and Publicist), though the ideas may germinate even earlier, during development of the property. The elements of the plan are collected primarily during the shoot, and rolled out on a schedule during post production and delivery that maximizes the production's visibility at time of release.

The parallel schedule, of course, means that the unit publicity team is competing to collect necessary publicity elements at exactly the same time that main unit is trying to shoot the film itself. Principal photography is already squeezed for time to capture the original scenes despite challenges that include limited Star or location availability. Nevertheless, the A.D.s need to be on board to integrate unit publicity opportunities into the main unit's shooting schedule. Without the publicity elements, such as photographs of the cast in character, how will there be any posters made? How will any audience know to go see this film?

As for a roll-out schedule, independent films with limited financial resources may wish to start word-of-mouth publicity as soon as possible. It will take time for the buzz to spread. In this case, it is essential to plan for as much lead time as possible.

Higher budget releases may choose to shoot under the cloak of silence in order to release publicity elements on a more strategically timed schedule. This scenario weighs heavily on a hefty P&A (prints and ads) budget to control, not only the timing as much as possible, but also the publicity messages.

If the content is controversial, it is best to start word of mouth when one can capitalize on the coverage, rather than leave a long, empty break between controversial discussion and release of film that could take the discussion to a new level.

Television series have a unique situation. Since their Internet presence is born with the launch of the first season, the publicity plan for season one may differ radically from season two. The audience – the core audience anyway – has been aware of the production for at least a year prior to airing of the first episode of the second season. The audience has existing expectations of the show and its web presence. The publicity plan needs to find new ways of capturing their attention and building on that audience.

TYPICAL UNIT PUBLICITY ELEMENTS

The number and range of unit publicity elements to be created during production will vary based on the publicity plan in mind, and the financial allowance in the production budget. Find out how extensive the publicity plan is in order to help facilitate their collection, though it is the Unit Publicist who will do the actual coordination of these following elements.

PRESS KIT

A typical press kit is crafted by the Unit Publicist and includes: bios of the main cast and crew; press releases; synopsis; background story of the production; a set of publicity photographs; transcriptions of interviews and/or a list of sample questions. Each production will also include other items that are deemed appropriate (visionary artwork is one example). Basically the press kit is structured so that a reporter or blogger can well prepare for an interview with a representative of the film, or even to write a news article without needing to meet anyone from the cast or crew. The kit needs to be both downloadable and in physical form.

PUBLICITY PHOTOGRAPHS

Several types of images can be collected: the cast in character in a studio setting (known as "gallery shots"); the cast in character in mid-scene (to look like a frame of action from the movie itself); and candid looking photographs from behind-the-scenes. The images are used not only in the press kit, but also for the creation of a poster and everywhere necessary for the visual design of the marketing campaign.

EPK ("ELECTRONIC PRESS KIT")

The electronic press kit is a motion picture extension of the traditional press kit, allowing reporters to insert footage and/or interviews from the set into their video news stories. An EPK typically includes: video interviews with key cast and crew; behind-the-scenes segments of the film being shot ("B-Roll"); and a teaser trailer as a visual synopsis of the film. Rather than being a polished single program, the EPK is clearly made up of individual, separated video clips for the user to select and edit as needed. For lower budget productions, careful planning of the EPK can contribute to the bonus features on the BluRay or DVD release.

PRODUCTION WEBSITE

Depending on the complexity of the site and its expected duration online, a separate company is typically hired to build and maintain the production's website. The site needs to be online as soon as possible so word of mouth can be germinated during the production's shoot. Otherwise, the web launch plan is linked to the release of other publicity and marketing elements.

Beyond being a kind of online press kit, what are the goals of the site? Does the production website expand on the film story in some way? Does it provide a forum for discussion of the controversial elements of the production? The budget, maintenance staff, and the multiplatform plan for the film story will determine how interactive or static the site will be. The visual design that the art department has forged for the production will be key in helping to design a complementary look for the online presence. Ensure that these two teams meet at some point early in website development.

SOCIAL NETWORK POSTINGS & INTERVIEWS

Beyond the press kit, social networks, blogs, and micro-blogs demand fresh content on a frequent basis. Postings and interviews need to be designed to keep with the theme of the production, and then collected and rolled out as planned. Also, someone needs to be available to address all interactions with the audience. Will the blog site be hosted by a cast or crew member, or will one of the fictional characters be the host?

MOBISODES, WEBISODES & SHORT FEATURES

If the project is truly multiplatform, mobisodes, webisodes or short features may be created to complement and expand the on-screen story. New stories may be told from secondary characters' point of view. A treasure hunt of clues could be revealed over time leading up to the film's release. Depending how extensive the multiplatform plan is, a separate company (and budget) may be engaged to run with this idea. Again, the short features could be end up as bonus features.

OTHER PUBLICITY ELEMENTS & ANCILLARY PROPERTIES

Imagination and budget are the only limiting factors as to what other publicity elements could be created. The more extravagant they are, the more likely a separate company, budget, and revenue plan will be needed. A companion video game, for example, could be as simple as limited-interaction bonus feature, an application for cell phones or smart phones, or a separate game title sold in the retail market. The line between publicity and new property can be blurry.

The Unit Publicist is constantly questioning how to reach the target audience with the news of this production. Since great ideas can come from anywhere, do not hesitate to share your ideas for this production with the Producer.

WHEN CONFIDENTIALITY IS THE PUBLICITY PLAN

If the production has the marketing heft to keep production a secret during the shoot and postproduction, the crew will no doubt need to sign confidentiality agreements as part of their start pack. At times like this, the blogosphere has an annoying ubiquitous presence. Visitors to set will not be allowed, or need to undergo a strict approval process. Increased security staff can help to protect the borders of the set against intruders. Production will use a working title for all production documentation, location signs, and so on. The actual title should never be used — even verbally — or never shared with the production team. Though the crew may sign confidentiality agreements in preproduction, you should remind everyone of the policy at the first full production meeting and again periodically throughout production.. You can seek the crew's input as to how to keep production a secret, and in so doing, make them part of the magic in keeping that secret.

— ⚋ —

The Unit Publicist finds ways to reach the audience through conventional channels (television, newspapers, magazines, and in some cases, set visits and personal appearances of key cast or crew) and through the host of new options provided by digital technologies (the production website, news sites, e-zines, blogs, micro-blogs, social networks, mobile platforms, and behind-the-scenes websites such as *www.movieset.com*). Knowing the publicity elements needed and facilitating their collection will help you to be part of building the buzz. A film does not end at postproduction. Give the film its best chance to find its audience.

THE BOX AT CUSTOMS

When it comes to shipping props, you can ship an incredibly wide variety of items. You have to know how to handle each one separately when it comes to customs clearances. One missing word can stop a shipment and delay a shoot.

On one show, we had to ship crates and crates of props to New Zealand for a period piece. All parts of the paperwork were carefully reviewed over and over again for accuracy and completeness. At the border one crate stopped dead.

But customs refused to open the case to examine the contents. They asked the shipper present if the contents were real or fake. The documents did not specify. The shipper refused to open the case to find out, too. They telephoned me back home to ask if I had forgotten to include the word "fake" on this contents list. I asked them to be more specific. They said they refused to open the case to find out; they just wanted my answer, and read to me the list of contents.

I held back my laughter and apologized for the oversight and insisted that yes, the props were indeed fake. The two items that had concerned them so deeply were: one human ear… and one baby's head.

COURIERS & CUSTOMS | 32

When production decides that there is a very special item for set that needs to be imported from another country, you know you cannot ship it as easily as you can across town. Knowing also that the item is required on set in a day or two, it is time to make friends with a Customs Broker. The Production Coordinator organizes the shipment, and the Production Manager tracks the costs associated with shipping, duties, and taxes.

COURIERS (LOCAL & INTERNATIONAL)

The Coordinator tends to be the one both to set up the account with the local and international couriers, and to deal with the day-to-day business of shipping and receiving packages. The PM can entrust the Coordinator to do this job and become involved in more complex shipping issues, as noted below.

TRACKING COURIERED PACKAGES

As the Coordinator, you are comfortable with the services of the courier companies you have chosen. You can call them after hours, they are quick to respond, and they are reasonably affordable. They have pre-printed your company name on a series of waybills. There is a bit more you should know to track the many packages you send daily and weekly.

FILL OUT WAYBILLS COMPLETELY

Whether local or international, get into the habit of filling out each waybill completely. If you think that packages are delivered without a telephone number, the date, or a complete description of the contents, you are right most of the time. Realize, however, that noting the telephone number aids the courier if he cannot find the address or the person, and noting the date and the contents aids you if someone forgets to enter the information into the distribution binder. Completed waybills only help you.

LOG OR KEEP WAYBILLS

Use a log form to record each couriered envelope or package. You will refer to this log. You send a lot of packages to numerous people and companies. Your memory cannot retain the information. Your memory cannot help you when you have to trace lost packages.

KNOW YOUR COURIER'S SERVICES

Find out what shipping options you have from overnight deliveries to expedited shipping to dedicated truck and so on. Know what time the last pick up is for your courier. Know where the drop boxes are and those last pick-up times. Know what is the last time you can take a package to their airport location and still make it into the plane that night. Due to the nature of the film industry, you will almost always be working on those last minute times.

TAXIS AS LOCAL COURIERS

Taxis deliver people or packages in town. They can be faster than the fastest service your courier can provide, but they tend to be more expensive. Taxi companies can set you up with an account and give you chits to fill out instead of handling cash. They charge an administration fee atop the price of each ride for this convenience.

THE EFFICIENT OFFICE P.A.

If you have an efficient Office Production Assistant, you will find you do not need your local courier very often. An Office P.A. who knows the city and can manage time, will cut your courier bill down to minimum. He is also equipped with more knowledge about production, and therefore production's priorities, than any courier or taxi driver could be. Use this to your advantage.

THE CUSTOMS BROKER

Documents easily cross borders, bypassing customs. Documents have no commercial value. Working for a film company, you will rarely be shipping only documents. There are many restrictions and many forms for items that have to pass through customs to enter your country. You need a Customs Broker to help you. The Production Manager tends to choose the Customs Broker. When choosing one, talk about their services, including accessibility after hours, as well as their rates.

Dealing with shipping and receiving, the Coordinator will more often be the one to deal with the Customs Broker on a day-to-day basis.

POWER OF AUTHORITY LETTER

When a Customs Broker is chosen, the Coordinator can produce a letter addressed to that Broker giving them the power of authority to clear packages through customs for you. The Production Manager needs to be the signing authority for this letter, of course, being a signing authority for the company. The letter is very short and can read like this:

(On letterhead)

Customs Broker
Customs Broker Address

To whom it may concern:

This letter authorizes (Customs Broker company) to act on our behalf of FILM COMPANY INC. ("FILM TITLE") relating to all customs clearances.

Sincerely,

(Production Manager Name)
Production Manager

COURIERS KNOW SIMPLE CUSTOMS PAPERWORK

International couriers know which customs paperwork is required for many typical shipments. If you ask, they will supply you with appropriate forms and directions for the do-it-yourself approach. Use this approach for repeated simple packages, like documents or digital viewing copies that you may be shipping to some of the Executives. If you are ever concerned about the correct paperwork or customs procedure, call your Customs Broker for advice.

DIGITAL VIEWING COPIES CROSSING BORDERS

Dailies, rough cuts, and delivered shows may have you shipping your share of digital viewing copies across international borders to sources that have no access to the FTP site. Confirm with the courier or the broker that no more paperwork is needed than a commercial invoice and a video/film declaration to accompany the waybill. The commercial invoice describes in more detail what the waybill explains, and the videotape declaration is your assurance that the videotapes do not contain material that is pornographic or treasonous. Some countries have censors from whom you will need approval at the border.

COMMERCIAL INVOICE – SMALL SHIPMENTS

The waybill often has a section that is called "commercial invoice." Completing this section is sufficient for international shipments of digital viewing copies, except for very large shipments. Note how many viewing copies and which format are in the package, then mark in large letters in this section that the tapes are: "FOR REFERENCE ONLY; NOT FOR RESALE." Presuming, of course, that you are indeed sending the material for approvals, then "for reference" is what they are.

COMMERCIAL INVOICE – LARGE SHIPMENTS

For large shipments, make a secondary, more detailed commercial invoice on letterhead, as shown here.

(On letterhead)

Date of shipment: (date)

To Whom: (name, address, phone, fax)

Description of Contents: (e.g., one DVD)

Value of Contents: (note value and currency)

Reason for Export: (e.g., Rough Cut of "Film Title" for reference only; not for resale)

How Shipped: (courier company name & waybill number)

Signed: (Production Coordinator name & title)

VIDEO/FILM DECLARATION

If you cannot download a form from the courier's website or obtain one from the broker, make one on the production company's letterhead like this:

(On letterhead)

Date of shipment: (date)

To Whom: (name, address, phone, fax)

Waybill Number: (number)

Description of Contents: (e.g., one DVD)

Length of Video or Film: (e.g., 30 minutes)

Reason for Export: (e.g., Rough Cut of "Film" for reference only; not for resale)

I/we declare that the FILM(S)/VIDEO(S) contain no obscene or immoral matter, not any matter advocating or urging treason or insurrection against (country of destination), nor any threat to take the life of, or inflict bodily harm upon any person in (country of destination).

Signed: (Production Coordinator name & title)

WARDROBE CROSSING BORDERS

Imagine sending a knife wrapped in a t-shirt (for safety) from one country to another, complete with customs documents for the knife. You may wonder why the package stops at customs. Customs will be looking for the proper documentation for the t-shirt. Okay, an overstatement, but at the border, they do need to know what the article of clothing is, its value, why you are shipping it, what fiber makes up the fabric, and where each of those fibers were made in the world. Each piece of information requires a separate form. When you ship clothing, seek the help of your Customs Broker.

REQUEST FOR REDUCTION OF DUTY LETTER

When you courier large shipments of rental costumes internationally, large duties and taxes are triggered because customs presumes the costumes are arriving to stay. To apply for reduction of these duty and taxes, because production is only renting the costumes, draft a letter to the customs office with the help of your Broker (who will know the latest procedure). Start with the following draft letter, customizing the information to your production.

(On letterhead)

Date: (date)

Collector
Customs Office

Dear Sir/Madam:

Please consider this letter an application for reduction of duty and taxes for the costumes (see attached lists). I am applying on behalf of the importer, FILM COMPANY INC., whose address is listed here. We are a (country of nationality) crew currently in production of a (type of film) entitled, "FILM TITLE" for (note where it will be distributed or broadcast). Below please find our responses to the questions regarding responsibility of the importer:

a.) **Name and address of importer**:
(film company's name, address, telephone, fax, email, Web address)

b.) **Contact within company**:
(Production Coordinator name, Head of Wardrobe name)

c.) **Financial Hardship**:
We believe that full duty and taxes would be excessive considering the short period of time that the costumes will be in the country. These goods are obtainable only from (the country of export) and will be returned immediately.

d.) **Why goods are required**:
We are filming "FILM TITLE" that requires authentic (describe originality of the costumes).

e.) **Goods not available from national suppliers**:
The above-mentioned goods could not be obtained from the top costume houses in (your country) due to their peculiarity within the time and budget allotted.

f.) **List of companies and persons contacted**:
(Name at least three companies in your country that you contacted looking for these costumes. Include letters from these companies reporting that they do not have these particular costumes.)

g.) **"Public Interest"**:
(Explain the big picture of how temporary importing of these costumes is beneficial, for example:) This production employs many people from the shooting crew to the support industries, such as (note appropriate suppliers you use, like: equipment houses, hotels, restaurants, airlines, limousines, postproduction and sound facilities, telephone systems, studio rentals, the unions and guilds, etc.). If we cannot obtain the goods within the required time and budget, we will have to shut down production until such time as we can have appropriate costumes made for filming, which would mean a shutdown of at least (mention an estimated time frame). This shutdown will affect in excess of (number of employees) people with a loss of income.

h.) **Statement**:
See attached letter from Production Manager. (The letter is described below.)

i.) **National Competitors**:
We have contacted everyone possible to obtain the required costumes and they are unable to provide the goods. Nor can anyone suggest anyone in (your country) that can.

j.) **Any objections to reveal company's name**:
Film Company Inc. does not have any objections to its name being revealed.

k.) **Description of what makes them special in nature**:
(Describe the costumes.)

l.) **Use of goods**:
As wardrobe for a (feature film or television movie).

m.) **Where goods to be used**:
"FILM TITLE" movie currently filming in (city).

n.) **Value of goods**:
(note overall value and currency)

o.) **Estimated date of arrival**:
Shipment from (costume company name) in (city, country) on (date of arrival).

If you require further information, I can be reached at the production number listed below. I look forward to hearing from you in the near future.

Signed, (Production Coordinator name and title)

WARDROBE SUPPLIER LETTERS (Item f.)

The Head of Wardrobe will usually arrange for these letters for you. If the supplier asks you to draft up the wording, since they are busy, start with the following: "Film Company Inc. has requested the rental of (specify costumes). We do not have such costumes in our stock and do not know of another company in (your country) that can assist them with this rental."

STATEMENT LETTER FROM PM (Item h.)

Create and attach a letter addressed to customs from the Production Manager that promises the film company will cover all duty and taxes should the request for reduction of duty be denied. Begin with the following wording: "This letter is to confirm that FILM COMPANY INC. would accept responsibility for payment in full of duties and taxes applicable under the (appropriate tax act), if the request for reduction of duty and taxes is not approved." In this case, when the items are exported back to the original country, you may be eligible for a duty drawback to reclaim the duty paid, so keep in touch with your Customs Broker.

COMMERCIAL INVOICE

Type up a commercial invoice on letterhead, just as you do for digital viewing copies, detailing exactly what items are being imported. The costume company will have a detailed list since they have to generate one for rental and accounting purposes anyway. Do not simply photocopy their forms (which you will also use for customs). Make the commercial invoice easy to read, listing the items clearly, and noting the overall value rather than individual values.

FILM EQUIPMENT CROSSING BORDERS & CARNETS

If you take film equipment to certain countries for the filming period and return with it, your Customs Broker will help you to obtain a carnet. If it is the whole equipment package, the equipment rental house will arrange for the carnet. A carnet is a document that lists every single item of film equipment (right down to each filter), all the serial numbers, every separate value, and every source country for each separate piece. This document is a promise to customs that this equipment will be in the country only temporarily. It works like a bond, which is why you need to return home with each piece of equipment you imported. This is a complex form to assemble. Beyond that, not all countries recognize a carnet, so you may have to arrange for another type of certificate of temporary import/export. When you are planning on shipping large quantities of equipment for the duration of (or part of) the shoot, talk first with your Customs Broker and with the equipment rental house you are using. They will both be of great help.

DIGITAL vs. FILM STOCK CROSSING BORDERS

Digital stock does not have the same critical problem film stock has at the airport since it is unaffected by radiation. Unexposed and unprocessed film stock, however, is.

Security at the airports may say that unprocessed film is unaffected by the security x-ray machine, but they are wrong. There is a very real risk of x-ray radiation on your raw stock or unprocessed film dailies every time you pass it through a security x-ray machine. X-rays, too, are cumulative in effect. Consider this effect when you add up all the machines you need to pass through on the journey. And, yes, the higher the ASA of the film, the higher the risk, as ASA measures the film's sensitivity to light (which is a kind of radiation). Therefore, as you cannot afford to have raw stock or unprocessed film dailies exposed to x-rays, it behooves you to send the film in lead cases when crossing borders, or arrange for some other cross-border arrangement wherein the film is not x-rayed. If you are hand-carrying unprocessed film across the border, remember to bring along a black changing bag in case you need to open a can at security for validation of the contents. You likely will.

OTHER ITEMS CROSSING BORDERS

You can ship almost anything: contact lenses, animals, props, antiques, and so on. Since countries have different restrictions and requirements for each shipment, contact your Customs Broker for the latest procedures for each item.

HAND-CARRYING ITEMS ACROSS BORDERS

Due to time constraints, sometimes the only remaining alternative is to fly a person across a border to hand-carry the item to its destination. Because this is a last resort method of shipping, any delay at the border is critical. Documentation must be perfectly complete and accurate. Review all the paperwork necessary with the Customs Broker. They may arrange for someone at the airport to aid you through customs. Along with all that paperwork, give a letter of identification to the person hand-carrying.

(On letterhead)

Date

To whom it may concern:

(Hand-carry Person name) is hand-carrying (describe item) for the film entitled: "FILM TITLE." (Describe reason for the export and if the item is being returned to the country.)

The value of (the item) for customs purposes is: (amount and currency).

Signed, (Production Coordinator name and title)

—⁙—

As the Coordinator, you will become used to foreign shipments, growing amazed by how similar the various customs forms actually are. Each one requires so much of the same information over and over again with one or two differences. You may never stop being amazed, but you will soon learn which forms are appropriate to which packages, and amaze the Production Manager, and crew, on your knowledge about customs. The PM will feel a level of comfort with the Coordinator shepherding anything and everything across town and across borders. When whatever it is needs to be on set, the PC is dealing with the details to ensure is shows up on time.

SING TO ME IN PUBLIC DOMAIN

Performers often invent unscripted business on set for their characters to add depth and personality to their performances. That's wonderful, unless the unscripted business is singing unscripted, copyrighted songs.

One Performer I worked with had this tendency, and the first two songs did not prove to be a big problem. After watching the dailies, I arranged for licenses to use the songs that he sang. Both licenses were reasonable. Twice lucky. But the third song...

Watching the dailies, I was relieved that the Performer had chosen to hum a piece of his own making. It was a totally unintelligible, nonsense collection of sounds. Not so, apparently.

The day before broadcast, the Assistant Coordinator was dubbing a copy of the show and commented how long it has been since she's heard that song. "Song?" I asked. She told me the title and the artist. It was no collection of sounds, as I originally thought; it was an obscure, old, and very copyrighted song.

The Producer asked me to get a quote on the license. I discovered a catch. The particular broadcaster we were using was not signatory with the performing rights company that covered the song. The performing rights company did not want to grant a license at any cost. They wanted the broadcaster to become signatory.

So, to this day, lawyers speak with lawyers about this song, and the particular Performer was never allowed to sing or hum unscripted songs on set again, unless it could be proven before call time that the songs were indeed in the public domain.

SCRIPT, MUSIC & OTHER LEGAL CLEARANCES

33

Sometimes the Producer does it. Sometimes Legal Counsel does it. Often either of you, the Production Manager or the Production Coordinator, does it. "It" is the clearing of the rights to copyrighted works, like songs or photographs, for use in a film production. This chapter cannot be an exhaustive description of legal rights and clearances, nor is it any form of legal advice; it does not intend to be – but it will help you to embark on another facet of filmmaking. Keep in contact with Legal Counsel for advice as you enter the world (or minefield) of rights and clearances.

THE SCRIPT CLEARANCE REPORT

Script clearance has been mentioned several times so far. You need to find a script clearance company to read and report on the script as it is, nearly ready for production. Read on to find out why.

E & O INSURANCE

As mentioned previously, in order to distribute or broadcast a film production, the Producer needs to arrange for E & O insurance (errors & omissions insurance) for the film. E & O insurance is a kind of "malpractice" insurance for Producers in case the Producer has mistakenly represented a real person or a company in this fictional film, and the actual person or company feels the representation is derogatory and harmful enough to them to sue the Producer. Now, these types of lawsuits never result in the suing party only suing the Producer, they will also sue the Distributor and the Broadcaster and the Studio and anyone else who has money to compensate them. This is why you cannot distribute the film without E & O insurance. Everyone needs to be protected.

Of course, the Producer (through the production company) must have conducted all the research during the script writing process to ensure that this fictional film indeed does not happen to portray a real person or company or take place in real locations. This is where the script research report comes in. Clearance companies read scripts and report on all the names, trademarks, logos, and other potentially litigious items in the script and comment on them for the Producer. The Producer must then act and change the references to keep the script legally clear. The Producer may consult with Legal Counsel to determine how much risk the production is willing to take. Some of the clearance report references will need to be changed whereas others will be deemed clear enough as they are.

HOW SCRIPT CLEARANCE REPORTS WORK

If, as mentioned before, the script has a character named John Smith who is a dentist from a particular city, the clearance company will research to see if such a man exists. If there are many John Smiths in that city, of which none of them are dentists, then the name "John Smith" is clear for use in the film. If, however, there is one John Smith who is a dentist in all of North America, or if there is only one John Smith in that city, then the clearance company will suggest your changing the character name in the script to avoid any possible lawsuit. The real John Smith may see the film, decide that the character is a derogatory portrayal of himself, and sue. Production needs to use "clear" names in the script. The same goes for names and trademarks on props, locations, set dressing, and wardrobe (like logos on baseball caps). These references will be in set descriptions and in dialogue references.

FIRST CONVERSATION WITH A CLEARANCE COMPANY

Decide between the Production Manager and Coordinator who is going to be the contact with the script clearance company. Then, when you first talk to the script clearance company, know where and when the script takes place. Is the film fictional or is it based on a true story? Where is the film going to be distributed or broadcast? From this information and other questions they will ask, the clearance company will determine the scope of the clearance you need, and the two of you can negotiate a price.

THE CLEARANCE COMPANY AND SCRIPT REVISIONS

It is truly important to keep the clearance company abreast of all script revisions as soon as possible. Once you are aware of how they read a script, you as the Coordinator — while you are preparing the next script revision for publication — can telephone in script changes as they happen. This process will give the clearance company extra time to research the new material.

THE RELUCTANCE OF CHANGING NAMES

Writers, Story Editors, and Producers may be reluctant to change names they deem trivial or absolutely essential to the story as is. Changing names is legal preventative medicine, so if you need to, involve Legal Counsel for persuasion. Together Legal Counsel and the Producer can evaluate the potential legal risk and come up with a decision to change the names or not, and take the risk of this item being an exclusion from the E & O insurance.

ADDRESSING THE SUGGESTIONS ON THE CLEARANCE REPORT

After distributing the clearance report, read it carefully and ensure that, somehow, the production team addresses each suggestion for change.

CHARACTER NAMES THAT DO NOT CLEAR

Have the Writers or the Story Editor generate a list of replacement names in descending order of priority to send to the clearance company for "re-clearing" immediately. Once a replacement name is cleared, send a memo to everyone who regularly receives the clearance report. The Coordinator needs to place an extra copy in the script revision desk file to remind him to include it when next revising the script. The immediacy of the memo will help the Wardrobe Department (for example) build clothing labels using correct, cleared names.

LOCATION NAMES THAT DO NOT CLEAR

If the script is fictitious, the names of the locations must also be fictitious. If an actual location (like a restaurant) with its name is used on screen, then the script, legally, is no longer located in a fictitious place. Actual locations make the clearing of character names more complex and iffy. Collect replacement names (typically from the Writer) and send them to the clearance company as soon as possible. The Art Department will likely need time to build signs to identify these fictitious buildings on screen.

TRADEMARKS THAT DO NOT CLEAR

Trademarks like "Kleenex" and "Xerox" are often mentioned in early drafts of scripts when what is actually meant is "tissue" and "photocopy." The clearance report will note these trademarks for you. If you do not change these words in the script, you must contact each company to negotiate written permission to use their trademarked name on screen. Since most corporate companies do not work at the speed of film companies, permissions can take up to six or eight weeks. For trivial on screen references, your time and effort are not worth wasting. Make the change.

REFERENCES THAT ALMOST DO NOT CLEAR

People who work at clearance companies seem to have seen every film ever made, read every book on the market, and speak every language in the world. These people are amazing. You may see a comment in the clearance report that notes a certain visual look is particularly like that of another film already made, or a certain phrase has been published in a book already on the market, or that a certain work or character name actually means something terribly rude in another language. Discuss these comments with the Producer and the Legal Counsel. Find out how these notes will be addressed.

CLEARANCES REFERENCES NOT IN THE SCRIPT

As you can imagine, not all references that need clearing are listed clearly in the script. While out shopping for production, the Wardrobe Department has the opportunity of purchasing clothing with rights-protected logos on them; the Set Dressing team has the opportunity of purchasing or renting televisions and wireless devices with rights-protected logos on them, too; and the Locations Department has the likelihood of showing other company names in the background of shots due to the location's proximity to other businesses. As a Production Manager, you need to hire a professional crew who is conscious of clearance issues, and not rely totally on the script clearance report. If in doubt, discuss these issues at the beginning of production, especially with the Art Department.

WHERE TO ASK FOR PERMISSION

You have a rights-protected name that you really want to use in the film but you do not know whom to ask for permission. If the contact name and the number are not already on the clearance report, telephone and ask the clearance company. Though they are not negotiators for you, they will find out where you have to go to obtain permission.

USING ACTUAL NAMES

In stories based on real people or companies, it is obvious that you need each person's and each company's permission to depict them in the film. But even in fictional films, you will sometimes use the names of real people or locations.

USING AN ACTUAL PERSON'S NAME

When the script uses the name of a person, be it a crew member or a friend who gives permission to the production company to do so, draft a short letter from that person confirming that permission. Legal Counsel needs all such permissions in writing in order to obtain the E & O insurance. Be simple in creating the letter with wording like: "I give Film Company Inc. permission to use my name in the film 'FILM TITLE.' I understand that my name will not be used in a derogatory manner." Review the wording with Legal Counsel for simplicity and full legal coverage.

USING AN ACTUAL LOCATION OR COMPANY NAME

Location agreements usually contain a clause to give the film company permission to use the company name on screen when filming there. Do not assume all location agreements specify this. Check with the Location Manager. If there is no such clause and you intend to see the company's name on screen, generate a letter granting the permission you need, and review the letter with Legal Counsel.

COPYRIGHT, TRADEMARK & PUBLIC DOMAIN

Copyright and trademarks are intellectual property rights that are attached to works of all kinds. In very simple terms, a trademark is used to distinguish your goods and services from the goods and services of others. You can trademark a word, phrase, or logo (think "title", "log line" or "character", for example). Copyright, on the other hand, is the right to copy, publish, exhibit, and modify an original work — plus the right to authorize others to do so. Copyright starts with the original creator, like an author, and does expire over time. If maintained, the registration of a trademark can last indefinitely, otherwise, it will become abandoned. Both copyright and trademark require that you secure a license to use the original work that it is protecting.

When copyright expires, the work goes into the public domain and is then free for use by the public at large, which is great for filmmakers. The trick with public domain, however, is that different countries have different time calculations to determine what is in the public domain, for example: 50, 100, or 120 years after publication date, or the life of the author plus 70 years and so on. Since your film is expected to be available internationally some day, you care about these international nuances. Copyrights can also be renewed under certain circumstances, and governments change public domain rules over time to address present realities and the introduction of new medias. So basically, there is no one calculation you can use to know if a work is definitively in the public domain without the help of your clearance sources and Legal Counsel.

CREATIVE COMMONS LICENSES

Creative Commons is a non-profit organization that developed a unique set of licenses for the sharing, and possible modification of creative works, including: music, websites, film, books, blogs, and photographs. Simply put, a Creative Commons license lies between copyright and public domain and also deals with authorship. It acknowledges copyright, but opens up some of the reserved rights for specific uses. When you think of copyright as "all rights reserved (always ask me for permission)", then a Creative Commons license is "some rights reserved (you may or may not need to ask me for permission)". You cannot have a Creative Commons license on a trademark, it works with copyright only.

Now, not all Creative Commons licenses are created equal. The allowable rights vary based on the particular license registered, and also vary from country to country. In general, there are six possible licenses, three allowing for commercial re-use of the creative work, while three keep strictly to non-commercial permissions. Some licenses allow for adaptation and modification of the original work, whereas others permit no changes (known as "no derivatives"). In all cases the author of the original work must be attributed (credited) in the new work.

If you plan to use material under a Creative Commons license, involve Legal Counsel to be sure you secure sufficient rights to exploit your finished film with the acquired, copyrighted material included.

MUSIC CLEARANCES

If there are a lot of songs in the script and the film company has the funds, hire a music clearance company to clear the songs for you. They will identify songs that are in the public domain (free) or under the right Creative Commons license (payment-free) and will save you from an enormous and time-consuming job. If, however, you have to (or want to) clear the music in the script – including such favorites as "Happy Birthday To You" – here are a few things you should know.

TYPES OF RIGHTS

Once you select a song to use, there are four types of rights you may need to buy before using that song.

PUBLISHING RIGHTS OR SYNCHRONIZATION RIGHTS

As the name suggests, you must contact a Music Publisher to purchase a publishing rights license. This license grants you permission to use the "sheet music" for a particular song. This license in hand, you can hum that song, sing that song, play that song, or arrange your own version of that song on screen and play that song in synchronization with the film you are producing.

RECORDING RIGHTS

As the name suggests, you have to contact a Record Company to obtain a recording rights license. This license grants you permission to play a particular recording of a song on screen. This license does not include the Publisher's permission. You must obtain a publishing rights license separately.

ARTIST RIGHTS

Sometimes the Record Company does not hold all the rights to a recording, because the Artist has retained some rights. Ask the Record Company if Artist's rights are applicable to this recording. Artist's rights are negotiated through the Record Company or through the Artist's manager. Again, you still have to obtain a publishing rights license separately.

ARRANGEMENT RIGHTS

Not all songs in the public domain are free to use. Some have arrangement rights attached to them. An Arranger can take a song in the public domain, publish his own arrangement, and copyright that arrangement. As the description suggests, you will need to contact a Publisher to negotiate arrangement rights.

SO, WHAT ARE MASTER RIGHTS?

You will hear the term "master rights" used frequently. "Publishing rights" are technically called "master rights" and "recording rights" are technically called "master recording rights" (but are often incorrectly also called "master rights"). By using the terms "publishing" and "recording" instead of "master" for both, you cannot mix up the two licenses, and people in the industry will understand you.

MUSIC DOWNLOADED FROM THE INTERNET

Just because you can easily download music from the Internet (for free or pay), does not mean the music is rights-free, or that you have the correct rights to use the music in your film production. Downloaded music typically grants rights for personal non-commercial use. To include music in your soundtrack — a purpose for which the music was not originally intended — you still need to secure publishing and recording rights from the rights owners.

WHERE TO LOOK FOR MUSIC RIGHTS

For publishing rights, call the Index Department of the music performer rights associations (ASCAP, BMI, SOCAN, or similar CMRRA) with the name of the song. They can furnish you with the name of the Publisher and will also know if arrangement rights apply.

For recording rights, refer to the CD cover for the name of the Record Company. Contact the Permissions or Legal Department and request permission. Postproduction will consider a CD adequate quality from which to duplicate the recording onto the soundtrack. For downloaded music, depending on the compression ratio, the file you download may also be adequate. If there is no CD or adequately uncompressed file of the song, ask the Record Company or owner to supply you with a master of the recording.

TERMS, TERRITORIES, USAGE, FEES

When you are set to negotiate for the rights, address the following criteria.

TERM

Often license fees are for a 5-year term, 10-year term, or perpetuity. Naturally, the longer the term is, the higher the price. Buy as much as you can afford. Distributors and Legal Counsels love the words "in perpetuity," so that a few years from now they do not have to buy the rights all over again in order to continue to show and sell your finished film.

TERRITORY

You can buy a license to cover one country or pay more and cover the world. Find out from the Producer the plan for the film's distribution. Will production or the Distributor pay for all those foreign territories?

USAGE

Is the song to be hummed, sung, or instrumental? Is it a record playing or a band miming to the recording? Is the song atmosphere in the background or a critical part of the scene's action? Have some script pages handy to demonstrate the song's usage in the scene when you ask for permission. The owners need to know how the song is to be handled. Is it being used in a derogatory manner?

FEES

A character hums an identifiable song in the script as he walks in the door. The Producer wants to know how much the use of that song will cost. Fees vary drastically, taking into consideration the range of terms, territories, and usages, the budget of your production, and the particularities of each Publisher. Some Publishers who do not want to participate in your film for whatever reason, may quote fees so far out of reach that they never need to say "no". Each song will be different. A price quotation is time-consuming for you and the Publisher, so be sure you really want that song before you start the process of asking for permission.

STOCK MUSIC

Stock music is generally low-copyright music. If you are specific about a song you want but not about a particular arrangement or Artist, contact a Stock Music Supplier to source stock music that will suffice. They charge research fees, so be specific. They also charge transfer fees, so be sure postproduction tells you exactly which delivery format is acceptable. The license fee is sold to you at a very discounted price compared to that of the big Publishers, and the license will be for the use throughout the world and in perpetuity.

PROMISE OF A SCREEN CREDIT

Song credits are not short. For each piece of music, count on three to four lines of text to credit any or all of the song title, the Composer, the Publisher, the Artist, and the Record Company. Be upfront with the record company about credits. It is standard to credit songs, but if the production is too small to warrant many credits of any kind, address this issue early. Do not wait for the license to arrive with credit wording expected and specifications defined.

WHEN YOU CANNOT FIND THE OWNER

Rights change hands. They expire. They revert back to the Composers. Publishers buy out other Publishers. Sometimes you cannot find the rights to a song no matter how hard you try. Keep notes of everyone you contact in your search for the owner. If after a few weeks your search has still been to no avail, Legal Counsel can review your notes and decide that enough effort went into the search, and the song can be used anyway.

SINGING UNSCRIPTED SONGS ON SET

Performers can be asked to ad lib a song on the set. Talk to the A.D.s and do not let any Performer hum a song that is not in the public domain! Clearing a song after it has been cut into the film is a nearly impossible task. With the film completed, you are no longer in a bargaining position. If the owner does not want to grant or sell you the rights, your only way out is to cut the offending song from the film.

CUE SHEETS

Postproduction is aware they have to forward cue sheets to the music performer rights associations (ASCAP, BMI, or SOCAN), as well as to the Distributors, the Broadcasters, and other places. Cue sheets report how many seconds of each song is played in the production and identify the respective owners. The associations use this information to calculate royalty payments to the Composers. Read the licenses you have purchased. They may also require that a copy of the cue sheets go to the Publisher and/or the Record Company. If so, send a memo to postproduction relating this information.

PHOTOGRAPHIC CLEARANCES

When you are arranging for permission to use a photograph from a stock library or a magazine, note that there are at least two kinds of rights that may apply: "publishing rights" and "photographer rights." The publishing entity is the magazine company, and the Photographer is equivalent to the Music Artist for music rights. The Magazine's (or Book's) Legal Department will know if the Photographer has retained any rights to the photograph you wish to use, not unlike Artist's rights. Online, the Photographer typically does hold rights, but it is the Web publisher who typically brokers the rights payment when you purchase a license. If the people depicted in the photograph are unrecognizable, there are no more rights to buy. Note, however, that if the people are recognizable, you must seek permission from each one of them, too. A simple letter granting permission to the film company will suffice, but it is wise to discuss this situation with Legal Counsel before pursuing photographic clearances, because, even descendants of people whose names are depicted on grave stones could have an issue with your including their ancestor's names in a fictional film.

In some cases, Stills Photographers you hire on set retain rights to the photographs they take (not unlike Artist's rights). In these cases, you will have to ensure you address these rights issues in their agreement/deal memo when you hire them.

As with downloaded music, know which rights you purchase when you download photographs for inclusion into the film. Do those rights cover re-purposing the images the way you plan, and do they cover the eventual exploitation plan and commercial intentions of your finished film? Yes, you will have to read the online fine print to find out.

OTHER CLEARANCES

Rights can be attached to numerous items: radio station call letters, posters, artwork, and so on. The script clearance report will note these copyrighted items and lead you to the source for chasing down the appropriate permissions. Unique fonts also tend to have purchasable rights attached to them, so be sure you purchase the rights you need, or choose a rights-free font instead.

MORAL RIGHTS

Very basically, moral rights are retained by the original Artist or Creator of the work (be it a sculpture, script, etc.) and ensure that the Artist has an ongoing right to the integrity of that work. An obvious example: you cannot deface a sculpture to suit the purpose of the film story. A more subtle example: though you can revise the script substantially, changing characters, scenes, scene order, locations and so on, you cannot distort the integrity of the original script from, say, a touching family drama to a high-action thriller — well, unless the original Writer has waived her moral rights. Moral rights, you see, cannot be purchased or transferred. It is therefore standard to see moral rights waived in all agreements related to production, since the making of a film is a truly collaborative experience. Still, keeping in mind the preservation of the integrity of the original work is good practice for whatever works your license.

TITLE SEARCHES

A title search is different and separate from script clearances. You need a legal firm that specializes in title searches to clear the title for your production. Again, this search is another requirement for the E & O insurance application, and you most certainly do not want your production to have the same name as another film just recently, or soon to be, released. Internet research can help you conduct the initial title search yourself, so you do not end up purchasing several title searches looking for a title that just will not clear.

PRODUCT PLACEMENT

By now you may expect to pay for all permissions you arrange. In some cases however, permission is granted free of charge and in other cases, they actually pay you. Product placement is when a company pays the production to show its logo on screen. It is a form of advertising for the company and a source of revenue for the production. Not all productions, however, want to advertise products in the course of telling a story, and not all Broadcasters appreciate what is basically a commercial during the story. Some broadcasters have a complete prohibition on product placement, for example. If production allows for product placement, you can approach companies directly or contact a Product Placement Agent from your reference sources. Product placement is rarely the source of income it appears to be, and you have to ensure the product's logo is clearly on the screen, which the Director may find restrictive, and may distract from the action of the story.

—⁂—

All kinds of legal clearances no longer mystify you. Though this chapter has not been an exhaustive explanation, the complexity of rights here should inspire you to not be a stranger to your Legal Counsel. She, too, will appreciate your contact and will be happy to share knowledge with you, as she will be up on the latest when it comes to intellectual property rights. Just be sure that you have all the necessary rights before committing anything to screen.

POSTPRODUCTION VIII

Do not fix it in post... create magic in post.

WHO'S IN CHARGE?

Though the hierarchy of a film production deems the Executive Producer most in charge, that is not true all of the time. At the wrap party, the Coordinator rules.

One wrap party, we rented a cruising boat to tour the harbor. The several decks supplied us with a wonderful buffet, danceable music, and incredible views of the city. The party was a great success, and the Executive Producer, along with the Producer and the Production Manager, decided that it should continue for another hour. The Executive Producer was willing to cover the expense on his own credit card.

The boat crew refused their request. They needed the permission of a woman named Deborah. This must be the boat's manager, the producing trio presumed. So a search went out for this Deborah. When she was found, she was escorted to the scene of the request.

The Executive Producer, the Producer, and the Production Manager were rather surprised to find out that the person who appeared was not the boat's manager, but their own Production Coordinator. In front of the trio, the boat crew asked Deborah for permission to extend the party. I quickly said, "Yes, of course!" then turned to the Executive Producer and said: "Sir, you have my approval to spend your own money."

WRAP & WRAP PARTY | 34

The last day of principal photography is here. Crew members are talking about their next jobs. But your mind is concerned with the last phase of production: wrap. In wrap you must return everything that you rented, sell everything that you bought, and pack all the files for head office storage. It is time to hand over your files of ongoing issues to head office and to postproduction. It is time to empty the office. It is also time to arrange a celebratory party.

THE PRODUCTION MANAGER WRAPS

Wrap does not mean production is completed. It is far from completed. Only principal photography is done. Postproduction continues. The Production Manager is responsible to wrap up the files of production and hand over the cost reporting responsibilities to the Postproduction Supervisor.

- ☐ Meet with the Coordinator daily
- ☐ Wrap Main Unit
- ☐ Wrap Second Unit
- ☐ Wrap the PM files
- ☐ Seek out and collect final invoices
- ☐ Wrap out petty cash
- ☐ Final production cost report
- ☐ Wardrobe & set sale or storage
- ☐ Check in with Accounting
- ☐ Prep for Audit
- ☐ Hand–over memo
- ☐ Post Mortem
- ☐ Tie up loose ends
- ☐ Move files to head office

MEET WITH THE COORDINATOR DAILY

First things first: meet with the Coordinator daily, especially during wrap. The PC was key to setting up the office in the first place, and will be heading up wrapping the office now. The PC will also be organizing the wrap party, so you will both need to speak frequently about wrap issues.

WRAP MAIN UNIT

How is the studio strike of the sets proceeding? How is the return of the equipment going? Are there any broken or lost items that need to be found or paid for by production? In everyone's rush to complete within days, and your needing to be at the office for a week or two, you must remember to supervise and be available during wrap to discover potentially costly issues. You want to be immediately available so you can corral crew into helping you deal with issues before they depart onto new productions and holidays. Note anything that will cost you money on the PM-only cost report.

WRAP SECOND UNIT

Second unit may be shooting a few days or a week into wrap. Do not forget about them. Have they achieved all their pickup shots? Their wrap issues will happen later, and you still need to be fresh to deal with them. Find out if they are having trouble securing access to key crew for decision-making while wrap of main unit is underway.

WRAP THE PM FILES

It is time to sift through all the PM files — both hard copy and electronically — and remove documentation that is unnecessary for future reference. Fax top sheets with "2 pages attached" as the only notation are useless now. You will now find out how incredibly useful those descriptive electronic file names and email subject headers are. If you would like, you can integrate the PM files into the Coordinator's production files now so that head office will have fewer sources of files to refer to when they are seeking information in the future. Even if the electronic files on are on a shared drive with head office, strike an electronic backup copy of them to store with the physical files. Preserve this moment in time.

SEEK OUT AND COLLECT FINAL INVOICES

You want to have all payables in the cost report as soon as possible. The Postproduction Supervisor should not have to chase down production invoices for you. Ask companies for invoices, even if they are supplied by email or fax, so that you can at least purchase order and close out all production costs on the cost report. Most companies will be thrilled to be able to invoice you quickly.

WRAP OUT PETTY CASH

As with invoices, it is time to ensure all crew have completed their petty cash and balance out. They will be eager to supply you with their petty cash anyway, unless they owe production money. Some crew will surprise you with receipts you never expected because they have been hoarding them throughout production. Expect this conduct now and then. The Production Accountant will no doubt hold onto the crew's last paycheck until their last petty cash is in.

FINAL PRODUCTION COST REPORT

All the final invoices and final petty cashes you have been collecting enable you and the Production Accountant to generate the final production cost report. You want to zero out as many production line items as possible, so everyone knows how much money and contingency is left in the Estimate To Complete column for postproduction.

WARDROBE & SET SALE OR STORAGE

Are you arranging for a wardrobe and set dressing sale or putting this material into storage? If production is a television series, you will most likely want to keep the sets and wardrobe in case the show is picked up for the next season. Make a notation to the Producer of how long you are storing the materials, because the budget will only pay for so many months. On other shows you may want to sell the items to generate a little income for the production company to offset some production overages in those categories. Sets are hard to sell, but you can always contact film companies starting up soon; they might be interested. The Art Department and the Coordinator will be pleased to arrange for and publicize the sale.

CHECK IN WITH ACCOUNTING

The Production Accountant will be busy wrapping the accounting files and preparing them to move to the Postproduction Accountant, and preparing the production reports for the audit. She will also ensure the payroll company completes all the tax forms for the crew. If the cast were paid on flat rates, the Accountant will have to calculate the union scale rates of the actual hours each Performer worked, to be sure the flat rate encompassed all those hours and all that overtime. You may find you will have to pay extra for even flat rate cast because of this situation. Do what you can to help the Accountant wrap all the accounting issues of production.

PREP FOR AUDIT

Prep for the audit has been mentioned, but will be discussed in more detail in Chapter 36.

HAND-OVER MEMO

Create a hand-over memo to the Producer, the Postproduction Supervisor, and the Postproduction Accountant summarizing anything and everything you would like to know if you were to take over the production from here. Include cost report notes, because the Postproduction Supervisor and the Postproduction Accountant will be generating the cost reports from now on. What is the history they need to know? What invoices may yet come in? What issues about unpaid bills do they need to know? Include a list of all accounts payable with explanations for why each is remaining unpaid. Include notations for issues that may arise in your absence. Identify the status of the ISAN registration. Discuss this memo with the Production Accountant, because she can help with information from her perspective. The Coordinator will be generating his own ongoing issues memo. Be sure your hand-over memo works well with it.

POST MORTEM

Whether production went well or did not, it is always good to conduct a post mortem so you can learn from both your good and bad experiences. Hindsight is a wonderful teacher. Knowing what you know now in wrap, if you could go back and do everything all over again, what would you do the same, and what would you do differently? Summarize these thoughts in a memo for the Producer and for yourself. If you are on a series, there may be another season where you can use this memo in early preproduction decisions. Encourage other keys to do post mortems too, or at least interview them during wrap about what would have been done similarly or differently: the First A.D., the Production Designer, the Production Accountant, others. Every job is a learning experience. Capitalize on it. Remember to be insightful. This is an opportunity to think and analyze, not to rant.

TIE UP LOOSE ENDS

Many other issues of an unpredictable nature will form in wrap. You will spend time chasing things down, calling people and companies, and basically tying up loose ends. The days will slow down, but you probably will not notice it for a week or so. There will be fewer and fewer people every day. Include whatever you cannot tie up in the hand-over memo.

MOVE FILES TO HEAD OFFICE

At the end of your wrap, move the electronic and physical files back to head office. You may end up moving back to head office yourself to complete wrap and to tidy up the last few loose ends. Remember to say your goodbyes.

THE PRODUCTION COORDINATOR WRAPS

You brought it all together here in the office. It is time to dispose of it all. Return it, sell it, close it out, hand it out, or accomplish whatever needs to be done. You also need to report on everything you are about to do.

☐ Meet the PM daily
☐ Arrange the Wrap Party
☐ Refer to Chapter 5 (Setting Up The Production Office)
☐ Report to the "wrap" file
☐ Inventory list
☐ Summary memo of returned items & ongoing issues
☐ List items for sale
☐ Wardrobe & set sale or storage
☐ Crew gifts arrived and distributed
☐ Crew photograph
☐ Seek out and collect final invoices
☐ Close accounts
☐ Be careful ordering office supplies in wrap
☐ Box up files for head office
☐ Forward telephone to head office
☐ When you do not have to empty the office entirely
☐ Take your kit home

MEET THE PM DAILY

As mentioned to the PM, you both need to meet daily. In wrap, the office quickly becomes a busy place again; then as people wrap day by day, the activity slows down. You both have to be on top of wrap issues immediately — before the crew goes home and can no longer help you with answers.

ARRANGE THE WRAP PARTY

Arranging the wrap party is discussed in more detail below.

REFER TO CHAPTER 5 (SETTING UP THE PRODUCTION OFFICE)

Since Chapter 5 lists all the items you arranged, such a list will not be repeated here. Review and reverse the items you acquired in that chapter.

REPORT TO THE "WRAP" FILE

You already have a file in the cabinet called "wrap." In this file, keep all the memos and the copies of letters reporting what happened to everything (from furniture to the linen delivery) at the end of the film.

INVENTORY LIST

Back in preproduction you created an inventory list (or kept a detailed P.O. log) of everything that you bought and rented as it happened. This list is invaluable to you now to double check that all items are indeed wrapping. Much time has elapsed since the beginning of preproduction, and your memory will need the assistance. The Production Accountant may be able to add to this list after reviewing the petty cash reports for inventory-type purchases.

SUMMARY MEMO OF RETURNED ITEMS & ON-GOING ISSUES

As you return items (from walkie-talkies and coffee machines to telephones and furniture), keep notes of when and how everything is returned. Draft a memo combining all these notes, sending it to the Producer, the Production Manager, the Production Accountant, and to yourself. Also note last working dates for all the office staff, and the status of issues that could not be completed by the end of your last workday. This memo will be a wonderful reference after your departure.

LIST ITEMS FOR SALE

Note every saleable item that production bought and each item's original purchase price. Other production companies just starting up will buy pretty much everything from folding tables to office supplies. Approve and price the sale list with the Production Manager, then contact other Production Coordinators to peddle your goods.

WARDROBE & SET SALE OR STORAGE

If production is a television series, you may have to help with arrangements to store the wardrobe, sets, set dressing, and props until the next potential season. If not, there may be a wardrobe & set sale to rid production of all their goods. Find out when the sales are planned and coordinate the office sale simultaneously. This tactic will help for attendance. You may even help with publicizing the sale by emailing, faxing or telephoning your contacts and other production companies starting up soon.

CREW GIFTS (OR "SWAG") ARRIVED AND DISTRIBUTED

Whether they are hats, bags, sweatshirts, pins, watches, or bathmats with the production title on them, make sure the crew gifts are delivered on time. Keep in touch with the supplier. The Producer may want them handed out on the last day of principal photography or at the wrap party. Handing them out without missing a crew member is actually a large undertaking, so here is advice on how to coordinate it.

> **Make Labels For Distribution**: Handing out crew gifts sounds easy, until you see the mountainous heap of crew gifts left on the office floor from the courier. If you have 200 sweatshirts to hand out, some will go to the set crew, some to the postproduction crew, some to cast that wrapped weeks ago, and some to Executives in another country. It is very easy to give too many gifts to one person, and run out before you have finished. If the gift is free, many crew members will ask you for an extra one or two for their families and friends. Just like scripts, label each gift before distribution. You have a list of who is entitled to a crew gift. On file folder labels, write one crew name per label (include size, if applicable). Then pre-organize the labels in groupings of: (1) those to be couriered out of country, (2) those to be delivered around town, (3) those to be distributed on set, and (4) those to be held for people coming into the office to pick them up. When the stacks of crew gifts arrive, slap a label on each one. Done. If not, have several spare gifts on hand, because those 200 identical sweatshirts after distribution on set are just that: identical. Some will become lost. Some people will take two.

> **Make Boxes For Distribution**: Though the crew gifts are labelled, they still may be a large bundle to handle. Decorate old photocopier paper boxes with wrapping paper and stow the crew gifts into the boxes in roughly alphabetical order (i.e., clump all the A's together in any order). Then label the boxes with the appropriate letters. Now you can hand out the gifts efficiently, or let the crew pick them up on their own.

> **When Crew Gifts Are A Surprise**: It is next to impossible to keep a surprise from an entire crew. If you want to try, use a code word with the supplier on the telephone to inform him that you cannot talk presently because someone else is in the room. On arrival, whisk the crew gifts into a pre-designated solitary room (with a lock) to store, label, and box them in private. You can also encourage a red herring rumor to steer the crew off track in guessing what the gifts might be.

> **When Handing Out Free Gifts On The Last Day Of Shooting**: Check with the Producer if the daily crew and the daily cast on the last day should receive a crew gift. Know the company's position before being put on the spot when someone who has worked for the company for nine hours asks to have a crew gift too.

> **When "Swag" Is Purchased By The Crew**: Review the choices and the prices with the Production Manager, and decide on an item or two. Make and distribute a flyer to the crew presenting all the information necessary,

including a picture or drawing if possible. Collect payment in advance, or ask Accounting if paycheck deductions can be effected. Keep a separate file to track the orders and the money. Because of the number of people involved and the sporadic way the money will filter in, this job will become very time-consuming. Be warned.

CREW PHOTOGRAPH

A crew photo may be taken on the last day, or during the shoot, and copied for distribution on the last day. Distribute these the same way you do crew gifts (with labels).

SEEK OUT AND COLLECT FINAL INVOICES

Now that you are emptying the office, telephone your suppliers to ask for final invoices immediately — especially suppliers to the wrap party. Have them email or fax the invoices so that payment can be effected while you are still in the office (to make sure it happens).

CLOSE ACCOUNTS

Discuss with the Production Manager which accounts need to be closed (from the office cleaners to the water delivery) and which ones remain open for head office and postproduction to use. Send written confirmation to those suppliers that the account has been closed because production is completed. Copy these confirmations to the Production Accountant and archive them in the wrap file. The courier account should remain active for use during postproduction. Send the remaining blank waybills to the Accountant and/or the Postproduction Supervisor.

BE CAREFUL ORDERING OFFICE SUPPLIES IN WRAP

Double check the crew requests for office supplies as you near production wrap. You will be ordering many storage boxes, but should not be ordering staplers and rulers. Ensure that production does not furnish crew home offices.

BOX UP FILES FOR HEAD OFFICE

The filing cabinet and computer drive are currently filled with a veritable ton of production documentation. As you prepare to move the files into boxes for storage and transfer to head office, make a point of looking through each file and folder one by one. Discard any duplicate or extraneous material. You may find that up to one third of the paper in the filing cabinet is expendable. The Production Manager may hand over his files to incorporate into the production files, too. Label each file box clearly with the production title, your title, and, the date. Include a digital backup copy of all your computer files and relevant emails that relate to the project. Finally, find out the name of the person to receive these files at head office. Have the Office P.A. personally deliver the materials to that person. These files are important. They tell head office everything that happened on the production. These files will be the reference about production for years to come.

FORWARD TELEPHONE & EMAIL ADDRESS TO HEAD OFFICE

When arranging for the telephone and Internet disconnection, forward the telephone number and production email address(es) to the head office number. This procedure helps people trying to find the company in a month or two.

WHEN YOU DO NOT HAVE TO EMPTY THE OFFICE ENTIRELY

If the office is a permanent production office, or if another production company is moving in when you are done, you may not have to empty the office down to the bare walls. You are lucky. With the Production Manager, decide what of the office can be emptied or simplified, and then do a scaled-down version of wrap.

TAKE YOUR KIT HOME

At the end of your last day, take home your kit. The longer you are on production, the more you will have brought in during the past weeks or months, so make sure the Office P.A. is still around to give you a hand. Do not forget to say your goodbyes.

THE WRAP PARTY

Though the wrap party is not the very last thing you do in wrap, it does signify the end of production; therefore, it is addressed last in this chapter. The Coordinator does most of the work arranging and hosting it, but the PM gets involved too, as every design and decision has its price.

THE UNEDITED INVITATION LIST

The Coordinator creates the unedited invitation list. Start with all the lists (crew lists, cast lists, credit lists) to create a mega, first draft invitation list to the wrap party. Include absolutely everyone you can think of so that you do not forget a soul. This list will be enormous.

DISCUSSIONS WITH THE PM

Review the first draft invitation list with the Production Manager and narrow it down to reality. Decide if spouses and guests are invited. Decide on a day of the week and discuss possible venues. Get an idea of the money you are allowed to spend.

SEE POTENTIAL PARTY VENUES

Research places to hold the party. Visit these venues. Just like hotel rooms, there is nothing like seeing the place in person to make discussing the party location easier.

WRAP PARTY BUDGET & CHECKLIST

It is your turn to generate a budget and track the costs. A wrap party has many costs associated with it. Make the party come in on budget, but with flare. Use the following checklist to prepare the wrap party budget. (See a wrap party budget form on pages 528-529.)

> Date of party
> Invitations
> Party room
> Decor of room
> Catering
> Bar
> License
> Notifications
> Music
> Other Entertainment
> Total

DATE OF PARTY

Note the planned date and time for the wrap party on the wrap party budget/checklist.

INVITATIONS

You can create invitations using the photocopier, or convince the Art Department to design invitations for professional printing. Decide if you will email, fax, mail, and/or deliver invitations. Invitations that people have to surrender at the door (for door prizes) are great both to ensure people bring them, and to cut down on gatecrashers.

PARTY ROOM

Make sure the room is big enough for the crowd. Note the features of the room, like a fireplace or billiard tables. These features may help sway you on choice of venue. Rental is usually free if a bar is supplied with the room. Know when you have to vacate at the end of the evening. Estimate the costs involved of supplying washroom supplies and/or a cleaning service. Find out if you or the venue will supply security. Consider public transit access to the site.

DECOR OF ROOM

Is the lighting appropriate to the party? You may want to arrange lights from your equipment supplier or buy miniature Christmas lights to create a mood. Decide how many tables and chairs you will need and price their rental. Table cloths and ashtrays are often supplied by the caterer, if you ask for them. Some decoration ideas to spark your imagination are: a snow machine at the entrance to the room that triggers with the door opening, strings of CD's hung from the ceiling, helium balloons held down by film reels or cores, film cans as ashtrays, and, of course, flowers. Budget some money to hire a Production Assistant or two to help you with the set up and to do the clean up. You will be so busy hosting the party, you will not have any time to "work" the party as well. Hire Assistants that have not worked on the show until now so that they will not be tempted to drink and socialize with the cast and crew.

CATERING

Decide what food you want to serve. Will you have a serve-yourself buffet of pizza or oysters shucked by catering staff? Order food for sixty percent of the attendees, as people do not eat as much as they drink, especially if the party is scheduled for after the dinner hour. For dessert, a cake with the film title in icing looks wonderful. To ensure people will actually eat the cake rather than just admire it all evening, arrange for the Producer (or someone) to cut the cake, then arrange for other people to physically hand out the slices. The Producer will appreciate the moment of focus to say a few words about the production. The caterer can supply napkins, plates, and cutlery for this purpose. Will you use paper plates or the real thing? Confirm when the caterer needs to set up, and when they will return to clean up.

BAR

Are you arranging for your own bar or will you use the room's bar? If you choose the room's bar, discuss the prices and deposit. Buy wine by the bottle instead of by the glass if you can. Decide how many bartenders you will need. Who is arranging for the ice and the ice containers? If you choose a full bar (beer, wine, and liquor), who is supplying the mixers? The caterer can supply you with more napkins and glasses if you ask. Know who is in charge of setting up and cleaning up the bar.

LICENSE

If you arrange for your own bar, you need a "no sale" liquor license. You cannot charge money for the drinks. Contact your local licensing office for the procedure and the fee.

NOTIFICATIONS

To have a large party, you should also notify the police, the fire department, the health department, and the buildings & inspections department. You may need these letters to complete your liquor license application. They do not cost anything and you can email, fax, or deliver them. You are showing these departments that you know how to run a safe party and when you are going to do it. Include in each letter when, where, and how many guests; also describe security, mention that you will be serving food, and explain that the party is an end-of-production party.

MUSIC

Will you have a band or a disk jockey? If a band, confirm if they are providing their own lights and equipment; ask if they can supply recorded music in between sets. Be clear when the music is to start and end. Discuss with the band or the disk jockey how they may feel about a possible extension to the end of the evening if the party is going well. Ask when they need access to the room for set up and clean up.

OTHER ENTERTAINMENT

Other entertainment could be door prizes, access to a skating rink, the showing of an outtake reel, or whatever your imagination can dream up. If you choose an outtake reel, give the editors enough time to complete one. When you rent the equipment to show the reel, hire enough technicians to take care of the set up, testing, and clean up of the equipment.

TOTAL

Approve the party choices and the prices with the Production Manger. Total the budget and copy it to the PM, the Production Accountant and you, the PC. You have to monitor and keep to these costs.

PC HOSTS THE PARTY

Now that the party is budgeted, arranged, and happening, the PC steps into the shoes of host. Be obvious so that your "party" Production Assistants can find you if they need to. Socialize and welcome everyone. But above all else, have a great time! This is your party, too! Tomorrow you will get to hear how wonderful the party was all over again as the crew talk about it. Enjoy!

—◊—

After the wrap party night, both the PM and the PC return to the office to complete wrapping the office. The hours slow down again and you eventually adjust to the pace of production wrap. Soon you too will be going home or moving onto your next production. Congratulate yourself for a job well done. You deserve it!

SMALL, DARK ROOMS

You have to wonder about postproduction people. They spend an awful lot of time alone and in small, dark rooms.

It was a difficult scene to cut. Apparently the picture editing of it was a painstaking process – the matching, the timing, the best performances, the reveal, the joke. The Editor had meeting after meeting with Director and Producer to work it through. He worked long and hard hours tweaking the scene over and over again. He would get it right. He was determined. The heat from the editing equipment in the small room was almost unbearable. But he ventured on. He was striving for editing perfection and nothing less.

Then it happened. Perfection.

He leapt out of his editing room into the middle of the production office to celebrate... sporting only Spandex pants, swinging shoulder length hair that would do any rocker proud, and playing the air guitar.

You have to wonder what those small, dark rooms do to a person. Still, it was quite a rocking good tune.

POSTPRODUCTION 35

Postproduction officially starts after principal photography wraps, but the Editor and Assistant have been on board already, synching and editing the main unit's output from the second day of shooting. Postproduction does stretch on longer after production is done, and it is usually up to the Postproduction Supervisor to shepherd the film through the final critical stages of post — and deliver the film to all the contracted sources on time and on budget. As Production Manager, you need to understand a little bit about postproduction, so that it does not become a "black hole" of knowledge to you. You do, after all, have to budget for post knowledgeably.

THE UNIQUENESS OF POSTPRODUCTION

There may be a Postproduction Supervisor or a Postproduction Coordinator or both. You have budgeted for them, and you will hand over the issues of production management (like the creation and the distribution of regular cost reports) to them for follow up and to continue during postproduction.

There is a whole different set of concerns during postproduction than during production. The pace is slower, for starters. While production spends heavily day by day, postproduction spends week by week, or event by event. You may have a five-week shoot, but a ten-week post. Production may have a crew of 75, while post may have about six. Production spends its time getting the movie magic "into the can," basically collecting the parts of the movie. Postproduction, however, is making movie magic in the editing room; they are literally making the movie from the parts that production supplies. Postproduction is indeed unique. Hire a Supervisor or a Coordinator who understands the particular issues of postproduction and of technical acceptances by various distributors, broadcasters, and countries.

THE STAGES OF POSTPRODUCTION

You can divide a film production into basically three technical stages: the shooting stage, the postproduction stage (editing), and the finish or delivery stage. You can use digital (data drive or videotape) or you can use film in any of these stages, but basically this section deals with the four most commonly used combinations. More than one of these combinations will be triggered when you decide on a shooting format, and review required finishing formats in your various financing agreements. For now, we will look at each stage separately from a work flow point of view.

SHOOT ON DIGITAL – POST ON DIGITAL – FINISH ON FILM

Even though you choose to shoot on digital — be it 3D or 2D, HD or mini-DV — you may find that you need a film finish so you can access certain world theatrical markets and festivals that will only accept film stock. In this case, the digital original is transferred at the post facility, typically on a daily basis, into a digital intermediate format for the postproduction stage. The final digital product undergoes a digital-to-film transfer, the price of which can be quite hefty and may even offset any savings you are expected to earn by shooting digital in the first place. Check that your expected savings are indeed valid on examination of both production and post/delivery costs, or better than that, ensure the choice to shoot digital is for creative reasons.

SHOOT ON FILM – POST ON DIGITAL – FINISH ON FILM

Many feature films shoot in this manner: shooting on film stock such as 35mm, then transferring to a digital intermediate format for editing, and conforming back to film stock again for the finished product. This method allows access to certain world markets and festivals that have no digital theatrical projection. If you shoot on Super 16, the optical track is missing to allow more celluloid for the widescreen image and you will be required to either finish digitally, or purchase a blow up to 35mm.

SHOOT ON DIGITAL – POST ON DIGITAL – FINISH ON DIGITAL

If you do not need to worry about a film finish, keeping to a digital format for the entire process from production to delivery is the most economical way to proceed. Not all digital, however, is the same; there are seemingly minor technical differences between many digital formats that require attention during transfers for compatibility in postproduction. Most documentaries and television-only projects are shot and delivered digitally, because that is the format of broadcasters. Digital theatrical projection will have to become even more mainstream worldwide before feature films can have an unlimited release without the need for a supplemental digital-to-film transfer.

SHOOT ON FILM – POST ON DIGITAL – FINISH ON DIGITAL

If you love the look of film stock but do not need a film finish for any festival or Distributor, then this combination works. Typically, however, the digital finish for a production shot on film is supplemental to the film finish.

THE POSTPRODUCTION WORK FLOW

Since you are the Production Manager, the best way to understand post is to run through the issues of production in reference to the budget. The budget is generally set up to look at the costs chronologically.

ABOUT "SHOOTING ON DIGITAL"

Before moving into the digital intermediate ("DI") work flow of postproduction, there are a number of post-related issues you deal with during production itself. Since digital is the most predominant shooting format, we will first look at digital shoot issues.

DIGITAL PICTURE STOCK

The picture stock is the hard drive, disk, memory card, or tape stock that captures the original images via the camera on set. Think of the image that is captured as "data" rather than "pictures" or "footage."

DIGITAL ORIGINAL

Once the images are captured, the digital picture stock becomes the digital original file or tape. This file or tape becomes "it" —— the only (and therefore precious) original capture of the shoot day's images (also known as the "raw scenes"). The Camera Assistants or DMT will be in charge of sending the digital original images to the post facility at the end of each shoot day, and sometimes throughout the day. Over the course of the day, the Camera team is checking for file corruption, dead pixels, or tape drop-outs that cause technically imperfect images.

ISO FILES OR TAPES

ISO stands for isolation. These files or tapes are used by the second camera or B-camera on production. By shooting with two cameras or more, you can capture multiple angles at the same time, but will need to reference this material differently on the Continuity Supervisor's documentation to know which is which.

BACKUP FILES OR TAPES

While you are shooting, you must backup the digital original immediately as a preservation copy. Alternatively, you can arrange for the post facility to archive or clone the digital masters overnight after each shoot day. The post facility can also store the digital original safely.

TRANSFER TO EDITING FORMAT

If the digital shooting format is not an exact match to the picture editing system, you will need to digitize the original scenes onto a compatible computer format to edit the picture. If need be, sound is also transferred at this stage from the recording format used on set into the file format used by the editing system.

DIGITAL DAILIES (RUSHES)

Synching picture to sound may not be required if sound was recorded on the digital original. Typically, however, every day during the shoot, the post facility during transfer, matches the picture to sound of the previous day's material using the time code slate at the beginning of each take as the synch reference (sometimes this is done by an Assistant Editor who is hired just to synch dailies). With picture and sound matched together for the first time, the new viewing copy can be made available on the FTP site for the production and head office to view locally. These viewing copies are called the "dailies" (also known as "rushes"). They may also be output to a portable digital format such as DVD. For feature films, projection of the dailies can be arranged at the post facility in order to preview the captured scenes on a screen that emulates public theatrical projection. The big screen affords superior evaluation of the raw scenes.

TIME CODE SLATE AND BURNED-IN TIME CODE

You will hear a lot about time code during postproduction. There are several times you use it, each one different. Time code is audio/visual reference that runs like a clock to give a time/frame address to every frame of the picture and audio thus enabling you to synch the two together. Since you can have time code that runs as time of day time or elapsed time, with or without drop frame, ensure that you have a compatible system between the post team, post facility, and on set team to minimize conversion costs and complications.

On set, the time code slate (a clap board with ever-updating electronic numbers on the front of it) freezes the time code numbers at the moment the slate is clapped shut. By displaying the slate on camera, you have effectively recorded time code on the picture. After processing and/or transfer, the audio can be synched quickly with picture by simply finding and matching the sound of the clap on the soundtrack (the audio representation of time code) to the first frozen number on the slate on the picture (the visual representation of time code). From take to take you will notice huge gaps in the numeric sequence since, more often than not, you will be using a time-of-day time code slate which displays time code like a clock, and on set you are never shooting 100% of clock time.

As you are synching the dailies, you will be laying the "synched" dailies down to a new master file. In order to have a visual time code reference in the picture editing process, you now need a new time code "burned-in" to the picture to give a visual address to each frame. Since this time code is laid down all at once, it will be sequential from the beginning of the footage to the end, and will therefore differ from the numbers used on the time code slate on set.

There is a third time code you will create, but that is later in the video editing process — after you lock the picture edit.

ABOUT "SHOOTING ON FILM"

Though a film shoot shares similar work flow issues to a digital shoot, there are nuances to understand between the two processes.

RAW STOCK

Raw stock is what unprocessed film stock is called before it is run through the camera.

EXPOSED FILM

Once the film has been through the camera, raw stock is now exposed film. Camera Assistants will label film cans accordingly, and production will ensure exposed film is dropped off at the lab every night. You do not want to be responsible for storing exposed film in uncertain weather conditions and risk ruining the original film.

ORIGINAL NEGATIVE

Once it was called raw stock, then exposed film, now that it has been through the processing at the lab, the same stuff is called the original negative. This is "it." Immediately transfer "it" to digital and then store the original negative safely at the lab and in an environmentally-controlled storage location, if possible.

NEG CHECK

Most labs process film overnight and digitally transfer early in the morning, which is why you can have a negative check the next morning. You want to know if the negative has any noticeable physical damage.

I/P (INTERPOSITIVE) AND I/N (INTERNEGATIVE)

If you are planning a film finish, and have the money to backup all your negative, process an I/P and I/N immediately. Typically, however, an I/P and I/N are not created at the time of dailies, even though the cost tends to show up at this stage of the work flow process in the budget template. Instead, you will strike an I/P and I/N after you cut the negative, much later in the work flow process. Having a backup of the negative allows you not to rely on the original negative for all your delivery elements. Every time you run film stock through a process at the lab, you risk further scratching and damaging the material through regular wear and tear — in this case, damaging the original negative. There are two steps to completing a backup of the negative: the first is to create a positive image of the negative (the "I/P") and only then can you make a new negative image (the "I/N") from the recently-created positive.

DIGITAL TRANSFER (AND ONE-LIGHT WORKPRINT)

To post digitally, you need to transfer the film to a digital format to start the digital intermediate ("DI") process. You can transfer a positive digital image straight from the film negative. The Assistant Editor will digitize those dailies onto the computer to access the footage in the editing software. At this stage, sound is also transferred from the original recording format into a computer file, and the synching of picture to sound may happen during the transfer. If you are finishing on film, you may wish to strike a "one-light" work print of some of the early dailies to view and analyze some of the film in its delivery format. "One-light" (one exposure) is sufficient since you do not need to perfect the exposure of each shot at this point in time.

SYNCHING THE DAILIES (OR RUSHES)

As with digital, each shoot day, the post facility during transfer, or an Assistant Editor, synchs the picture to sound using the time code slate at the beginning of each shot as the synch reference. The post facility or Editing department outputs the final dailies via the FTP site or onto a portable digital format (such as DVD) for reference and analysis. For feature films, projection of some, if not all, of the dailies can be arranged at the post facility on a large screen.

EDGE CODING OR EDGE NUMBERING

These numbers are tiny and run down the edge of the original negative. They serve as a reference later in the DI process when you cut the negative to match the locked picture. Using this reference, you can match, not only the desired edit order, but also the exact frame choice.

TIME CODE SLATE AND BURNED-IN TIME CODE

As described above in more detail for the digital process, there are three sets of time code applicable to your production: (1) the on-set time code of the slate; (2) the time code laid down onto the synched dailies; and (3) the time code that laid down when the picture is locked.

Now that you have the dailies in hand — whether you shot them on digital or film — you are technically finished with production costs and are off in the land of official postproduction.

ABOUT "PICTURE POSTING ON DIGITAL"

The "posting" section has been divided into picture post and sound post, since there are two separate editing teams involved with different processes and costs.

Computer editing systems (like Final Cut Pro and Avid) afford editors two major bonuses: the ability to save and examine many different edited sequences at the same time; and the ability to edit faster than on film. The freedom to preview multiple versions of edited sequences is probably the single most valuable advancement of computer editing systems. However, the faster editing process can be a false savings if not budgeted correctly. Sufficient time is required to properly edit a film. Much thought has to go into each cut, and no speedy equipment can shorten the thought process. So budget well for the thought process, not only for the more obvious equipment costs. Data storage costs are also taken for granted, so be sure to address the storage needs of your production sufficiently.

Though you may never picture post on film, you will notice a few film terms in the following section, because digital editing was originally set up to emulate how picture post happened on film many years ago.

COMPUTER LOAD LIST

The Continuity Supervisor takes notes of which takes are "selected" on set. The computer load list (a computer file) identifies these takes so that the Editors can digitize only the "selected" ones into the computer.

OFFLINE (OR "ROUGH CUT")

Since the Editor starts just after shooting has begun, he edits scenes and sequences while the film is still being captured. These sequences are the genesis of the first rough cut. The Editor will start with a chronological assembly of all the best wide shots, then add close-ups to highlight story points and emotions. There is no fine-tuning in offline editing and little concern for the required length of the production; this stage is about creating the film in broad strokes and finding the right performances in the right takes. The offline is the chance to experiment in the editing process... though it takes decisive people in the approval path to ensure you can move on to the next editing stage in a timely manner.

For feature films, if you have the time, you can hold rough cut screenings complete with rough sound mix using music similar to what you have in mind for the final version. There is nothing like a full audio/visual preview of the film on a big screen with temporary music to best examine how the story is forming. A test audience can provide you with excellent feedback as to what is working in the story and what is not.

Because the rough cut is filled with broad strokes, big changes can happen from cut to cut. The film may have slugs (black leader with white text headings) to fill in for unfinished scenes or undelivered CGI or effects shots. Financiers and others may have contractual approval of the rough cut, so the post schedule needs to allot time for these people to review the cut and give their approval, plus sufficient time to make required changes.

DIRECTOR'S CUT & PRODUCER'S CUT

The Editor is allowed a "cut" of the film, as are the Director and the Producer. Who has the final cut (i.e., final decision) will have been contracted prior to shooting and committed to in an agreement. Beyond who has final cut, guild rules will often have other clauses that protect the Director's participation in postproduction. For example, the rough cut or Director's cut may not be viewable without the permission of the Director.

ISAN VERSION NUMBERS

With ISAN you can register multiple versions of the project. If, for example, you foresee the possibility of finishing and releasing the Director's Cut at some point in the future, now is the time to register a new version to your ISAN number. Other delivery versions can also be added to your ISAN number later in the post work flow.

FINE CUT AND PICTURE LOCK

Offline ends with fine-tuning the latest approved rough cut. Scene timing is tightened. Missing CGI shots are included. Other minor changes happen. Even though there may be more than one fine cut, as financiers may have a say in fine cut approvals, the changes from cut to cut are basically minor by this stage.

The last fine cut is picture lock. Offline is now completed and the picture will have no more changes from here on. This procedure allows the Sound Department to add tracks of sound to the locked cut, synching them frame for frame to the picture. Provide a copy of picture lock to the Sound team. Also, since no more editing changes may happen to the picture after lock, you can arrange for the digital original or film negative to be edited into this final order too.

E.D.L.

The "edit decision list" is an automatic printout of the picture editing system detailing all the chosen shots in the chosen order, along with a notation of exactly which frame starts and ends each shot. The E.D.L. also includes directions for effects such as fades and dissolves. Obviously, this list is essential to conform the digital original or the film negative to match the locked cut. Picture-wise, you are now ready to move into the finishing stage of post.

ABOUT "SOUND POSTING ON DIGITAL"

You can arrange with a sound facility to set up a package to include the sound edit staff as well as the equipment, or you can hire people separately and deal with the sound facility only for the studio time.

Sound can accumulate a myriad of soundtracks to be mixed together. The more soundtracks, the richer the sound landscape is to the ear. It is not unusual to hear of productions having from 75 to 200 tracks of sound: dialogue, sound effects, foley, atmosphere, and music tracks. To orchestrate such a wide, rich soundtrack, you may hire a Sound Designer.

DIALOGUE EDITING

Recorded dialogue needs to be split into several tracks to separate the various voices, so the sound quality of each can be treated separately during the sound mix. Dialogue Editors may even steal sound from another take to apply to this take because the sound or the voice performance is better.

ADR OR LOOPING

ADR stands for additional dialogue recording. When the dialogue is unacceptable in the sound edit, you may need to call in the Performer to re-do some of his lines. ADR is done in a sound studio where the picture is "looped" to repeat over and over again, so the Performer can lip synch his lines to the picture. More on the specifics of the ADR session and required cast contracts are in Chapter 24.

NARRATION OR VOICE OVER RECORD

Voice over may also be recorded during post for the dialogue edit. This recording is a Performer's voice that does not synch with any picture, so you can use a smaller sound studio to record the voice.

WALLA

Walla is a team of Performers who work together in a sound studio to provide you with background group sounds for the soundtrack. These sounds include cheers and background restaurant mumbling.

SFX EDITING OR SOUND EFFECTS EDITING

Sound Effects Editors gather sounds from various sources to match to the picture. Oddly enough, the actual recorded sound of a gun firing is way too tinny to sound right on film, so Sound Effects Editors become inventive and create sounds the way we think they should sound. There are many sound effects libraries to tap into as a resource. So that each sound can be treated separately during the mix, Sound Effects Editors use multiple tracks to lay down these effects. Sound effects can also be layered and layered from separate tracks to make one sound incredibly rich and complex.

ORIGINAL FX RECORDING

When Sound Effects Editors are not sourcing existing sounds from libraries, they are outside the editing room recording brand new sounds and being their inventive best.

ATMOSPHERE TRACKS

Sound Effects Editors also add separate atmosphere tracks for every room or space. Atmosphere is the background "white noise" that every room possesses and that would be noticeably missing if absent.

FOLEY EDITING

The Foley Artist is the person in a foley studio at the sound facility who watches the film, and while watching it, supplies another layer of sounds to add to the richness of the soundtrack. A foley studio, for example, has several floor sections of differing qualities: one of gravel, one of pavement, one of tile, and another of wood, so the Foley Artists can time footstep sounds to the picture on appropriate surfaces. They also add clothing sounds, door sounds, kissing sounds, and a host of others.

MUSIC COMPOSER

The Music Composer and the Sound Designer will come on board rather early in production to discuss the way the music is planned to fit into the final film. At no later than rough cut stage, the Music Composer needs to do the music spotting with at least the Director to decide what music needs to be added and where. A spotting session basically generates a "to do" list for the Music Composer (but is also a useful planning tool for the entire post sound team as the sound landscape is designed). Next the Composer writes and/or sources the music for each of those screen moments and transitions. Often you can hire a Composer who has her own studio and will create the music for the soundtrack as a one-stop supplier.

MUSIC EDITING

The Composer does not supply the music cut to the picture frame-ready. The Music Editor needs to lay the music onto various tracks so the fades and dissolves and other sound treatments to the music can be addressed during the mix. The Music Editor may also move some of the music around to fill in spaces that need to be filled to smooth out a scene or a transition.

PRE-MIX

The Sound Editors have created timing sheets, graphically plotting where each sound is laid on each separate track for reference for the Sound Mixer as the tracks are mixed together. Since it is expensive to rent a mixing theater for the final sound mix, you will end up doing a pre-mix to iron out the problems that always seem to show themselves when you combine all the tracks of sound for the first time. You will fire through the sound mix like a dry run during a pre-mix, merely identifying the problems to address now. To minimize costs at the mix and later, you need to be well prepared for the mix with tracks flexible enough to address the needs of all the delivery versions.

SWEETENING

After the pre-mix you have some editing time to fix the problems identified in the pre-mix, or replace sounds that just do not work. This process is called sweetening.

MIX

The final mix is when all the various soundtracks finally come together to match with the final picture. There is a rocking motion to sound mixing. The film moves forward and some tracks are mixed together for a few seconds or minutes, then the film is rewound to review the mix or to take another pass at getting it right. This happens over and over and over again. It can be a bit hypnotic if you arrive at the mix sleepy, so make sure you get a good night's sleep beforehand.

Mixing theaters have total recall of all the sound editing decisions made to date, enabling easy revisions and the automation of hundreds of sound elements at the mix. If, however, you have many, many tracks, the mix may take a few passes as you mix several tracks down to a few, then the few down to one or two.

You can mix in mono or stereo, or if you have arranged for a license, you can mix in Dolby Stereo, THX, or other noise-reduction systems. The Sound Designer, the Sound Editors, and the Music Composer will have addressed preparing for these noise-reduction systems prior to the mix, of course, but here is where it all comes together.

M&E TRACK

You need to generate a music and effects (M&E) track separate from the dialogue track, so that you leave the project available to international sales. With an M&E track, any country can dub the voices into any language accompanied by the rich M&E track underneath. This is typically a required deliverable to distributors.

BACKUP OR PROTECTION COPY

Just as you have backups for the picture throughout postproduction, always create a master backup of the final mix on a digital protection format.

TRANSCRIPT

The transcript is another necessity for international dubbing and is nearly always a required deliverable. It accompanies the M&E track, allowing other countries to translate the script for dubbing purposes. Ensure the transcript is made from the final, locked picture and soundtrack. Your distribution and broadcast agreements will identify if you need the more simple "as broadcast script" transcription, or the more detailed and costly "action/dialogue/continuity script" transcript.

Sound is now ready for the finishing stage of post, and to marry itself to the picture. If you finish on digital, sound rejoins the DI work flow process at layback to picture. If you finish on film, sound rejoins the process in time to create the optical negative.

ABOUT "FINISHING ON DIGITAL"

Let us start with the easiest finish. If the final product is planned exclusively for television broadcast, or for festivals and theaters that can promise digital projection, then you do not need a film finish and can stay on digital for completion and delivery. The Sound team may still be posting while some of these finishing tasks take place, so long as they are ready in time to marry the sound to final picture.

First, a note about generation loss. Now that the finished film stage is rapidly approaching, and the picture will be duplicated numerous times, aim to preserve the finest source of the original images: the digital master. Repeated duplication results in generation loss, especially the further you stray from the original. Dubbing copies from copies of consumer formats such as VHS was great to clearly demonstrate this kind of resolution loss. Broadcast formats (like Digital Betacam) have remarkably less generation loss with each copy, but the principle still applies. Preserve the digital master and make duplicate masters for all the delivery duplication work in case something should happen to the original.

ONLINE OR CONFORM

Once the picture is locked, the online or conform can begin. You go back to the digital original (camera originals or transfer masters) to edit together the digital master of the film, making it match the choices made in the locked picture cut. The E.D.L. (Edit Decision List) is used as the road map for all the required details about what to cut, fade, and dissolve — and where to find all the necessary original material.

You will likely have to move into a higher-end editing suite (at the post facility) to do the online. Here you can also add final CGI shots along with simple effects like fades, dissolves.

COLOR CORRECTION OR COLOR GRADING (DURING ONLINE)

The DP tends to come back to deal with the color timing of each scene. Just as in a sound mix where you addressed the sound level and the quality of each sound, in the color timing you adjust the color and the exposure on each shot of the film. Many color correction notes are taken during the online, but it is afterward, in a separate session, that you commit to the color corrections in order to create a new, color-corrected master.

TITLES (DURING ONLINE)

Also during the online, the final credit list is now turned into on-screen main and end titles and is added to the picture. Being on a digital format already, is it easy to superimpose titles over picture during the online. You can input text from the post facility's computer, add video clips from other sources, and add computerized or video logos of financiers to complete the package. If you choose to supply your own font, be sure that it was either created for production or that there are no outstanding rights to be purchased for the privilege. Now is the last time to ensure the credits are correct. Input errors are not infrequent, so beware. Though it is cheaper to show credits on sequential pages, it is traditional to have a credit roll for a feature film.

TIME CODE AFTER PICTURE LOCK (DURING ONLINE)

As mentioned previously, you will be laying down a new (third) time code after picture lock. Since the synched dailies had their own consecutive time code, by the time you make it to picture lock, there is a complete mishmash of time codes from all the edits. During the online, you are laying down the final edit to a new tape, so lay it down with a new, continuous time code.

LAYBACK SOUND TO PICTURE

Now the final sound mix is added to the final picture creating a new color-corrected and titled digital master — in effect the first complete copy of the finished production with both sound and picture.

VERSIONING (INCLUDING TRANSFER TO PAL, NTSC, OR SECAM)

There are many reasons you will need to create extra versions of the finished film — the requirements all stem from the financing agreements that brought you this far. Broadcast delivery formats differ in specifications from broadcaster to broadcaster, country to country. For example: some require commercial blacks within the delivery master for future ease to insert televised ads. Naturally you do not want commercial blacks in the feature film version. Dubbed or subtitled language versions will be addressed later in the work flow.

For videotape especially, different countries have different formats. You know from travel that electricity itself varies between countries; the differing cycles of electricity affect videotape formats the same way. NTSC is used in places like North America, whereas PAL is used in places like the UK and Western Europe, and SECAM in places like France, Asia, Africa, and Eastern Europe. Basically, each format is hugely different from each other. Due to electricity being 60 cycles per second in the UK and 50 cycles per second in North America, PAL runs 4% longer in screen time than NTSC if you were to do a straight transfer. You can either remove a frame here and there (through a mathematical calculation, of course) to match length during the transfer, or transfer the videotape expecting the different length, as long as you are not too picky about the change in pitch of the sound being either higher or lower at the new speed. Some conversion techniques will create credit rolls that jitter, so it is better to plan for the delivery versions in preproduction when reading the financing agreements so you can minimize conversion needs and headaches later in the work flow process.

These are just some of the issues you will deal with during versioning.

Register an ISAN version number for each of these versions so during distribution the Producer can track them (and their revenues) separately.

DELIVERY MASTERS

With all the postproduction parts assembled, you can now make the delivery masters or delivery clones. To prevent generation loss, you may need to duplicate many of them from the same digital master. Due to localization and differing technical specifications between the distributors and broadcasters, you may find that the list of required delivery clones is quite long. You may also encounter compatibility issues at post and conversion facilities, since, for example, not all HD is the exact same format (i.e. HDCAM differs from HDCAMSR).

BACKUP OF MASTER OR PROTECTION COPIES

For each unique delivery clone you send out, you need to duplicate a backup master or protection copy in case something goes wrong with the one sent. If you have numerous delivery requirements, the prerequisite dominoes into a lot of protection copies, for example: one on BluRay, two on DVD (one for the international version and another for the domestic version), two on Digital Betacam (one being NTSC and the other being PAL), another with commercial blacks, one without, a version at 23 minutes, and another version at 28:30 minutes, and so on. Data, of course, can be backed up on hard drives. Beyond the backups themselves, consider and plan for long-term storage of these archival treasures.

VIEWING COPIES

Viewing copies are typically consumer (not broadcast) quality, and are made on BluRay or DVD. You will need plenty for all the Financiers, the Producers, and other crew or cast or suppliers to whom you promised copies of the finished product. To ensure the best bulk duplication rate, you may wish to strike promotional copies for Publicity and screening copies for festival entries at the same time you are duplicating the contractual viewing copies.

CLOSED CAPTIONING

If you are broadcasting the program, you may need a closed-captioned version as another deliverable. Find out from your financing agreements which type of closed-captioning is required, for example pop-up captioning or open captioning. There are facilities to go to as a one-stop supplier. Closed captioning, however, is a two-step process: one to create the captions and the other to encode the captions onto the master.

VERSIONING – OTHER LANGUAGES

If you are versioning to other languages, you can also find suppliers that do this as a one-stop package. Even if you are not versioning to other languages in the production budget, you will likely need a transcript of the final edited film so that distributors in the future can arrange for dubbing or subtitling.

The number and variety of post deliverables will be spelled out in the financing, distribution, and broadcasting contracts. Examine the lists to budget sufficiently for the big job that the Post Supervisor will need to shepherd.

ABOUT "FINISHING ON FILM (FROM DIGITAL MASTER)"

If the film is going to be screened at a festival or in a theater somewhere in the world without digital projection, you obviously need a film finish, no matter which format you shot on.

As described above, you have completed the online, added titles, laid down the new time code, color corrected, and laid back the sound to picture.

DIGITAL TO FILM TRANSFER

Now that the digital master exists as a complete sound and picture experience, it is time to arrange for a digital to film transfer. The transfer is typically an expensive process but that is becoming more affordable over time. The higher the resolution and less compression of the digital master (and the digital original before it), the higher quality is of the finished film print.

The print you strike will be considered an answer print, and you may need to repeat the transfer a couple of times to tweak the colors or quality of the transfer before you have a Release Print that makes you happy. If you are striking only a few finished film prints, you can potentially make them all directly from the DI negative. If, however, you need more than a small handful of prints, you would do well to strike an I/P (Intermediate Positive print) and I/N (Intermediate Negative print) from which you will create the final, wet gate release prints, and so preserve the integrity of the original elements.

OTHER DIGITAL DELIVERABLES

The film print will never be your only deliverable. Consult the "Finishing on Digital" section (above) for information about the host of other contractually required elements that do not need a transfer to film stock.

ABOUT "FINISHING ON FILM (FROM THE NEGATIVE)"

If the production was shot on film stock, there are a number of other steps to include, and with some of them, a slight change of order. The online, for example, is divided into three film stages: negative cut, opticals and titles, and finally color correction. Chances are the sound team is still posting. Their objective is to have the sound mix completed in time to create the optical soundtrack and marry it to the finished film.

PREPARE FOR NEG CUT (CONFORM TO NEGATIVE)

On the E.D.L. the Editor has included notations of all the fades and the dissolves and the other optical effects for the negative cutter's reference. The E.D.L. is a blue print to permanently cut the negative.

NEGATIVE CUT

If you have an inter-negative, you cut it, saving the original negative untouched. The process of negative cutting removes a frame on each side of the shot for each cut, as the negative is literally cut, the emulsion is scratched off the frame prior to and after the shot, and the now-clear negative is glued onto other film for permanence. Once the negative is cut, there is no turning back. The negative will be split into A&B rolls, separating each shot onto the next roll to be dealt with separately in the rest of the completion process (for adjusting color and exposure of each shot separately, for example). When you see the shot on roll A, you will see black leader on roll B, then when you see the next shot on roll B, black leader will be on roll A, and so on. The final product ends up looking like a checkerboard of shots between the two rolls.

INTERPOSITIVE & INTERNEGATIVE

If you have decided to strike a backup I/P and I/N of the cut negative only, now is the time to do it. Store the original cut negative safely in the lab's vault.

CHECK PRINT

This is the first print of the cut negative, used to see if there are any problems that need to be fixed. It also gives the opportunity to make notes on the color timing needed to fix certain shots, or to bathe certain sequences in a wash of color to complete the look of the film.

FILM OPTICALS & TITLES

Simple opticals are the fades and dissolves between scenes. Titles superimposed over picture are more complex and more expensive. White text on black background are the simplest titles to make when dealing with film stock. As mentioned earlier, credits shown on sequential pages are also cheaper than a credit roll; however, a credit roll is traditional for a feature film.

COLOR CORRECTION OR COLOR GRADING

The DP tends to come back to deal with color timing of each scene at the lab in time for the final printing process.

PRINT OPTICAL TRACK

Once the sound track is mixed, it needs to be printed on a separate optical track to marry to the final finished film.

ANSWER PRINT (& WET GATE)

The first answer print (a wet gate answer print) could be the first time sound and picture are printed together and you have a completed film you can screen… well, if the colors are acceptable. More typically, you will need to fine-tune the color timing and end up printing more than one answer print in the process, only adding sound to the final answer print.

WET GATE

Every time film goes through a process at the lab, there is always the danger of light surface scratches appearing on the base (acetate) side of the negative. The film goes through a lot of equipment, so it is only natural that this type of wear and tear will happen. To prevent seeing these light scratches on the finished film, you can send the film through a wet gate process every time you print. A wet gate is literally a printing gate where the film — as it passes through — is immersed in a solution that fills light scratches during printing.

RELEASE PRINT (& WET GATE)

Once the final answer print is approved, the release print (a wet gate release print) can be struck. Now it is time to print multiple copies for the distributor, film festivals, national archive, and other sources that require a film deliverable. If you have used the original negative all the way through the process, you may well have sent the original negative through the lab's equipment at least six times already (for processing, transferring, check printing, answer printing twice, and release printing), exposing it each time to the danger of permanent scratches. You are well on the way to wearing out the original negative when now you need to have a pristine negative to create all those release prints. If you had printed an I/P and I/N, your original negative will only have been through the lab's process about four times by now (for processing, two answer prints and inter-positive printing). The I/P and I/N process is invaluable, as you cannot replace damaged original negative without shooting the film again.

BLOW-UP PRINT

If you shot on Super 16, you cannot finish the film until you blow it up to 35mm. Super 16 uses the space where the optical track should be to expose more picture. The proportions of the frame on Super 16, however, better match that of a 35mm negative than regular 16mm does. If money is driving the choice of using Super 16 instead of 35mm, remember to check into the cost of the blow up. You may find the cost is high enough to warrant your shooting the film on 35mm in the first place.

TRANSFER TO DIGITAL

Now that the completed film is on film stock again, you need to transfer back to digital in order to create digital masters for versioning and duplication (use the I/P to do so). No doubt you will have a long list of required broadcast masters, international versions, and viewing copies to create in order to honor the various financing, distribution and broadcast agreements. Consult the "Finishing on Digital" section (above) for more information.

VAULTS & STORAGE

Whether you have a digital original, a digital intermediate master or original negative, you need to consider storage of the original in an environmentally-controlled vault for safekeeping. The post facility can accommodate you for short-term storage while you are making the film, but after delivery, arrangements need to be made for long-term storage. Who is going to pay for these extended storage costs? Ensure the information about the storage is given to head office.

DELIVERY

Delivery triggers more cash flow to production, so you will be especially concerned that the film is delivered on time to all parties. Of course, delivery does not only mean you have to deliver one master clone to each party. The various financing agreements will list a host of items required as "deliverables" that may include digital masters, an M&E track, a transcription, publicity photos, biographies of the key cast and crew, a cost report, and a host of other possibilities. The Postproduction Supervisor should have a list of all the deliverables, but it is wise to review again the list to be sure all elements make it to the appropriate parties in a timely manner to affect a quick turnaround of the delivery payments.

Broadcasters may reject delivery for technical (quality control) reasons once they have screened the delivered master. Delivery is not considered completed until the broadcaster (or distributor) accepts the finished project. Be sure the technical issues are addressed immediately. Have technical folk talk with technical folk to ensure a speedy resolution. The Postproduction Supervisor will be the lead dealing with these issues.

It is possible to arrange for a technical evaluation of your final delivery materials prior to delivery. This will help you address technical issues before they become a real problem after delivery to the broadcaster.

AIR DATES & RELEASE DATES & FESTIVALS

On a series, you may still be working in production when the show has begun delivery and even airing. If the information becomes available to you, publish an email and memo to all concerned informing them of the air dates. Crew and cast love to pass around this information to family and friends. If you are aware of a festival screening date, also inform "all concerned" via email and memo.

Also on a series, if you are working on a subsequent season, you may find that you will also become involved in submitting the show to festivals. Production and postproduction has all the historical documentation and technical elements to duplicate speedy screening copies and copy or print relevant information for the submissions.

It is unlikely you will be around for the release date of a feature, but you can keep in touch with the Producer to find out when the film will be released. Prepare a contact list to spread the word when you do have information about the film's release or broadcast. Positive word of mouth attracts larger audiences, and you want the film to be seen.

—⁂—

This has been a mere nutshell look at postproduction. Recognize the importance of the Postproduction Supervisor and the Postproduction Coordinator in dealing with these many complex issues, and appreciate them as part of the team.

WELL-TRAVELED WARDROBE

Cost report pop quiz.

You're on a multi-international co-production. You have to keep track of costs being spent in Toronto, Nova Scotia, New Zealand, and the UK — all separately.

You rent costumes in London, England. Ship them to Toronto, Canada for fittings, organization, and repackaging. Then ship them to Nova Scotia for shooting. Ship them back to Toronto for further organization and repackaging. Then ship them on to New Zealand for shooting. Ship them back to Toronto for further organization and repackaging. And finally, ship them back to London, England, at the end of the shoot. Got it?

The question is... on which country's cost report do you report the wardrobe costs? Ugh.

AUDIT

The audit. It happens long after production. It happens after delivery and all the costs of production are being reported as really and totally final. Neither the Production Manager nor the Coordinator are involved on a production when it comes to audit, but the Production Manager — being so involved in reporting production costs — needs to be aware of the audit, as you and the Production Accountant are basically preparing for the audit from your first day's work.

MUST YOU ALWAYS AUDIT?

You may not always have to go to audit. On very small films, you may only need a final cost report at audit stage; on others you may be allowed a review engagement, while most of the time you will be arranging for an audit.

A final cost report is just that: a report from the Production Accountant on the final costs. A review engagement is a review of the books by an outside, unrelated accounting source, to double-check the plausibility of those numbers. A full audit is also conducted by an outside, unrelated accounting source, where they not only check the plausibility of the books, but examine all the accounting files — spot-checking to cross reference the numbers in the books to original receipts, to see if all the official backup is present to validate the numbers in the books. Naturally, the more work an outside accounting source has to do, the more expensive the report.

The Financiers of production will determine if production requires a final cost report, a review engagement, or a full audit. Their decision will be influenced by the budget size of your production, and by the experience and the past history of the producing team. Find out what your production will require at the very end of the day.

THE VARIOUS REVIEWS OF AN AUDIT

There may be more than one type of review to make up your audit. You are designing the accounting system and, in essence, preparing for the audit in preproduction. Factor in the requirements of all the financing sources. Do your financing sources require the Auditor to only review the final costs, or do they also require the Auditor to do one of many possible compliance reviews, to see that you really did do what you promised to do in the financing agreements? Compliance reviews can vary from a review of Writer's Guild payments (as in the USA), to a review of third country costs and of the creative contribution by nationals (as in the UK), to a review of related party costs, a nationality list of key creative personnel, and a list of the financing sources (as in Canada). If tax incentives based on labor are part of your financing, you may also need the Auditor to review the labor costs during the audit. Basically, the audit can easily become very complex. In preproduction, factor in these "end of the day" needs so that you can extract this information quickly and easily. Have you factored in the accounting complexity of a multi-country co-production? Take time to think through the accounting needs of your production and talk it through with the Production Accountant and with the chosen Auditor.

THE DOCUMENTATION NEEDED FOR AN AUDIT

Since the audit is the most detailed of reports, here is a list of the documentation typically required for an audit review. Prepare to assemble these documents during production. Prepare the production accounting files to collect and display this information clearly and easily. Neither of you will be around for the audit review, and do not want an Auditor calling you at home for an explanation of accounting anomalies or incomplete files and reports.

AN OVERVIEW OF THE GENERAL LEDGER

The Accountant can write an explanation of how the general ledger was set up and any other notes the Auditor may need to readily read the general ledger, especially notes on what coding system was used for various type of costs.

CHART OF ACCOUNTS

A bit like a table of contents, this is a printout of the budget account codes (and account descriptions) used in the general ledger. The Accountant can generate this report.

GENERAL LEDGER

This is obvious, because this is "the books." It is generated from the accounting software.

FINAL COST REPORT

The Postproduction Accountant will be generating this final cost report, because it happens after delivery to the Distributor and/or the Broadcasters. By the time you leave production, there should be the final production cost report (complete with explanation memo) in this file.

VARIANCES FROM ORIGINAL BUDGET

You have made many explanation memos for the cost reports. Look them over and summarize why the large variances happened on various budget lines.

PAYMENT SCHEDULE FOR PURCHASE ORDERS & ESTIMATES TO COMPLETE

Though the cost report has columns that clearly identify the purchase orders yet to be paid and the remaining estimates to complete, draft a list that also projects when these costs will realistically be spent.

LIST OF DEFERRALS INCLUDED IN PRODUCTION COSTS

No deferrals should be counted as production costs, but in case they are, the Auditor needs to know what "non-costs" you have considered to be money spent, so they can deduct this amount from true production costs.

LIST OF NON-MONETARY TRANSACTIONS

If there were any production costs that were non-monetary transactions (like services provided in exchange for screen credit or other benefit), you have to declare them to the Auditor, too.

SYNOPSIS OF THE PLOT

If there is no brief synopsis of the plot already, it is likely that the Producer or the Publicity Department already have one that you can use.

INVENTORY LIST OF THE ACCOUNTING BOXES SENT TO THE AUDITOR

Since the accounting files will take up a number of boxes and/or electronic files, create an inventory list for each accounting box and electronic source, so that the Auditor can refer to this list to quickly find any information.

COPY OF ALL PRODUCTION REPORTS

As production is done, all the DPRs will be done, too. You can assemble this set of production reports in wrap, or the Production Accountant has already prepared a file in prep, and the DPRs are already in the accounting files because he has been collecting them during production. Do not forget to include Second Unit's production reports.

COPY OF ALL CALL SHEETS

Just like the production reports, you can assemble a set of call sheets in wrap, or have the Production Accountant prepare a file and collect them for the audit during production. Again, do not forget Second Unit's call sheets, too. These are usually optional, but can be helpful to the Auditor.

LIST OF FINANCIERS

List all the Financiers of production, complete with their names and all their contact information.

COPY OF ALL FINANCING AGREEMENTS

Ensure the accounting files have a complete set of all the latest in financing agreements, co-production agreements, distribution agreements, broadcasting agreements, interim loan agreements, and tax credit approvals or certificates.

COPY OF ALL DEFERRAL AGREEMENTS

Whenever you defer funds, you have an agreement. Copy all of these in one place and summarize the deferrals for the Auditor. If you have deferrals on all the crew, this is a long report and a big file.

ORIGINALS OF ALL BANK STATEMENTS WITH CANCELLED CHECKS

These originals justify the general ledger. The Production Accountant will ensure that they are filed appropriately and accessibly.

VIEWING COPY OF THE COMPLETED FILM

Yes, the Auditor needs to see the actual film. Send a digital screening copy.

OTHER DOCUMENTATION THAT MAY BE NEEDED

As mentioned, there may be a few or many more compliance reviews that need to take place during the audit. Discuss what is needed with the Auditor, but here is a sampling of other reports you may need to generate prior to the audit for review:

> A list (or cost report) of non-country charges

> A calculation of the Writer's or the Performer's payments

> A list of key creative personnel, their nationality, screen credit & total remuneration

> A copy of the citizenship declarations for the key personnel

> Deal memos and/or agreements for key personnel

> A copy of all screen credits

> A delivery schedule to all Distributor(s)/Broadcaster(s)

> A list of related party expenditures
  (costs associated with non-arm's length companies,
  the Producers, their relations, and companies related to them)

> A list of labor costs
  (detailing crew names/companies, employee/corporate status,
  company ownership status (single-owned or multi-owned),
  citizenship(s), residency, total labor cost by country and state or province)

> Chain of Title documentation

> Corporate documentation, like incorporation documents, shareholder
  information, etc.

—⁓—

The more work the Production Accountant and you do to prepare for the audit, the faster — and therefore cheaper — the audit will be. The Producer does not typically have excess funds after delivery to pay for an Auditor to sort through badly prepared accounting files, to find out officially what happened to all that money. Remember that the audit review triggers the final drawdowns that will pay back a lot of the interim financing loan. If you have prepared for the audit well, you will save the Producer money even in your absence. Only when the audit review is done, can you really, truly say your job as Production Manager is really, truly done.

CLOSING NOTES

Congratulations! You did it! You have just managed or coordinated a film production!

As the PM, you were trusted with the production's money to see that the production was produced on time and on budget. As the Coordinator, everyone looked to you to keep production running. You made it happen. Be proud. If you feel like you have just dealt with absolutely everyone and everything during the course of making the film, you are right. You did. Both Production Management and Coordination can be all-encompassing and stressful experiences. When the stress gets to you, remember: It is only a movie. Take a deep breath and try to relax. You do not have to be an expert, but you do need to think clearly. You have the ability and you are prepared. You can carry on.

Keep a balance between working on documentation and keeping in personal contact with the crew. Though you have a desk in the production office, your job is much more than shuffling paperwork. Recognize your job as one critical part of the magical wheel of making a film story come to life. No matter what your job, you will always be learning. Ask questions. Continue to build on your skills and abilities — your tool set — with every production completed. Adapt this book to create your own personal style of management or coordination. Make the job yours.

Congratulations again as you embark on a very exciting adventure: the exotic lifestyle of filmmaking! Get the most out of it. "Now" will never happen again, so enjoy every minute of it… from prep all the way to post.

But before I go, I have one more story for you…

THE EXOTIC LIFESTYLE

Many of us choose the film industry because we are looking for an exotic lifestyle. None of this nine-to-five work complete with benefits for me! Oh no! I want an interesting job! An exotic career!

So we work in film. Black becomes the key color of our wardrobes. We work so many hours on set or in the production office that most of our friends are filmmakers. We date filmmakers. We watch films. We talk about films. We make films. We eat on set or at film parties. We swap film rumors with our friends and help each other with contacts for future work.

Yet, no matter how much we work from contract to contract, at the end of every job we wonder... will I ever work again? Exotic equals unstable. We recognize that now. So that's why our parents always wished us to find a "real" job! Never mind. We love it here. We are filmmakers.

So when I go to film parties, I naturally bring my fellow along with me. He dresses in black just like me and everyone else. Little do they know he is here in disguise. For the time always comes during conversation that they ask him what department he works in. Of course he is a filmmaker. Aren't we all? But my fellow smiles and tells them what he does (he doesn't work in the industry).

Shock comes to their faces first. Then they respond: "Wow. You have a real job." You can see their eyes light up and a look of admiration come to their faces. A "real" job... with benefits! How exotic!

Now go out and enjoy YOUR exotic lifestyle!

APPENDIX IX

GLOSSARY

Please note that only the industry terms mentioned throughout this book are included in this glossary. You can find more terminology in the index. If, however, you are looking to truly immerse yourself in industry terminology, you can surf through numerous online glossaries or seek out the comprehensive book: *A to Z Guide to Film Terms* by Tim Moshansky.

1/8ths of Pages: Due to simple division of a script page (divide it in half, then in half again, and then in half once again) you come up with the magic 1/8th of a page. Also, with script format done correctly, you cannot fit more than eight scenes on a page. You will see the 1/8ths on the schedules, DPRs, and continuity documentation because the number of pages scheduled and shot each day helps plan the schedule and monitor if the production is on time and on budget. Using the common denominator of 1/8 makes the numbers easier to add.

A&B Pages: Once the production script is considered locked, and especially once shooting has begun, you can no longer re-paginate the script when adding new material because the script is used "as is" for continuity and editing departments. Therefore, when adding new material demands more script pages, you need to add pages in between existing pages using "A, B, C" and so on. Your page numbers could therefore look like this: page 13, 14, 14A, 14B, 14C, 15....

A&B Rolls: In postproduction, the film negative is cut and split into two separate rolls — each shot checkerboarded to the "other" roll — so that each shot may be addressed separately for color timing during the post process. Where you see negative on Roll A, you see black leader on Roll B, and where you see black leader on Roll A, you see negative on Roll B.

A&B Scenes: Once the production script is considered locked you can no longer re-number the scenes of a script when adding new scenes to the story. Many departments from the art department to editing have been preparing their breakdowns based on the scene numbers of the locked script. Therefore, when adding new scenes in between existing numbered scenes, you use "A, B, C," and so on, in the scene number. For example Scene 6A will happen after Scene 6 and before Scene 7. Scene A1, however, will happen prior to Scene 1 on the first page.

A&D: Assignment and Direction. For an interim financing loan, you have technically sold some of the Financier's drawdowns to the Lender in order to receive the money up front. Through the A&D, you "assign" certain drawdowns to the Lender, and "direct" the affected Financier(s) to pay the Lender instead of you, and so pay back the loan.

A.D.: Assistant Director. Though the term sounds like this team assists the Director — and the First A.D. does work closely with the Director — they are actually the Producer's or PM's representatives on set. They make the shooting schedule, organize, and supervise all the logistics of the shoot day. A.D.s generate the call sheet and DPR — key documents to know how production is faring. They do an awful lot of running around, and they are very good at using walkie-talkies. Because of the A.D's "take-charge" presence on set, visitors often mistake the First A.D. for the Director.

ADR: Additional Dialogue Recording. Also known as "Looping." When dialogue is unacceptable in the sound edit, you may need to call the Performer back during postproduction to re-do some of his lines. ADR is done in a sound studio where the picture is "looped" to repeat over and over again, so the Performer can lip synch his lines to the picture.

Advanced Schedule: At the end of the call sheet, the advanced schedule projects the scenes and schedule order of the following day's call sheet to aid crew in preparing more than one day in advance. Sometimes the advanced schedule will project a few days at a time for the same reason.

Ancillary Property: This type of property is a secondary product or property that is related to the film production but is not the film production itself, nor one of the delivered versions. Ancillary properties are typically merchandised (sold to the public) to generate alternative sources of revenue to the production. Examples of ancillary properties include: a book based on the film story; clothing with the production title on it; a companion video game of the film story; an interactive production website and so on.

Arm's Length Entity: An arm's length entity (company or individual) is an entity that is unrelated to the ownership or control of the production company or its parent company. Most Financiers require declarations of related (also known as non-arm's length) parties and how much money each of them is receiving from the production budget.

ATL: Above-The-Line. *See* Line (the "Line").

Atmosphere (for Picture): Handled by the Special Effects or Props department, atmosphere is smoke that creates a very light, soft and even haze across the image. This kind of smoke is generated by a smoke machine — not cigarettes — and the Special Effects or Props department will run the machine.

Atmosphere (for Soundtrack): No room or location in the world is 100% quiet, for even in what you think is the quietest of spaces you have the main unit crew breathing. Every space has some kind of white noise no matter how subtle, and it is most noticeable when absent. The sound department will record atmosphere wild (without the camera running) on the shoot day for the post sound team's use.

Audit Review: This report is a comprehensive look at how you spent the production money to say the very least. Typically, once 95% of the budget is spent, an accounting company unrelated to the production company can examine and test the validity of the production's accounting records with an audit review. During the examination, they spot-check to cross-reference numbers in the accounting records (the books) to the original receipts to see if all the official backup is present that validates the numbers in the books. Financiers tend also to require the auditor report on various expenses, like budget categories that were locked by the Financiers during preproduction, or declarations of assets required, and so on.

B+C: Two sections of the budget that sum up direct production costs ("B") and postproduction costs ("C"), but do not include Above-The-Line costs (like Writer, Producer, Director, and Star expenses) or indirect production costs (like publicity, insurance, and financing expenses).

B-Camera: When more than one camera is used on set to capture images simultaneously, the secondary camera is labeled as B-Camera in order to track the images it captures all the way from the continuity notes to the end of the post work flow.

B-Roll: B-Roll is a secondary camera on the set, but B-Roll is not recorded by B-Camera. Publicity arranges for a camera team on set to record B-Roll: behind-the-scenes footage and interviews to be used for publicity purposes.

Base Camp: Also known as the circus, base camp is made up of the hair/makeup/wardrobe and dressing room trucks when shooting on location.

Best Boy: When the term Best Boy is used as the entire job title, reference is to the crew member who is second in charge in the Electric department. The Best Boy Grip is the second in command in the Grip department, and the Best Boy SPFX is second in command in the Special Effects department.

Black Wrap: A thick black bendable material that is heat-resistant; it is one of the expendables that is used by the Grips and Electrics to shade and direct lights on set.

Blog: A blog is a website with frequent updates or new stories that encourages reader interaction with comments and sharing.

Blogosphere: All the blogs of the Internet and their social interaction, like a network within a network.

Breakdown: Though all departments break down the script into elements that relate to their department (props looks for required props in the script, locations looks for required locations, etc.), the A.D. breakdowns are most widely known and quite comprehensive. In creating the schedule, the A.D.s identify the on-set needs of each scene including: a list of characters and Background Performers; required props; stunts; lighting effects, and so on. A budget breakdown is less detailed than the A.D. breakdowns and is conducted by the PM for purposes of costing out a production budget.

BTL: Below-The-Line. *See* Line (the "Line").

CGI: Computer Generated Image or Computer Graphic Imagery. These computer effects can be 2D, like painting smoke into the image or painting tethers out, or they can be 3D like painting a solid animated object into the scene. The Previs team makes entire scenes using computer animation to visually test the Director's vision during preproduction. CGI is also known as Visual Effects (VFX).

Circus: *See* Base Camp.

Circled Takes: Also known as Selected Takes. Not all takes on the shoot day are considered good for postproduction, so the Camera and Continuity departments will track which takes are desirable and circle them on their documentation in order to pass the information along the post work flow to the Editors.

Clone: This term is typically used when referring to copies of delivery masters. Due to localization and differing technical specifications between the distributors and broadcasters, you may find that the list of required delivery clones is quite long at time of delivery of the finished film.

Copro: This term is short for Coproduction, but more typically short for International Coproduction.

Copyright: An intellectual property right that is the right to copy, publish, exhibit, or modify an original work — plus the right to authorize others to do so. Copyright starts with the original creator, such as an author of a written work, and expires over time, but it can be renewed under certain circumstances. If copyright does expire, the work falls into the public domain.

COT: Chain of Title. For a film production, it is a collection of agreements that starts with the creator and copyright holder of the original work (the origin of the Title), follows all the legal assignments of that copyright (the Chain), and ends with the agreement that includes sufficient rights to the final copyright holder to make and distribute the movie (the end of the Title). Early in development the entire chain could be captured in one agreement between Writer and Producer.

Coverage (Insurance): An insurance policy is coverage that insures the production against unforeseeable happenings that cost the production money. For example, office contents coverage would pay for new computers in the office were they stolen during production — well, minus the deductible.

Coverage (Scene): Scene coverage is a term used on set. Once the scene is captured on camera in a wide shot, the camera moves in closer to the action to capture the same action in close-up. The close-up shots are coverage, and provide the choice of camera angle options in postproduction in order to tell the story.

Craft Service: Reference is either to the department or short for the actual Craft Service person who provides the service. Craft service is refreshments available to the crew and cast between meals. An entry level position, the Craft Service person is also typically a ticketed first aid representative.

CV: Curriculum vitae. Also known as your resume or bio.

D4N: Day For Night. A shooting technique used to simulate night on screen while shooting instead during the day.

Dailies: Depending on the context, Dailies are crew members who are hired on a daily basis in any department, or they are the captured image and sound from set that have just been transferred and synched together and are ready for first viewing (also known as Rushes). Dailies still include the slate that identifies the start of each take. Typically, dailies (rushes) are screened on a television monitor, but for feature films they may also be viewed on a large screen at the post facility to simulate the big screen experience.

Day Out Of Days: A type of schedule output by the A.Ds that tells you simply if a certain element or person is required on a particular shooting day, without cluttering you with details of the scenes or other required elements for those days. D.O.O.Ds can be used for any element the A.Ds breaks down in the script, but are most usually for the Performers' and Background Performers' schedule (especially for booking talent through a Casting or Extras Casting Director).

Deferral: When a crew member, for example, works on deferral, their earned salary is postponed to be paid out of revenues when the finished film is complete and in distribution. Deferrals are paid as directed in the Financier agreements, and are paid prior to the production moving into profit. It is also possible to make a partial-deferral arrangement where the crew member receives a small, defined salary during production, with the balance of the salary being deferred.

Deliverable: Each Financier, broadcaster and distributor will have a list of elements that are required to fulfill their agreement — these are the deliverables and they can include items such as: a digital master, an M&E track, a closed-captioned master, a transcription, publicity photos, a press kit, 100 publicity stills, an audit review, a copy of all financing agreements, a completion bond, to name a few. Some deliverables trigger drawdown payments on financing agreements during the course of production whereas other deliverables are due at the very end when the film is completed and the production accounting books are ready to be closed. The deliverables due to the distributor or broadcaster at time of delivery are also known as delivery materials.

Delivery: Delivery is the date that the distributor or broadcaster accepts all the delivery materials required to distribute or broadcast the final production. It is possible to arrange for technical evaluation of your final delivery materials in advance of delivery in order to address any technical deficiencies quickly and thus speed up final acceptance of delivery.

DI: *See* Digital Intermediate.

DIT: *See* DMT.

Digital Original: The original media — be it a tape or file — that has captured the original images on set.

Digital: A data-based recording that stores the data on memory cards, discs, hard drives, or videotape.

Digital Intermediate: Also known as "DI," digital intermediate is the postproduction work flow process in a digital format. The original scenes (captured on film or digital) are sent nightly to the post facility for transfer to an intermediate digital format for postproduction until it is time to finish the film for delivery.

Digital Master: Once the edited picture is combined with the mixed soundtrack on a single file or tape, you have a digital master. For delivery to various distributors and broadcasters you may have to create a number of different digital masters to address their various technical requirements. Digital masters are also known as digital clones.

DMT: Data Management Technician. Also known as the Digital Image Technician ("DIT") this camera department crew member backs up the footage on set and ensures the image is indeed captured.

Dolly: A piece of equipment on which the camera can be mounted and moved around set while filming — used to follow the action in a scene. Typically the dolly moves along track pre-laid by the Grips to ensure the camera movement is smooth. The Dolly Grip operates the dolly.

D.O.O.D.: *See* Day Out Of Days.

DOP: *See* DP.

DP: Director of Photography. This crew member designs the technical look of the production, and on smaller shoots may also double as the Camera Operator. Also known as DOP.

DPR: The Daily Production Report is the official record of what transpired on set each shoot day. The DPR summarizes all the daily status reports from each department including: continuity, camera, sound, A.Ds, and production office. From reading it, the Production Accountant can estimate costs as they are spent, while the PM, Producers, and Financiers can evaluate if the production remains on time and on budget. In an insurance claim or legal battle, the DPRs are especially referenced and scrutinized. You may also generate DPRs for each rehearsal day during preproduction and for each second unit day during wrap.

Drawdown: Financing agreements tend to pay out their investment to the film in installments scheduled over the course of the production. Triggering events, like first day of principal photography, delivery of fine cut, delivery to the distributor, or completed audit review will effect a payment of one of those installments — known as drawdowns. For an interim financing loan, a drawdown is when you take out the loan up front, recognizing, of course, that you will have to pay it back when you have triggered payments from the financing agreements later in the process.

E & O: Errors and Omissions Insurance. E & O is a kind of producer malpractice insurance. For example, once you have conducted sufficient research to declare that the work you have produced is original, E & O insurance covers you should someone try to sue you claiming that the work is theirs, but stolen. Your exposure to the risks of E & O increases as you exhibit the production to a wider audience, and since lawsuits are typically aimed at parties with the most money (i.e.: distributors and broadcasters), you will need E & O insurance if you wish to distribute your film.

E.D.L.: Edit Decision List. An automatic printout of the picture editing system, it is a road map of all the required details about what to cut, fade, and dissolve to conform the digital original to match the locked cut — and where to find all the necessary original material to do so.

EFC: Estimated Final Costs. A column on the cost report that adds "Total Costs" to "Estimate to Complete (ETC)".

Emotional Arc: The characters in a script undergo some kind of transformation over the course of the screen story. This transformation, no matter how extreme or subtle, is the emotional arc of that character. Filming scenes out of script order creates a unique challenge for Performers: act the emotional arc on screen even if it is out of sequence to suit the schedule. The arc must appear natural and progressive when cut into order in the editing room.

EPK: Electronic Press Kit. A promotional tool, the EPK is an extension of the press kit that allows reporters to insert footage and/or interviews from your set into their video news stories. An EPK typically includes: video interviews with key cast and crew; behind-the-scenes segments of the film being shot ("B-Roll"); and a teaser trailer as a visual synopsis of the film. Rather than being a polished single program, the EPK is clearly made up of multiple, separated video clips for the user to select and edit as needed.

Equity: To have some equity participation in a film is to own a portion of that film, for example, to own a portion of its copyright.

Escrow: More completely identified as Fees in Escrow or an Escrow Account. If allowed by the Financiers, it is one of the alternatives to arranging a full (read "more expensive") completion bond. To give the Financiers comfort that the production will be completed, you place a negotiated amount of cash into a separate, locked bank account that the Financiers will release to you at time of delivery. Typically the cash is what will be used for the producer fees and corporate overhead. If production spending goes over-budget, the Financier will direct the Producer to use the funds in the escrow account to pay for the over-budget items thus reducing payment of the producer fees and corporate overhead.

ETC: Estimate to Complete. A column on the cost report for the PM to declare how much more money is required to be spent for each budget line item in order to complete the production.

Extras: Also known as Background Performers. Extras are cast who have no speaking parts and who fill the background of scenes. On screen, they pass by, walk dogs, or comprise crowds. Special Skills Extras (or Special Business Extras) are paid slightly higher rates because they have a unique skill to perform on screen; for example, they play hockey, ride horses, and do other things on film that require some special skill.

Flat Rate (& Flat Picture Rate): Rather than pay a cast or crew member for their services on a hourly basis, you can negotiate a fixed rate per week or a fixed rate for the entire shoot. When a union is involved, the flat (or fixed) rate must exceed minimum scale, so work hours and overtime hours must still be logged for the Accountant to compare the flat rate against what the person would have made working hourly at the end of production, and then arrange payment for the balance owed, if appropriate.

Flying Wall: A temporary wall of the set built for location or studio that can be moved, typically to allow for camera placement.

Foley: While watching the final cut of the film on screen in a special studio, the Foley Artist acts out and records many sound effects in order to supply another layer of richness to the soundtrack. Typical foley sound effects include: footsteps, door sounds, clothing rustling, kissing sounds, and a host of others. The foley studio is filled with props and devices to help create these sounds, for example, the floor is sectioned into different qualities: one section of gravel, another of pavement, one of tile, and yet another of wood. A Foley Artist in a foley studio records foley.

FTP Site: A File Transfer Protocol Site. Basically a web-hosted data warehouse. FTP software allows you to upload and download files from such a website.

Gaffer: This crew member is the head of the Electric department on set. Also known as the Chief Lighting Technician.

Gallery Shoot: The Stills Photographer captures publicity photos of the Performers dressed in character in a studio-like setting.

Gels: Colored gelatin sheets or rolls that are placed in front of studio lights in order to change the light's tint. Clothes pegs are used to hold gels onto the lights.

Generation Loss: Especially noticeable with consumer grade video, when you duplicate a copy of a video from a copy of a video, the picture and sound quality degrades. The quality degradation is generation loss and it increases the further you are from the original source.

Greek ("to greek an object"): When, for example, you cover or otherwise make illegible a product name that you do not have permission to show on screen, you are "greeking" that product name.

Grip: Grips move all sorts of things around on the set, and build rigs to enable the camera to move around. They also set up flags to block or pattern some of the lights. The Key Grip heads the department, the Dolly Grip pushes the camera dolly, and there can be a Best Boy Grip who is second in charge.

Guide Track (or "GT"): When it is impossible to record high quality sound on set (for example due to loud motors or loud location sound), the Sound Recordist will capture the sound on set anyway and call it guide track. The guide track is a temporary recording that will be used in postproduction until the Performers can return to replace their lines in an ADR session.

HD: High definition. There are many high definition formats, so expect to deal with conversion and compatibility issues throughout the process.

Hiatus: The hiatus is the break taken between episodes when shooting a television series. Typically a week long, hiatus allows for script writing to catch up to the speed of the shoot and during this time the preproduction crew is still at work, but the shooting crew has time off.

Hot Costs: Created by the Production Accountant, hot costs are recorded on a daily basis for Producers and Executives. The focus is only on costs that fluctuate the most on a daily basis (like how much overtime was worked) for a quick overview.

I/N (Internegative): Like the digital intermediate, the internegative is the second step in backing up the original film material, so you do not have to rely on the original negative for all your delivery elements. In this case it is a backup of the interpositive. Every time you run negative through a process at the lab, you risk further scratching and damaging through regular wear and tear. You can create an I/P and I/N of the entire negative, but more likely — due to budget — will strike the I/P and I/N after you have cut the negative, later in the postproduction process.

In The Can: The day after the end of principal photography. This moment is when all the original images and sound have been captured, backed up and transferred to an editing format. The shooting crew moves into wrap, and the postproduction team takes center stage to finish the production.

I.P. (Intellectual Property): Copyright and trademarks are examples of intellectual property rights that are attached to works of all kinds.

I/P (Interpositive): Like the digital intermediate, the interpositive is the first step in backing up the original film material, so you do not have to rely on the original negative for all your delivery elements. After the interpositive you will need an internegative of this element to complete the backup. Every time you run negative through a process at the lab, you risk further scratching and damaging through regular wear and tear. You can create an I/P and I/N of the entire negative, but more likely — due to budget — will strike the I/P and I/N after you have cut the negative, later in the postproduction process.

ISAN: International Standard Audiovisual Number. A global, numeric identifier for your production (not unlike ISBN numbers are for books) that can be represented by a number or by a visual bar code. The ISAN is useful in distribution of the finished film to identify your project across borders and languages. Because you can register various versions of the same project, you can track, for example, the director's cut separately from the producer's cut from the international version and so on. The number can be assigned early in preproduction but cannot be registered until the credits are locked.

Key: Depending on the context, a Key is the crew member who is the head of a department, otherwise it is the main light that illuminates the majority of the Performer's face on camera.

Kit: If a crew member is expected to come to work on set with a specific set of tools for their work (that the production budget will rent), then those tools are the kit. Typically heads of departments, construction crew, grips, and electrics have kits to rent to the production.

Line ("The Line"): The Line is in the production budget and marks a division between the costs associated with the people and elements who made up the creative package that was assembled in development to attract financing to make the production: the Producer, the Director, the Writer and story rights, the Star, the other development costs (known as Above-The-Line costs), and the costs associated with everything else in the budget (known as Below-The Line costs).

Long Form: More completely known as Long Form Agreements. Beyond a one or two page deal memo that summarizes certain elements of their employment, some cast and crew members will have a more extensively written agreement attached to the deal memo to clarify all the details of their work contract, rights assignments, and screen credit expectations.

Looping: *See* ADR

LM: Location Manager. Head of the Locations department that finds the on-screen locations for the production and manages the agreements, logistics and public relations related to those locations.

M&E: Music and Effects. A music and effects track is a required deliverable that the post sound department arranges that allows your project to be sold internationally. With an M&E track, any country can dub the voices into any language accompanied by the rich M&E track underneath.

Main Unit: The main unit is the cast, crew, and equipment that is shooting all the primary story scenes of your film.

Meal Penalty: Unions and guilds specify a maximum number of work hours before the cast and crew must break for lunch. Should production continue to work into the required lunch break, the production company must pay a monetary meal penalty to each affected person. The size of the penalty will be determined by how long lunch is delayed.

Mobisode: A typically short narrative production that is delivered to the audience primarily on a mobile device. Think of merging the words "mobile" plus "episode".

MOW: Movie Of the Week. It is a term for a feature-length film that premieres on television.

NCR: No carbon required. Multi-part forms that make instant copies without the use of carbon paper between sheets.

Office P.A.: Office Production Assistant. The Office P.A. is an entry-level position in the production office, and one of the only non-union positions on a union shoot.

Option: Rather than buy all the rights during development to produce and exhibit a movie of a script (a "script purchase" — read "expensive"), the Producer can purchase a few rights from the copyright owner (an "option" — read "affordable") to develop the script and seek financing for the project. Typically books, scripts, and plays are optioned, and the option lasts for anywhere from a few months to two years before naturally expiring. Option fees paid are deducted from the overall purchase price should the project move into production.

OT or O/T: Overtime.

P.A.: Production Assistant. More typically referred to as the Office P.A., but may also be a reference to the Set P.A. or Location P.A.. Each of these positions is entry-level, one in the office, one on set in the A.D. Department, and the other on set in the Locations department.

Pacing: A term used in the script, and also in the editing room, to discuss the timing of scenes and shots within scenes. Action pictures are typically fast paced, whereas touching dramas have slower pacing. If the pacing is too fast, the audience can become confused, if too slow, the audience can become bored.

PC: Production Coordinator. Need I say more?

Period Piece: A story that takes place in an historical era.

Pickup Shot: A shot, not involving the key cast, that main unit did not capture on the shoot day, or a shot that the Editing department determined was necessary after roughly editing a scene. Typically these shots are close up, for example: hands opening a letter or the sign on the building;. As the list of missing or pickup shots increases over the course of the shoot, a second unit, smaller than the main unit crew, can capture these necessary shots.

Picture Vehicle: A vehicle that is filmed on screen, whether it is the main character's car used daily, or a collection of cars in the background to decorate a street scene.

Pink Slip: A written notification of the end of production sent to the regular cast and crew. It is provided usually one week in advance of wrap in the paycheck envelopes. Unions often require such official notification, even if production is very short in duration. It is usually taken as an opportunity of thanking the crew for their hard work and dedication to the project.

Plate Shot: One of the picture layers that the visual effects team requires to work their magic. For example, to insert an animated character into a live action shot with a live Performer, at least three layers are required: (1) the animated character; (2) the live Performer acting and moving around the set; and (3) the plate shot of the set with no Performer in it at all. These layers provide sufficient visual information to place the animated character in the set and either in front of or behind the live Performer.

PM: Production Manager. Enough said?

PMP: Poor Man's Process. A shooting technique used to simulate a character or two in a moving vehicle while actually shooting inside a studio with a screen behind the false vehicle. Rear-screen projection, fans, creating moving shadows with the lights, and rigging the false vehicle to jostle, all contribute to the illusion. Also known simply as "process shot."

P. O.: Purchase Order. When signed by the PM, it is a promise that the production will pay the price listed for the goods or the services ordered, even though no invoice has yet been created. The Accountant will set aside the money promised on the P.O., and when the invoice arrives, will match the purchase order to the invoice. The P.O. forms part of the backup to justify the cost in the accounting files.

POC: Production Office Coordinator. What else is there to say?

Pre-calls: Pre-calls are the time for selected crew to report to set in advance of the general start-work time ("call time") on a given shoot day. For example: Makeup, Hair, and Wardrobe need a pre-call along with certain Performers to prepare them for first shot; Drivers need a pre-call to bring the Performers to the set for their pre-call and to park the many trucks that make up the unit; and Craft Service needs a pre-call to ensure the coffee is hot and ready for the all the first arrivals on set.

Previs: Previsualization. The Director's vision, shot list, and DP's camera angles can be previewed, tested, and visually explored through previsualization. A small CGI team can generate preliminary versions of shots and sequences using interactive computer-animated models or sequences, or a Storyboard Artist can draw 2D images, or the Art department can construct miniature models of selected sets or locations (inside which you can place and move toy characters). Action sequences are nearly always previewed and tested in one of these manners, although it is possible to previsualize the entire production using some or all of these methods. Previs facilitates valuable communication and collaboration between the Director, DP, and Picture Editor.

Production Media: A generic term to cover whichever media the production used to capture picture and sound (digital file, film stock, videotape, DAT, etc.) and often also encompasses the original images and sound once captured on that media.

Production Stills: Photographs taken on the set by the Stills Photographer to be included in the publicity materials. Typically, shots will include both behind-the-scenes photographs and gallery shoot pictures. The poster shot may emerge from these stills.

Production Value: Overall quality. Production value is typically in reference to the quality of the finished film — both picture and sound quality, but high production value can also be in reference to a location that has excellent set dressing already present.

Public Domain: When copyright expires, the work goes into the public domain and is then rights-free for use by the public at large; however, different countries have different time calculations to determine what is in the public domain, for example: 50, 100 or 120 years after publication date, or the life of the author plus 70 years and so on.

Review Engagement: A Review Engagement is an examination of and report on the production accounting books by an outside, unrelated accounting source to double-check the plausibility of the numbers within. It is not as thorough as an audit review. It is typically conducted once 95% of the budget is spent. Financing agreements will specify if a review engagement or a full audit review is required.

Rights: There are many rights related to a production including, but not limited to: copyright, moral rights, and master recording rights. Instead, consider this example to explain the overall concept of rights: first, you pay a Performer for his acting services on the shoot day and once the shoot day is over and payment is made, the transaction is complete. The Performer, however, still retains the right to their image and voice. You must now purchase the right to use that image and voice when exploiting your finished film around the world. You can purchase these rights in advance for a fixed number of years (known as the "front end"), or use a royalty system that will pay a percentage out of any revenue generated during exploitation of the project (known as the "back end").

RPT: Related Party Transactions. These are expenses in the production budget that are paid to companies or individuals who are related to the ownership or control of the production company or its parent company, for example: the Producers and their family members; companies sharing ownership with the same parent company; and so on. Most Financiers require a declaration of RPTs and lock these expenses in preproduction to prevent their going over budget without the Financier's approval. Related parties are also known as non-arm's length entities.

Rushes: *See* Dailies (Rushes).

Scale Rate: The minimum pay rate as set by a union or guild for a cast or crew member's services.

Scenes: A script is made up of a number of scenes to tell the story — a change in script location (like from a living room to a kitchen) or a change in time will effect a new scene in the script. In between scenes, for example, the main unit may have to move to a new set or location, or a Performer may have to change clothes. *Also see* "Setups;" "Shots and Takes."

Script Day: Several scenes in a script may take place on the same day within the story (the "script day"). Continuity declares the list of script days in the entire script, and this information is useful to plan, for example, how many wardrobe changes are required for a given character.

Second Unit: A small crew and their equipment that captures pickup shots, establishing shots, stunts, animal shots, or special effects that do not require the Director's presence or lead cast. They work simultaneously with main unit, but in different locations. They may be working a few days into wrap to collect all required pickup shots missed by main unit or requested by the Picture Editor.

Set: Wherever the main unit is currently shooting.

Setups: A setup relates to the camera placement and the action in a scene that is captured on set by one or multiple camera setups. For example, start with a wide shot and then move the camera physically closer to capture the Performer in close-up for the same action. This is two setups. A change in the camera placement or a change in the scene will trigger a new setup (because new lighting may be required for the new scene). If you are shooting with two cameras, each camera is providing a separate setup, so you could have the action of Scene 1, Shot 1 covered by two separate setups. *Also see* "Scenes;" "Shots and Takes."

SFX: Sound Effects. Sound Effects Editors gather sounds from various sources to match to the picture. Oddly enough, the actual recorded sound of a gun firing is way too tinny to sound right on film, so Sound Effects Editors create sounds the way we think they should sound, using libraries and/or inventing and recording new sounds themselves.

Shots: A scene can be captured in one shot (known as a "long take") or in many shots (known as "coverage"). A shot is most frequently a division of a scene. The Director and DP will have a list of camera angles they plan to use to capture all necessary viewpoints on the action of the scene. Each camera angle is a shot. *Also see* "Scenes;" "Setups and Takes."

Short Ends: Unexposed partial rolls of film stock that are long enough to be used in the future to capture images.

Sides: When used on set, sides are the selected scenes from the script as declared on the day's call sheet. They are reduce-photocopied so they can be carried around in a pocket and used as reference on set as a prompt. When used in auditions, sides can be full-sized and will be an excerpt of the script for screen testing the potential Performer.

Slugs: Used in postproduction to preserve the time duration of a missing shot, slugs are black leaders with white descriptive text. Typically slugs are used in place of finished CGI shots that take longer to deliver to the Editors than live action shots from main unit.

SPFX: Special Effects. Also known as Physical Effects in order to differentiate them from Visual Effects. They can range from the use of dry ice, steam, or smoke as atmosphere, to the creation of a waterfall, snowfall, rainfall, wind, blazing fire, or explosions on set. Simple effects are typically handled by the Props department, whereas more complex ones are handled by a Special Effects company.

Spotting Session: The Music Composer, Sound Designer, and Director come together to watch a cut of the film in postproduction and generate a "to do" list of music to source or write for the Composer. This screening is the spotting session.

Stand-In: A Background Performer who stands in place of the Performer while the technical team lights the set. Doing so allows the Performer to complete preparation for the shoot in Hair, Makeup and Wardrobe. The Stand-In does not show up on screen.

Storyboard: *See* "Previs."

Strip Board: The first shooting schedule an A.D. makes is the strip board (also known as production board). Created on computer with software to emulate the look and interaction of the old physical board, the strip board is made up of a "header board" strip (a legend) followed by numerous colored strips, each strip representing one scene from the script and each strip coded with essential scene requirements, like list of characters, number of pages per scene, and so on. The colors code the strips into day versus night and interior versus exterior scenes to aid with developing an efficient shooting schedule.

Swag: Purchased or gifted to the crew at the end of production, swag can be hats, bags, sweatshirts, pins, watches, bathmats or whatever you can dream up with the production title on it. Typically they are distributed on the last day of principal photography or at the wrap party. Also known as crew gifts or wrap gifts.

Synch: To be "in-synch" is to have the picture and sound running together and matching, for example, voice to lip movements. To "synch" is the act of bringing the sound and picture together so they match.

T.A.D.: Trainee Assistant Director. This position is an entry-level job on the Assistant Director team.

Take: A take is an attempt to capture the scene's action on camera for a given shot. The action of Scene 1, Shot 1, for example, could be captured five times (meaning "5 takes") before the main unit is happy with the results. *Also see* Scenes; Setups and Shots.

Target Scenes: Scenes that are not scheduled to be shot on a given shoot day; however, scenes that could be shot if time permits.

Tie-in: Using the power outlets at a location for the set's lighting needs is to tie-in to that location's power. Expect to pay the owner's power bill later.

Top Sheet: A summary sheet. Budgets, cash flows and cost reports all have top sheets to summarize the broad cost categories of the document in a page or two. Detail pages follow that explode each category into numerous sub-categories, and sometimes into exacting calculations. The Continuity Supervisor also supplies a daily top sheet to provide an overview of the shoot day's continuity information, for example: number of scenes and shots captured, estimated running time of the entire picture, and so on.

Trademark: An intellectual property right that distinguishes your goods and services from the goods and services of others. You can trademark a word, phrase, or logo (think "title", "log line" or "character", for example). The registration of a trademark must be maintained to prevent the trademark from becoming abandoned (and therefore no longer protected by trademark law).

Transition: Editing commands that carry you visually from one scene to another, including: cut directly to the new scene, dissolve between them, fade out and then fade in, and so on. Required sound transitions are typically identified in a spotting session.

Turnaround: Defined by a union or guild, it is the number of hours cast or crew is required to have between going home at night after one shoot day and starting work on the next shoot day. If turnaround is too short, monetary penalties ensue to all affected cast or crew.

Unit: *See* "Main Unit" or "Second Unit."

VFX: Visual Effects. *See* "CGI."

VOIP: Voice Over IP. A system that uses the Internet connections instead of telephone wires to connect telephone sets.

VPN: Virtual Private Network. Also known as Virtual Private Office (VPO). The network of computers primarily in the production office.

VPO: Virtual Private Office. *See* "VPN."

Walla: A team of Performers who work together in a sound studio to provide you with background group sounds for the soundtrack; for example, cheers and background restaurant mumbling.

Weather Cover: An interior location or studio that is ready for shooting and on standby in case poor weather conditions forces a change of schedule at the last minute for an exterior shoot. The interior location or studio will be scheduled later in principal photography, so triggering weather cover is only about changing the shooting order of scenes, not changing the location for certain scenes.

Webisode: A typically short narrative production that is delivered to the audience over the Internet. Think of merging the words "web" plus "episode."

Wet Gate: Every time film goes through a process at the lab, there is always the danger of light surface scratches appearing on the acetate side of the negative from regular wear and tear. A wet gate in the lab machinery literally prints the film through a printing gate filled with a clear solution that temporarily fills any possible light scratches.

Wet Signature: An original signature on an agreement, not a facsimile or scan of one.

Wild Sound (or Wild Lines): Sound or Performer's lines recorded on set but not with the camera rolling.

Wrangler: A Trainer and/or Handler who prepares an animal to perform certain actions on command — even if those actions are what that animal does already. The Wrangler then cares for and works with the animal on set on the shoot day to achieve those shots. "Animal" could, however, mean anything from a horse, dog or cat to a spider, ant colony, or anything else you can imagine.

Wrap: At the end of every day in principal photography you wrap the shoot day by tidying up and going home. If you are returning to this set the next day, you will probably have security on station overnight. At the end of using a location or a set, you also wrap the location or set by restoring it to its original (or better) condition and sending thanks to the location owners. At the end of principal photography, you wrap the production by doing the big tidy-up, returning equipment, finishing paperwork, having a party and handing over the production to the post team.

SAMPLE FORMS

A list of these forms can be found in the Table of Contents on pages xv-xvi.

These forms can be downloaded in full size (8.5" x 11") at
www.mwp.com, click on "Virtual Film School," click on "Resources."

DEVELOPMENT TO PRODUCTION BUDGET SAMPLE #1

Development to Production Budget Sample #1

"Film Title"

The figures on this form are for demonstration purposes only and are not to be taken as financial advice.

Acct	Description	Amount	Sub-Total	Total
1.00	**STORY RIGHTS / ACQUISTIONS**			
1.01	Story Rights	7,500		
	Paid in Development	(7,500)	0	
	TOTAL STORY RIGHTS			**0**
2.00	**SCENARIO**			
2.01	Writer	75,000		
	Paid in Development	(25,000)	50,000	
2.20	Story Editor	6,000		
	Paid in Development	(4,500)	1,500	
2.25	Research	5,000		
	Paid in Development	(2,532)	2,468	
2.27	Clearances / Title Search	2,000	2,000	
2.60	Writer Travel & Living	2,968		
	Paid in Development	(2,968)	0	
	TOTAL SCENARIO			**55,968**
3.00	**DEVELOPMENT COSTS**			
3.95	Story Rights	7,500		
	Writer	25,000		
	Story Editor	4,500		
	Research	2,532		
	Travel & Living	2,968		
	Producer Fees	3,750		
	Overhead	3,750	50,000	
	TOTAL DEVELOPMENT COSTS			**50,000**

DEVELOPMENT TO PRODUCTION BUDGET SAMPLE #2

Development to Production Budget Sample #2

"Film Title"

The figures on this form are for demonstration purposes only and are not to be taken as financial advice.

Acct	Description		Sub-Total	Total
1.00	**STORY RIGHTS / ACQUISTIONS**			
1.01	Story Rights	7,500		
	Paid in Development	(7,500)	0	
	TOTAL STORY RIGHTS			0
2.00	**SCENARIO**			
2.01	Writer	75,000		
	Paid in Development	(25,000)	50,000	
2.20	Story Editor	6,000		
	Paid in Development	(4,500)	1,500	
2.25	Research	5,000		
	Paid in Development	(2,532)	2,468	
2.27	Clearances / Title Search	2,000	2,000	
2.60	Writer Travel & Living	2,968		
	Paid in Development	(2,968)	0	
	TOTAL SCENARIO			55,968
3.00	**DEVELOPMENT COSTS**			
3.95	Financing Company #1	10,000		
	Financing Company #2	35,000		
	Financing Company #3	5,000	50,000	
	- Story Rights ($7,500)			
	- Writer ($25,000)			
	- Story Editor ($4,500)			
	- Research ($2,532)			
	- Travel & Living ($2,968)			
	- Producer Fees ($3,750)			
	- Overhead ($3,750)			
	TOTAL DEVELOPMENT COSTS			50,000

BLANK BUDGET TOP SHEET #1

Blank Budget Top Sheet #1

"Film Title"
Type of Production (ie: Feature Film, # Episode Series…)

Shoot [Format] / Post [Format]
[List of Unions or Non-Union]
Budget prepared by: [Name]

Shoot [Month] & [Year]
Location vs. Studio
Budget dated: [Date]

Acct	Description	Total	Acct	Description	Total
1.00	Story Rights / Acquisitions		45.00	Camera Equipment	
2.00	Scenario		46.00	Electrical Equipment	
3.00	Development Costs		47.00	Grip Equipment	
4.00	Producer		48.00	Sound Equipment	
5.00	Director		49.00	Second Unit	
6.00	Stars		50.00	Digital Stock	
Total "A" (Above The Line)			51.00	Production Lab / Digital Dailies	
10.00	Cast		**Total "B" (Below The Line Production)**		
11.00	Extras		60.00	Editorial Labor	
12.00	Production Staff		61.00	Editorial Equipment	
13.00	Design Labor		62.00	Digital Post Production (Picture)	
14.00	Construction Labor		63.00	Digital Post Production (Sound)	
15.00	Set Dressing Labor		64.00	Post Production Laboratory	
16.00	Property Labor		65.00	Film Post Production (Sound)	
17.00	Special Effects Labor		66.00	Music	
18.00	Wrangling Labor		67.00	Titles / CGI / Opticals / Stock Ftg	
19.00	Wardrobe Labor		68.00	Versioning	
20.00	Makeup / Hair Labor		69.00	Amortization (Series)	
21.00	Video Technical Crew		**Total "C" (Below The Line Post Prdn.)**		
22.00	Camera Labor		70.00	Unit Publicity	
23.00	Electrical Labor		71.00	General Expenses	
24.00	Grip Labor		72.00	Indirect Costs	
25.00	Production Sound Labor		**Total "D" (Other)**		
26.00	Transportation Labor		80.00	Completion Guarantee (%)	
27.00	Fringe Benefits		81.00	Contingency (%)	
28.00	Production Office Expenses		82.00	Cost of Issue (%)	
29.00	Studio / Backlot Expenses		**GRAND TOTAL**		
30.00	Location Office Expenses				
31.00	Site Expenses				
32.00	Unit Expenses				
33.00	Travel & Living Expenses				
34.00	Transportation				
35.00	Construction Materials				
36.00	Art Supplies				
37.00	Set Dressing				
38.00	Props				
39.00	Special Effects				
40.00	Animals				
41.00	Wardrobe Supplies				
42.00	Makeup / Hair Supplies				
43.00	Video Studio Facilities				
44.00	Video Remote Technical Facilities				

BLANK BUDGET TOP SHEET #2

Blank Budget Top Sheet #2

"Film Title"

Type of Production (ie: Feature Film, # Episode Series…)

Shoot [Format] / Post [Format]

[List of Unions or Non-Union]

Budget prepared by: [Name]

Shoot [Month] & [Year]

Location vs. Studio

Budget dated: [Date]

Acct	Description	Total
801-00	Story & Other Rights	
803-00	Writing	
805-00	Producer & Staff	
807-00	Director & Staff	
809-00	Talent	
810-00	Fringe Benefits (ATL)	
Total Above The Line		
811-00	Production Staff	
813-00	Camera	
814-00	Art Department	
815-00	Set Construction	
816-00	Special Effects	
817-00	Set Operations	
819-00	Electrical	
821-00	Set Dressing	
823-00	Action Props	
825-00	Picture Vehicles & Animals	
826-00	Computer Graphics	
827-00	Special Photography	
829-00	Extra Talent	
831-00	Wardrobe	
833-00	Makeup & Hair	
835-00	Sound	
837-00	Location	
838-00	Digital Capture Stock	
839-00	Transportation	
841-00	Film & Lab	
843-00	Tests	
845-00	Facility Expenses	
847-00	Second Unit	
848-00	Special Unit	
849-00	Fringe Benefits (Prdn.)	
Total Below The Line Production		

Acct	Description	Total
851-00	Editing & Projection	
852-00	Digital Picture (Post Production)	
853-00	Music	
855-00	Sound (Post Production)	
857-00	Film, Tape & Library	
858-00	Visual Effects	
859-00	Titles & Opticals	
860-00	Fringe Benefits (Post Prdn.)	
Total Below The Line Post Production		
861-00	Insurance	
862-00	Publicity	
864-00	Product Placement	
865-00	General Expenses	
866-00	Fringe Benefits (Other)	
867-00	Insurance Claims	
869-00	Completion Costs	
870-00	Contingency	
Total Other		
GRAND TOTAL		

BLANK BUDGET TOP SHEET #3

Blank Budget Top Sheet #3

"Film Title"
Type of Production (ie: Feature Film, # Episode Series...)

Shoot [Format] / Post [Format]

[List of Unions or Non-Union]

Budget prepared by: [Name]

Shoot [Month] & [Year]

Location vs. Studio

Budget dated: [Date]

Acct	Description	Total		Acct	Description	Total
A	Story & Script			O	Insurances	
B	Producer / Director			P	Social Security & Fringes	
BE	Main Cast			Q	Publicity	
Total A+B+BE (Above The Line)				R	Miscellaneous Expenses	
C01	Production Management			S1	Construction Labor	
C02	Assistant Director / Continuity			S1A	Construction Materials	
C03	Technical Advisors			S2	Set Dressing Labor	
C04	Camera Crew			S3	Operating Labor	
C05	Sound Crew			S4	Striking Costs	
C06	Editorial Staff			S5	Lighting / Spotting Labor	
C07	Stills Camera Staff			S7	Foreign Labour	
C08	Wardrobe Staff			S8	Properties	
C09	Makeup Staff			T	Special Effects	
C10	Hair Dressing Staff			U	Location Facilities	
C11	Casting			**Total O thru U**		
C12	Production Accountancy			Y	Finance & Legal	
C13	Projectionists			Z	Overheads	
C14	Miscellaneous Studio Staff			**Total Y+Z (Other)**		
C15	Foreign Unit Technicians				Completion Insurance (%)	
D	Art Department			**GRAND TOTAL**		
E1A	Cast (Non-Principals)					
E2	Stand-Ins / Doubles / Stunts					
E3	Crowd					
F	Music					
G	Costumes & Wigs					
H	Miscellaneous Production Store					
I	Production Media / Post Services					
J	Studio Rentals (Prdn. & Post)					
K	Equipment					
L	Power					
M1	Travel & Transport					
M2	Studio & Other Transport					
N1	Hotel & Living Expenses					
N2	Studio Hotel & Living					
Total C01 thru N2						

A Film Production Management 101 form

BUDGET BREAKDOWN SAMPLE #1 "THE LISTS"

Budget Breakdown Sample #1 - "The Lists"

Locations	Cast
Hilary's Galley – I I I I	Hilary – I I I I I I I I I I I I I I I I I I I I I I I I I I I I I I I I I I I I I I I I I I I
Huw's Workshop – I N N I I I I	Huw – I I I I I I I I I I I I I I I I I I I I I I I I I I I I I I I I I
Hilary's Livingroom – I I I N N I I I I I N I	Max - I I I I I I I I I I I I I I I I I I I I I I I I I I
Park – I I I I I I I I N N I	Thug - I I I I I I I I I I I I
Ext. Max's House – I N N N N I I N	Little Girl - I I I I I I I I I I I I I I I I I I I I I I I I
Indoor Playground – I I I I	
Hospital Room – I I I	
City Establishing - I	
Max's Back Porch – I I N N N N N I	
Huw's Forge – N N N N	
Solarium – I I	

Extras	Vehicles
Man with Dog – I I	Max's car – I I I I I I I I
Indoor playground kids – I I I I	Hilary's car – I I I I I I I I I I I
Drivers of passing cars – I I I I	Huw's Truck – I I I I I I
Nurse – I I	Mini-bus – I
Gardening Grandmother – I I I I I I I	Backhoe – I
4 Bridge Players – I	Tank – I I I
Backhoe Operator - I	

Other pages may track: Children, SPFX, CGI, Stunts, Songs, Animals, Other Special Notes...

BUDGET BREAKDOWN SAMPLE #2 "THE SPREADSHEET"

Budget Breakdown Sample #2 - "The Spreadsheet"

Sc#	Set	D/N	# Pg	Cast	Extras	Animals	Vehicles	Other Notes
1	City Skyline	N	0.5	-	peds,drivers		cars	
2	Office	N	1	M,Hw		dog		
3	Parking Lot	N	2.5	M,T			M,T,cars	gun fire
4	City Streets	D	1	M,T,Stunt drivers	peds,drivers		M,T,cars	car chase
5	Indoor Playground	D	2	M,Hy,F	kids,parents			
6	Forge	N	2	Hw,Hy		dog		atmosphere
7	Boat Galley	D	1.5	Hy,F		seal		smoke

Leger
M = Max
Hw = Huw
Hy = Hilary
T = Thug
F = Friend

DETAIL PAGE OF A BUDGET

"Film Title"

The figures on this form are for demonstration purposes only and are not to be taken as financial advice.

Acct	Description	Amount		Rate	Sub-Total	Total
10-0	**CAST**					**89,438**
10-1	**Principal Cast Members**					
	Character #1					
	- Shoot Days	20	days	1,000	20,000	
	- OT	20	hours	200	4,000	
	Sub-total				24,000	
	- Rights Pre-buy	50	%	24,000	12,000	
	- Prep Fittings/Rehearsals	2	days	500	1,000	
	- H/M/W	20	hours	130	2,600	
	Character #1 - Total				**39,600**	
	Character #2					
	- Shoot Days	15	days	600	9,000	
	- OT	15	hours	100	1,500	
	Sub-total				10,500	
	- Rights Pre-buy	50	%	10,500	5,250	
	- Prep Fittings/Rehearsals	2	days	300	600	
	- H/M/W	15	hours	70	1,050	
	Character #2 - Total				**17,400**	
	Total 10-1 Principal Cast Members					57,000
10-4	**Casting Director**		Allow			15,000
10-4.5	**Casting Facilities**		Allow			2,000

… and elsewhere in the budget …

Acct	Description	Amount		Rate	Sub-Total	Total
20-2	**Production Manager**					
	- Prep	5	wks	3,500	17,500	
	- Shoot	5	wks	3,500	17,500	
	- Wrap	2	wks	3,500	7,000	
	- Hiatus	0	wks	3,500	-	
	- Stat Holidays	0.2	wks	3,500	700	
	See Fringes in Category 45-0					
	Total 20-2 Production Manager					42,700
20-5	**Production Coordinator**					
	- Prep	4	wks	2,000	8,000	
	- Shoot	5	wks	2,000	10,000	
	- Wrap	2	wks	2,000	4,000	
	- Hiatus	0	wks	2,000	-	
	- Stat Holidays	0.2	wks	2,000	400	
	See Fringes in Category 45-0					
	Total 20-5 Production Coordinator					22,400

CHECKLIST OF QUESTIONS/NOTES FOR BUDGET CREATION (PAGE 1 OF 2)

Checklist of Questions/Notes for Budget Creation   Page 1 of 2

Project Title   _____
Type (MOW, FF, series, #eps)   _____
Budget size (estimate)   _____
When shoot   _____
days shoot   _____
When delivery/# months post   _____
Shoot: 3D, HD, digital, 35 or 16   _____
For Distributors/Broadcasters   _____

ATL - Script Rights
Original vs. cost of rights/who   _____
Nationality of original work   _____

ATL - Writer(s)
Names/rates/nationality   _____
Union   _____
Rights to be bought   _____
Travel: who/when/where   _____

ATL - Development
Spent to date/by who   _____
To be spent/by who   _____
Budget/bkdn _____;   Travel _____; Tax estimates _____; Loc scout _____

ATL - Producers
List names/Co's/rates/nations   _____
 /restrictions (ie: 5% of budget)   _____
XP(s)   _____
Producer(s)   _____
Assoc Producer(s)   _____
Line Producer   _____
Other(s)   _____
Producer Asst(s)   _____
Travel: Who/When/Where   _____

ATL - Director
List name/confirmed?/rate   _____
Rights to be bought   _____
Union   _____
Travel: When/Where   _____

ATL - Stars
List names/Roles   _____
 /Rates/Nationality   _____
Rights to be bought   _____
Travel: who/when/where   _____
Rehearsal/wdb/MU tests   _____

(cont)

A Film Production Management 101 form

CHECKLIST OF QUESTIONS/NOTES FOR BUDGET CREATION (PAGE 2 OF 2)

Checklist of Questions/Notes for Budget Creation – Page 2 of 2

BTL - Production
Union for cast _____

Union(s) for crew _____

SPFX _____

Stunts _____

Animals _____

Night shoots _____

Location vs. studio _____

Distant location _____

Period wardrobe/sets _____

# of Extras _____

Child Actors _____

Second Unit _____

B-Camera _____

Cranes/camera cars/etc _____

Previs _____

Other special notes _____

BTL - Post
Union for post crew _____

Facilities deals? _____

CGI _____

Music Composer - name/rate _____

Music rights _____

Stock footage _____

Titles - how fancy _____

Opticals _____

Delivery version(s) _____

BTL - Other
Publicity - how much _____

Insurance - E&O # of yrs _____

Legal - how much _____

Post Acctg - how much _____

Audit - how many _____

Corporate overhead - how much _____

Interim financing - what items _____

Est. interim loan size _____

Foreign currencies _____

Completion Bond
Company history _____

Contingency - %
_____

Which Financiers involved? _____

(inc. Distributors, Broadcasters) _____

Contact info _____

A Film Production Management 101 form

TIME SHEET

Production Company Ltd.   **TIME SHEET**

Soc.# _____

Name/Co.: _____

Address: _____

Rate: _____   For Week Ending: _____

APPROVALS			
Exec.P:	_____	PM:	_____
Dept.Head:		Acct:	

Day	Call	Lunch		Dinner		Wrap	HRS	ST	1.5	2.0	2.5	3.0	MP	TA	HRS
Sun															
Mon															
Tue															
Wed															
Thu															
Fri															
Sat															
Total															
Equivalent ST Hours:															

Notes:	Item	Account	Amount
	AMOUNT PAID		

A Film Production Management 101 form

ACCIDENT REPORT FORM

ACCIDENT REPORT	
Date of Accident:	Time of Accident:
Date/Time Reported:	By Whom:
Description of Location:	
Injured Person (Full Name):	
Age:	Occupation:
Address:	Telephone:
Nature/Extent of Injuries:	
Attending Physician:	Address:
First Aid Rendered: Y / N	By Whom:
Hospital Name:	Conveyance (Name):
Witnesses Names/Addresses:	
Description of Incident:	
Reported by:	Signature:

A Film Production Management 101 form

WALKIE-TALKIE SIGN-OUT FORM

Prdn Title: **WALKIE-TALKIE SIGN-OUT**   Page:

Name/Dept	Walkie #	Serial #	Accessories	Date Taken	Date Return	Sign

A Film Production Management 101 form

CELL PHONE SIGN-OUT FORM

Prdn Title: **CELL PHONE SIGN-OUT**   Page:

Name/Dept	Cell Phone #	Serial #	Accessories & Plan Info	Date Taken	Date Return	Sign

A Film Production Management 101 form

KEYS & SECURITY CARDS SIGN-OUT FORM

Prdn Title: **KEYS & SECURITY CARDS SIGN-OUT**   Page:

Name	Dept	Key(s) / Security Card	Date Taken	Sign	Date Return	Sign

A Film Production Management 101 form

EQUIPMENT RENTAL LOG

Prdn Title:		**EQUIPMENT RENTAL LOG**				Page:
Date	**Rental Co.**	**Eqt Rented**	**Dept**	**Ep#**	**Start/End Rental Dates**	**Price**

A Film Production Management 101 form

COURIER LOG

Prdn Title:	COURIER LOG				Page:
Date Sent	**To Whom (From)**	**Reason/Contents**	**Ep#**	**Dept**	**Courier Co / Waybill #**

A Film Production Management 101 form

LONG DISTANCE LOG

Prdn Title:		LONG DISTANCE LOG		Page:	
Date	**Time**	**Phone Number**	**Your Name**	**Personal**	**Business**

A Film Production Management 101 form

COPIER PAPER COUNT

Prdn Title: _____   **COPIER PAPER COUNT**   Page: _____

Date	white	pink	blue	green	yellow	gold	purple	Legal	11x17	no-hole
Fri.										
Fri.										
Fri.										
Fri.										
Fri.										
Fri.										
Fri.										
Fri.										
Fri.										
Fri.										
Fri.										
Fri.										
Fri.										
Fri.										
Fri.										
Fri.										
Fri.										

A Film Production Management 101 form

DEVELOPMENT COST REPORT

Development Cost Report

"Production Adventure For Me"
Development Cost Report
as of 1 Dec 2015

The figures on this form are for demonstration purposes only and are not to be taken as financial advice.

Code	Description	Actual Cost	Dev Budget	Difference
1.00	Story Rights	10,000	10,000	-
2.00	Script Writing & Fringes	30,000	30,000	-
3.00	Story Editor & Fringes	5,000	5,000	-
4.00	Research	1,794	2,000	206
5.00	Budget/Breakdown	3,000	3,000	-
6.00	Travel & Living	2,312	2,000	(312)
7.00	Office Overhead & Accounting	4,894	5,000	106
8.00	Producer Fees	13,000	13,000	-
	TOTAL	**70,000**	**70,000**	**-**

A Film Production Management 101 form

CREW LIST (PAGE 1 OF 2)

"Film Production Adventure"

Production Company Ltd.
Address
Telephone/Fax/Email/Website

Parent Company Ltd.
Address
Telephone/Fax/Email/Website

Co-Production Company Ltd.
Address
Telephone/Fax/Email/Website

Key Funding Company Ltd.
Address
Telephone/Fax/Email/Website

CREW LIST

GREEN REVISED

3 Dec 2013

executive producer	**NAME** c/o Company name	office phone # email address
executive in charge of production	**NAME** c/o Company name	office phone # email address
supervising producer	**NAME** c/o Company name	office phone # email address
associate producer	**NAME** c/o Company name	office phone # email address
producer	**NAME** home address	home/cell phone # email address
line producer	**NAME** home address	home/cell phone # email address
director	**NAME** home address Agent: Agency & address Agent's name	home/cell phone # email address agency phone # agency fax #
writer	**NAME** home address Agent: Agency & address Agent's name	home/cell phone # email address agency phone # agency fax #

Continuing with contact information for:

PRODUCTION OFFICE
production manager
assistant production manager
production coordinator
assistant coordinator
office P.A.
assistant to producer
tutor

ACCOUNTING DEPARTMENT
production accountant
assistant accountant

(cont)

A Film Production Management 101 form

CREW LIST (PAGE 2 OF 2)

CASTING DEPARTMENT
casting director (leads)
casting director (on location)
extras casting

PUBLICITY
publicist
stills photographer
digital media team

PRODUCTION - ON SET
1st assistant director
2nd assistant director
3rd assistant director
set production assistant
continuity supervisor

LOCATION DEPARTMENT
location manager
assistant location manager
location assistant

ART DEPARTMENT
production designer
art director
1st assistant art director
2nd assistant art director
computer graphics
draftsperson

PREVISUALIZATION
previs team
storyboard artist

SETS DEPARTMENT
set decorator
lead set dresser
set dresser
on-set set dresser

PROPS DEPARTMENT
property master
lead props
props buyer

VISUAL EFFECTS
effects supervisor
computer animation
special effects
prosthetics

WARDROBE DEPARTMENT
wardrobe designer
wardrobe mistress
seamstress

HAIR/MAKEUP DEPARTMENT
hair designer
makeup artist

CAMERA DEPARTMENT
director of photography
camera operator
1st assistant camera
2nd assistant camera
data management technician
camera department trainee

SOUND DEPARTMENT
sound recordist
boom operator

ELECTRICAL DEPARTMENT
gaffer
best boy
electric
generator operator

GRIP DEPARTMENT
key grip
dolly grip
grip

STUNTS DEPARTMENT
stunt coordinator

TRANSPORTATION DEPARTMENT
transport coordinator
picture vehicle coordinator
transport captain
head driver
driver

CATERING/CRAFT SERVICE
caterer
craft service

CONSTRUCTION DEPARTMENT
construction manager
head carpenter
carpenter
scenic painter
construction labor

POST-PRODUCTION
post production supervisor
music composer
picture editor
assistant editor
sound effects editor
dialogue editor

CAST LIST

(On Letterhead)

"Film Production Adventure

CAST LIST

BLUE REVISED - 2 Dec 2013

1. Max   **PERFORMER'S NAME**   Talent Agency
                          Home address   (Agent's Name)
                          Home/Cell phone   Agency address
                          Home email   Agency phone / fax
                                                     Agency email

2. Huw MacConneach   **STAR'S NAME**   Talent Agency/Manager
                          c/o Hotel   (Agent/Manager Name)
                          Hotel address   Agency address
                          Hotel phone   Agency phone / fax
                                                     Agency email

3. Friend   **PERFORMER'S NAME**   Talent Agency
                          Home address   (Agent's Name)
                          Home/Cell phone   Agency address
                          Home email   Agency phone / fax
                                                     Agency email

4. Little Girl   **PERFORMER'S NAME**   Talent Agency
                          Home address   (Agent's Name)
                          Home/Cell phone   Agency address
                          Home email   Agency phone / fax
                          (Parent's names)   Agency email

STUNTS - **Stunt Agency**, address, phone, fax, email, web page

51. Stunt Coordinator   **STUNT PERFORMER NAME**   Home/Cell phone
                          Home address
                          Home email

STAND-INS

Female Stand-in   **STAND-IN'S NAME**   Home/Cell phone
                          Home address   Email

Male Stand-in   **STAND-IN'S NAME**   Home/Cell phone
                          Home address   Email

N.B. Character numbers match A.D. character number assignments (i.e., on all schedules and call sheets).

A Film Production Management 101 form

CONTACT LIST (PAGE 1 OF 2)

"Film Production Adventure"

Contact List

PINK REVISED   4 December 2013

Air Conditioning	**Company Name** Address Website Contact Person	Telephone # Fax # Email
Apartment Rental	**Company Name** Address Website Contact Person	Telephone # Fax # Email
Batteries	**Company Name** Address Website Contact Person Account #	Telephone # Fax # Email

Continuing with this format, list suppliers, contact names, and account numbers for the following subjects:

Casting Facility

Cell Phones & Wireless

Cleaners

Coffee Machine/Supplies

Computer Rental

Conference Operator

Courier (in town)

Courier (international)

Customs Broker

Doctor

Disposal & Containers

Drafting Equipment

Electrician

Equipment (camera/grip/elec.)

Equipment (scaffolding)

Expendables (gels, etc.)

(cont)

A Film Production Management 101 form

CONTACT LIST (PAGE 2 OF 2)

Florist	Script Research Company
Funding Agencies	Security
Furniture Rental	Stock Footage
Guarantor Company (the Bond)	Studio
Hotel	Tables & Chairs Rental
Image Capture Stock (Film, Drives..)	Taxi
Immigration	Telephone Rental
Internet ISP/FTP	Telephone: Long Distance
Limousine	Towel Service
Location Supplies	Travel Agent
Music Rights Clearances	Tutor
Moving & Storage Company	Unions & Guilds
Nurses/Ambulance Attendants	Vehicle Rental
Office Rental	Vehicles: Honeywagons
Office Supplies	Vehicles: Winnies
Payroll Service	Vehicles: Winnie pump-out
Photofinishing	Vehicles: Road/Traffic Info
Plumber	Vehicles: Tow Truck/Repairs
Post: Laboratory	Video Rental
Post: Editing Facility	Video Stock
Post: Sound Editing Facility	Walkie-Talkies
Post: Transfers	Wardrobe Supplier/Builder
Printer/Scanner/Fax Machine	Washer/Dryer
Printing Company	Water Machine
Product Placement	Weather Information
Recycling	
Safety Supplies	

A Film Production Management 101 form

CALL SHEET SAMPLE #1

"FILM PRODUCTION ADVENTURE"	**CALL SHEET**	Day:	11
Production Company Inc.		Date:	FRIDAY 31 OCTOBER 2014

Office #: 555-1212

		BREAKFAST READY:	**0630**
Producer/Director:	(Name)	LEAVE FOR SET:	0730
Production Manager:	(Name)		
Assistant Director:	(Name)	**On Location:**	**0800**
		Shooting Call:	0915
LOCATION: MAPS HANDED OUT AT BREAKY		Lunch:	1300

WEATHER: Cloudy, windy, Rainy, hi:14, lo:6, POP:90%   SUNRISE/SET: 0712-1801

POLICE: (Telephone #)		AMBULANCE: (Telephone #)			FIRE: (Telephone #)

SC#	SET	D/N	CAST	PGS	SYNOPSIS
*** MORE "DRIVING & PROCESS" BLOCK SHOOTING THE FOLLOWING "HUW CAR" SCENES ***					
8pt	INT HUW'S CAR	Day	2.4.	6/8	Next day, same route
9pt	INT HUW'S CAR	Day	2.4.	1 7/8	Hilary gives advice on better sleep
10pt	INT HUW'S CAR	Ev'g	2.4.	1 0/8	Magic hour: Arriving to work
Reduced unit...					
26	INT HILARY'S CAR	D4N	4.	---	Isn't that the same street sign?
Target of opportunity...					
1	INT HUW'S CAR	Morng	2.4.	2/8	Gosh, ya gotta love these hours
2	INT HUW'S CAR	Ev'g	2.	1/8	Home so soon?

⏰ ⏰ ⏰ **C L O C K S   G O   B A C K   O N E   H O U R   T O N I G H T** ⏰ ⏰ ⏰

CHARACTER	ARTIST	LV.COTT	H/M/W	SET
2. HUW	**(Name)**	0730	0800	0900
4. HILARY	**(Name)**	0730	0800	0900

SET REQUIREMENTS

VEHICLES		-Huw's car on tow rig for block shooting, then home for processing
		-Hilary's car on set for "Flashlight scene"
		-Hilary's car on standby for reduced unit
LIGHTING/GRIP	9:	Glare of sun passes
	10:	Door opens to beam of diffuse light, Car moves into sun
ART DEPT	8-10:	Huw's littered car dressing, Bug splat on windshield
	26:	Street sign: "The Middle of Nowhere"
MAKEUP/HAIR	10:	Huw looks haggard
WARDROBE	8-9:	Huw's gym clothes, Huw's watch
	10:	Huw's gym shoe (left)
NOTES	26:	Dry ice

TUESDAY ADVANCE SCHEDULE					Cloudy windy cool hi:10 lo:2 POP:60%(0650-1714)
4	EXT MAX'S HOUSE	Morng	---	1/8	Establishing shot
23	INT LIVING ROOM	Morng	1.	4/8	Max breaks in to his own house
25	INT LIVING ROOM	Morng	1.	2/8	Max asleep out on the couch
24	INT KITCHEN	Morng	1.	3/8	Max learns all about hot chocolate
28	INT LIVING ROOM	Night	1.	2/8	Max slept through the whole day?!?

Call sheet joke here...

CALL SHEET SAMPLE #2 (PAGE 1 OF 2)

"FILM PRODUCTION ADVENTURE"	**CALL SHEET**	Day:	14
Film Company Inc.		Date:	FRI., FEBRUARY 14, 2014

Address
Telephone
Night Line Telephone #

		CALL:	**3:00am**
Exec. Producers	(Name)	Gennie Op x2:	2:30am
	(Name)	Honeywagon:	2:30am
Producers	(Name)	MU/Hair:	3:00am
	(Name)	Wdb:	2:30am
Prdn. Manager	(Name)	Craft:	2:15am
Director	(Name)	Substantials:	5:30am No:85
		Lunch:	9:00am No:85 Box:300

Episode #5 "It's a N-Ice World"

	Sunrise:	6:39am
	Sunset:	5:36pm
Set Cell: (Tel.#)	Weather:	sunny, windy, warmish
Loc Cell: (Tel.#)		POP 0% Lo:-5 Hi:+5

LOCATION: (SEE MAP)
1. Hockey Arena, (Address)

SC#	SET/DESCRIPTION	CAST	D/N	PGS	LOC
34-B	INT ICE SURFACE The dream-game	1,4,6,12,Black team x15, White team x12,Refs x3,Coach x1, Fans x298, Photographer x1	N10	3 4/8	1
34-F	INT STANDS Fans cheer them on	12,Fans x300	N10	1/8	1
34-A	INT BLACK BENCH But we're bad guys?	1,2(vo),4,6,Black team x15, Fans x300	N10	1 0/8	1
34-D	INT BLACK BENCH Somebody wake me?	1,2(vo),4,6,Black team x15, Fans x300	N10	3/8	1

* 2ND CAMERA DAY   TOTAL: 5 0/8

CHARACTER	ARTIST	PU	H/M/W	SET	LOC
1 Max	(Name)	3:15am	3:30am	4:00am	1
2 Huw V/O	(Name)	--	N/A	N/A	
4 Hilary	(Name)	--	3:30am	4:00am	1
6 Thug	(Name)	--	3:30am	4:00am	1
12 Reporter	(Name)	--	3:00am	4:00am	1

PHOTO DOUBLES

1A Max Double	--	2:30am	3:00am	1	
4A Hilary Double	--	2:30am	3:00am	1	
6A Thug Double	--	2:30am	3:00am	1	

EXTRAS

Cast of thousands! ... uh, hundreds! Fans x298	--	4:00am	1	
Coach x1, Photographer x1	--	4:00am	1	
Black team x15, White Team x12	2:30am	3:00am	1	
Refs x3	3:00am	4:00am	1	

1st AD:(Name/Phone)   **2nd AD**:(Name/Phone)   **Transport**:(Name/Phone)

CALL SHEET SAMPLE #2 (PAGE 2 OF 2)

Call Sheet Day #14 - Page 2 of 2

DAILY CREW
2:30am - P.A. Daily x1, TAD Daily x1 to report to set.
3:00am - 2nd Camera x1, 2nd Focus Puller x1 to report to set.

TRANSPORTATION
2:30am - Honeywagon hot and cooking!
3:15am - Transport to pick up "Max" at the hotel

ADVANCE SCHEDULE - DAY 15 - THURSDAY, FEBRUARY 22, 2001

30	INT ARENA STANDS	1,4	D9	4/8	1
45-A	INT STANDS	12,Fans x35	N11	1 0/8	1
45-C	INT STANDS	Fans x35	N11	1/8	1
45-B	INT WHITE BENCH	1,2(vo),4,7,Fans x35	N11	7/8	1
35	INT ARENA CORRIDOR	1,2(vo),7	N10	1/8	1

RUSHES OF DAY 13
4:30pm - at the Lab

Crew Rep: (Name)   **Performer's Union:** (Name/Phone)   **Safety Rep**: (Name)

Callsheet joke here...

Map to location (with closest hospital noted) here...

PRODUCTION REPORT FORM #1 (BLANK)

DAILY PRODUCTION REPORT – [Production Company]										DAY		of	

Title

Producer

Director

Sets

Locations

Date

Scheduled Dates

Weather

Crew Call | **Lunch** | **Wrap**

#1 Shot AM | #1 Shot PM

	Scenes	Pages		Minutes		Setups
Script			Prev		Prev	
Taken Prev			Today		Today	
Today			Total		Total	
To Date			Avg		Avg	
To be taken						
Avg/Day				Running Time	

Scene #'s

Wildtracks

#	Cast	Character	SWF	Call	Set	Lunch out	Lunch in	Wrap	Sound Stock Usage
									of
									Avg Total Pic Stock Use/Day

Position	Crew Name	Set	Wrap	Lunch out	Lunch in	Pic Stock Usage	HDD/stock	HDD/stock	HDD/stock
Director						Received Previous			
Prdn Mgr						Received Today			
Loc Mgr						Total Received			
1st AD						Use Previous			
2nd AD						Used Today			
Continuity						Total Used			
DOP						On Hand			
1st AC						NOTES:			
2nd AC									
Gaffer									
Electric									
Key Grip									
Grip									
Sound									
Boom Op									
Art Dir									
Set Dec									
Prop Mstr									
Costumes									
Cost. Asst									
Hair/MU									
Stills Photo									
PA's						1st AD:	PM:		

PRODUCTION REPORT FORM #2 (BLANK) (PAGE 1 OF 2)

[Production Company Name]	MAIN UNIT DAYS _____ of _____
DAILY PRODUCTION REPORT	2ND UNIT DAYS _____ of _____
Page 1 of 2	TOTAL DAYS [____] of [____]

Title _____   Date _____

Producer _____   Director _____

Start date _____   Finish date _____

Sets _____

Locations _____

Weather

Crew Call [____]   Lunch [____]   Wrap [____]

#1 Shot AM [____]   #1 Shot PM [____]

Script Running Time [____]

Scene #'s

	Scenes	Pages		Minutes		Setups
Script			Prev		Prev	
Taken Prev			Today		Today	
Today			Total		Total	
To Date						
To be taken			Avg		Avg	

Pic Stock		Prev	Today	Total
[HDD/	Gross			
Stock]	Print			
	NG			
	Waste			
[HDD/	Gross			
Stock]	Print			
	NG			
	Waste			

Wildtracks

Pic	Total Rec'd	Today	Used	On Hand
[HDD/Stock]				
[HDD/Stock]				
GRAND TOTAL				

#	Cast	Character	SWF	Call	Wrap	Lunch out	Lunch in

Sd Stock	Prev	_____
Usage	Today	_____
	Total	_____

Cash Extras	Wdb-Set	Wrap	Amt

Qty	Act/Per/App	Type of Extra	H/M/W	Set	Wrap	Lunch out	Lunch in

TOTAL AMT CASH EXTRAS:

Asst Director

Prdn Mgr:

PRODUCTION REPORT FORM #2 (BLANK) (PAGE 2 OF 2)

DAILY PRODUCTION REPORT – Page 2 of 2		Title	0	
Director	Day	0	Date	0
1st AD	Prdn Coord		Gun Wrangler	
2nd AD	Coord Asst		Animals	
3rd AD	Office PA		Wrangler	
Set PA	Art Director		Nurse	
Continuity	1st Asst Art		Ambl. Attend	
Craft Serv	2nd Asst Art		Security	
DOP	Art Trainee		Policemen	
Cam.Op	Set Dec		ETF	
1st A.C.	Lead Sets		Vehicles (list):	
2nd A.C	Set Dresser			
DMT	On Set Dress			
Cam.Trainee	FX Super			
Gaffer	FX Asst			
Best Boy	3D Artists			
Electric	2D Artists			
Gennie Op.	Computer Artist			
Key Grip	Prosthetics			
Best Boy Grip	SPFX			
Grip	SPFX Asst		Pic.Vehicles:	
Sound Mixer	Stunt Coord			
Boom Op	Stills Photog.			
Props Master	Post Super.		Substantials at:	x
Lead Props	Editor		Lunches at:	x
Props Buyer	Asst Editor		Dinners at	x
Cost. Design	DAILIES:			
Ast Cost.Des.				
Wdb Asst				
Seamstress				
Hair Design				
MU Artist				
Trans Coord				
Trans Captain				
Drivers				
NOTES:				

LOCATION RELEASE FORM

LOCATION RELEASE

*This form is a sample to inspire you to design one with your own legal counsel
appropriate to your production, and is not to be taken as legal advice.*

To: Production Company Inc.
       Address
       Telephone / Fax
       Email / Website

In consideration of the sum of _____, and for other good and valuable consideration, the receipt and sufficiency whereof is hereby acknowledged:

I hereby grant Production Company Inc., its affiliates, licensees, successors and assigns (hereinafter collectively the "Company") the irrevocable right, in perpetuity, to use the footage taken of the premises (the "Footage") located at:

_____   (the "Premises")

on the following date(s):

_____

in connection with the production, distribution and exploitation of the feature film presently entitled "Film Production Adventure" (the "Film"), to edit, delete, alter and amend the Footage in any manner and to juxtapose the Footage with any other material. The Film and/or the Footage may be exploited throughout the world, in perpetuity and in any and all media now or hereafter devised without any further payment to me. The Company has no obligation to use the Footage in the Film.

The Company will insure the Premises for damages as a result of accident or negligence on the part of the Company.

Should the Company need to return to the Premises for retakes for whatever reason, I agree to accept terms no less favorable than the terms stated herein.

I do hereby release and forever discharge the Company of, from and against all actions, causes of action, claims, suits, judgments and demands which may by made against the Company by virtue of the appearance of the Premises, in any manner whatsoever, in the Film.

I warrant that I have the right to grant the above rights to the Company and enter into this Release.

Dated this _____ day of _____, _____.

Witness: _____   Signature: _____

                                          Name: _____

                                          Title: _____

                                          Address: _____

                                          _____

                                          Tel: _____

A Film Production Management 101 form

LOCATION LETTER

Location Letter

(on letterhead)

(Date)

TO THE BUSINESSES, PATRONS AND RESIDENTS OF MAIN STREET, FILM AVENUE AND NEW STREET:

Film Company Inc. is presently filming scenes in and around (City) for an independent feature film presently entitled "Film Production Adventure." This production is a family comedy about an unlikely threesome who while making a movie about Grandma's bad cooking, learn how to live life to the fullest at the same time.

On January 4, 2014, we will be filming at 123 Main Street on the corner of Main Street and Film Avenue. We will also be filming in the park on Main Street at the same corner. The shots at 123 Main Street will be exterior shots of the building. The shots in the park will be of our hero, Max, confronting his nemesis with hilarious results.

We will be filming between the hours of 3:30 p.m. and 10:00 p.m. We will be parking our vehicles on Film Avenue and on New Street.

We are an experienced crew and we are aware of the need for street access and a calm atmosphere with as little disruption as possible while working in your neighborhood.

We hope that our presence does not cause you any inconvenience and appreciate your patience in this matter. If you have any questions, please call me on my cell phone (telephone #) or my assistant (Name) at the production office (telephone #). On the day, either I, or my assistant, will be on site during the set-up and shooting if you have an immediate concern.

Sincerely,

(Name)
Location Manager
contact number(s)

PETTY CASH REPORT

Petty Cash Report

Name _____   Production Title _____

Dept _____   Date _____

#	DATE	TO WHOM	PURPOSE	ACCT	NET AMT	TAX	TOTAL
1							
2							
3							
4							
5							
6							
7							
8							
9							
10							
11							
12							

APPROVALS		TOTALS:			
Ex.P:	PM:	MINUS ADVANCE:			
DEPT:	ACCT:	BALANCE DUE:			

DISTRIBUTION:

A Film Production Management 101 form

PURCHASE ORDER (P.O.) SAMPLE

"Film Production Adventure"
Production Company Ltd.
Production Company Address
Production Company Phone
Production Company Fax

Purchase Order No.   007

To: *Supplier Company* *Supplier Address* *Supplier Phone, Fax, Email*	Ship to: *Studio* *Studio Address* *Contact Person*
Contact Name: *Person Name*	**Delivery Date:** *7 Dec 2015*
Ordered by: *Wilhelm*	**Tax #:** *Attached Exemption Form*
Date ordered: *5 Dec 2015*	**Terms:** *Invoice*

Qty	Description	Unit	Total
5	*Really Necessary Items (Rental)*	*7.50/day*	*225.00*
	2 week rental (3-day week)		
	Delivery to Studio		*N/C*
	Pick up from office on 21 Dec 2015		*N/C*
	RE: LOCATION DEPARTMENT		
Approval: *DP*			*225.00*

Copy – Supplier   Copy – Production Company   Copy - Accounting

A Film Production Management 101 form

PURCHASE ORDER (P.O.) (BLANK)

"Film Production Adventure"
Production Company Ltd.
Production Company Address
Production Company Phone
Production Company Fax

Purchase Order No. ____

To:	Ship to:
Contact Name:	**Delivery Date:**
Ordered by:	**Tax #:**
Date ordered:	**Terms:**

Qty	Description	Unit	Total
Approval:			

Copy – Supplier   Copy – Production Company   Copy - Accounting

A Film Production Management 101 form

P.O. LOG

Prdn Title:		**P.O. LOG**				Page:	
PO#	To Whom	For What	Ep#	Dept	Date	Amt	

A Film Production Management 101 form

CHECK REQUISITION

"Film Production Adventure"
Production Company Ltd.
Production Company Address
Production Company Website
Production Company Phone / Fax / Email

CHECK REQUISITION

Date: _____   Required: _____   Amount/Currency: _____

PAYABLE TO: _____

_____

_____

TELEPHONE: _____

CONTACT: _____

FOR: _____

Mail Check: _____   Hold for P/U: _____   Give Check to: _____

APPROVALS:

Dept. Head: _____   PM: _____   Allocation: _____

Do not write below this line - for Accounting use only
* *

A Film Production Management 101 form

CASH FLOW SAMPLE (DETAIL)

Cash Flow Sample (Detail)

The figures on this form are for demonstration purposes only and are not to be taken as financial advice.

Code	Description	Budget	Dev/Prep4	Prep 3	Prep 2	Prep 1	Shoot 1	Shoot 2	Shoot 3	Shoot 4
1-1	Story Rights	7,500	7,500							
1-0	**STORY RIGHTS**	**7,500**	7,500							
2-1	Writer	85,000	25,000				50,000			
2-3	Story Editor	6,000	4,500	1,500						
2-4	Script Clearance	2,000			2,000					
2-9	Fringes	14,080	4,360	120			8,000			
2-0	**SCRIPT WRITING**	**107,080**								
4-1	Executive Producer	90,000	5,000				10,000			
4-2	Producer	90,000	5,000	5,000	5,000	5,000	5,000	5,000	5,000	5,000
4-7	Producer's Assistant	20,000	1,000	1,000	1,000	1,000	1,000	1,000	1,000	1,000
4-8	Producer Travel/Living	5,968	2,968			2,000	1,000			
4-9	Fringes	2,800	140	140	140	140	140	140	140	140
4-0	**PRODUCERS**	**208,768**								

... and further down the cash flow ...

Code	Description	Budget	Dev/Prep4	Prep 3	Prep 2	Prep 1	Shoot 1	Shoot 2	Shoot 3	Shoot 4
75-1	Contingency	150,000				7,500	7,500	7,500	7,500	7,500
75-0	**CONTINGENCY**	**150,000**								
79-1	Union Bonds - out	40,000			40,000					
	Union Bonds - in	(40,000)								
	Location Deposits - out	20,000		10,000	10,000					
	Location Deposits - in	(20,000)								
	Art Deposits - out	10,000	7,500	2,500						
	Art Deposits - in	(10,000)								(2,000)
79-0	**REFUNDABLES**	**-**								
	TOTAL OUTFLOWS	**2,500,000**	114,050	53,396	106,290	169,455	497,310	192,309	221,873	198,550

CASH FLOW SAMPLE (SUMMARY PAGE)

Cash Flow Sample (Summary Top Sheet)

[Boxed numbers are Financier's drawdowns assigned to the Bank for the interim financing loan.]

The figures on this form are for demonstration purposes only and are not to be taken as financial advice.

Acct	Description	Budget	Dev/Prep4	Prep 3	Prep 2	Prep 1	Shoot 1	Shoot 2	Shoot 3	Shoot 4
	TOTAL OUTFLOWS	1,500,000	68,430	32,038	63,774	101,673	298,386	115,385	133,124	119,130
INFLOWS										
	Financier #1	750,000	10,000	187,500			187,500			150,000
	Financier #2	375,000	35,000				225,000			
	Financier #3	150,000	5,000				45,000			
	Financier #4	175,000	20,000		20,000		20,000		20,000	
	Producer Deferral	50,000								
	TOTAL INFLOWS	1,500,000	70,000	187,500	20,000	-	477,500	-	20,000	150,000
	Inflows Minus Outflows		1,570	157,032	113,258	11,585	190,699	75,314	(37,810)	(6,939)
	INTERIM FINANCING	246,250							46,250	
	Running Balance		1,570	157,032	113,258	11,585	190,699	75,314	8,441	39,311

Acct	Description	Shoot 5	Shoot 6	Wrap 1	Wrap 2	Post Mo1	Post Mo2	Post Mo3	Post Mo4	Total
	TOTAL OUTFLOWS	131,346	110,117	57,745	18,778	41,249	64,803	87,890	56,133	1,500,000
INFLOWS										
	Financier #1			112,500			56,250		46,250	750,000
	Financier #2						75,000		40,000	375,000
	Financier #3			50,000			25,000		25,000	150,000
	Financier #4	20,000		20,000		20,000		20,000	15,000	175,000
	Producer Deferral								50,000	50,000
	TOTAL INFLOWS	20,000	-	182,500	-	20,000	156,250	20,000	176,250	1,500,000
	Inflows Minus Outflows	(118,285)	(228,402)	(103,647)	(122,425)	(143,674)	(52,227)	(120,117)	(0)	(0)
	INTERIM FINANCING	100,000	100,000				(100,000)	(20,000)	(126,250)	-
	Running Balance	27,965	17,848	142,603	123,825	102,576	94,023	6,133	(0)	(0)

COST REPORT SAMPLE (TOP SHEET)

Cost Report Sample Top Sheet (showing sample numbers and sample cell references/formulas)

The figures on this form are for demonstration purposes only and are not to be taken as financial advice.

COST REPORT Film Title: ___ Production Company: ___ For Period Ending: ___

	A	B	C	D	E	F	G	H	I	J
	Code	Description	This Period	Cost To Date	P.O.s	Total Costs	ETC	EFC	Budget	Variance
1	1.00	Story & Writer				=D+E	=H-F			=I-H
2	2.00	Producer				=D+E	=H-F			=I-H
3	3.00	Director				=D+E	=H-F			=I-H
4	4.00	Star				=D+E	=H-F			=I-H
5		Total ATL	=C1+2+3+4	=D1+2+3+4	=E1+2+3+4	=F1+2+3+4	=G1+2+3+4	=H1+2+3+4	=I1+2+3+4	=J1+2+3+4
6	10.00	Cast								
7	11.00	Crew								
8	12.00	Location/Studio								
9	13.00	Equipment								
10	14.00	Supplies								
11	15.00	Production Lab								
12		Total BTL Production								
13	20.00	Pic & Sound Edit								
14	21.00	Music & Rights	-	2,500	5,000	7,500	147,500	155,000	150,000	(5,000)
15	22.00	Post Lab	500	1,500	960	2,460	124,540	127,000	125,000	(2,000)
16	23.00	Publicity	4,500	12,500	2,250	14,750	30,250	45,000	45,000	-
17	24.00	General Costs	3,756	48,224	-	48,224	399,776	448,000	450,000	2,000
18		Total BTL Post/Other	8,756	64,724	8,210	72,934	702,066	775,000	770,000	(5,000)
19	30.00	Contingency	-	-	-	-	30,000	30,000	35,000	5,000
20		GRAND TOTAL	=C5+12+18+19	=D5+12+18+19	=E5+12+18+19	=F5+12+18+19	=G5+12+18+19	=H5+12+18+19	=I5+12+18+19	=J5+12+18+19

Sample Portion of Detail Page

COST REPORT Film Title: ___ Production Company: ___ For Period Ending: ___

Code	Description	This Period	Cost To Date	P.O.s	Total Costs	ETC	EFC	Budget	Variance
21.10	Music Composer	-	1,500	-	1,500	83,500	85,000	85,000	-
21.50	Music Rights	-	-	750	750	34,250	35,000	32,500	(2,500)
21.75	Stock Footage	500	-	210	210	6,790	7,000	7,500	500
21.00	MUSIC & RIGHTS	500	1,500	960	2,460	124,540	127,000	125,000	(2,000)

PM-ONLY COST REPORT #1 (SPREADSHEET FROM ACCOUNTING)

PM-Only Cost Report – Version #1 (Spreadsheet From Accounting)

The figures on this form are for demonstration purposes only and are not to be taken as financial advice.

COST REPORT

Film Title: _____

Production Company: _____

Code	Description	This Period	Cost To Date	P.O.s	PM ONLY	Total Costs	ETC	For Period Ending: EFC	Budget	Variance
218.10	Props Labor	2,650	5,300	-	160	5,460	18,550	24,010	24,750	740
	Shoot Wk 2 Overtime				160					
218.50	Props Purch/Rentals	1,250	19,576	350	2,000	21,926	3,074	25,000	20,000	(5,000)
	#1 Petty Cash Float				1,000					
	#2 Petty Cash Float				1,000					
218.80	Props - Kit Rental	200	400	-		400	800	1,200	900	(300)
218.0	**PROPS**	**4,100**	**25,276**	**350**		**27,786**	**22,424**	**50,210**	**45,650**	**(4,560)**
220.10	Camera Labor	9,050	18,100	-	544	18,644	45,250	63,894	62,300	(1,594)
	Shoot Wk 2 Overtime				544					
220.50	Camera Eqt Rental	7,200	7,200	-		7,200	36,000	43,200	45,000	1,800
220.55	Camera Daily Rentals	-	-	225	1,500	1,725	775	2,500	2,500	-
	Steadicam (maybe)				1,500					
220.70	Camera Expendables	1,294	1,339	37		1,376	1,124	2,500	2,500	-
220.80	Camera Kit Rentals	425		210		210	2,340	2,550	2,700	150
220.0	**CAMERA**	**17,969**	**26,639**	**472**		**29,155**	**85,489**	**114,644**	**115,000**	**356**

... and further down the cost report ...

Code	Description	This Period	Cost To Date	P.O.s	PM ONLY	Total Costs	ETC	For Period Ending: EFC	Budget	Variance
400.10	Insurance	-	23,500	-	(1,500)	22,000	8,500	30,500	30,500	-
	Pkg Insurance savings				(1,500)					
400.15	Medicals	150	675	75		750	-	750	750	-
400.50	Corporate Overhead	-	-	-		-	150,000	150,000	150,000	-
400.60	Legal	-	7,500	-		7,500	32,500	40,000	40,000	-
400.70	Post Accounting	-	-	-		-	4,800	4,800	4,800	-
400.75	Audit	-	-	-			5,000	5,000	5,000	-
400.90	Bank/Financing	-	374	-	54,000	54,374	20,626	75,000	75,000	-
	Interim Interest Estimate				54,000					
400.0	**GENERAL COSTS**	**150**	**32,049**	**75**		**84,624**	**221,426**	**306,050**	**306,050**	**-**

PM-ONLY COST REPORT #2 (SPREADSHEET MADE BY PM)

PM-Only Cost Report – Version #2 (Spreadsheet Made by PM)

The figures on this form are for demonstration purposes only and are not to be taken as financial advice.

COST REPORT   Film Title: _____

Code	Description	Total Costs	PM ONLY	PM + Total	ETC	EFC	Budget	Variance
						For Period Ending:		
218.10	Props Labor	5,300	**160**	5,460	18,550	24,010	24,750	740
	Shoot Wk 2 Overtime		160					
218.50	Props Purch/Rentals	19,926	**2,000**	21,926	3,074	25,000	20,000	(5,000)
	#1 Petty Cash Float		1,000					
	#2 Petty Cash Float		1,000					
218.80	Props - Kit Rental	400		400	800	1,200	900	(300)
218.0	**PROPS**	**25,626**		**27,786**	**22,424**	**50,210**	**45,650**	**(4,560)**
220.10	Camera Labor	18,100	544	18,644	45,250	63,894	62,300	(1,594)
	Shoot Wk 2 Overtime		544					
220.50	Camera Eqt Rental	7,200		7,200	36,000	43,200	45,000	1,800
220.55	Camera Daily Rentals	225	**1,500**	1,725	775	2,500	2,500	-
	Steadicam (maybe)		1,500					
220.70	Camera Expendables	1,376		1,376	1,124	2,500	2,500	-
220.80	Camera Kit Rentals	210		210	2,340	2,550	2,700	150
220.0	**CAMERA**	**27,111**		**29,155**	**85,489**	**114,644**	**115,000**	**356**

... and further down the cost report ....

Code	Description	Total Costs	PM ONLY	PM + Total	ETC	EFC	Budget	Variance
400.10	Insurance	23,500	(1,500)	22,000	8,500	30,500	30,500	-
	Pkg Insurance savings		(1,500)					
400.15	Medicals	750		750	-	750	750	-
400.50	Corporate Overhead	-		-	150,000	150,000	150,000	-
400.60	Legal	7,500		7,500	32,500	40,000	40,000	-
400.70	Post Accounting	-		-	4,800	4,800	4,800	-
400.75	Audit	-		-	5,000	5,000	5,000	-
400.90	Bank/Financing	374	54,000	54,374	20,626	75,000	75,000	-
	Interim Interest Estimate		54,000					
400.0	**GENERAL COSTS**	**32,124**		**84,624**	**221,426**	**306,050**	**306,050**	**-**

PM-ONLY COST REPORT #3 (BUDGET FORM)

PM-Only Cost Report – Version #3 (Budget Form)

The figures

Code	Description	Amount		Rate	Sub-Total	Total
218.0	**PROPS**					**50,210**
218.10	**Props Labor**					
	PROPERTY MASTER					
	- Prep	2.4	weeks	1,800	4,320	
	- Shoot	6	weeks	1,800	10,800	
	- Wrap	0.6	weeks	1,800	1,080	
	SHOOT WEEK 2 - OVERTIME				104	
	Total Property Master				**16,304**	
	PROPERTY ASSISTANT					
	- Prep	2.4	weeks	*850*	2,040	
	- Shoot	6	weeks	*850*	5,100	
	- Wrap	0.6	weeks	*850*	510	
	BUDGET AT $950; AGT AT $850					
	SHOOT WEEK 2 - OVERTIME				56	
	Total Property Assistant				**7,706**	
	Total 218.10 Props Labor					24,010
218.50	**Props Purchase/Rentals**		Allow		20,000	25,000
	ESTIMATED OVERAGE		*Allow*		*5,000*	
	(N.B. PETTY CASH FLOAT $1,000 X2)					
218.80	**Props Kit Rental**					
	2 kits x $75 each	6	weeks	150	900	1,200
	KITS @ $100 EACH (+$25 X2/WK)	*6*	*weeks*	*50*	*300*	

... and further down the "budget-format" cost report ...

Code	Description	Amount		Rate	Sub-Total	Total
400.0	**GENERAL COSTS**					**104,000**
400.10	**Insurance**					
	Entertainment Package		Allow		23,500	
	ENT. PKG BUDGET NOT $40,000 (TAKE $1(					
	E&O Insurance		Allow		5,500	
	Total 400.10 Insurance					29,000

... and further down the "budget-format" cost report ...

Code	Description	Amount		Rate	Sub-Total	Total
400.90	**Bank/Interim Financing**		Allow		75,000	75,000
	INTEREST RESERVE EST $54,000					
	$21,000 ALLOWABLE FEES/LEGALS					

PM-ONLY COST REPORT #4 (PENCIL COPY)

PM-Only Cost Report – Version #4 (Pencil Copy)

The figures on this form are for demonstration purposes only and are not to be taken as financial advice.

COST REPORT

Film Title:

Production Company:

For Period Ending:

Code	Description	This Period	Cost To Date	P.O.s	Total Costs	ETC	EFC	Budget	Variance
218.10	Props Labor	2,650	5,300	OT WK2= $160 —	5,300	18,550	23,850	24,750	OT OVG $160 900
218.50	Props Purch/Rentals	1,250	19,576	Float $1000x2 350	19,926	5,074	25,000	20,000	(5,000)
218.80	Props - Kit Rental	200	400	—	400	800	1,200	900	(300)
218.0	**PROPS**	**4,100**	**25,276**	**350**	**25,626**	**24,424**	**50,050**	**45,650**	**(4,400)**
220.10	Camera Labor	9,050	18,100	OT WK2= $544 —	18,100	45,250	63,350	62,300	OT OVG $544 (1,050)
220.50	Camera Eqt Rental	7,200	7,200	S/cam $1500 ? —	7,200	36,000	43,200	45,000	1,800
220.55	Camera Daily Rentals	—	—	225	225	2,275	2,500	2,500	—
220.70	Camera Expendables	1,294	1,339	37	1,376	1,124	2,500	2,500	—
220.80	Camera Kit Rentals	425	—	210	210	2,340	2,550	2,700	150
220.0	**CAMERA**	**17,969**	**26,639**	**472**	**27,111**	**86,989**	**114,100**	**115,000**	**900**

... and further down the cost report ...

Code	Description	This Period	Cost To Date	P.O.s	Total Costs	ETC	EFC	Budget	Variance
400.10	Insurance	—	23,500	—	23,500	7,000	30,500	30,500	Sav $1500 ? —
400.15	Medicals	150	675	75	750	—	750	750	—
400.50	Corporate Overhead	—	—	—	—	150,000	150,000	150,000	—
400.60	Legal	—	7,500	—	7,500	32,500	40,000	40,000	—
400.70	Post Accounting	—	—	—	—	4,800	4,800	4,800	—

A Film Production Management 101 form

DEAL MEMORANDUM (ESPECIALLY FOR NON-UNION CREW)

DEAL MEMORANDUM

BETWEEN: Prdn. Company: _____

_____

AND: Company/Name: _____

Address: _____

_____

Telephone: _____

Co.Tax#/Soc.#:   _____

* *

CONCERNING THE FOLLOWING FILM PRODUCTION:

_____

* *

CATEGORY: _____

SHOOT DATES: _____

START / END WORK DATES: _____

PAY RATE: PER DAY: _____

OTHER: _____

_____

PAYABLE BY: _____   INVOICE: _____   PAYROLL: _____

* *

_____   _____

Company/Employee   on behalf of
                                                 Production Company

_____   _____

Date   Date

EXTRAS RELEASE FORM

EXTRAS RELEASE FORM

This form is a sample to inspire you to design one with your own legal counsel
appropriate to your production, and is not to be taken as legal advice.

To: Production Company Inc.
        Address
        Telephone
        Fax
        Email
        Website

For good and valuable consideration, the receipt and sufficiency whereof is hereby acknowledged:

I hereby grant Production Company Inc., its affiliates, licensees, successors and assigns (hereinafter collectively the "Company") the irrevocable right, in perpetuity, to use the footage taken of me (the "Footage") in connection with the production, distribution and exploitation of the feature film presently entitled "Film Production Adventure" (the "Film"), to edit, delete, alter and amend the Footage in any manner and to juxtapose the Footage with any other material. This grant of rights includes the right to use my image, voice and all instrumental, musical or other sound effects produced by me contained in the Footage without restriction of any kind or nature whatsoever. The Film and/or the Footage may be exploited throughout the world, in perpetuity and in any and all media now or hereafter devised without any payment to me. The Company has no obligation to use the Footage in the Film.

I do hereby release and forever discharge the Company of, from and against all actions, causes of action, claims, suits, judgments and demands which may by made against the Company by virtue of my appearance, in any manner whatsoever, in the Film.

Dated this _____ day of _____, _____.

Witness: _____   Signature: _____

                                         Name: _____

                                         Address: _____

                                         _____

                                         Tel: _____

A Film Production Management 101 form

PERFORMER'S CHANGE OF DATE FORM

PERFORMER'S CHANGE OF DATE FORM
(to attach to all copies of Performer's Agreement)

To: _____
Person Spoke To

_____
Talent Agency

_____
Talent Agency Address / Telephone / Fax / Email

RE: _____
Re: Performer's Name playing "Character Name"

From: _____
Production Company

_____
Address

_____
Telephone / Fax / Email / Contact Name

This is to confirm our TELEPHONE CONVERSATION of:

_____ at _____
Date   Time

concerning a change of date(s) for the following work day(s):

From: _____   To: _____

From: _____   To: _____

and/or additional work day(s) as follows:

_____

_____

_____
Signature

_____
Name

_____
Date

A Film Production Management 101 form

LETTER OF AGREEMENT (CATERING)

LETTER OF AGREEMENT

This form is a sample to inspire you to design one with your own legal counsel appropriate to your production, and is not to be taken as legal advice.

between:

PRODUCTION COMPANY LTD.   AND   **CATERING COMPANY LTD.**
Address   Address
Telephone   Telephone
Fax   Fax
Email   Email
Website   Website

Date

This is to confirm that Catering Company Ltd. ("The Caterer") agrees to cater **"Film Production Adventure"** Television Movie for Production Company Ltd. ("The Production") for the period: _Start Date - End Date_.

The Caterer agrees to provide meals for cast and crew for _Price_ plus tax per person and substantials for _Price_ plus tax per person.

In addition, The Caterer will provide their own vehicle.

The Production agrees to supply tables and chairs and all beverages.

The Production agrees to provide The Caterer with a deposit of _Amount_.

With regard to changes in location, meal time and number of meals to be served, The Production agrees to give The Caterer best effort for twenty four (24) hours notice.

Invoices to be submitted weekly.

Signed and agreed,

_____
Production Manager
on behalf of
PRODUCTION COMPANY LTD.

_____
Date

Name: _____
on behalf of
CATERING COMPANY LTD.

_____
Date

FEATURE FILM TITLE PAGE

```
        FINAL (WHITE) DRAFT -  1 December 2014
        PINK REVISED        -  2 December 2014
        BLUE REVISED        -  3 December 2014
        GREEN REVISED       -  4 December 2014
        YELLOW REVISED      -  5 December 2014
        ORANGE REVISED      -  8 December 2014
        BUFF REVISED        -  9 December 2014
        TAN REVISED         -  9 Dec 2014 (PM)
        GOLDENROD REVISED   - 11 December 2014
        LAVENDER REVISED    - 11 Dec 2014 (PM)
        WHITE AGAIN REVISED - 12 December 2014
      * PINK AGAIN REVISED  - 15 December 2014
```

"Film Production Adventure"

written by

Deborah S. Patz

based on a story by

Laura J. C. Sousa

```
            Production Company Ltd.
            Address
            Telephone
            Fax Number
            Email
            Website
```

Copyright notice & disclaimer

TV SERIES TITLE PAGE

<u>**FILM PRODUCTION ADVENTURE**</u>

Episode #2

<u>"It's a N-Ice World"</u>

teleplay by

Deborah S. Patz

based on characters by

Laura J. C. Sousa

Second Draft - 27 April 2015

Production Company Ltd.
Address
Telephone
Fax Number
Email
Website

Copyright notice & disclaimer

DRAMA SCRIPT PAGES (PAGE 1 OF 2)

"**Film Production Adventure**"   Blue-5 Dec 14
by Deborah S. Patz

FADE IN:

Sc.1 **EXT - HILARY'S HOUSE - NIGHT**   Sc.1

Establishing shot. It is raining softly.

                                        CUT TO:

Sc.2 **INT - LIVING ROOM - NIGHT**   Sc.2

HILARY (30) sits amid piles of scripts and script notes,   *
working on them, but the biscuit tin on the coffee table   *
keeps drawing her attention.   *

                    HILARY (V/O)
            After she died, I inherited my
            grandmother's recipe tin. Now, for   *
            most people, this would be a precious
            gift. My only problem was: my
            grandmother couldn't cook.

                    YOUNG HILARY (V/O)
                    (sniffing)
            What's that smell?

                    GRAN (V/O)
            Oh! The roast!

The SOUND of footsteps rush up stairs.

                                        CUT TO:

Sc.3 **INT. KITCHEN (FLASHBACK) - NIGHT**   Sc.3

Smoke is seeping out of the oven. GRAN (55) puts on oven
mitts and opens the oven door, removes a blackened char
of meat on a platter. Smoke billows from the oven.

                    GRAN
            Ooo, just in time!

                                     (CONTINUED)

A Film Production Management 101 form

DRAMA SCRIPT PAGES (PAGE 2 OF 2)

```
"Film Production Adventure" - Pink Again - 15 Dec 14          -2-

3.  CONTINUED:

        YOUNG HILARY (8) watches, unbelieving, from the kitchen
        door.

                              HILARY (V/O)
                     It never was.

                                                 CUT TO:


Sc.4 INT. KITCHEN (FLASHBACK) - NIGHT (LATER)              Sc.4

        A questionable meal, including the blackened meat, is
        placed on the table. YOUNG HILARY tests the meat with a
        fork, starts eating the vegetables.

        HILARY'S MOM (33), HILARY'S DAD (37) and GRAN are also
        at the table, eating. Everyone has trouble cutting the
        meat, but no one addresses the issue.

                              HILARY (V/O)
                     There was a reward, though, for making
                     it through one of Gran's meals, and
                     that was dessert. As much as Gran
                     couldn't cook. She sure could bake.

                                              DISSOLVE TO:


Sc.5 INT. KITCHEN (FLASHBACK) - NIGHT                     Sc.5

        GRAN serves up a slice of lemon meringue pie, spilling
        it in pieces onto the plate.

                              HILARY (V/O)
                     And Lemon Meringue Pie was my all
                     time favorite.

        YOUNG HILARY grins, widely.

                                                 CUT TO:


Sc.6 OMITTED                                      Omit Sc.6 *
                                                           *
                                                           *
```

COMEDY SCRIPT PAGE

"Film Production Adventure: Ep.#2" - Blue - 19 Dec 14   -5-

6. CONTINUED:

MAX ROUNDS THE CORNER AND COMES FACE TO FACE WITH
HUW, ALREADY WITH FOOD IN HAND FROM THE 'FRIDGE.

                         HUW
              A little hungry, perhaps?

                         MAX
              Sort of...

                         HUW
              Would that be "sort of yes" or

              "sort of no?"

                         MAX
              Uh... "sort of yeah."

HUW DIVES INTO THE 'FRIDGE FOR SOME FOOD FOR MAX. HE
PASSES OUT ITEM AFTER ITEM FOR AN AMAZING SPREAD.
MAX RELAYS THE FOOD TO THE TABLE.

                         HUW
              You know, I've heard all the stories,

              but faced with her Gran's cooking,

              it takes a braver man than me to eat it.

                         MAX
              Yeah. Me too.

HILARY ENTERS THE KITCHEN AND SURVEYS THE FEAST IN THE
MAKING. SHE LOOKS HUNGRY. PAUSE.

                         HILARY
              What amazes me, is that I had actually

              forgotten what her food really tasted

              like. Gosh, I miss those days.

                                   (CONTINUED)

SAMPLE STRIP BOARD

Sample Strip Board

			INDOOR PLAYGROUND	INDOOR PLAYGROUND	Day 1 – End – 2 5/8 pages	KITCHEN	DRIVEWAY	MAX'S HOUSE	Day 2 – End – 5/8 pages
	Sc.#		1	26		14	11	6	
	Day/Night		N	D		D	D	D	
	Int/Ext		Int	Int		Int	Ext	Ext	
	Continuity Day #		1	3		3	2	2	
	Pages		1 1/8	1 4/8		1/8	2/8	2/8	
Title: Director: Producer: A.D.: Script date:	Film Prdn Adventure Jane Doe John Smith John Doe Pink								
Character	Artist	No.							
Max		1	1	1		1	1	1	
Huw		2	2	2		2			
Hilary		3	3	3		3			
Little Girl		4	4	4		4			
Roommate		5	5	5				5	
Thug		6		6			6		
Mother		7	7	7					
Father		8	8	8			8-vo		
		9							
		10							
		11							
		12							
		13							
		14							
Spot (Dog)		15					15		
		16							
Extras			X	X			X	X	
			Max sure knows how to play!	Everyone celebrate... big time!		Chocolate milk shaken, not stirred	Make friends with thug, not dog	All is quiet arriving home	

A.D. BREAKDOWN PAGE

Breakdown Sheet # 28	**A.D. BREAKDOWN SHEET** Prdn Title: **FILM PRODUCTION ADVENTURE**	Scene # 23

Int / Ext **INT**	Set **MANAGER'S KITCHEN**	Day / Night **N-4**	Pages **2 3/8**

Description **MANAGER DESPERATELY TRIES TO MAKE DINNER**	Location	Studio **STUDIO**

Cast 1. PRODUCTION MANAGER	Extras STAND-IN FOR MANAGER	Stunts 51. STUNT COORDINATOR MANAGER SLIPS ON BANANA PEEL CRASH PAD

Props LOTS OF COOKING POTS BLACKENED FOOD NON-SLIP BANANA PEEL SMOKE IN OVEN BRIEFCASE COMPUTER IN BAG PENS & PENCILS (TO FALL OUT OF BRIEFCASE) PHOTO OF JORDAN & NATALYA	Costumes DOUBLES FOR STUNT NEVER-USED APRON NEVER-USED OVEN MITTS	Vehicles

Notes

<u>ANIMALS</u>: BIRD AT WINDOW WATCHES THE MESS; WRANGLER

<u>ELECTRICS</u>: D4N

<u>NOTE TO ALL</u>: SMOKE IN OVEN

<u>MAKEUP</u>: MANAGER LOOKS VERY, VERY TIRED

A.D. BREAKDOWN PAGE (BLANK)

Breakdown Sheet #	**A.D. BREAKDOWN SHEET**		Scene #
	Prdn Title:		

Int / Ext	Set		Day / Night	Pages

Description			Location	Studio

Cast	Extras	Stunts

Props	Costumes	Vehicles

	Notes	

A Film Production Management 101 form

ONE-LINE SCHEDULE

| | **"Film Production Adventure"** | | | Blue Revised |
| | One-Line Schedule | | | Date: 9 Dec 2014 |

Sc#	Description	D/N	Cast	Pages	Loc
DAY 1 - MON. JAN. 05, 2015				1.=STUDIO, 2.=123 MAIN ST	
24	INT HOME OFFICE	N5	1,2,3	1 4/8	1.
4	INT HOME OFFICE	N1	1,3-vo	1 0/8	1.
	* * * * * * * * * * * U N I T M O V E * * * * * * * * * * *				
2	EXT HOUSE	D1	1,X	1/8	2.
			END DAY ONE - 2 5/8 PAGES		
DAY 2 - TUE. JAN. 06, 2015				1.=FUN PARK, 2.=CITY PARK	
1pt	EXT WATERPARK	D1	1,2-vo,4,X	6/8	1.
26	EXT WATERPARK	D7	1,2,3,4,X	4/8	1.
	* * * * * * * * * * * U N I T M O V E * * * * * * * * * * *				
8	EXT PARK	D2	1,4,X	2/8	2.
12	EXT PARK	D2	1,2,X	1 2/8	2.
			END DAY TWO - 2 6/8 PAGES		
DAY 3 - WED. JAN. 07, 2015				1.=123 FIRST AVE	
6	INT/EXT MAX'S CAR	D2	1,51,X	4/8	1.
10	EXT/INT MAX'S CAR	D2	1,2,51,52,X	2/8	1.
9	EXT CITY STREETS	D2	51,52,X	3/8	1.
11	EXT CITY STREETS	D2	1,2,X	1 0/8	1.
			END DAY THREE - 2 1/8 PAGES		
DAY 4 - THU. JAN. 08, 2015				1.=STUDIO	
1pt	INT LIVING ROOM	D1	1-vo,2	3/8	1.
3	INT LIVING ROOM	N1	1,2-vo	3/8	1.
19	INT LIVING ROOM	N4	1,2,3	7/8	1.
	* * * * * * * * * * * TARGET OF OPPORTUNITY * * * * * * * * * * *				
18	INT LIVING ROOM	N4	2,3	1 2/8	1.
			END DAY FOUR - 2 3/8 PAGES		
DAY 5 - FRI. JAN. 09, 2015				1.=STUDIO, 2=COOL GARDEN	
18	INT LIVING ROOM	N4	2,3	1 2/8	1.
	* * * * * * * * * * * U N I T M O V E * * * * * * * * * * *				
21	INT INDOOR WATERFALL	D5	1,2,3,4	1 3/8	2.
			END DAY FIVE - 1 5/8 PAGES		

Characters
1. Max
2. Huw
3. Hilary
4. Little Girl
X Extras

SHOOTING SCHEDULE

"Film Production Adventure"
Shooting Schedule

Pink Revised
Date: 12 Dec 2014

DAY 1 - MON. JAN. 05, 2015

LOC.#1 - STUDIO - 111 FILM ST.

| 24 | INT HOME OFFICE
Max figures it all out | N5 | 1 4/8 | 1.MAX
2.HUW
3.HILARY | Props: Really cool computer,
Homework, Stacks of paper,
Flowers, Tapioca pudding
to eat
Set Dressing: Secret wall
switch
Lighting: Computer light effect
Music: Radio gets turned off |

| 4 | INT HOME OFFICE
Getting the mission | N1 | 1 0/8 | 1.MAX
3.HILARY'S
VOICE | Props: Really cool computer,
Homework, Stacks of paper
Lighting: Computer light effect
Sound: Computer bell |

---

* * * UNIT MOVE TO LOC.#2 - 123 MAIN ST. * * *

| 2 | EXT HOUSE
Max arrives home, wet | D1 | 1/8 | 1.MAX
EXTRAS
Man with
dog x1 | Props: Max's cell phone,
Wet towel roll, Backpack,
Dog toy
H/M/W: Max is wet from the
water park |

END DAY ONE - 2 5/8 PAGES

DAY 2 - TUE. JAN. 06, 2015

LOC.#1 - FUN PARK - 1001 PLAY WAY

| 1pt | EXT WATERPARK
Max meets the girl | D1 | 6/8 | 1.MAX
2.HUW'S
VOICE
4.LITTLE
GIRL
EXTRAS
Kids x30
Parents x7
Lifeguard x2 | Props: Max's cell phone,
Water to splash on Max,
Pool toys a'plenty, Max's
towel (dry), Toy manatee
H/M/W: Max gets wet
(triples of Max's dry clothing) |

(Day 2 - cont'd Page 2...)

CREDITS STYLE #1 (PAGE 1 OF 4)

Credits Style #1   Page 1 of 4

"Film Production Adventure"
Credits - 4th Draft

December 15, 2014

OPENING CREDITS

CARD #

1	Company Name Presents	0:03
2	Script Revision Nightmare	0:03
3	Performer	0:02 *(single card, 1st)*
4	Performer	0:02 *(main titles, 2nd)*
5	Performer	0:02 *(single card, 3rd)*
6	Performer Performer	0:02 *(shared card)*
7	and Performer as Character Name	0:02 *(single card, last, "and-as")*
8	Screenplay by	0:02
9	Directed by	0:02

Total= 0:20

A Film Production Management 101 form

CREDITS STYLE #1 (PAGE 2 OF 4)

"Film Production Adventure"
Credits - 4th Draft

END CREDITS (CRAWL)   Total= 5:00

Executive Producer

Producer

Co-Producer

Director Of Photography

Production Designer

Editor

Music by

Casting by

Costume Designer

Featuring
(in alphabetical order)
Performer   as   Character Name
Performer   as   Character Name
Performer   as   Character Name
Performer   as   Character Name

Stunt Coordinator
Stunts

Production Manager
First Assistant Director

Associate Producer
Executive in Charge of Production

Art Director
Assistant Art Director
Set Decorator
Property Master
Previsualization
Script Supervisor

Camera Operator
Focus Puller
2nd Assistant Camera
Digital Image Technician

CREDITS STYLE #1 (PAGE 3 OF 4)

Credits Style #1 - Page 3 of 4

Assistant Costume Designer
Costumers
Hair Designer
Key Makeup Artist

Chief Lighting Technician
Best Boy
Electric
Generator Operator
Key Grip
Best Boy Grip
Grip
Sound Recordist
Boom Operator

Unit Manager
Location Manager

Production Coordinator
Assistant Coordinator
Production Accountant
Production Assistants
Assistant to [Name]

Second Assistant Director
Second Second Assistant Director

Special Effects

Lead Set Dresser
Set Dressers
Props Assistant
Props Buyer

Unit Publicist
Stills Photographer

Construction Manager
Head Carpenter
Carpenters
Scenic Artist
Painters

Location Casting
Extras Coordinator
Catering

Transportation Coordinator
Driver Captain
Drivers

2nd Unit

CREDITS STYLE #1 (PAGE 4 OF 4)

Post Production Supervisor
Assistant Editor

Sound Designer
Dialogue Editor
A.D.R. Editor
Folet Artist
Sound Mixer
Post Services Supplied by

Music Editor
Music Recorded & Mixed by
Music Recorded at

Visual Effects

Main Titles Design
Opticals
Digital Intermediate
Colorist
Negative Cutter

Song Title
Written by
Performed by
Courtesy of

The producers gratefully acknowledge
the support and assistance of

Produced by (Co-Production Companies)

A (list countries) Co-Production

Produced with the participation of

Produced in association with

Developed with the assistance of

(Union, Guild, equipment & supplier logos)

© (year, in numbers or Roman numerals) Production Company Ltd.

(Legal disclaimer, ie:
This film is based on true events, however, some of the names in this film were changed and some events fictionalized for dramatic purposes. This motion picture is protected under the laws of the United States, Canada and other countries, and its unauthorized duplication, distribution or exhibition may result in civil liability or criminal prosecution.)

(Co-Production Companies logos)

CREDITS STYLE #2 (PAGE 1 OF 3)

Credits Style #2   Page 1 of 3

"Film Production Adventure"
Credits

EPISODE #2 - "Oh no! Not Again!"

Opening Credits

FONT STYLE: VENETIAN 521 GOUDY EXTRA BOLD

Final Draft - 19 Dec 2014

Card #

#		
1	Film Production Adventure	0:02
2	starring Lead Performer	0:02 *(single card, 1st,* *"starring")*
3	Lead Performer	0:02 *(single card, 2nd)*
4	and Lead Performer as Character Name	0:02 *(single card, last,* *"and-as")*
5	series created by	0:02
6	based on characters by developed for television by	0:02
7	supervising producer	0:02
8	producer	0:02

Shown over the first frames of Act One:

#		
9	Oh No! Not Again!	0:02
10	written by	0:02
11	directed by	0:02

Total= 0:22

CREDITS STYLE #2 (PAGE 2 OF 3)

"Film Production Adventure"
Credits

EPISODE #2 - "Oh no! Not Again!"

Tail Credits   Total= 1:00 +logos

Final Draft

Card #

Card #		Time
1	executive producer	0:02
2	executive in charge of production	0:02
3	guest starring Star Name as Character Name and featuring Performer Name as Character Name	0:03
4	director of photography production designer	0:02
5	editor music theme by performed by	0:02
6	casting director wardrobe designer	0:02
7	production manager assistant production manager first assistant director second assistant director third assistant director continuity supervisor	0:02.5
8	art director 1st assistant art director 1st assistant art director art department trainee set decorator lead set dresser lead set dresser set dresser	0:02.5
9	special effects design props master props builder props assistant art department coordinator	0:02.5

CREDITS STYLE #2 (PAGE 3 OF 3)

Credits Style #2 - Page 3 of 3

10	camera operator 1st camera assistant 2nd camera assistant digital management technician sound mixer boom operator	0:02.5
11	assistant wardrobe designer wardrobe mistress makeup artist hair designer	0:02.5
12	gaffer best boy key grip dolly grip construction manager head carpenter scenic painter	0:02.5
13	production coordinator production accountant business affairs production secretary production assistant craft service catering	0:02.5
14	post-production supervisor post-production coordinator post-production assistant sound editors 1st assistant editor foley artist sound assistant	0:02.5
15	rerecording postproduction facilities rerecording studio online editor colorist sound editing facility	0:02.5
16	© (Year) Production Company Ltd. (Disclaimer) (Piracy Clause) (Union, Guild, Equipment, Supplier logos)	0:02.5
17	Produced with the participation of	0:03 x2
18	produced by in association with	0:03 x5
19	Co-Production Company logos	0:03 x3

DOCUMENT DISTRIBUTION BINDER - TRACKING FORM

DOCUMENT DISTRIBUTION BINDER - TRACKING FORM

Script	White Dec.1	Pink Dec.2	Blue Dec.4	Green	Yellow
Research Company	E - Dec.1	E - Dec.2	E - Dec.4		
Exec Producer	E - Dec.1	E - Dec.2	E - Dec.4		
Producer	D - Dec.1	D - Dec.2	D - Dec.4		
Director	D - Dec.1	D - Dec.2	D - Dec.4		
Story Editor	D - Dec.2	D - Dec.2	D - Dec.4		
Casting Director	C - Dec.2	N/A	N/A		
DP	D - Dec.1	D - Dec.2	D - Dec.4		
"Rest of Crew"	D - Dec.1	D - Dec.2	D - Dec.4		
"The Cast"	D - Dec.1	D - Dec.2	D - Dec.4		
Distributor	C - Dec.1	F - Dec.5	F - Dec.5		
Broadcaster	C - Dec.1	F - Dec.5	F - Dec.5		
Funding Agency	E - Dec.1	E - Dec.5	E - Dec.5		
XP/Head Office	C - Dec.1	C - Dec.5	C - Dec.5		
Editors	D - Dec.1	D - Dec.2	D - Dec.4		
Completion Bond	C - Dec.1	E - Dec.5	E - Dec.5		
Publicist (major only)	C - Dec.1	N/A	N/A		
Performer Union (major only)	C - Dec.1	N/A	N/A		
Gov't Agency (major only)	C - Dec.1	N/A	N/A		

C: via courier   D: hand-delivered   E: via email   F: via fax

A Film Production Management 101 form

DOCUMENT DISTRIBUTION BINDER - TRACKING FORM (BLANK)

DOCUMENT DISTRIBUTION BINDER - TRACKING FORM

	White	Pink	Blue	Green	Yellow

C: via courier   D: hand-delivered   E: via email   F: via fax

A Film Production Management 101 form

WALL ENVELOPE DISTRIBUTION - TRACKING FORM

WALL ENVELOPES DISTRIBUTION - TRACKING FORM

HEAD OFFICE (Contact Name)	White	Blue	Pink	Yellow	Green
Script (Ep.#1)	C-Dec.1	F-Dec.2	F-Dec.4		
Script (Ep.#2)	C-Dec.5				
Script (Ep.#3)	C-Dec.9				
Script (Ep.#4)					
Script (Ep.#5)					
Script (Ep.#6)					
Research Report (Ep.#1)	E-Dec.8				
Research Report (Ep.#2)					
Research Report (Ep.#3)					
Research Report (Ep.#4)					
Research Report (Ep.#5)					
Research Report (Ep.#6)					
Crew List	C-Dec.1	F-Dec.8			
Cast List (Ep.#1)	C-Dec.1				
Cast List (Ep.#2)	D-Dec.5				
Cast List (Ep.#3)					
Cast List (Ep.#4)					
Cast List (Ep.#5)					
(etc.)					

C: via courier   D: hand-delivered   E: via email   F: via fax

A Film Production Management 101 form

WALL ENVELOPE DISTRIBUTION - TRACKING FORM (BLANK)

WALL ENVELOPES DISTRIBUTION - TRACKING FORM

	White	Blue	Pink	Yellow	Green

C: via courier   D: hand-delivered   E: via email   F: via fax

A Film Production Management 101 form

WRAP PARTY CHECKLIST & BUDGET FORM (PAGE 1 OF 2)

Wrap Party Checklist & Budget   Page 1 of 2

Date of party: _____

Item/Activity	Description/Notes	Price
WRAP PARTY INVITATIONS		
Number invited		---
Invitation costs		
Mailing costs		
PARTY ROOM		
Room rental		
Capacity		---
Special features		
Closing time		---
Security		
Washroom supplies		
Clean up		
DECOR OF PARTY ROOM		
Lights rental		
Tables/Chairs		
Linen/Ashtrays		
Balloons/Helium		
Flowers		
Other decorations		
Set up / Clean up		
MUSIC		
Band		
DJ		
Set up needed		---
When clean up		---

A Film Production Management 101 form

WRAP PARTY CHECKLIST & BUDGET FORM (PAGE 2 OF 2)

Wrap Party Checklist & Budget   Page 2 of 2

Item/Activity	Description/Notes	Price
OTHER ENTERTAINMENT		
Entertainment type		
Outtake reel avail.		
Playback equipment		
Other entertainment		
Set up / Clean up		
WRAP PARTY CATERING		
Bartenders		
Deposit required		---
Beer		
Wine		
Liquor		
Mixers & others		
Ice & container		
Glasses (type)		
Napkins & access.		
Set up / Clean up		
LICENSE		
Liquor license		
NOTIFICATIONS		
Police		---
Fire department		---
Health department		---
Building/Inspection		---

GRAND TOTAL PARTY COSTS	

A Film Production Management 101 form

INDEX

ABOUT THE AUTHOR

DEBORAH S. PATZ has been a filmmaker on award-winning productions since the mid-80s, primarily as a production manager and coordinator, and then as production executive. She has worked with LucasFilm, IMAX, MCA/Universal, Alliance/Atlantis, Nelvana, BBC, CBC, Disney Channel, and the list goes on. She has shot on everything from 3D to 35mm to digital video. Having worked on numerous international coproductions and shot in several countries around the world, Ms. Patz has even sent a camera

into space. Her first book *Surviving Production* (on coordination) was published worldwide by Michael Wiese Productions in 1997, and then was included into this, her second book which was first published in 2002.

A graduate Producer Resident of the Canadian Film Centre and with a Banff Centre Executive Program certificate, Ms. Patz has also ventured to the financing side of the business as an Investment Analyst at the funding agency Telefilm Canada. There, she also increased her exposure to digital and interactive medias prompting her to attend UBC and achieve a certificate in digital media and web development.

Based on her books, Ms. Patz regularly participates on panels and conducts workshops and seminars wherever aspiring filmmakers reside. She hosts Deb's F.I.L.M blog to share further production insights and stories under the categories of "Fun," "Inspiration," "Life," and "Management" and provides production resource links for managers and coordinators at *www.debpatz.com*. Readers may also connect with her on Facebook at *www.facebook.com/DebPatzBooks*.

Ms. Patz currently resides in Vancouver, BC, Canada.

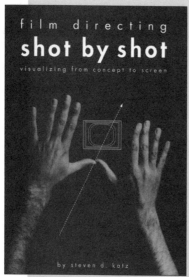

FILM DIRECTING: SHOT BY SHOT
VISUALIZING FROM CONCEPT TO SCREEN

STEVEN D. KATZ

BEST SELLER
OVER 200,000 COPIES SOLD!

Film Directing: Shot by Shot — with its famous blue cover — is the best-known book on directing and a favorite of professional directors as an on-set quick reference guide.

This international bestseller is a complete catalog of visual techniques and their stylistic implications, enabling working filmmakers to expand their knowledge.

Contains in-depth information on shot composition, staging sequences, visualization tools, framing and composition techniques, camera movement, blocking tracking shots, script analysis, and much more.

Includes over 750 storyboards and illustrations, with never-before-published storyboards from Steven Spielberg's *Empire of the Sun*, Orson Welles' *Citizen Kane*, and Alfred Hitchcock's *The Birds*.

"(To become a director) you have to teach yourself what makes movies good and what makes them bad. John Singleton has been my mentor... he's the one who told me what movies to watch and to read Shot by Shot."
— Ice Cube, *New York Times*

"A generous number of photos and superb illustrations accompany each concept, many of the graphics being from Katz' own pen... Film Directing: Shot by Shot is a feast for the eyes."
— *Videomaker* Magazine

"... demonstrates the visual techniques of filmmaking by defining the process whereby the director converts storyboards into photographed scenes."
— *Back Stage Shoot*

"Contains an encyclopedic wealth of information."
— *Millimeter* Magazine

STEVEN D. KATZ is an award-winning filmmaker and also the author of *Film Directing: Cinematic Motion*.

$27.95 · 366 PAGES · ORDER NUMBER 7RLS · ISBN: 9780941188104

24 HOURS | 1.800.833.5738 | WWW.MWP.COM

PRODUCER TO PRODUCER
A STEP-BY-STEP GUIDE TO LOW BUDGET INDEPENDENT FILM PRODUCING

MAUREEN A. RYAN

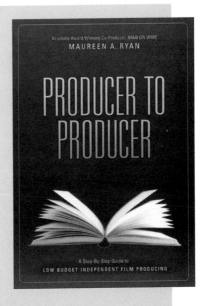

Everything you need to know – all in one place – to produce your independent film or documentary, from last year's Academy Award-winning co-producer of *Man on Wire*.

All the steps are clearly stated so that you can produce your low budget independent film. Save time and money by following the advice and information in Producer to Producer to make the most successful film possible.

This book is a definitive step-by-step guide for low budget independent film producing. Filled with practical advice award-winning producer Maureen Ryan has culled from her 20-plus years of production experience, it takes you through the entire process of bringing a film into the world. From development and script breakdown, to budgeting and preproduction, to production and post, and to sales and distribution, *Producer to Producer* gives you all the information you need in easy-to-follow, chronological order.

Emerging and professional producers alike will benefit from this comprehensive guide to low budget film producing. *Producer to Producer*, which outlines every aspect of film producing in detail, is designed to take to production meetings. It includes checklists to keep you on track from 12 weeks before shooting to the first day of principal photography and through postproduction.

"This does what no book on production has done before — you actually can go out and make a movie after you read it. Maureen Ryan is one of the best independent producers working today and this book will show you why. Like her, it's thorough, thoughtful, and highly enjoyable. Whether you are a novice or a professional, there is much to learn here."

— Ben Odell, Producer, *Padre Nuestro*, Partner, Panamax Films

MAUREEN RYAN has been a film producer for over 20 years with experience in narrative film, documentary, short film, commercials, music videos, and industrials. Other films she produced have won a BAFTA Award, a Peabody Award, and an Emmy nomination. She has taught film producing at Columbia University's School of the Arts Graduate Film Program since 1999 and also teaches producing at NYU's Tisch School of the Arts.

$39.95 · 350 PAGES · ORDER NUMBER 144RLS · ISBN: 9781932907759

FILM & VIDEO BUDGETS – 5TH EDITION

DEKE SIMON

BEST SELLER
OVER 45,000 COPIES SOLD!

Film & Video Budgets 5th Edition is a budget-making toolkit. Whether you're making a feature, a short, a documentary, an industrial or corporate, a music video, or a student film, you'll find sample budgets, complete explanations for budget line items, and tons of useful background information on High-Definition workflow updated for the 5th edition that will apply to every project you do. Plus, purchasing the book grants you access to the MWP website, where you can download all the budget templates for free. Adapt these for your own use, saving yourself hundreds of hours of tedious data entry.

For over a decade, this classic budgeting book has helped filmmakers figure out:

· How do I put a budget together?
· How much will my project cost?
· How do I build an impressive-looking budget
  for investors and funders?
... and answers to hundreds of questions you may not have thought of yet!

The 5th edition of this all-time standard includes NEW material on preproduction and High-Definition, as well as an update of all budgets.

"Wow, just when you think you know everything about developing and producing a film, along comes another edition of Film and Video Budgets *to make you even smarter. I love those Desperate Measures sections, too."*

> — Mary J. Schirmer, screenwriter, instructor
> *www.screenplayers.net*

"The information here is truly invaluable for starting film producers. Easy to read, this gives you what you need to know to better budget your film. The new edition provides up-to-date info, so that whether you're making anything from shorts to features, you'll be well prepared."

> — Erin Corrado, *www.onemoviefiveviews.com*

DEKE SIMON is a writer/producer/director of documentary, dramatic, and informational programs for television and education. His work has been honored with numerous awards, including two L.A. Emmy Awards, and four L.A. Emmy nominations.

$29.95 · 477 PAGES · ORDER NUMBER 143RLS · ISBN: 9781932907735

THE SOUND EFFECTS BIBLE
HOW TO CREATE AND RECORD
HOLLYWOOD STYLE SOUND EFFECTS

RIC VIERS

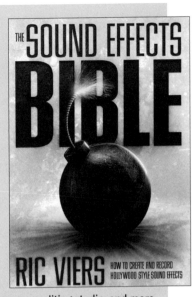

Learn how to record amazing Sound Effects in your own home from the world's leading expert.

Create the sounds of 10,000 alien soldiers or a jet fighter using just the simple recording techniques of the trade.

The Sound Effects Bible is a complete guide to recording and editing sound effects. The book covers topics such as microphone selection, field recorders, the ABCs of digital audio, understanding Digital Audio Workstations, building your own Foley stage, designing your own editing studio, and more.

Industry secrets are shared by sound effects veteran Ric Viers (along with the companion website *www.soundeffectsbible.com* that offers free sound samples referenced in the book). Whether you're a beginner or an audiophile, this book will show the tools and tricks of creating sound effects for your films, television shows, video games, webisodes, and multimedia productions.

"Ric's book is an excellent introduction to techniques for producing professional sound effects for films, games, etc. It's packed with nuts-and-bolts information that beginning and intermediate level sound designers/editors will find useful."
> — Randy Thom, Director of Sound Design, Skywalker Sound

"The SFX Bible is the go-to resource for anyone serious about sound creation! Viers generously shares his real-world experience in an absorbing and hard to put down guide to this fascinating corner of the entertainment industry."
> — Aaron Marks, Composer/Sound Designer and author of *The Complete Guide to Game Audio*

"Ric Viers eats, drinks, and breathes sound effects. If you're a sound designer, editor, or filmmaker, you'll need the Bible!"
> — Tasos Frantzolas, founder of *Soundsnap.com*

RIC VIERS has worked in the film & television industry for over ten years. His location sound credits include nearly every major television network, Eminem, Kid Rock, Dateline, Good Morning America, and many others. His sound design work has been used in major motion pictures, television shows, radio programs, and video games. In 2007, Viers launched his own label, Blastwave FX, to celebrate the release of his 100th sound effects library. He is considered to be the world's largest independent provider of sound effects with over 100,000 sounds and more than 120 sound effects libraries to his name.

$26.95 · 260 PAGES · ORDER NUMBER 90RLS · ISBN: 9781932907483

MASTER SHOTS
100 ADVANCED CAMERA TECHNIQUES TO GET AN EXPENSIVE LOOK ON YOUR LOW-BUDGET MOVIE

CHRISTOPHER KENWORTHY

Master Shots gives filmmakers the techniques they need to execute complex, original shots on any budget. By using powerful master shots and well-executed moves, directors can develop a strong style and stand out from the crowd. Most low-budget movies look low-budget, because the director is forced to compromise at the last minute. *Master Shots* gives you so many powerful techniques that you'll be able to respond, even under pressure, and create knock-out shots. Even when the clock is ticking and the light is fading, the techniques in this book can rescue your film, and make every shot look like it cost a fortune.

Each technique is illustrated with samples from great feature films and computer-generated diagrams for absolute clarity.

Use the secrets of the master directors to give your film the look and feel of a multi-million-dollar movie. The set-ups, moves and methods of the greats are there for the taking, whatever your budget.

"Master Shots gives every filmmaker out there the blow-by-blow setup required to pull off even the most difficult of setups found from indies to the big Hollywood blockbusters. It's like getting all of the magician's tricks in one book."
— Devin Watson, producer, *The Cursed*

"Though one needs to choose any addition to a film book library carefully, what with the current plethora of volumes on cinema, Master Shots is an essential addition to any worthwhile collection."
— Scott Essman, publisher, *Directed By* Magazine

"Christopher Kenworthy's book gives you a basic, no holds barred, no shot forgotten look at how films are made from the camera point of view. For anyone with a desire to understand how film is constructed — this book is for you."
— Matthew Terry, screenwriter/director, columnist
www.hollywoodlitsales.com

Since 2000, CHRISTOPHER KENWORTHY has written, produced, and directed drama and comedy programs, along with many hours of commercial video, tv pilots, music videos, experimental projects, and short films. He's also produced and directed over 300 visual FX shots. In 2006 he directed the web-based Australian UFO Wave, which attracted many millions of viewers. Upcoming films for Kenworthy include *The Sickness* (2009) and *Glimpse* (2011).

$24.95 · 240 PAGES · ORDER NUMBER 91RLS · ISBN: 9781932907513

{ THE MYTH OF MWP }

In a dark time, a light bringer came along, leading the curious and the frustrated to clarity and empowerment. It took the well-guarded secrets out of the hands of the few and made them available to all. It spread a spirit of openness and creative freedom, and built a storehouse of knowledge dedicated to the betterment of the arts.

The essence of the Michael Wiese Productions (MWP) is empowering people who have the burning desire to express themselves creatively. We help them realize their dreams by putting the tools in their hands. We demystify the sometimes secretive worlds of screenwriting, directing, acting, producing, film financing, and other media crafts.

By doing so, we hope to bring forth a realization of 'conscious media' which we define as being positively charged, emphasizing hope and affirming positive values like trust, cooperation, self-empowerment, freedom, and love. Grounded in the deep roots of myth, it aims to be healing both for those who make the art and those who encounter it. It hopes to be transformative for people, opening doors to new possibilities and pulling back veils to reveal hidden worlds.

MWP has built a storehouse of knowledge unequaled in the world, for no other publisher has so many titles on the media arts. Please visit www.mwp.com where you will find many free resources and a 25% discount on our books. Sign up and become part of the wider creative community!

Onward and upward,

Michael Wiese
Publisher/Filmmaker

FILM & VIDEO BOOKS
TO RECEIVE A FREE MWP NEWSLETTER, CLICK ON WWW.MWP.COM TO REGISTER

SCREENWRITING | WRITING

And the Best Screenplay Goes to... | Dr. Linda Seger | $26.95
Archetypes for Writers | Jennifer Van Bergen | $22.95
Bali Brothers | Lacy Waltzman, Matthew Bishop, Michael Wiese | $12.95
Cinematic Storytelling | Jennifer Van Sijll | $24.95
Could It Be a Movie? | Christina Hamlett | $26.95
Creating Characters | Marisa D'Vari | $26.95
Crime Writer's Reference Guide, The | Martin Roth | $20.95
Deep Cinema | Mary Trainor-Brigham | $19.95
Elephant Bucks | Sheldon Bull | $24.95
Fast, Cheap & Written That Way | John Gaspard | $26.95
Hollywood Standard, The, 2nd Edition | Christopher Riley | $18.95
Horror Screenwriting | Devin Watson | $24.95
I Could've Written a Better Movie than That! | Derek Rydall | $26.95
Inner Drives | Pamela Jaye Smith | $26.95
Moral Premise, The | Stanley D. Williams, Ph.D. | $24.95
Myth and the Movies | Stuart Voytilla | $26.95
Power of the Dark Side, The | Pamela Jaye Smith | $22.95
Psychology for Screenwriters | William Indick, Ph.D. | $26.95
Reflections of the Shadow | Jeffrey Hirschberg | $26.95
Rewrite | Paul Chitlik | $16.95
Romancing the A-List | Christopher Keane | $18.95
Save the Cat! | Blake Snyder | $19.95
Save the Cat! Goes to the Movies | Blake Snyder | $24.95
Screenwriting 101 | Neill D. Hicks | $16.95
Screenwriting for Teens | Christina Hamlett | $18.95
Script-Selling Game, The | Kathie Fong Yoneda | $16.95
Stealing Fire From the gods, 2nd Edition | James Bonnet | $26.95
Talk the Talk | Penny Penniston | $24.95
Way of Story, The | Catherine Ann Jones | $22.95
What Are You Laughing At? | Brad Schreiber | $19.95
Writer's Journey, – 3rd Edition, The | Christopher Vogler | $26.95
Writer's Partner, The | Martin Roth | $24.95
Writing the Action Adventure Film | Neill D. Hicks | $14.95
Writing the Comedy Film | Stuart Voytilla & Scott Petri | $14.95
Writing the Killer Treatment | Michael Halperin | $14.95
Writing the Second Act | Michael Halperin | $19.95
Writing the Thriller Film | Neill D. Hicks | $14.95
Writing the TV Drama Series – 2nd Edition | Pamela Douglas | $26.95
Your Screenplay Sucks! | William M. Akers | $19.95

FILMMAKING

Film School | Richard D. Pepperman | $24.95
Power of Film, The | Howard Suber | $27.95

PITCHING

Perfect Pitch – 2nd Edition, The | Ken Rotcop | $19.95
Selling Your Story in 60 Seconds | Michael Hauge | $12.95

SHORTS

Filmmaking for Teens, 2nd Edition | Troy Lanier & Clay Nichols | $24.95
Making It Big in Shorts | Kim Adelman | $22.95

BUDGET | PRODUCTION MANAGEMENT

Film & Video Budgets, 5th Updated Edition | Deke Simon | $26.95
Film Production Management 101 | Deborah S. Patz | $39.95

DIRECTING | VISUALIZATION

Animation Unleashed | Ellen Besen | $26.95

Cinematography for Directors | Jacqueline Frost | $29.95
Citizen Kane Crash Course in Cinematography | David Worth | $19.95
Directing Actors | Judith Weston | $26.95
Directing Feature Films | Mark Travis | $26.95
Fast, Cheap & Under Control | John Gaspard | $26.95
Film Directing: Cinematic Motion, 2nd Edition | Steven D. Katz | $27.95
Film Directing: Shot by Shot | Steven D. Katz | $27.95
Film Director's Intuition, The | Judith Weston | $26.95
First Time Director | Gil Bettman | $27.95
From Word to Image, 2nd Edition | Marcie Begleiter | $26.95
I'll Be in My Trailer! | John Badham & Craig Modderno | $26.95
Master Shots | Christopher Kenworthy | $24.95
Setting Up Your Scenes | Richard D. Pepperman | $24.95
Setting Up Your Shots, 2nd Edition | Jeremy Vineyard | $22.95
Working Director, The | Charles Wilkinson | $22.95

DIGITAL | DOCUMENTARY | SPECIAL

Digital Filmmaking 101, 2nd Edition | Dale Newton & John Gaspard | $26.95
Digital Moviemaking 3.0 | Scott Billups | $24.95
Digital Video Secrets | Tony Levelle | $26.95
Greenscreen Made Easy | Jeremy Hanke & Michele Yamazaki | $19.95
Producing with Passion | Dorothy Fadiman & Tony Levelle | $22.95
Special Effects | Michael Slone | $31.95

EDITING

Cut by Cut | Gael Chandler | $35.95
Cut to the Chase | Bobbie O'Steen | $24.95
Eye is Quicker, The | Richard D. Pepperman | $27.95
Film Editing | Gael Chandler | $34.95
Invisible Cut, The | Bobbie O'Steen | $28.95

SOUND | DVD | CAREER

Complete DVD Book, The | Chris Gore & Paul J. Salamoff | $26.95
Costume Design 101, 2nd Edition | Richard La Motte | $24.95
Hitting Your Mark, 2nd Edition | Steve Carlson | $22.95
Sound Design | David Sonnenschein | $19.95
Sound Effects Bible, The | Ric Viers | $26.95
Storyboarding 101 | James Fraioli | $19.95
There's No Business Like Soul Business | Derek Rydall | $22.95
You Can Act! | D. W. Brown | $24.95

FINANCE | MARKETING | FUNDING

Art of Film Funding, The | Carole Lee Dean | $26.95
Bankroll | Tom Malloy | $26.95
Complete Independent Movie Marketing Handbook, The | Mark Steven Bosko | $39.95
Getting the Money | Jeremy Jusso | $26.95
Independent Film and Videomakers Guide – 2nd Edition, The | Michael Wiese | $29.95
Independent Film Distribution | Phil Hall | $26.95
Shaking the Money Tree, 3rd Edition | Morrie Warshawski | $26.95

MEDITATION | ART

Mandalas of Bali | Dewa Nyoman Batuan | $39.95

OUR FILMS

Dolphin Adventures: DVD | Michael Wiese and Hardy Jones | $24.95
Hardware Wars: DVD | Written and Directed by Ernie Fosselius | $14.95
On the Edge of a Dream | Michael Wiese | $16.95
Sacred Sites of the Dalai Lamas– DVD, The | Documentary by Michael Wiese | $24.95